MASON-DIXON

MASON

DIXON

CRUCIBLE OF THE NATION

EDWARD G. GRAY

Harvard University Press

Cambridge, Massachusetts & London, England   2023

First printing

Library of Congress Cataloging-in-Publication Data

Names: Gray, Edward G., 1964– author.
Title: Mason-Dixon : crucible of the nation / Edward G. Gray.
Description: Cambridge, Massachusetts : Harvard University Press, 2023. |
    Includes bibliographical references and index.
Identifiers: LCCN 2022059423 | ISBN 9780674987616 (cloth)
Subjects: LCSH: Borderlands—Northeastern States—History—19th century. |
    Borderlands—Southern States—History—19th century. | Slavery—United
    States—History—19th century. | Mason-Dixon Line—History.
Classification: LCC F157.B7 G73 2023 | DDC 975 / .03—dc23/eng/20230118
LC record available at https://lccn.loc.gov/2022059423

For Norman Fiering and Gordon S. Wood

What satire on government can equal the severity of censure conveyed in the word politic, which now for ages has signified cunning, intimating that the state is a trick?

—Ralph Waldo Emerson, "Politics"

CONTENTS

PART IV   THE AGE OF THE MASON-DIXON LINE

LIST OF MAPS AND ILLUSTRATIONS

NOTE ON TERMS

Until the latter half of the twentieth century, the Mason-Dixon Line was generally referred to as "Mason and Dixon's line." In its earliest eighteenth-century usages, that name referred to the portion of the boundaries between Maryland, Delaware, and Pennsylvania surveyed by the English astronomers Charles Mason and Jeremiah Dixon. Beginning with the debate over Missouri's admission to the Union in 1819 and 1820, politicians, such as Virginia congressman John Randolph, used "Mason and Dixon's line" in a more familiar, metaphoric sense, to refer to the national divide between free and slave states. (On nineteenth-century usages of "Mason and Dixon's line," see Richard H. Thornton, *An American Glossary: Being an Attempt to Illustrate Certain Americanisms upon Historical Principles* [Philadelphia: J. B. Lippincott, 1912], vol. II, 573.) Except when quoting historical sources or referring directly to Mason and Dixon's survey in Chapter 6, I use the modern "Mason-Dixon Line," or just "the Line."

MASON-DIXON

Prologue

NEAR THE END of 1764, the first full year of their great American surveying expedition, Charles Mason, Jeremiah Dixon, and their party briefly camped on the banks of the Nanticoke River. The surveyors spent a few days at the site awaiting supplies from Philadelphia. Mason used the time to explore his surroundings. What he discovered, in the heart of the peninsula separating the Delaware and Chesapeake Bays, was spectacular natural beauty. The flora of the nearby Pocomoke Swamp took Mason's breath away. "There is," he observed, "the greatest quantity of Timber I ever saw." And that timber was not merely abundant, it was also majestic: giant oaks, beeches, poplars, hickories, hollies, and bald cypresses. Above them all towered "the lofty cedar," its trunk shooting skyward, a colossal wooden vessel, whose "green conical top . . . seems to reach the clouds."[1]

During the preceding three months, the surveying party had slowly made its way south, plotting the eighty-two-mile meridian line that would separate Maryland from the Lower Counties, also known as the Delaware colony. The party had traversed a landscape bearing the marks of centuries of human habitation. Much of what had once been heavily forested coastal plain and wetlands was now cleared and drained, first by Native farmers and dugout canoe makers and later by English tobacco planters and their servants and slaves. By the time Mason and Dixon's party traversed the peninsula, many of those farms had begun abandoning tobacco for grain, but the effects of a century of intensive tobacco farming were plain. Only at the Pocomoke Swamp, a remnant of primordial wetlands that once enveloped the peninsula's southern reaches, did Mason glimpse American nature's sublime majesty. In the coming century, that remnant would shrink further, drained by farmers and cleared by loggers.[2]

From spring 1765 to late fall 1767, Mason and Dixon plotted the West Line separating Maryland and Pennsylvania and carrying the surveyors deep into the North American woodlands. Few Englishmen would have a better grasp of the stunning topographical range of eastern North America. From the coastal plain of the Delmarva Peninsula, as the entire Eastern Shore peninsula would later come to be known, the surveyors passed into the rolling northern Piedmont of Cecil County in Maryland and Chester and Lancaster Counties in Pennsylvania. What they saw of the human-made landscape differed from Eastern Shore Maryland. In place of small tobacco and grain plantations, worked by white farmers, their servants, and African American slaves, the region was a patchwork of forests and the family farms of English, Scots-Irish, and German migrants.

As the surveyors moved west, through the fertile Piedmont to the North American continent's aged eastern mountains, they crossed the broad, shallow Susquehanna River. By the end of September 1765, they had hauled their party up and down South Mountain, the northernmost of the Blue Ridge Mountains. On South Mountain's western face, they found a brief reprieve in the Great Cumberland Valley, known further south as the Shenandoah Valley, and separating the eastern Blue Ridge from the Appalachian plateau—that vast assemblage of mountains, valleys, and waterways through which runs North America's eastern continental divide. The further inland the surveyors traveled, the smaller and more widely dispersed the farms— longer, colder winters meant shorter growing seasons and more time devoted to surviving the fallow months. Dense deciduous forest still abounded, requiring the surveyors to employ teams of axe men to cut lengthy channels through the woods. As the surveying party traversed the hills and valleys between South Mountain and the foothills of the Allegheny Ridge, they used wagon roads and trails originally cleared by Native hunters and traders, but few of these paralleled the Line for long. The Forbes Road, named for British general John Forbes, traveled well north of the West Line. Braddock's Road, beginning deep in the Shenandoah Valley and named for Edward Braddock, another British general, ran parallel to the Line for a little over fifty miles, between Fort Cumberland in western Maryland and the site of the first battle of the French and Indian War, Fort Necessity, just over the Line in Pennsylvania. Mason and Dixon ultimately cut their own path. Nothing in either the human-made or natural contours of the region suggested a straight line, let alone a straight east-west line.

As autumn deepened, the surveyors returned east. The following spring they would ascend the Appalachian Mountains and spend the summer hacking their way through mountainous terrain to the survey's end point, a little over ten miles outside present-day Morgantown, West Virginia. The West Line covered 230 miles from the northeastern corner of Maryland, roughly the distance between Philadelphia and Providence, Rhode Island, or between Baltimore and the eventual location of Wheeling in West Virginia. About half that journey was through mountains. The Appalachian plateau sits across the Line at an oblique southwest-to-northeast angle, a giant boomerang-shaped range of mountains and valleys about 150 miles wide and rising to a height of over 3,200 feet above sea level, many of its dense coniferous forests more akin to the boreal forests of Canada than those of the Cumberland Valley or the Piedmont. The rivers and streams flowing down from the mountains also cross the Line at oblique angles. On the eastern face, they flow in a mostly southeasterly direction, dozens of them, toward the meandering Potomac River. Further east, they drain into branches of the Susquehanna River before it disgorges into the Chesapeake Bay.

For centuries before the arrival of Europeans, and for about a century after, the waterways and mountains bisecting the Mason-Dixon Line had dictated the movement of people and goods. Native peoples, traveling the mid-Atlantic river systems in swift and lightweight birchbark canoes, moved produce to and from coastal communities. Copper, animal skins, and furs traveled south and east; wampum, stone pots, tobacco pipes, and maize traveled north and west. European-made goods began arriving in the sixteenth century—glass beads; leather belts, straps, and shoes; metal tools, textiles, and firearms. These, too, traveled far inland, carried by Native traders in search of ever-scarcer beaver pelts. Indigenous travelers never limited their movement to water routes. They carved hundreds of paths through the eastern woodlands, many following creeks and rivers, but many also moving inland, across the Piedmont to the high country. With European settlement, these arteries of commerce and transit remained in use, traversed by Native and European fur traders, military personnel, and migrants, the last in search of fertile farmlands, often overgrown with dense forest, long abandoned by native agriculturalists.

In the years Mason and Dixon traveled through these colonial borderlands, fewer descendants of the region's original Native inhabitants remained. The Susquehannocks had once controlled most of the southern Susquehanna River valley. Their ancestors had arrived from the north, a dissident band of Iroquoian peoples drawn to the region's rich woodlands. An early seventeenth-century account, written by the English explorer Captain John Smith, referred to these people as "Sasquesahanoughs," a name Smith learned from an Eastern Algonquian–speaking interpreter. To Dutch and Swedish colonists, these inland Indians would come to be known as "Minquas," another term of Eastern Algonquian origins. What they called themselves is unknown, but historians and archaeologists have retained a version of the name Captain Smith used, mostly because the broad river near their villages came to bear a version of that name as well.

Smith and his party are the first Europeans known to have made contact with the Susquehannocks, although in fact it was the Susquehannocks who made contact with the Englishmen whose barge had stalled near the mouth of the Susquehanna. The river, originating in two branches, a northern one flowing out of the mountains of what is now southeastern New York State and a western one flowing down from the Pennsylvania mountains, had left too much sediment and too many rocky shoals near its mouth to afford passage for the English watercraft. But Susquehannock envoys readily paddled their canoes downriver to meet the visitors. Smith described the Susquehannocks as giants whose speech sounded "as a voyce in a vault" and who came dressed in bear and wolf skins. These striking men brought gifts of bows, arrows, wampum beads, swords, and tobacco pipes, clearly prepared to forge commercial relations with this latest party of foreigners to visit their homeland. Smith learned that that homeland was extensive and vibrant. The Susquehannocks lived in several palisaded villages, all defended by several hundred able-bodied warriors.[3]

Smith's account leaves little doubt that the Susquehannocks were a formidable presence—but it comes nowhere near capturing the full scope of Susquehannock military and economic power. Years of playing eastern Indian nations and their European trading partners against one another allowed the Susquehannocks to dominate trade across the northern Chesapeake and lower mid-Atlantic. Through their connections to the Iroquoian Wyandots, commonly known as the Hurons, the Susquehannocks triumphed in the great race to harvest beaver pelts from the forests of inland North America. Susquehannock successes in the fur trade would also account for the decline of Susquehannock power. Disease and war, products of the contest for inland commercial primacy, took their toll, and by the end of the seventeenth century there would be little left of the vibrant lower Susquehanna Indian villages. Some Susquehannocks would remain, but even they had mostly fled by the time Mason and Dixon first traversed the region. Just a few years earlier, Indians living near the site of the original Susquehannock villages had been nearly wiped out by a group of murderous Pennsylvania vigilantes known as the Paxton Boys.[4]

To the east, the Algonquian-speaking Lenape people had built thriving towns, with a population roughly comparable to their Susquehannock neighbors—probably a few thousand. The Lenape lived along the lower Delaware River, their influence reaching south, down the shore of the Delaware Bay. The Lenape were also traders but, like most eastern Native societies, they engaged in a variety of sustenance practices—they grew maize, they hunted deer, turkeys, bears, and other game, and they harvested oysters, clams, and fish from nearby rivers and coastal waters. To the English, the Lenape, along with all the other Algonquian peoples living near the Delaware River, were known simply as Delawares. That the English named the Delaware River and the Native peoples living near it for a governor of the Virginia colony, Thomas West, 3rd Baron De La Warr, known for his brutal treatment of Native peoples, was an irony lost on most. Mason and Dixon made no mention of the Lenape. After the onslaught of European settlement, enabled by fraudulent land claims and epidemics, most descendants of the seventeenth-century Lenape had migrated north, settling in the upper Susquehanna River valley. Others traveled west, and by the time Mason and Dixon traversed Lenape country, these Delawares were living in villages along the Ohio River and its tributaries.

In the half century following Mason and Dixon's survey, the mountainous western portion of the Line would remain a place of sparse Euro-American settlement. The area to the east, across the Cumberland Valley and the Piedmont ridge, would emerge as one of the Western world's most productive grain-producing regions. Gristmills would proliferate, and with those mills would come towns of dry-goods merchants, artisans, and manufacturers. By the 1830s, new networks of roads, canals, and railroads would carry all this economic expansion across the Appalachian Mountains to the Monongahela and Ohio River valleys. By the middle of the nineteenth-century, those areas bore the marks of industrialized agriculture. The woodlands Mason and Dixon traversed had been largely consumed, cleared for farmlands or their timber burned as fuel to heat homes and feed iron furnaces and steam engines.

Defying nature's dictates, the Mason-Dixon Line cut through eastern North America, its purpose to bring peace to a region racked by war. The Line never brought peace. It brought war of another kind. Mason had acquired a vague sense of the violence preceding his arrival in America, but unlike the enlightened colonial proprietors who hired him, he had little hope that a mere line on the land would bring peace to the Maryland-Pennsylvania borderlands. Violence, it seemed, had infected those lands to their very depths, leaving their immigrant inhabitants callous and cruel. The Indians recently slaughtered near the old Susquehannock homelands, Mason learned, "had always lived under the protection of the Pennsylvania Government and had Lands allotted for them a few Miles from Lancaster by the late celebrated William Penn, Esquire, Proprietor. They had . . . fled to the [Lancaster] Gaol to save themselves. The keeper made the door fast, but it was broken open; and two men went in and executed the bloody scene; while about 50 of their party sat on Horse Back without; armed with Guns, etc." The people of Lancaster "never offered to oppose" the murderers, despite the nearby presence of sympathetic British troops. This cruel indifference followed decades of internecine warfare. As early as 1736, a Pennsylvania official informed Mason, settlers, sent by the proprietors of Maryland and Pennsylvania, "were . . . at open war." The surveying party, it had become clear, traversed a battle zone as old as any in eastern North America.[5]

During a break from surveying activities, Mason traveled into Maryland to visit a giant cave used for church services. The cave's majesty impressed Mason in a way the great Pocomoke Swamp had not. Here was sublime nature with a very different, darker connotation. What Mason experienced was a natural cathedral whose vaulted ceiling drew the eye downward, toward some sort of mortal abyss, "striking its visitants with a strong and melancholy reflection: That such is the abodes of the Dead: Thy inevitable doom, O stranger, Soon to be numbered as one of them."[6]

Introduction

THIS BOOK TELLS THE STORY of a geopolitical boundary. That boundary marked the jurisdictional and territorial limits of the colonies—which would become the states—of Maryland, Pennsylvania, and Delaware, and it still bears the name of the two English astronomers, Charles Mason and Jeremiah Dixon, who worked between 1763 and 1767 to establish its definitive location.

Nestled in pastoral suburbs and gently rolling mid-Atlantic farmlands, the original Mason-Dixon Line and its innocuous stone markers, many first placed by Mason and Dixon, hardly suggest a boundary, let alone a border once as fraught as some of the world's most contested international borders. As you pass east along I-95, from Maryland into Delaware, or south from Chambersburg, along I-81 toward Hagerstown, there is barely a sense of border crossing at all. Signs bear the laconic welcome of state governors, rest stops have a few extra displays of tourist brochures, or there is a state-line liquor store—little else marks one's transit across the Line.

And yet, through the feverish middle decades of the nineteenth century, the Mason-Dixon Line, much like so many other territorial demarcations, became a locus of tension and conflict and a source of many of the very same kinds of anxieties and failed, futile policies that modern borders have produced in our own day. The most contentious such policies were those established under the Fugitive Slave Act of 1850, a law designed to weaken northern states' powers to stop the kidnapping and rendition of runaway slaves by giving the federal government primary jurisdiction in fugitive slave cases. Individual states could no longer determine the terms by which southerners reclaimed slave property. And with a federal government beholden to southern slaveholding interests, the liberty of self-manumitted former slaves was in true legal jeopardy everywhere in the continental United States.

As has happened in other border regions when distant authorities attempt to assert control, after 1850, the borderlands adjoining the Mason-Dixon Line witnessed a surge of vigilantism and violence.[1] In one notable instance, on September 11, 1851, the Maryland slave owner Edward Gorsuch and a group of slave catchers who had crossed into Pennsylvania entered the small border town of Christiana. They had come to retrieve a group of runaways and carry them back to a life of slavery. Gorsuch and his party were met by a large group of locals, outraged that one of their own—William Parker, an African American farmworker and self-manumitted slave—had been targeted for harboring fugitives. In the ensuing melee, Gorsuch was killed and another member of his party seriously injured.

Authorities referred to the incidents at Christiana as a riot, deserving of the American equivalent of the old English Riot Act, established in the early eighteenth century and giving magistrates the right to disperse or punish threatening mobs. One hundred forty-one alleged rioters were arrested, and thirty-nine were charged with treason against the United States. Although the government's case fell apart, the crisis at Christiana marked a new chapter in the history of the Line. Much like undocumented immigrants in our own day, African Americans north of the Line lived with the mortal fear of a species of deportation. As the federal government increased police activity north of the Line, enslaved African Americans to the south saw hopes for freedom within the United States dim as well. In response, a decades-old network of African Americans and white abolitionists now known as the Underground Railroad redoubled its efforts to take enslaved African Americans across the Line and, eventually, to safety in Canada.

In 1854, Maryland antislavery activist, lawyer, and historian John H. B. Latrobe, son of the celebrated neoclassical architect Benjamin Henry Latrobe, observed that the Mason-Dixon Line "was always expressive of the fact that the states of the union were divided into slaveholding and nonslaveholding—into Northern and Southern; and that those, who lived on opposite sides of the line of separation, were antagonistic in opinion upon an all engrossing question, whose solution . . . had been supposed to threaten the integrity of the republic." In Latrobe's mind, the survival of the world's most admired democratic republic would depend on whether it could alter what the Mason-Dixon Line had become—a border between North and South, slave states and free states. The border had lost any real significance as a boundary between specific states. "Men cared little," Latrobe explained, "where it ran or what was its history—or whether it was limited to Pennsylvania, or extended, as has, perhaps, most generally been supposed, from the Atlantic to the Pacific." Now "it suggested the idea of negro slavery; and that, alone, was enough to give it importance and notoriety."[2]

Latrobe's assessment echoes through the historical record to the present day. But as he recognized, it represented only part of the Line's story. As much a metaphor for a United States divided by the issue of slavery, the Line was a geopolitical border whose origins far predated the nineteenth-century fugitive slave crisis. Latrobe's insight frames my own interpretation of the Line's history. America's age-old reputation as a nation whose history has been driven by the defiance of boundaries and borders rests on deep historical amnesia. From very early in its history, the United States has been defined by borders and boundaries and all the tangled political struggles they reflect.[3]

Because my story is mostly one of government and politics, its central characters are agents of governance. English colonial proprietors and their various court patrons; Native American diplomats and traders; colonial governors, justices of the peace, tax collectors, and other officials—these are the primary actors in the first two parts of the book. The second two shift emphasis.

In 1780, the new republic of Pennsylvania enacted the world's first statutory act for the gradual abolition of slavery. From this point, in addition to a boundary between American states, the Line became a boundary between slave states and a free state. What that legal change meant for the borderlands adjoining the Line, and how it transformed a boundary between colonies into something resembling a border between slave states and an antislavery state—that is the story of the book's second half. As much a story of age-old policy struggles and jurisdictional confusion, this part of the book is also the story of a captive labor system and a federal republic whose legal treatment of that system varied widely from state to state. At the center of that story are slavery's opponents, Black and white Americans whose efforts had a profound impact on the legal and political regimes that had long sustained the institution of chattel slavery. But their impact on the Line itself, on the political and legal culture of the counties and towns adjoining the Line, would be much more incremental. As I explain in Part III, the gradual abolition of slavery had very little impact on the peoples of the Maryland-Pennsylvania borderlands. Of far greater consequence was the movement of goods from the borderlands to markets, mostly in the young boomtown of Baltimore. Only in the 1850s did the work of abolitionists and hundreds of African American fugitives from slavery take hold and transform the region adjoining the Line into one divided over the institution of slavery. That division, covered in the book's concluding two chapters, produced unlikely political alignments that explain why the states of Maryland and Delaware became so-called border states, or slave states that never seceded from the Union.

Among the challenges of structuring the story of the Mason-Dixon Line has been a subject that lies at the center of my career: the American Revolution. This familiar series of events figures prominently in the Line's story, but less as a profound historical rupture than as a period of political realignment—realignment that afforded Pennsylvania's radical statutory enactment of gradual abolition. Beyond this act, and its limited reverberations in the slave states adjoining the Line, the Revolution does not figure prominently. Of greater significance in the Line's history are events that precede the Revolutionary War.[4]

For much of the eighteenth century, the borderlands adjoining what would become the Line were among the most war-racked and violent areas in the British colonial world. The politics of war and security, far more than independence from Great Britain and the forging of America's federal republic, would reverberate through the region to the Civil War era. As I tell it, the story of the Line is really a story of Americans and their relationship to government. That relationship was frequently a profoundly antagonistic one. But that antagonism, an eighteenth-century variety, bore very little resemblance to the familiar modern hostility to the federal government.

There is very little evidence that the peoples of the borderlands were animated by anything like an ideological or libertarian antagonism toward

government. If anything, the opposite was the case: insofar as they were unified by politics, it was a politics of disappointment and aggrievement. The
white, property-owning men who dominated the region's electoral politics
demanded, over and over, more government. For most of the eighteenth
century, those demands centered on security, as settlers and homesteaders
fought Native peoples and rival colonizers for possession of land. In the latter
decades of the eighteenth century and the early decades of the nineteenth,
those demands centered on the closely aligned matters of internal improvements and tax relief.

That the demands of borderlands voters rarely translated into coherent
government policy was symptomatic of another perennial problem: the
eastward emphasis of state politics. This was more so in Pennsylvania than
in the other states adjoining the Line, but as by far the largest of those states,
Pennsylvania exerted a disproportionate influence over the politics and
economy of the borderlands. As eastern Pennsylvanians and their financial
supporters pushed for control of the produce of America's countryside, the
farmers and producers of the borderlands lost. This perception, driven
by the divisive commercial politics of the region, would draw together the
commercial basin between the Susquehanna River and the Appalachian
Mountains, from central Pennsylvania south through Maryland to the Potomac. This region, which I call greater Baltimore, defined the politics of
the borderlands, and those politics were, above all, a politics of sectional
grievance.

By the end of the eighteenth century, greater Baltimore was also a place
of relative ethnic and religious uniformity. Although Maryland and Delaware were slave states, relatively few slaves lived in the border counties of
those states. Free African Americans lived along the Line, but the vast majority of the borderlands' population were descendants of German-speaking
and Scots-Irish settlers. This latter point is crucial. The ethnic composition
of the borderlands was a legacy of the ethnocidal slaughter that enveloped
them during the middle decades of the eighteenth century. Among the consequences of all that violence and slaughter was the displacement of Native
American communities who had long controlled the borderlands and their
abundant natural and human-made wealth. The story of the Line is as much
a story of the colonial assault on these Native peoples as it is of the emergence of greater Baltimore. Had it not been for the lengthy, systematic
dispossession of Native nations, Mason and Dixon's work would never have

been undertaken, and even then the surveyors' work was directly shaped by remaining Native control of the borderlands. Envoys from the Iroquois League provided Mason and Dixon passage through Indian country but refused them passage across an Iroquois warpath, stopping the survey thirty-one miles short of its planned end point.

Readers familiar with early American history might justifiably wonder about the appropriateness of associating the term "border" with the Mason-Dixon Line. In modern usage, borders usually mark the territorial limits of sovereign geopolitical entities. As part of an international order that has prevailed in the European world since the seventeenth century, such entities, the most persistent of which have been states and empires, are assumed to have ultimate legal jurisdiction over bounded territorial claims. In their more modern iterations, nation-states also tend to be coterminous with ethnolinguistic groupings—or at least they have sought to achieve contiguousness with such groupings. The entities separated by the Line never possessed sovereign control over historically delineated territories, and their respective populations had nearly identical ethnolinguistic compositions. Moreover, far from possessing independent and distinct legal and political systems, they were subordinate provinces of a single federated empire, governed first by Great Britain and later by the United States.

Readers might also wonder how a border between colonies or American states could serve the primary function of territorial borders, at least as they have functioned since the nineteenth-century rise of the industrialized nation-state. That function, enabled by the sovereign exercise of governing power, centers on the power to control the movement of people. For most of its history, the Mason-Dixon Line had no effect whatsoever on the movement of people. No walls or fences have ever been associated with the Line. Similarly, the legal significance of the Line never included any capacity to dictate insider-outsider status. For white Americans at least, one's legal status was similar on both sides of the Line. Although one might be subject to the jurisdiction of colonies or states adjoining the Line, wherever one stood one was a subject of the king of Great Britain or, later, a citizen of the United States. The situation would be very different for Americans of African descent, but the distinction had less to do with the Line itself than with the peculiar political economy of slavery. Insofar as movement back and forth across the Line was at all regulated, it was regulated because the Line corresponded with legal limits on a particular commercial activity—chattel slavery. The states of Maryland and Delaware permitted slavery; the state of Pennsylvania severely restricted it. Only because of this interstate legal distinction does the Line become at all meaningful as a regulator of travel and migration. As a means of establishing national affiliation or citizenship and, in turn, regulating the movement of human beings, the Line was not, in any modern sense, a border.

If the Line is considered in the context of other efforts to mark and limit territory from the seventeenth through the mid-nineteenth centuries, the term becomes more appropriate. Early America was a largely border-free place. There were no routinely regulated and policed geopolitical borders anywhere in North America until the twentieth century.[5] Much like Europe before the Napoleonic Wars, the American continent was generally a place of vaguely defined jurisdictions, frontiers, and marchlands. A traveler (not constrained by subservient status as pauper, servant, apprentice, felon, slave, or Native American—the last ostensibly restricted to Native territories and trade routes by deeds and treaties) could move freely through the countryside, back and forth across the territorial claims of different colonies, states, empires, and Indigenous nations, oblivious to political geography.[6] In times of war, identity papers or passports were often necessary, but these rarely contained declarations of citizenship or national allegiance. They were akin to letters of introduction—documents endorsed by government officials or other persons of note testifying to the good character and peaceful purpose of the traveler—and they were usually needed for passing through ground claimed in war rather than across anything like a static international border.[7]

In Europe, the experience would have been much the same until one approached a river crossing or city. Remnants of the age of siege warfare, medieval walls and gates persisted into the eighteenth and early nineteenth centuries. A traveler crossing the Rhine into France or approaching a city could thus expect to confront gates and sentries demanding justification for entry, or perhaps requiring customs payments. This security apparatus was about as close as the premodern world came to something like a modern international border. As the architectural critic Lewis Mumford observed, "far more than a mere opening," the city gate "offered the first greeting to the trader, the pilgrim, or the common wayfarer; it was at once a customs house, a passport office and immigration control point, and a triumphal arch, its turrets and towers often vying . . . with those of the cathedral or town hall." In overwhelmingly rural eighteenth-century mainland British North America, Boston had its gate and New York its wall (of Wall Street fame), but otherwise there was very little of this kind of regulatory architecture. The sovereign limits of empires, cities, and states were rarely discernible.[8]

Insofar as premodern states and empires had territorial limits, they tended to be referred to as frontiers rather than borders. This was indicative of the fact that, much like the city-states and the kingdoms they succeeded, premodern states and empires had neither the inclination nor the means to articulate and defend precise lineal boundaries. The result was a kind of sovereignty that made only the vaguest claims to territory, especially territory far from the geographic loci of power. In a seminal study of the boundary between France and Spain in the Pyrenees, Peter Sahlins writes that through the eighteenth century, "the French monarchy continued to envision its sovereignty in terms of its jurisdiction over subjects, not over a delimited territory, relying on the inherited notions of 'jurisdiction' and 'dependency' instead of basing its administration on firmly delineated territorial circumscriptions."[9] While "zonal boundaries," or frontiers, were evident in the early modern Pyrenees and elsewhere in Europe, particularly in the plains and forests along Russia's western frontier, the vastness of the Americas and the limits of mapping technology meant that they were particularly abundant in the Western Hemisphere.[10] Even when maps suggested otherwise, imperial borders in the Americas tended more toward the zonal than the lineal. In an assessment that could be applied to any early modern Euro-American boundary, historian J. H. Elliott notes that "the straight line drawn on a map made the frontier of Brazil the most clear-cut frontier in all the Americas, but nobody in the seventeenth or early eighteenth century had any accurate idea of where in practice Portuguese territory ended and the Spanish viceroyalty of Peru began." This disjunction between cartographic ideal and geopolitical reality was never more evident than in Britain's ill-fated 1763 attempt to partition its mainland North American claims. The so-called Proclamation Line of 1763 was the cartographic answer to Britain's attempt to separate its Euro-American subjects from Native nations by somehow arresting the flood of colonists across the Appalachian Mountains into Indian territory. On maps, the Proclamation Line looks like any carefully mapped boundary line: a stark imposition along the Appalachian spine. On the ground, of course, the line was invisible. British military officials charged with policing the line threw up their hands in frustration as settlers flooded through the Ohio River valley into Indian country. As a partition between Native and European nations, the Proclamation Line was, like most such partitions, a near total failure.[11]

Within European imperial claims, particularly the mainland North American claims of Great Britain, lineal boundaries were far more common. But these were not, strictly speaking, borders, or at least they were never conceived of as territorial borders. They were instead much more akin to the kinds of fences, walls, and other spatial boundaries that separated private land claims or that separated private estates from commons. Only in their scope did the boundaries between Pennsylvania and Maryland—or North Carolina and Virginia, or New York and Connecticut—differ, at least in a legal sense, from the boundaries that demarcated commons from a feudal manor or that separated one manor from another. Both manorial boundaries and colonial boundaries marked the limits of land title, licensed by royal authority, to the various interests granted exclusionary rights to the Crown's overseas possessions. Much as in Britain, where titled lords controlled manors and incorporated bodies controlled some municipalities, the colonies were held by lords, such as William Penn and Cecil Calvert, the second Lord Baltimore, and by private corporate entities such as the Massachusetts Bay Company or the Lords Proprietors of Carolina. Insofar as these proprietary estates were bounded, they were bounded by cartographic decisions made by agents of the Crown, on the basis of only fragmentary geographic data and in the service of a domestic political agenda unrelated to the realities of colonial life.

The results of this arbitrary and narrowly instrumental approach to boundary making are readily apparent in maps of the eastern United States: colonial British America was largely a place of straight lines.[12] In their Euclidian perfection, the boundaries separating the American colonies and most of their successor states betray a purpose that had very little at all to do with bounding sovereign territory. Colonial boundaries reflected neither military conquest nor natural barriers to sovereignty—in the way that, say, the Pyrenees did for France and Spain. Instead, they reflected the arbitrary, top-down division of a monarchical domain. These boundaries, usually established by the Lords of Trade, a committee of Charles II's Privy Council, and later by the Board of Trade, a royally appointed advisory board, reflect the very narrow mandate of the king's colonial agents: to reward a small number of loyal subjects with landed estates, something European monarchs had been doing with ever more elaborate pomp and ritual since the early Middle Ages. Early America may have been a place of boundaries, but it was not a place of borders.

The boundary that would become the Mason-Dixon Line was different. In comparison to the frontiers and boundaries that crisscrossed early America, it looked and acted very much like a modern territorial border. Although the boundary that became the Mason-Dixon Line was much like the various colonial boundaries created by British government officials in the seventeenth and early eighteenth centuries, the boundary established by Charles Mason and Jeremiah Dixon had origins in military conflict and its associated fiscal demands, much as was the case with the boundaries of territorial nation-states.

The French and Indian War brought new and onerous fiscal problems to the colony of Pennsylvania. Those problems were exacerbated by the fact that without a clear border between Maryland and Pennsylvania, taxes, both direct (in the form of poll and property taxes) and indirect (in the form of militia and public service musters, ferry and turnpike fees, trade imposts, and excise taxes), became very difficult to levy. The fact that colonists living along the Line often had no idea if they lived in Delaware, Maryland, or Pennsylvania also made it very difficult for courts to adjudicate civil disputes or enforce criminal law. Without functioning courts, these regions left colonial lawmakers with the convenient perception that the Mason-Dixon borderlands were unworthy of public expenditure, feeding a politics of aggrievement and alienation. As a geopolitical demarcation, in other words, the Mason-Dixon Line may not have separated territorial nations, but its historical origins in problems of taxation and security were very much akin to the origins of international borders that did do this.[13]

Similarly, the colonies and states bounded by the Mason-Dixon Line were never recognized as sovereign, independent members of an international community of sovereign and independent states. But this did not mean they were somehow the opposite of independent nation-states. They were not vassal states. Their internal affairs were never controlled by exogenous authorities. Not until the very end of the last period covered here, the American Civil War, did either the British Empire or the United States aspire to achieve that kind of authority over its member provinces. If anything, the constitutional apparatuses underpinning both the British Empire and the new

American republic contained an array of mechanisms for the devolution of central imperial-style authority. Britain's American colonies possessed legally constituted governing institutions with powers associated with the modern state. They could tax, they could wage war, and they could treat and trade with certain quasi-foreign nations—the last reflective of the fact that neither Great Britain nor the United States was ever entirely consistent in their relations with autonomous Native American nations. The colonies did all of these things. For this reason, historian Patrick Spero has referred to colonial Pennsylvania as a "colony-state." The designation could as easily apply to all of Britain's mainland colonies.[14]

The revolution that transformed these colonies into confederated states began in part because the British government set out to reverse constitutional precedent. The constitutional order linking Great Britain to its mainland colonies was much more like a league of nations than a Roman-style empire. The colonies had always been responsible for their internal affairs, which is precisely why so many saw the stamp tax as unconstitutional: it was a tax levied by Parliament on goods made within the colonies themselves. Of course, the colonies' assertion of constitutional autonomy gave way to a new push for an external, imperial-like authority. That push culminated in a new federal constitutional power to levy taxes within formerly independent American states. The unraveling of the autonomy enjoyed by the former British colonies would nevertheless be a long and slow process. The authority to tax, for example, did not necessarily translate into effective tax policy. The Whiskey Rebellion, a 1794 Pennsylvania rebellion against a federal tax on distilled spirits, left little doubt about the political challenges of federal taxation.

William Penn and Charles Calvert, the third Lord Baltimore, initially faced their boundary troubles in the late seventeenth century through diplomatic channels. The two colonial proprietors used emissaries—ambassadors—to begin negotiations, and they approached the problem of their disputed boundary as a diplomatic one, undertaken by two geopolitical entities relating to each other through the protocols and rituals of treaty making. During the eighteenth century, the proprietors' descendants would redefine the dispute as one over private property and would seek redress through the king's courts. Once these proprietary colonies became states and their boundary conflicts were taken up by the respective governments of the new states, an old seventeenth-century pattern returned: the Maryland-Pennsylvania boundary dispute left the civil courts and returned to the provincial capitals. Diplomatic delegations, deputized by governors of the adjoining states, would again be called on to resolve the boundary question.

The point here is that although the boundary line separating Maryland, Delaware, and Pennsylvania, was not, strictly speaking, an international border, for much of its history those charged with administering the Line acted as if, in fact, it was. The colonies separated by the Line defy easy historical classification. They bear some resemblance to a variety of antiquated geopolitical entities. Much like European palatinates, duchies, principalities, and some cities, they were essentially controlled by proprietary families. Much like city-states, they exerted political influence far into their hinterlands, but that influence was more likely to be over persons and goods than territory. In their territorial boundaries, their taxation policies, their military conduct, and their diplomacy, they also have characteristics consistent with territorial nation-states. We call them colonies, but exactly what this means has never been clear. Perhaps the best way to think about them is in light of what legal historians have identified as the layered and often composite nature of sovereignty in early modern empires. Whatever the American colonists may have claimed in their 1765 rejection of the stamp tax or their ultimate declaration of independence from Great Britain, the British Empire had always been a place of competing and overlapping powers and jurisdictions, and those powers and jurisdictions, whatever their legal source, were sustained through appropriation of lands and the income generated from those lands. It was precisely these facts that led to the creation of the Mason-Dixon Line. The proprietary mode of government produced geopolitical conduct very much like that more commonly associated with sovereign, territorial states, precisely because the burdens borne by proprietary government were, in large measure, equivalent to those borne by sovereign territorial states.[15]

Although the Mason-Dixon Line originated from historical circumstances commonly associated with international borders, there was one quality associated with those borders the Line acquired only very late in its history. That particular quality was, paradoxically, the one that most separates the Line from colonial-era British-American boundaries. In the half century following the Revolutionary War, the Line was incorporated into a system of discipline and surveillance that distinguished between insiders and outsiders—between full members of the national community and human beings long denied membership in that community. Those insiders and outsiders did not carry the designations we most commonly associate with legally sanctioned membership in a national community: citizens and non-citizens (or aliens). Instead, they carried arcane designations that are, at least superficially, very much unlike the designations associated with rights-bearing subjects or citizens at the territorial limits of nation-states. The insiders and outsiders designated by policy surrounding the Mason-Dixon Line were, respectively, free Americans and enslaved Americans of African descent. What dictated insider-outsider status thus had less to do with one's capacity to demonstrate legal affiliation with a given territorial entity than it did with one's capacity to demonstrate a very different kind of legal status, that of a free or enslaved person. For white Americans, this meant that the Line remained, in effect, as it had always been. These Americans' associational status was more or less unchanged, whichever side they found themselves on. For Americans of African descent, the story was obviously completely different. One's legal status was entirely conditional. On the south side of the Line, African Americans were either free or enslaved. On the north side of the Line, where slavery was gradually abolished, a resident Black American would be either a free Black or a fugitive from slavery.

Although African Americans legally crossed the Line, they did so under the onus of a legal regime that looked very much like one we might associate with modern international borders: they were required to carry identity papers, and they bore the burden of demonstrating legal status before ordinary whites as well as state and federal magistrates. Those lacking suitable documentation faced a species of deportation into a life of slavery. The fact that, as a demarcation of insider-outsider status, the Line limited the movement only of one particular group might suggest a geopolitical demarcation very much unlike modern international boundaries. The latter, in theory at least, establish insider status equally for all naturalized citizens. Of course, the reality is very different. Whites on both sides of the nineteenth-century Line were much like citizens of wealthy, developed countries, able to travel unimpeded by the walls and fences and security personnel marking the territorial limits of nation-states. For the global poor, political refugees, and other victims of political instability and economic insecurity, in contrast, boundary crossing obviously means something very different. In the present-day United States, undocumented migrants live with ethnic and legal stigma, in addition to the fear of imprisonment and deportation. For Americans of African descent, life north of the Line came with very similar hazards.

These counterfactuals can obviously only go so far. Although the experience of African Americans across the Line may have had similarities to the experience of modern migrants, the legal and political apparatus surrounding the movement of these groups were very different. While many migrants are denied citizenship, some wealthy industrialized states accord them basic human rights. The degree to which undocumented migrants actually enjoy such rights obviously varies widely. Similarly, some have argued that human rights have come into being primarily as a means of easing the international movement of cheap labor. Liberal governments, according to this reasoning, can justify denying migrant laborers citizenship because they accord them the purported right not to suffer torture, unjust imprisonment, enslavement, and assorted other cruelties.[16] Alleged runaway slaves could claim no such rights. For a time, some northern states afforded African Americans a species of state citizenship. Northern personal liberty laws allowed accused fugitives from slavery to argue against claims on their persons in state courts, but no national or international legal order guaranteed them rights to anything like habeas corpus or freedom from cruel and unusual treatment.

In arguing that the Mason-Dixon Line bore hallmarks of borders between modern nation-states, my purpose is to uncover a long-overlooked chapter in early American history. The story of the Mason-Dixon Line will also, I hope, reinforce what has been a far-reaching development in early American history writing. From a place once studied for what made it exceptional, what made it different from European progenitors, scholars have come to understand early America through the networks linking its peoples to the Old World societies and states that sponsored its colonization. Understanding the history of the Mason-Dixon Line less for what made it distinctly *American* and more for what made it reflective of larger, transcontinental, transoceanic processes that shaped the early modern and nineteenth-century worlds reinforces just how important that boundary was, not only to the history of the United States but also to the broader global history of state making and political development. If the story of America's founding divide resonates with similar stories elsewhere, I will have achieved one of my core ambitions: reminding readers that ours is not a history sui generis but a history of processes and peoples far transcending anything so fleeting as a line on the land.[17]

PART I

MARCHLANDS IN MOTION

Although Pennsylvania was founded nearly a half century after Maryland, the two colonies were very similar geopolitical entities. Both were founded by prominent Englishmen with dissenting religious views. Both were unmistakably commercial ventures. Both faced existential security threats—from dissident factions within and from Native and Euro-American nations without. And both were, according to the royal charters that authorized their creation, defined by strict, lineal boundaries. Those boundaries were intended to function in much the way boundaries between nations function: they were to mark the jurisdictional limits of distinct semisovereign governments. But a combination of limited cartographic knowledge and divergent political pressures meant that the intended function of these colonial boundaries would be almost entirely aspirational. Royal authorities deferred to colonial proprietors to resolve the ensuing jurisdictional disputes. As intercolonial diplomacy proceeded, violent rivalries with the Dutch and the dominant Native powers of Maryland's far north, the Lenape and the Susquehannocks, would lead to lasting demographic change.

CHAPTER 1

Lord Baltimore's
Northern Problem

GEORGE CALVERT, English founder of the Maryland colony and the first Lord Baltimore, was born in late 1579 or early 1580 in Yorkshire, a region dense with Catholic recusancy. The Catholic Calverts would bear witness to the stark confessional realities of the region's anti-Catholic persecution. Local authorities ordered the disbanding of the Catholic school George and his brother Christopher had attended, and the Calvert family was forced to employ a Protestant tutor to bring the boys around to the established creed. George's Catholic father, Leonard, capitulated to official pressure and entered the Church of England, but his mother, Alice, seems never to have done so. For the Calvert boys, the family's confessional divisions must have been deeply troubling and surely had something to do with George's quest to found a Catholic refuge in America. Born into the church of their mother but now seeing their father leave for England's church, the younger Calverts would have to make a difficult choice. For young George, clearly an ambitious child, the path would be clear. At age twelve he followed his father into the English church, and several years later he matriculated at Trinity College, Oxford. Until 1624, Calvert would maintain his adherence to Anglican rites.

After completing additional studies in the law at Lincoln's Inn, Calvert came under the tutelage of an exceptionally powerful patron, Sir Robert Cecil, the Earl of Salisbury. Although "dwarfish in stature," Cecil was to become a titanic player in the royal court.[1] Following his father, William, Queen Elizabeth's principal secretary, Robert entered the queen's inner circle, initially serving as secretary of state and eventually replacing his father as the queen's closest advisor. By far Robert Cecil's greatest achievement was managing the succession to the English throne of James Stuart, the king of Scotland and the queen's second cousin. For his role in bringing James to power, Cecil was showered with lucrative offices and titles and in 1608 was appointed lord treasurer, which was, along with lord chancellor and lord keeper of the privy seal, the highest office in English government.

With so powerful a patron, George Calvert's ascent was swift. In 1606, shortly after the birth of Calvert's son Cecil, named for his father's patron, the king appointed Calvert to the office of clerk of the Crown and assizes in the province of Connaught, County Clare, Ireland. In 1609, Cecil arranged for Calvert to take a seat in Parliament for the Cornish borough of Bossiny. He also arranged an appointment for Calvert as clerk in the king's Signet Office. The following year Calvert received the ultimate promotion, becoming a clerk of the king's Privy Council. Proximity to power and power itself were of a piece in the early modern English court. Calvert was far from being a mere clerk; short of being on the Privy Council itself, he could rise no further in the ranks of royal officeholders.

Calvert's prominence at court would lead to an assortment of important diplomatic missions, and in 1612, after Cecil's death, Calvert would begin work as an executor of the earl's estate. The pinnacle of Calvert's time in the king's service came in 1619, when James I appointed him one of his secretaries of state. The former Catholic boy from North Yorkshire, who had been knighted in 1617 and who was now a member of the king's Privy Council, found himself with easy access to the monarch himself, by far the most valuable asset to which any Englishman could aspire—and a worthy tribute to Calvert's late patron, the Earl of Salisbury, a master courtier. Although Calvert had prospered in Cecil's service, his wealth was not what it would become after he joined the circle of the king's closest advisors. In a fitting display of Sir George's new stature, he purchased the Yorkshire estate Kiplin Hall, which would become the Calverts' English family seat until 1722, when it was sold by Calvert's great-great-grandson and future proprietor of Maryland, Charles Calvert, the fifth Lord Baltimore.

Although he served the king during the initial age of English overseas expansion, for most of his first decade in royal service Calvert treated this burgeoning empire as did most other members of the king's court: another benefit of employment in the royal household. He purchased shares in several colonial ventures, including the East India Company and the private company that established the Virginia colony in 1607, but Calvert took no special interest in these novel enterprises.

The great mystery in George Calvert's life is his return to the Catholic Church. It appears to have happened around the time he sold his seat on the Privy Council to Sir Albertus Morton for the substantial sum of £3,000. His patron hardly seems to have begrudged so loyal a servant's return to Rome. As a final emolument, the king made Calvert lord of the Irish Barony of Baltimore.

Exactly how the first Lord Baltimore's Catholicism figured in his overseas ambitions remains as opaque a matter as his return to the church. The only certainty is that when Calvert began pursuing his colonial plans, those plans showed a distinct sympathy for England's Catholic minority. Even before his Catholicism became public, Calvert entertained thoughts of an overseas Catholic refuge. The province of Avalon, a colony in Newfoundland, established on lands Calvert purchased in 1620 from a bankrupted former Oxford friend, Sir William Vaughan, would receive a small number of settlers prepared to brave the harsh conditions of America's far-north Atlantic coast. In exchange, these colonists would face no formal restrictions on their confessional inclinations. The colony's charter, granted to Calvert in 1623, would reflect the general religious attitudes of the court of James Stuart. There would be no bold assertions of religious tolerance, but neither would there be vigorous enforcement of the supremacy of the English church. A colony with Catholics was far from a Catholic colony.

Another characteristic of the Avalon colony, while not exactly controversial, proved far more important, at least for Calvert's future. The colony was to be a feudal palatinate, a type of land tenure characterized by one authority as affording its lord "a very close relation to the person of the sovereign." What this meant was not so much political proximity as manorial authority: the lord or earl palatine would effectively possess powers over his feudal grant undifferentiated from those of the king over his kingdom.[2] He could create manorial estates or enfeoff smaller holdings. He could appoint and oversee magistrates; he could levy taxes; he could dictate ecclesiastical affairs; he could make and enforce law, in consultation with his subjects; and he was otherwise empowered to govern and defend his fiefdom. This palatinate model represented a departure from earlier colonial charters. As a means of encouraging private investment, these had been granted to limited-liability joint stock companies controlled by a board of investors. That board would, in effect, be the highest court of appeal and would have substantial influence over lawmaking. With unitary ownership, governance of the Avalon colony would also be unitary—it would reside with the person of a vice-regal Sir George Calvert, Lord Baltimore.

The unitary propriety of a palatinate served aims consistent with ancient practice: the rewarding of a favorite with hereditary title to some portion of the realm. But the Crown's decision to include a palatinate clause in Avalon's colonial charter had little to do with rewarding Calvert and much to do with colonial geopolitics. The palatinate originated as a means of maintaining control in regions far beyond the reach of ordinary institutions of government. England's palatinate counties, Chester, Lancaster, and the oldest of them, Durham, were all in the north of the country, far from the seat of monarchical authority. The bishop of Durham, the ruler of that county-palatinate, had much broader powers to assemble armies and organize military action than did other feudal lords, and this proved vital in mobilizing defenses against Scottish invaders. In exchange for policing English borders, the bishops of Durham could expect general immunity from royal writs and other proclamations. With no representation in Parliament, lawmaking was left to the bishops and their courts. Relations with the Crown came not through the usual networks of royal patrons and parliamentarians but through quasi-diplomatic agents.[3]

The Avalon colony was never able to attract more than about a hundred English and Irish settlers, most of whom endured horrific deprivation and sickness. Writing from Ferryland, his feeble colonial seat, Calvert apprised the Crown of his colony's dire circumstances. His own "house hath beene an hospital all this wynter, of 100 persons 50 sick at a time, myself being one and nyne or ten of them died."[4] To prevent further loss of life, Calvert and his family abandoned Ferryland to search for a more hospitable Avalon, eventually making their way south to the Virginia colony.

With the collapse of the Virginia Company in 1624, local officials now served at the pleasure of King Charles I, who had succeeded his father and Calvert's patron in March 1625. A more temperate colony controlled by clients of the Stuarts, Calvert concluded, was the best available alternative to an unsustainable Calvert-owned colony in the frigid north. Although happy for such an esteemed courtier as Lord Baltimore to join their colony, Virginians were less happy about the arrival of a powerful and influential Catholic. Calvert might have allayed their concerns by swearing oaths of allegiance to the English king and to the king's supremacy over England's church. As a member of Parliament, the Protestant Calvert had done so. But now he refused; the governing council of Virginia, anxious about rising religious disorder, could hardly indulge such egregious dissent and began pressuring Calvert to leave the colony.[5]

Calvert returned to England, where he spent the final two years of his life planning a new Avalon, one that avoided both the climatic constraints of Newfoundland and the religious ones of the king's existing colonies. Because of his loyalty to the king's late father, Calvert remained a royal favorite and somebody whom Charles I saw as a worthy agent of his realm's American expansion. With the help of friends on the Privy Council, Calvert petitioned the Crown for a chartered colony south of the James River. The scheme ultimately failed after former directors of the Virginia Company complained that it violated their claims to Virginia Company lands.

It is a measure of how arcane and improvised the legal apparatus of English colony building was that such a claim had any validity at all. The Crown had, after all, revoked the Virginia Company's charter. But the former holders of that charter argued that royal control did nothing to alter their property rights. Like any feudal conveyance, the charter granted permanent title to portions of the king's realm. In revoking the charter, the only thing the king had done, according to this logic, was affirm his authority to govern his dominions. Investors still owned Virginia, at least as stipulated by the colony's founding documents, and a grant to Calvert on lands so close to the company's original settlements clearly violated this fundamental agreement. The idea that former shareholders would give over portions of their rightful claims to another colonizer was all the more alarming when that colonizer was a Catholic who had already refused to subscribe to Virginia's Protestantism. Rather than litigate the claims of Virginia Company investors, the Privy Council accepted the opposition argument and proposed a new location, this one north of Virginia. Here, it seemed, there was less danger of intruding on the former Virginia Company claims, but a northern location would also accomplish a pressing new strategic end.[6]

Thriving Dutch Atlantic trade, a byproduct of the Netherlands' long dominance of the Baltic trade and its more recent entry into the Asian spice trade, transformed the United Provinces into a commercial juggernaut. The influx of commercial wealth allowed the Dutch West India Company, a private corporate behemoth designed to exploit the mercantile and financial zeal of Dutch merchants, to wrest New World silver and land from the provinces' Iberian enemies. In the twenty years after its founding in 1621, the company took control of Curaçao as well as several other Caribbean islands and began laying claim to Portuguese Brazil. For the English court, the more immediate concern was Dutch colonization along North America's Atlantic coast. The Dutch colony at New Amsterdam had shown itself to be as avaricious and expansive as its English counterparts in Massachusetts and Virginia. From its beachhead on Manhattan Island, its traders established fur-trading posts far up the Hudson River near present-day Albany and south, on the east banks of the Delaware River in the vicinity of present-day Camden, New Jersey. A northern location for Lord Baltimore's new colony could thus counter Dutch expansion into the lower Delaware Valley.[7]

George Calvert died on April 15, 1632, at age fifty-two, two months before the charter for his new colony received its final royal seal. The charter would be granted to Calvert's eldest son, Cecil, the second Lord Baltimore, and it would look very much like that awarded George for an earlier Calvert family venture. Like Avalon, the colony of Maryland—named for the queen consort, Henrietta Maria—was to be a palatinate. Cecil Calvert would have sweeping powers not only over the government of his new colony but also, much like the bishops of Durham, over its ecclesiastical affairs. In fact, he would have far more control—at least in theory—than the seventeenth-century bishops of Durham had. After 1536, King Henry VIII had constrained the judicial autonomy of the Durham bishops, and royal magistrates would subsequently assume control of that palatinate's legal system. In Maryland, the second Lord Baltimore and his heirs would be empowered "by judges by them delegated, to award Process, hold Pleas, and determine in those Courts . . . and Tribunals, in all Actions, Suits, Causes, and Matters whatsoever."[8]

Whatever the precise political origins of the Maryland palatinate, the political consequences of a chartered entity enjoying extensive constitutional autonomy were far-reaching. For Virginia's supporters, the fact that Cecil Calvert had such sweeping powers only made the Maryland colony more threatening. The first Lord Baltimore had already proven reluctant to disavow any papal allegiances, and now the second Lord Baltimore was being granted a minor kingdom in territory claimed by the directors of the former Virginia Company. Able to conduct his own diplomacy and warfare, Lord Baltimore could ally his colony with Catholic Spain or perhaps even build direct ties to Rome. Even more troubling, there was no constitutional clarity whatsoever about the palatinate's powers relative to other colonies. Should Virginia and Maryland come to dispute their respective boundaries, for example, the terms of the palatinate suggested that Maryland would negotiate as a quasi-independent state, while Virginia, now a royal colony, would have to defer to royal authority. For the Virginians, this might have been a mere technicality had there been a different king. But Charles I's court, with its well-known Catholic sympathies, could not be trusted to insulate faraway Virginia from the machinations of English Catholics.[9]

In its efforts to appease Virginia Company partisans, the Privy Council and its lawyers employed a new method for parceling out the Crown's American domain. The Lords Baltimore and their heirs would have title to a clearly defined tract, or at least as clearly defined as seventeenth-century cartographic knowledge afforded.

Maryland would include the Delmarva Peninsula (excluding its southern tip, which remained in Virginia and was separated from the colony by a boundary line running from Watkins Point on the west due east to the Atlantic coast). The colony's northern boundary, and the one that would eventually be the point of contestation with William Penn and his heirs, would begin "unto that part of the Bay of Delaware . . . which lieth under the Fortieth degree of North Latitude" and would follow a direct path to Maryland's western boundary, a north-south meridian line running between the fortieth parallel and the "first Fountain of the River of Pattowmack." The southern boundary would then track the Potomac's far bank to "a certain place called Cinquack, situate near the mouth of the said River, where it disembogues into the aforesaid Bay of Chesapeake, and thence by the shortest

N

40°N · 40°N

Schuylkill River

Fort Nassau ◇

LORD BALTIMORE

1632 GRANT

Susquehanna River

SUSQUEHANNOCKS

LENAPE

Christina River

Delaware River

◇ Fort Christina
◇• New Amstel
Fort Casimir

Patapsco River

Severn River

Patuxent River

DELAWARE BAY

Potomac River

Kent
Island

39°N

39°N

Cape May

Whorekill

Cape Henlopen
(Swanendael)

Rappahannock River

CHESAPEAKE BAY

Potomac River

St. Mary's
City •

VIRGINIA

38°N

38°N

Watkin's
Point

James River

ATLANTIC
OCEAN

Jamestown
•

Cape Charles

Point Comfort

37°N

Map Key

LENAPE Tribal area

• Village

◇ Fort

Maryland, c. 1660

Line unto the aforesaid Promontory of Place, called Watkin's Point."[10] In the history of American boundary making, the Maryland charter was momentous. It represents the first time England attempted to confine a colony within lineal boundaries.

In some ways the cartographic progression of England's mainland colonies suggests growing sophistication: from the Virginia colony, an amorphous grant between two parallels of latitude, defined in space primarily by nature's dictates and the expansion of fortress-like outposts, England's colonies came to have lineal boundaries made possible by improved cartographic knowledge. But progress would be the wrong frame through which to view Maryland's boundaries. Maryland was, at base, a feudal conveyance. It represented a monarch's efforts to reward a favorite while serving larger geopolitical aims. In this way, it was no different from the medieval palatinates or really any other feudal conveyance. Although the palatinate carried no ongoing obligation to the monarch—no knightly service or socage—it was, like all other forms of feudal land tenure, a portion of the king's dominions granted to a royal favorite as reward for service to the court. That it was a bounded grant reflected the fact that this particular colony, however necessary a prize for the Calverts and however useful as a bulwark against Dutch expansion, was created at a time of continued confessional strife.

The second Lord Baltimore was an unlikely lord for this new palatinate. Although he inherited a title, he never held government office, and his reputation at court was paltry compared to his father's—he was at best a shadowy factotum to the celebrated first Lord Baltimore. But perhaps Cecil's relative insignificance turned out to be beneficial. Lacking his father's association with James I, he would have been a much less alarming neighbor for Virginia. At the same time, without his father's influence at court, and without the former secretary of state's experience in foreign affairs, Cecil would have to rely on very different resources if his family's new American venture were to avoid fatal political entanglements. A less devoted son or a less opportunistic subject might have abandoned the whole business altogether. An Irish baronage was modest by English baronial standards, but in conjunction with Cecil's English estate and his family's name, it gave him ample wealth for an aristocratic style of life.

And yet abandoning the new American colony was something Cecil seems never to have considered.

Eight years into its founding, a total of around five hundred English had come to Maryland; fewer than four hundred survived long enough to appear on the colony's tax rolls.[11] St. Mary's City, Maryland's first official English settlement, consisted primarily of agricultural laborers, tenants, and small freeholders. Although this relative concentration of English colonists adhered to the authority of the second Lord Baltimore and his king, by the early 1640s that authority was in decline. By the middle of the decade, the colony's government, such as it was, would collapse and the colony would descend into chaos, raising the threat of a writ of quo warranto dissolving Maryland's royal charter.

Adding to Maryland's challenges were a few hundred colonists, a diverse and motley collection hailing mostly from Holland, Sweden, Finland, and England. They built fortifications along the Christina River in the lower Delaware Valley under the auspices of an entity known as the Swedish West India Company, but in fact these colonists were agents of Dutch commercial ambition. Although the Dutch West India Company had abandoned its colonizing efforts at the far southern reaches of New Netherlands, the Indian trade continued to attract Dutch merchants. With the endorsement of the Swedish Crown and a group of Swedish investors, Peter Minuit, the German-born former director general of the New Netherlands colony, established a new Swedish-sponsored settlement on the southwestern banks of the Delaware River. During the middle decades of the seventeenth century, this nominally Swedish colony would become the focus of a global conflict between Native groups and European powers. That conflict would conclude with far-reaching geopolitical realignments. In place of a Dutch threat, Maryland confronted a very different kind of threat, this one from its own English countrymen. And far from the powerful fur traders they had been during the first few decades of Maryland's existence, the Susquehannocks would become refugees, driven from their home villages deep into Maryland, where they would be victimized by the fateful events known as Bacon's Rebellion. This tumultuous chapter in Maryland's history accompanied profound demographic change. While Chesapeake Maryland looked more or less as it had twenty or thirty years earlier—still a place of small, isolated plantations—a critical change had begun occurring in the colony's workforce. From one dominated by English indentured servants, it was increasingly populated by enslaved laborers of African descent.

Following the English Civil War, advisors to the restored Stuart monarch, King Charles II, began contemplating action against a very weak link in the Dutch West India Company's commercial empire. A declining fur trade had driven the company to redirect its activities from trade to settlement. In the contest for territorial expansion, the company proved no match for its English counterparts. English settlers had already begun occupying Dutch-claimed Long Island and portions of Connecticut. Puritan families from New Haven, meanwhile, took advantage of ever-shifting claims along the lower Delaware to settle there as well.

Given its impotence in the face of foreign settlement, Charles II's advisors reasoned that New Netherlands was ripe for English annexation, and in March 1664, the king granted his brother James, the Duke of York, a patent for a vast new American estate, incorporating New Netherlands. This included all territory west of the Connecticut River and east of the Delaware River, in addition to Dutch claims in the upper Hudson Valley, the English-claimed islands of Long Island, Nantucket, and Martha's Vineyard.

To seize control of his new colony, the Duke of York appointed Richard Nicolls, a distinguished former cavalry commander and close advisor. Nicolls was to lead a small invasion fleet, carrying several hundred English troops, some of whom had been promised American estates in exchange for military service. These costly preparations proved unnecessary. By the end of August 1664, after some shrewd diplomacy by Governor John Winthrop Jr. of Connecticut, Peter Stuyvesant, director general of the New Netherlands colony, surrendered his charge to England, and the colony of New York came into being. In October, a member of Nicolls's invading party, Sir Robert Carr, accompanied by his son Captain John Carr, sailed two ships up the Delaware River to the Dutch Fort Casimir, not far from the old Swedish colony on the Christina. The Carrs demanded the surrender of the remains of the fort and the nearby Dutch village of New Amstel, to be rechristened New Castle by the English. Carr, a ruthless colonizer with little regard for legal formality and much regard for himself, proved indifferent to the fact that these Dutch settlements were situated on the Delaware's western shore and thus were beyond the limits of the duke's grant. When the region's inhabitants resisted, Carr and his men killed and injured several of them and seized all of New Amstel, including a number of enslaved Africans, a sawmill, a brewery, and livestock.[12]

The assault on a peaceful settlement infuriated Governor Nicolls, who had been commanded by the Duke of York to accommodate Dutch settlers so long as they swore allegiance to their new English lord. Were it not for Carr, in fact, the English seizure of New Netherlands would have involved precisely what the Duke of York and his brother the king had hoped for: a peaceful transition in colonial lordship. Nicolls traveled to New Amstel to reassure settlers that, despite Carr's outrages, they would be left in peace, on condition that they demonstrate allegiance to their new English lord. But Nicolls did little to compensate the former Dutch colonists for Carr's plunder and in a pattern that would define royal policy toward Maryland, never accounted for the fact that the attack took place outside the duke's formally recognized claims, never mind that they were actually within the competing claims of a fellow Englishman.

Things could hardly get worse for the second Lord Baltimore. For decades he had little success countering Dutch claims to the northeastern corner of his colony. But at least his battle was consistent with the aims of his charter—contending with threats from a foreign power. There could only be political gain in an English lord's advances at Dutch expense. But now those advances would come at the expense of the king's brother. Whatever Lord Baltimore's charter may have indicated, there was little guarantee that the crown would choose to overrule the Duke of York's agents and restore Maryland's claims to the New Castle settlements.

By the late 1660s, the eastern coast of North America from the Carolinas to Maine was at least nominally part of the dominions of the king of England, and all of this vast territory had been parceled out among various proprietors and private companies. Any further grants near coastal North America would thus intrude on existing grants or would involve interstitial lands on the margins of those grants. The absence of any systematic accounting of the territorial limits of existing grants made it difficult for the Lords of Trade and Plantations, the Privy Council committee charged with administering colonial affairs, to identify with any real clarity the limits of those interstitial lands. In an attempt to inform the lords about the spatial extent of England's proliferating American colonies, William Blathwayt, the lords' secretary, assembled a collection of colonial maps into what is now known as *The Blathwayt Atlas*. The collection is a treasure, the definitive cartographic accounting of England's overseas conquests, but still numbers only a few dozen maps in total, many fragmentary and inaccurate.

Augustine Herrman, a Czech religious refugee who settled in New Netherlands and became a prosperous fur trader and colonial official, was responsible for one of the most important of the *Atlas*'s maps—at least from the vantage of Maryland's proprietor. Herrman came to know Lord Baltimore's younger brother Philip in 1659 when the mapmaker and another Dutch official traveled to Maryland to negotiate an agreement over competing claims to the lower Delaware Valley. The negotiations achieved little, but they did make clear to Herrman, Philip Calvert, and the second Lord Baltimore that, whatever the intent of the Privy Council clerks and lawyers who drafted Maryland's charter, the actual boundaries of the colony remained abstractions, enshrined in an obscure legal document. In an effort to strengthen his claims to the lower Delaware and the Delmarva Peninsula, Lord Baltimore commissioned Herrman to prepare a definitive map of Maryland, including contiguous lands and waterways. In exchange for the map, Lord Baltimore granted Herrman the right to several thousand acres along the Oppoquimimi River (whose name Herrman would change to the Bohemia River, in recognition of his central European origins), on the far northeastern shore of the Chesapeake. Herrman, with his long-standing connection to New Netherlands, saw the location in terms of its commercial potential. His Maryland manor would be near an easy portage between the nearby Elk River and the Christina River (or Mincquas Kill, as it was known to the Dutch).

The map Herrman created, acquired by Blathwayt several years before William Penn petitioned the Crown for his American colony, established an unprecedented level of cartographic clarity about the coastal contours of the Eastern Shore of Maryland, the Chesapeake Bay, and the lower Delaware Valley. A dotted line just along the map's solid right-hand border (the map has a western orientation) depicts the fortieth parallel of latitude, Maryland's northern limit as understood by the colony's proprietor. This feature of Herrman's map bore heavily on Herrman's own commercial fortunes, since it

"Virginia and Maryland as it is Planted and Inhabited this Present Year 1670" by Augustine Herrman. The west
orientation suggests a Maryland as unbounded as its southern neighbor. Maryland's northern boundary, along
the right margin and vital to Lord Baltimore's claims along the lower Delaware, is barely visible.
Reproduction courtesy the John Carter Brown Library.

proved that Cecil County, where Herrman's Bohemia Manor was located,
was in fact in Maryland.

Herrman's map, a cartographical masterpiece by any standard, was not
entirely accurate in its placement of Maryland's northern boundary. The
actual fortieth parallel crosses the Schuylkill River south of the mouth of
Wissahickon Creek, just south and west of present-day Germantown. Herrman depicted the parallel a number of miles to the north, intersecting the
Delaware River above present-day Rancocas Creek (called by Herrman the
Remkokes) near modern Burlington, New Jersey. Herrman was closer
to the mark with the western limits of Maryland's northern boundary. He

located the line at Fort Susquehanna, the Susquehannock settlement on the west bank of the river, just north of the mouth of the Conestoga River (called by Herrman the Onestego River, perhaps owing to a printer's misreading of Herrman's original) and not far from the actual fortieth parallel.

In addition to its confusing placement of Maryland's northern boundary, Herrman's map entirely ignored the festering tangle over rightful control of former New Sweden. In Herrman's depiction, the colony was firmly part of Maryland. The one concession Herrman made to the contested nature of Maryland's northern border was his depiction of Cecil County. Instead of extending the county north to Maryland's northern boundary, Herrman left its northern limit unmarked. This may have been Herrman's way of ac-knowledging the claims of his former Dutch employer, Peter Stuyvesant, or it may have been an acknowledgment of the claims of the Native nations on which his own business interests depended. None of this can be known for certain, but what is certain is that the printed version of Herrman's map demonstrates that even the most accurate contemporary maps afforded royal officials only a marginally improved grasp of the precise territorial limits of England's mainland colonies.[13]

It had been a generation since a tiny Dutch outpost known as Swanendael had been obliterated by its Lenape neighbors. Settlers had, since the destruc-tion of the colony, avoided the area near remote Cape Henlopen at the mouth of the Delaware Bay. It was too vulnerable to storms, Dutch and Spanish pirates, and the Lenape, who retained control of the region. Most settlement was higher up the Delaware River, between present-day New Castle and Philadelphia, and almost entirely on the Delaware's western bank. Other than the occasional Dutch sentry stationed at the remains of the original Swanendael fort and, after 1658, a few Dutch traders, the colony had been completely abandoned. But in the early 1660s, Swanendael, which the Dutch called Hoere-kil and the English Whorekill (the origins of the name are unknown, but its literal translation from the Dutch is "whores' creek") and which, by decree of William Penn, eventually became Lewes, Delaware, would receive a new and very hopeful band of European settlers.

Pieter Cornelisz Plockhoy, a Dutch religious radical, spent the 1650s gath-ering financial support for a new heavenly kingdom in America. Well situ-ated to take advantage of trade and whaling in the Delaware Bay, but far enough from the corrupting influences of the various mongrel Protestants residing in the region, Plockhoy hoped that Whorekill—the name being no deterrent to his pious followers—could avoid the fate of Swanendael. Seeking to encourage American settlement, and perhaps deploy Protestant zealots to counter Lord Baltimore's claims to the Delaware, Amsterdam city officials had embraced Plockhoy's scheme, and in July 1663 a tiny advance guard of forty-one colonists arrived off Cape Henlopen. But unfortunately a little over a year after the Dutch returned to Whorekill, Sir Robert Carr embarked on his expedition of conquest and plunder along the South River, as the Dutch called the Delaware. Whorekill did not escape the Englishman's rampage. Carr seized property, terrorized colonists, and is alleged to have sold some of them into slavery. Plockhoy himself vanishes from the record around this time, presumably victimized by disease or intercolonial violence.[14]

The failure of Plockhoy's colony should have been a great gift for Lord Baltimore. An enemy outpost on his colony's far eastern edge was gone; Cape Henlopen was now free for full incorporation into the Maryland colony. In addition to giving Lord Baltimore control of his colony's easternmost coast, the cape had immense strategic value. Lying at the mouth of the Delaware Bay, it afforded control over maritime traffic through the bay. Lord Baltimore never saw these benefits.

Having long understood Whorekill to lie well within his territorial jurisdiction, in 1662 Lord Baltimore ordered the area incorporated into Maryland as part of the new Worcester County. Although briefly deterred by the Duke of York's conquests, by 1669 he was again taking action to prevent future foreign annexations, ordering his son Charles, who was now Maryland's governor, to "use all means Possible to procure that some persons be seated upon the Sea board side on the Eastern Shoar and on Deleware Bay within the Degree forty Northerly Latitude and particularly the Whore Kill." Maryland's proprietor further instructed his son to establish a new county, to be called Durham and divided into two manors of six thousand acres each, encompassing the western shore of the Delaware Bay, from Whorekill to the fortieth parallel of latitude. The whole was to be protected by a new militia force, headquartered in Worcester County. Should any inhabitants of these newly incorporated areas oppose Lord Baltimore's rightful rule, Charles was "to maintain his Lordships right by force if Need be."

What was happening in Maryland's far north could hardly have escaped any remotely aware observer. Lord Baltimore was preparing for the first actual border war in Maryland's long history of border wars. There had been fighting in the colony's northern borderlands since its founding, but most was conducted by Native proxies, and even when English settlers engaged in direct combat, there was little about the fighting that could be defined as territorial. These were wars of trade and alliance. Similarly, very little of the combat involved direct European-on-European conflict, let alone direct conflict between subjects of the English Crown. Now, Cecil Calvert, the second Lord Baltimore, was preparing to wage war against subjects of the king of England—insofar as all former Dutch colonists were now English subjects—and he was doing so purely to secure his colony's territorial claims.[15]

Given the frequency with which colonial Englishmen resorted to extrajudicial violence, we should not be surprised to find colonial militiamen interpreting Lord Baltimore's instructions as a much-sought opportunity for glory. In 1672, newly commissioned Worcester militia Captain Thomas Jones led an attack on Whorekill. Jones's conquest took a familiar form: a ruthlessly destructive rampage, followed by demands for oaths of allegiance—not to Parliament or the king but to the second Lord Baltimore. When news of the attack reached New York's governor, Francis Lovelace, he urged colonists in New Castle to prepare for war against Maryland. He also registered his outrage with Governor Calvert. "Sir," wrote Lovelace, "you cannot but imagine his royal highness will not be satisfied with those violent proceedings . . . neither can you but believe it is as easy an undertaking for me to retaliate the same affront on Jones's head and accomplices as he did to those indefensible inhabitants." For Lovelace, though, Lord Baltimore's attack was not just an offense against the king and his brother, nor was it simply the work of an obnoxious, rogue militia officer. It was also illegal. Maryland had no claim to lands "so long [in] quiet posession" of the Duke of York's deputies "and by other nations before that, several years before the date of the Lord Baltimore's patent." In other words, the stipulated boundaries of Lord Baltimore's grant were, as far as Lovelace was concerned, superseded by competing colonial claims. Because all of New Netherlands had come under the duke's control, and because the Delaware River colonists had been subject to Dutch jurisdiction, these colonies would now be part of New York, whatever Lord Baltimore may have believed.[16]

Governor Lovelace recognized that the Crown was unlikely to intervene and that Lord Baltimore was unlikely to rest with the conquest of Cape Henlopen. The "portending invasion" from Maryland would persist as long as ownership of the lower Delaware remained contested. For this reason, New York's governor urged his agents in New Castle to "stand well upon your guard," and if Lord Baltimore's troops "first break the peace by firing upon your guards, or any such hostile action, then use all possible means to defend yourselves and the place."[17]

A few months after Dutch marines reestablished Dutch rule over New York, Governor Calvert ordered a second Whorekill attack. With England and the Netherlands now effectively at war, the assault would be an attack on an enemy nation. Militia captain Thomas Howell and his force of about forty men showed ruthless indifference to civilians and their property. The Marylanders destroyed what was left of the Whorekill settlement and harassed its remaining inhabitants, many former followers of Peter Plockhoy, now mistaken by the English for radical Quakers. One Whorekill colonist recalled that after ranging through the settlement, Howell and his men "left all the inhabitants naked to the m[e]rcy of the Heathen," and "all the Cruelties afore mentioned was acted and done where & when no opposition was or ever had been made by any of this County against the Lord Baltimore nor his agents, officers, or men." The militia captain himself seems to have been especially sadistic and venal. One of his victims recalled that Howell "caused a burning match to be held to [his] fingers and there kept it until he . . . did confess whare his peltrey Beaver & ferr was."[18]

While the second Lord Baltimore's quest to secure territory accounts for the Whorekill raids, without the strategic cooperation of his colony's Native neighbors, any territorial gain would be temporary. Following the restoration of Charles II, an Indian alliance was all the more urgent. Calls for direct royal rule had been loud; chaos and war would surely be the end of proprietary governance. Among colonial officials, the new governor of New York, Edmund Andros, was proprietary government's harshest critic. In the fall of 1678, as he faced discontent in New England, he confided in fellow colonial official William Blathwayt, "All my hope is Regulations and Orders from the King, as the only means to keep us well in peace and preserve or defend us."[19] Given Lord Baltimore's attacks on the Duke of York's southern claims, and given that no colonial official was closer to the king than Andros, Maryland's independence was already in danger. Indian war would likely spell its end.

The entire Susquehannock nation—several hundred people—arrived in Saint Mary's City in early 1675. Governor Calvert had invited his colony's northern neighbors to resettle in Maryland after several decades supporting their battle against Iroquois enemies. The governor's gesture carried great political risk. Some colonists feared the Susquehannocks would draw friendly Potomac Indians into some sort of pan-Indian rebellion; others feared that in giving their northern neighbors refuge, Maryland would incur the wrath of the Susquehannocks' Iroquois rivals. But Governor Calvert prevailed and welcomed his colony's northern Indian allies to a new Maryland homeland, on the site of an abandoned Piscataway Indian village, just south of present-day Washington, DC.

Six months after the Susquehannocks' migration, some thirty Virginia militiamen crossed into Maryland in search of Doeg Indians believed to be responsible for a series of livestock thefts. Mistaking the Susquehannocks for the alleged thieves, the Virginians attacked the new village, killing at least a dozen Indians. Over the course of the next few months, several Englishmen were murdered, allegedly by aggrieved Susquehannocks or Doegs. For Virginia's governor, William Berkeley, pressured by a fiercely anti-Indian faction, the killings had to be avenged, and in September, Virginia militiamen, this time supported by militia from Maryland, laid siege to the Susquehannock village. The culminating battle resulted in dozens of Indian and English deaths, with the surviving Susquehannocks and Doegs fleeing across the Potomac into Virginia. In January 1676, Susquehannocks and Doegs began a counteroffensive. Starting in the Potomac valley, they attacked settlers on both sides, in Virginia and Maryland, killing some thirty-six English. Drawing to their ranks sympathetic Potomac-valley Indians along the way, the Indian attackers moved south, destroying English homesteads, killing colonists and their livestock.

Among the victims of the violence was an overseer on the James River plantation of Nathaniel Bacon, a young Cambridge dropout who had lived in Virginia for less than two years. Dismayed by Governor Berkeley's inadequate response to the Indian attacks, Bacon took matters into his own hands, leading his band of vigilantes in ruthless attacks on Chesapeake Indians, making little effort to discriminate between enemies and friends.

Unsatisfied with ethnocidal violence, Bacon and his supporters turned against Virginia's royal government, chasing Governor Berkeley from his seat at Jamestown. What has come to be known as Bacon's Rebellion left the Susquehannock nation homeless. Maryland could hardly allow its one-time Indian allies back into the colony. But the alternative was for them to return to their old Susquehanna Valley homeland, where they would be vulnerable to renewed Iroquois raids. In the end, the Susquehannocks accepted a jaundiced arrangement with Governor Andros, who took advantage of Bacon's Rebellion to assert his patron's southern claims. In exchange for protection from the Iroquois, some Susquehannocks returned to the Susquehanna Valley as adjuncts of an Iroquois–New York alliance. Their descendants would come to be known as the Conestogas, an Anglicization of "Gandastogues," the French name for the Susquehannocks.[20]

For Charles Calvert, who had succeeded his father, Cecil, as the third Lord Baltimore in 1675, the culminating reality of Bacon's Rebellion was a complete absence of external Indian allies. The Susquehannocks were now effectively tributaries of the Iroquois League, allied by proxy with the antiproprietary Andros. The Lenape, aggrieved by Maryland's bid to conquer Whorekill, remained neutral during the recent crisis. But the more serious problem was that control of Maryland's far north was now in the hands of rival English colonists and their Iroquois allies. Lord Baltimore's "absolute prerogative Royall Right and Power," attributes of "owr gratious souveraigne in England," could no longer be excused as a foreign policy necessity. Arcane palatinate powers, according to Lord Baltimore's ever-bolder opponents, merely enabled Maryland's proprietor to act "within the compass of treason." In an overwhelmingly Protestant colony, governed by a Catholic governor, Charles Calvert, and his mostly Catholic council, these claims proved widely persuasive. After the Glorious Revolution of 1689 drove the Catholic James II from the English throne, Lord Baltimore's enemies faced little meaningful resistance, and by 1691 they had succeeded in forcing the revocation of Maryland's charter. The former Calvert family estate would now join Virginia as a royal colony. Charles Calvert would be just another lord, presiding over his manors, and enjoying the fruits of his tenants' labors.[21]

Maryland's political struggles were inseparable from its boundary problems. As the southern portions of the colony were settled by tobacco planters, the only remaining frontiers for expansion were the colony's far north and Whorekill, neither of which promised the kinds of tax revenue, rent, and land transfer fees produced by the colony's tidewater counties. Between 1650 and 1674, the colony incorporated eight new counties. Three of them (Somerset, Dorchester, and Talbot) were on the Chesapeake's Eastern Shore, and two (Baltimore and Cecil) incorporated the far northern reaches of the Chesapeake. Without economic incentive to lure settlers, these assertions of territorial control did little to secure Maryland's far north, and without clear and recognized claims in the far north, little could be expected in the way of revenue from geographic expansion of the colony.

In the face of this reality, as early as 1668, the second Lord Baltimore began urging his son to establish a seaport to enable the collection of trade duties. While little came of this early call for urbanization, in 1695 Governor Francis Nicholson, a former deputy of Edmund Andros's, moved the colony's capital from St. Mary's City to the banks of the Severn River, near an old village settled by Virginia Puritans. Annapolis, named for Anne, England's crown princess, would soon become colonial Maryland's largest port. With limited western lands in which to invest tobacco profits, Marylanders turned to trade, shipbuilding, and small-scale manufacturing. But the benefits of this new economic expansion would be greatly impeded by another territorial battle, this one with a new northern rival, William Penn.[22]

CHAPTER 2

William Penn's Unlikely Empire

THE LORDS BALTIMORE and the founder of Pennsylvania embraced faiths at the institutional margins of England's confessional state. They also founded colonies to benefit their fellow religionists. The religious parallels go no further. William Penn's church emerged from the ferment of the English Civil War, when radical Protestants fell in behind dozens of seers and self-styled prophets. To their many detractors, the resulting bands of believers were often little more than what their iconoclastic behavior and defiant preaching suggested they were: Ranters, Seekers, Diggers, and Levellers, the last a fissiparous agglomeration emblematic of these groups' revolutionary leanings in its calls for political transformation. "Inevitably, utterly inevitably," writes Christopher Hill in a classic study of seventeenth-century English radicalism, discussions among these various dissenting Protestant sects "spread over from religion to politics. In the intoxicating new freedom of the early 1640s no holds were barred."[1] Such was very much the case with Penn's sect, known as the Quakers—a name of uncertain origins, but perhaps a pejorative reference to the alleged gyrations of early adherents. As understood by George Fox, its founder, the church began with a church of one: it is in the soul and the self that true faith resides, and it is in the self and the soul that true worship must originate. There is no need for didactic sermons or hellfire and damnation, no need for any sort of clerical hierarchy or abstract and alien doctrine; there is just fierce inner devotion. Parishioners came together not as acolytes but in communion, mutual witnesses to God's inner light.

So powerful was Quaker inner light that for its quietist branch, it penetrated even silence. Through that silence, Quaker devotion reflected its radical and leveling spirit: the Quaker church subscribed to no worldly lord, a precept seen by some as an overt rejection of the God-given authority of the English Crown. Membership was achieved not through anything so familiar as sacrament or conversion but through quotidian love and friendship; hence its members were not Quakers but simply Friends, and their church was the Society of Friends. A society, in the corporate, fraternal sense, was precisely what they were: literally a society of friends, brought together in communal godliness through no coercion of any kind—no monetary obligation, no chivalric imposition, no debt at all.

This radical vision fits awkwardly with the person of William Penn, a man whose mastery of the arcane politics of the English state allowed him to establish an enormous and long-lasting proprietary colony at a time when the Crown had begun abandoning the proprietary model of colony building. Much like George Calvert, Penn deployed his political gifts and family connections on behalf of the often-competing claims of both his lord and sovereign, the king of England, and his dissenting church. Penn managed these conflicting imperatives with unusual success. Although in 1692 the Crown would take control of Pennsylvania, the proprietor's charter was restored two years later. By the time Pennsylvania was chartered in 1681, Cecil Calvert, the second Lord Baltimore, had already lost control of Maryland during the age of the Cromwellian Protectorate. His son Charles, the third Lord Baltimore, would do so again, this time for twenty-five years, beginning in 1691.

The chronic turmoil of the seventeenth-century Delaware Valley makes Penn's achievement all the more remarkable. One can hardly imagine a man who presented himself to the world as a meek and homely follower of God bringing stability to one of the least stable places in England's far-flung dominions. Though he may have been a modest Quaker, William Penn was also a canny empire builder, as his Maryland counterpart would discover. He was, in fact, a far better builder of empire than he was a colonial proprietor. For all his achievements in America, the Pennsylvania colony was a

financial disaster for Penn, and would eventually land him in London's Fleet
Prison, a debtor's prison.

Penn's Quakerism may not have suggested empire builder, but his family
background did. Penn's paternal grandfather, Captain Giles Penn, was
among Stuart England's most successful merchant adventurers. His lucrative trade centered on North Africa and the Mediterranean and allowed him
to build a small personal fleet. His gifts to the Crown, which included Ara-
bian horses and hunting falcons, earned him the esteem of Charles I, who
rewarded the elder Penn with a commission as Mediterranean consul. Giles's
primary diplomatic responsibility was to negotiate the release of English captives taken by North African pirates. William Penn's father and Giles's
second son, also William, came of age in the family business and spent his
later teen years aboard his father's ships, plying the trade between various
Mediterranean ports and Bristol. In 1640, after his older brother George was
imprisoned by Spanish authorities, William left the family business for the
Royal Navy. Within two years he was promoted to ship's captain, and by
1644 he had risen to the rank of vice admiral.

William's first son and namesake was born in London that same year.
The two would see very little of each other over the coming two decades. The
elder Penn was mostly at sea, first in the Parliamentary Navy and then the
Navy of the Commonwealth and the Protectorate under Oliver Cromwell,
a former commander of the Parliamentary Army. Given Giles Penn's service to
the king, and given that Vice Admiral Penn's own initial naval commission
came from Charles I, his commission in Cromwell's navy meant that,
should the Royalists prevail in England's Civil War, he would surely face
the traitor's fate. Parliamentary victory also offered little certainty for the
long-term prospects of Admiral Penn. Although his commander, Cromwell,
valued the experienced navigator for his mastery of seaborne warfare, he
would also remain suspicious of the elder William's earlier royalism. The
dilemma was somewhat lessened when Penn was given command of Parliament's Irish fleet, responsible for patrolling the Irish Sea and repressing
rebellion on the Irish mainland. In this capacity, Vice Admiral Penn avoided
direct engagement with the king's naval forces and the hazard of exacerbating
royalist antipathy or, should his leadership fail, Parliamentary suspicion.
The elder William Penn would ultimately liberate himself from these dilemmas

in the first Anglo-Dutch War. His victories earned him the rank of general at sea, the highest in the Commonwealth Navy, although a rank intended to secure the navy's subordinate status to Cromwell's New Model Army. Vice Admiral Penn's triumphs also earned him an ignominious role as naval commander for Cromwell's ill-fated Western Design.

Emboldened by the Commonwealth's triumphs in the Anglo-Dutch War, and pushed by members of the mercantile community to continue the forceful expansion of English empire, Cromwell turned to the Spanish Caribbean. If success against the Dutch could be replicated in the Catholic New World, not only would Cromwell, now lord protector, vastly expand England's mercantile range, but he would do so at the expense of the very Catholic power so long reviled and still widely thought to be conspiring against Protestant England. Cromwell's colonial scheme involved the capture of Hispaniola and its silver reserves, thought sufficient to finance the whole venture. Under the command of army general Robert Venables, the English invaders were readily repelled by Spanish forces. Rather than return in defeat, Venables and Penn turned to the much smaller, much less well-fortified Spanish island of Jamaica. Although Jamaica would eventually become a stronghold of the English Caribbean, a chastened Cromwell saw the expedition as a failure and, in typical fashion, blamed its commanders. Forced to acknowledge disobedience for the unauthorized conquest of Jamaica and to resign his naval commission, the former vice admiral and general at sea retreated to the Penn family's Irish estate. He also began contemplating a change of allegiance and made known his support for a restored Stuart monarch. When Charles II assumed the throne in 1660, Penn was rewarded with a commission on the king's Navy Board, presided over by the lord high admiral and the king's brother, the Duke of York.

As a close advisor of the duke, Vice Admiral Penn could hardly have been better placed to enjoy the fruits of the restored monarch's new push for overseas empire. But the senior Penn was a navy man, with little interest in the administrative and political burdens of empire. Samuel Pepys, the great Restoration diarist who served with Penn on the king's Navy Board, and who periodically remarked on his colleague's generally morose demeanor, observed that Penn's Dutch wife, Margaret, "hath more wit than her husband." More damning was Pepys's abiding suspicion of Penn senior's politics. On July 5, 1662, he confided to his diary that he hated the man "with all my heart for his base treacherous tricks." Although Pepys was referring to Penn's maneuvers on the Navy Board, it is hard not to conclude that the hostility was at least partly of historical origin. Even so manifestly skilled a naval commander as Vice Admiral Penn could not overcome the costs of his wartime shifts in allegiance. Had he sought to capitalize on his king's imperial ambition, this Penn would have faced serious political barriers. The likes of Pepys might have tolerated Penn for his naval expertise but was unlikely to support him in other overseas ventures.[2]

The younger William Penn had none of his father's political baggage but all of his connections—which he cultivated with great acuity. William was only four when Charles I was executed. He spent the first few years of the Civil War with his mother at the family's home in Wanstead, Essex, northeast of London. In 1654, aged ten, Penn entered the Chigwell Free Grammar School, not far from his family's Wanstead home. He was an exceptional and precocious student, mastering Latin and Greek grammar, math, geography, and history, and seems to have gone about his life oblivious to the political upheavals around him. The main aspect of his formal schooling shaped by the Commonwealth was the absence of mandatory Anglican prayer and catechism. Penn's early education never included the stilted and gloomy rituals of high-church Anglicanism. Nor did it present him with the stark choice between dissent and conformity, as it had for the first Lord Baltimore. It included instead a level of spiritual latitude possible only in the religious ferment of the Interregnum, as England's time without a monarch came to be known. "I never addicted myself to S[c]hool-learning to understand religion by," William later remembered. "I never had any other religion than what I felt."[3]

Penn attended Chigwell School for only two years. His father's decision to leave the capital after the Western Design debacle meant that the younger Penn would spend the rest of his childhood on the family estate in County Cork, Ireland, mostly in the company of his mother, his younger brother Richard, perhaps his sister Margaret, and assorted tutors. These proved to be years of unhappiness, and Penn began yearning for "knowledge of God." In 1660, at his father's insistence, sixteen-year-old William matriculated at Christ Church College, Oxford. For the son of a benighted parliamentarian, Oxford was the politic choice. The younger William would be educated in a firmly royalist and Anglican institution. But for an unresolved religious seeker, long detached from conforming Anglicanism, the choice was a terrible one.[4]

After two years, the college banished Penn for nonconformity. The episode did little to diminish his growing religious yearning. If anything, Penn's short college experience had the opposite effect. There could be no conformity "in the midst of that hellish darknes & debauchery" that was seventeenth-century Oxford. William's failure to follow the path laid out by his father, himself struggling against Civil War political demons, led to a great split between the two. As Penn remembered, "The bitter usage I underwent when I returned to my Father, whipping, beating, & turning out of Dores," only heightened an appetite for greater spiritual wholeness.

In 1665, Penn settled in London and began studying law at Lincoln's Inn. It was during this period that he turned to Quakerism. After witnessing the horrors of plague in the summer of 1665, Penn began announcing his membership in the Society of Friends. He later remembered that during this time, "the lord visited me with a certain sound & testimony of his eternal word through one of those . . . called a Quaker." Penn's path had become clear. For "the Lord had preserved me to this day, & had given me . . . the Assurance of life everlasting." Scorned by his Oxford classmates and by a father whose own religious views prompted Pepys to call the elder Penn a "hypocritical rogue, and . . . an atheist," Penn's religious quest forced on him a quiet resolve—the kind of resolve a Freudian might interpret as compensatory reaction to an overbearing father.[5]

More than most other dissenting branches of Protestantism, Quakerism resided at the cultural margins of English society. In its hostility to civic oaths and public ritual, including the proceedings of the king's courts, Quakers challenged the very moral foundations of the English governing order. As the Quaker propagandist Edward Burrough acknowledged, the Quaker was widely viewed as "a sower of sedition, or a subverter of the laws, a turner of the world upside down, a pestilent fellow."[6] That such sentiments were widespread is hardly surprising. The suspicions of Reformation England died hard. While fantasies of Romish conspiracy remained, and would in fact find new fervor with the restoration of the Stuarts, Anglicans, royalists, and even many Puritans found in Quakers an additional menace. After all, if the Friends refused oaths, on what grounds could Quaker loyalties be established? They may not have subscribed to the dicta of a papal lord, but to what dicta did they subscribe? These sorts of questions elicited a torrent of anti-Quaker propaganda, drawing Penn's fellow religionists into ceaseless high-stakes confessional debate.

Only a few years after his Quaker conversion, the twenty-four-year-old Penn entered the fray with an anti-Trinitarian tract that briefly landed him in the king's prison, the Tower of London. Imprisonment did little to deter Penn. By 1680, he had published nearly fifty pro-Quaker tracts; he traveled extensively, in the British Isles and abroad, advocating for Quaker causes; and he lobbied the Crown and Parliament on behalf of the Friends— all on his own dime. Given the scope of his commitment, there were surely other expenditures that never entered Penn's fragmentary business records. What is clear is that Penn's membership in the Society of Friends had been costly. Following his imprisonment, he had been forced to sell portions of the Kent estate of his wife, the Quaker heiress Gulielma Springett. What is also clear is that Penn was prepared to incur monetary indebtedness in support of a faith that utterly rejected the sorts of dependencies debt entailed.[7]

With the very worldly danger of bankruptcy intruding on his spiritual pursuits, Penn began planning an ambitious New World venture. That venture would be equally a Quaker colony and a Penn colony. For Penn, there was no meaningful distinction between his personal wealth and the wealth of his church. It could be no other way. In an essay advising his children on civil and religious conduct, Penn warned of the dangers of worldly wealth. For, improperly understood, it produced in "youth and middle age, pleasure and ambition; old age, avarice. Remember, I tell you, that man is a slave where either prevails." These hazards were best averted by turning monetary and material capital into spiritual capital and this was best done by placing commerce in the service of faith.[8]

Penn's involvement in American affairs began in West Jersey, the southernmost portion of the Duke of York's American claims. In anticipation of Nicoll's seizure of New Netherlands, in June 1664 the duke granted two longtime Stuart loyalists, Sir George Carteret and Sir John Berkeley, the tract of Nova Caesaria or New Jersey. In the sense that New Jersey came into being as a reward for loyalty, it was typical of colony building during the Restoration. In the sense that the legal terms of those rewards were uncertain, it was also typical. Although the Duke of York's charter entitled him to govern his colony, there was no provision in the Berkeley and Carteret grant to allow them to do the same. The Dutch reconquest of New Netherlands in 1673 invalidated the New Jersey grants, and the Treaty of Westminster, which restored English rule to New York in 1674, made no particular provision for governing the colony either.

After Edmund Andros took control of the Duke of York's recovered American possessions, the Jerseys were divided diagonally between the far northern reaches of the Delaware River and a point roughly halfway down the colony's Atlantic coast near Little Egg Harbor. Carteret retained nominal control of the eastern portion of the grant, and Berkeley was left with the western portion. Rather than face the continued territorial battle of the lower Delaware, Berkeley sold his interest to two Quaker gentlemen, John Fenwick and Edward Byllynge. From the moment it transpired, the transaction raised questions. Because the nature of the original grant from the Duke of York was never clear, the legality of the sale was never settled. As far as Andros was concerned, West Jersey, as Berkeley's New Jersey tract would be known, remained as it had been since England first conquered New Netherlands: a dependency of the Duke of York's, answerable solely to the duke's American agents.

Hence, although West Jersey had in some sense become a Quaker colony, its new Quaker proprietors had very little formal control over the colony. Moreover, whatever Quakerism meant, it did very little to defeat the tensions that lurk behind most any business partnership. That of Byllynge and Fenwick was no different. They feuded bitterly over control of their colony and, faced with financial dissolution, were forced to cede control to three trustees, the most active and influential of whom was William Penn. Under his stewardship, West Jersey attracted a small number of settlers, too few to do much more than satisfy Byllynge's creditors. What Penn learned in his role as trustee was a fundamental tenet of English colony building: law was no mere formality. It was the foundation for proprietary income. The bewildering layers of claims and counterclaims in West Jersey could hardly have been better conceived to reinforce this truism.

As Penn began contemplating his own colony, he envisioned a royal bequest unencumbered by prior legal claims. This would, of course, prove hopeless. In addition to the Calvert family and the Duke of York, the Native nations of the Delaware and Susquehanna valleys retained—by treaty or title—much of the land Penn expected to colonize. Another truism of Restoration colony building was that it was, above all, a mercantile undertaking. Settlement and the extraction of marketable commodities—primarily furs and timber—remained vital but insufficient to satisfy the Lords of Trade. The value of colonized lands would come from their role in England's rise as a global trading power. That meant providing staples for English manufacturing as well as reliable markets for English goods. West Jersey lacked the kind of deep-water ports that would have tied it to oceanic trade, and even with extensive access to the Delaware River its commercial prospects were limited. The river's eastern and southern shores were much less navigable than its northern and western ones. At best, West Jersey would be a settlement colony—perhaps generating for its proprietors rent, quitrents (as proprietary taxes were called), and fees from title transfers or land sales. But this income would do little to earn the colony the good graces of the Crown. For that, Penn, an astute student of imperial policy, recognized a colony would need deep-water ports and ready access to oceanic trade routes. It would also need the direct endorsement of his father's Stuart patrons.

Penn sought that endorsement, along with a vast American tract, as compensation for expenses his father incurred during the Second Anglo-Dutch War. He calculated that those expenses, mostly for naval victualling, along with subsequent interest payments would total £16,000, roughly the value of an American colony. Although there is some indication that the Lords of Trade had doubts about Penn's proposal (they sat on Penn's petition for almost a year), the king's lawyers would eventually prepare a charter for the Pennsylvania colony.[9] The king's hand had no doubt been forced by domestic political considerations. In the year William Penn petitioned the Crown for a colony, it was embroiled in an explosive succession crisis. The Duke of York, next in line for the throne, was Catholic. Swayed in part by lasting hysteria over the so-called Popish Plot, a phony Catholic conspiracy ginned up by a charlatan named Titus Oates, Parliament acted to exclude the Duke of York from the throne.

Whether Penn timed his petition to coincide with the Exclusion Crisis is uncertain. What is certain is that in 1680, as the Lords of Trade considered his petition, the English Crown faced the most serious crisis of legitimacy since the Civil War.

King Charles II granted William Penn a charter for Pennsylvania in March 1681, almost a year after Penn initially petitioned the sovereign. The terms of Penn's charter represented a mix of old and new. In terms of the new, there were no specific references to the bishops of Durham, and the charter made explicit provisions to accommodate new trade policies. Penn would be required to enforce new English trade regulations and facilitate the collecting of customs. He would also retain a representative in London who could consult directly with Crown authorities. The absence of a palatinate clause meant that many of the familiar powers enjoyed by the Lords Baltimore would not be conferred on Penn: Penn would have limited pardon power, and the king would retain the right to hear appeals of cases decided in Pennsylvania's courts; Penn would have limited military authority, and notably would lack the authority to build and maintain forts; he would have no authority to grant honors or titles; and he would be required to admit a representative of the Church of England to his colony.

In practice, these new limits were cosmetic. Penn and his heirs still retained vast powers over their new dominions. Indeed, in terms of the material basis for colonial power—control over the titling of land—Penn's charter differed hardly at all from Lord Baltimore's. He and his heirs had complete authority to convey and utilize their colonial property as they saw fit, which meant they could transfer ownership of that property, rent it, and tax it. Similarly, much like the Lords Baltimore, they had the power to initiate legislation, in consultation with some sort of representative body. They could issue ordinances. They had full power to appoint local officials, including magistrates. In exchange, Penn and his heirs owed the monarch the utterly token sum of two beaver skins, to be paid yearly on the first of January.

The primary constitutional constraint on William Penn's power was, in the end, precisely the same as that on the first Lord Baltimore's. Pennsylvania would be bounded in space.

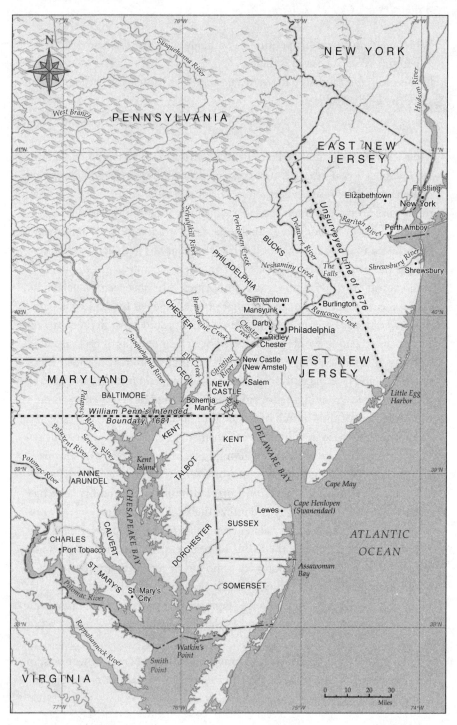

N

NEW YORK

PENNSYLVANIA

Susquehanna River

West Branch

EAST NEW
JERSEY

Elizabethtown
Flushing
New York
Perth Amboy
Raritan River
Hudson River
Delaware River
BUCKS
Schuylkill River
Perkiomen Creek
PHILADELPHIA
Neshaminy Creek
The
Falls
Unsurveyed Line of 1676
Shrewsbury River
Shrewsbury
Germantown
Mansyunk
Burlington
Rancocas Creek
CHESTER
Brandywine Creek
Darby
Mansyunk
Philadelphia
Chester
Creek
Ridley
Chester
New Castle
(New Amstel)
WEST NEW
JERSEY
Susquehanna River
Elk Creek
CECIL
Christina River
NEW
CASTLE
Salem
Little Egg
Harbor
MARYLAND
BALTIMORE
Bohemia
Manor
*William Penn's Intended
Boundary, 1681*
KENT
KENT
DELAWARE BAY
Patapsco River
Severn River
Patuxent River
TALBOT
Kent
Island
Potomac River
ANNE
ARUNDEL
Cape May
CHESAPEAKE BAY
Cape Henlopen
(*Swanendael*)
Lewes
SUSSEX
*ATLANTIC
OCEAN*
CALVERT
CHARLES
Port Tobacco
DORCHESTER
*Assawoman
Bay*
ST. MARY'S
SOMERSET
Potomac River
St. Mary's
City
Rappahannock River
Watkin's
Point
Smith
Point
VIRGINIA

0   10   20   30
Miles

Pennsylvania, c. 1685

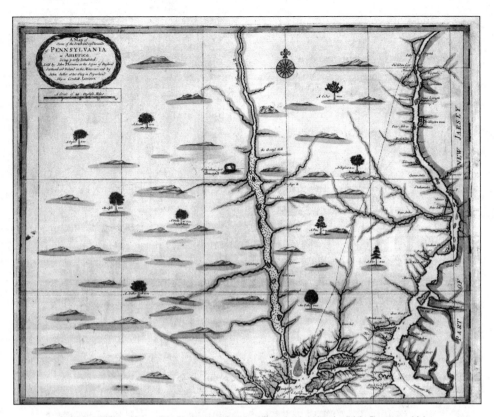

Detail from "A Map of Some of the South and eastbounds of Pennsylvania in America," John Thornton and John Seller, London, 1681. As part of his promotional campaign, William Penn commissioned London mapmakers John Thornton and John Seller to prepare this map of Pennsylvania. It shows a southern boundary about fifty miles south of the fortieth parallel of latitude, Maryland's northern boundary. Its sole indications of the region's Native inhabitants are a "Demolished" fort on the west side of the Susquehanna and an "Old Indian field," upper right, near the Delaware.
Reproduction courtesy the John Carter Brown Library.

The colony would lie along the western banks of the Delaware River; its northern boundary would lie along the forty-third northern parallel of latitude and its southern boundary would be coterminous with the fortieth parallel, the northern boundary of Maryland. To accommodate the small portion of New York situated west of the Delaware River, Pennsylvania's southern boundary would be truncated. At its eastern terminus, it would begin with "a circle drawne at twelve miles distance from *New Castle* Northward and Westward unto the beginning of the fortieth degree of Northern Latitude, and then by a straight Line Westward." Pennsylvania's boundary would thus circle around the duke's claims, becoming what came to be known as the Delaware Curve, the only circular boundary in the continental United States. It all made perfect sense—accounting for conflicting claims with a cartographic carve-out. Except, in fact, the carve-out created a raft of new problems. New Castle was about thirty miles south of the fortieth parallel, an error that gave rise to the lengthiest and costliest border dispute in colonial American history.[10]

As part of his efforts to secure the full territorial scope of his lord's colony, in 1676 Edmund Andros took control of a general court at New Castle and established another at Whorekill. By 1680, as settlement spread out along the Delaware Bay and settlers found it ever more difficult to reach either Whorekill to the south or New Castle to the north, Andros established a third court at the mouth of the St. Jones River. These courts would become the seats of New York's three Lower Counties (New Castle, Kent, and Sussex) and would secure the Duke of York's control of the Delaware and its sea lanes.[11]

Aware that without that same access, his colony would effectively be landlocked, Penn began lobbying for control of the Lower Counties. But this would not be a simple matter, even by the standards of English colonial politics. The Duke of York had never received any kind of formal patent or charter securing his control of the Lower Counties. John Werden, the duke's secretary, laid out the problem for Penn's friend and agent, the Scottish Quaker Robert Barclay. The duke had no right "to give a grant of what he has not a patent for himself." Penn was undeterred and after a year of haggling persuaded the duke's representatives to accept an alternative means of conveyance. Instead of transferring nonexistent charter rights, the duke would deed the Lower Counties to Penn, in the fashion of a manor deeded by any other colonial proprietor. The precise legal nature of this property transfer has been a puzzle to historians. Four legal documents seem to have been signed by the duke and Penn. Two of these were ordinary land deeds. The first granted Penn freehold ownership over the town of New Castle. The second granted him title to lands along the Delaware between Newcastle and Cape Henlopen. These deeds were granted enfeoff, carrying clear obligation of the new owner to his lord, and leaving Penn with few of the proprietary privileges afforded by a royal charter. The duke and Penn also signed leases of ten thousand years for each parcel. Here too, the arrangement left Penn with no proprietary authority and acknowledged that his claim to the Lower Counties involved obligation to a lord. The nature of that obligation is unclear, but the leases acknowledged the Duke of York's rights to quitrents collected in the Lower Counties.

Exactly why the duke and Penn applied two different modes of conveyance has never been explained. Most likely, because the duke's claims over the Lower Counties were themselves ambiguous—the duke's charter did not include the Lower Counties, but Lord Baltimore's did—and because the commercial prospects of Pennsylvania so clearly rested on control of the Delaware, Penn pursued what were, in effect, improvised charter rights. Should a future court decide the Duke of York lacked the right to deed the territory to Penn, it would perhaps accept the validity of the leases. The legal reasoning, if this is in fact what it was, would have been contorted even by seventeenth-century standards, but in any case it appears to have had no real merit, at least as far as the Crown was concerned. In March 1683, the Lords of Trade lawyers drafted a patent granting the Duke of York proprietary control of the Lower Counties. This seems to have been an ex post facto effort to secure the arrangements the duke made with Penn. Such a gesture would have been understandable.[12]

William Penn was surely aware that Maryland's charter, bearing the royal seal, had more legal weight than his hodgepodge arrangement with the Duke of York. Should opponents of a Catholic monarch again gain control of Parliament and perhaps even succeed in the push for exclusion, the court would have little grounds for preserving Penn's claims to the Lower Counties. Doing so would mean, in effect, upholding the claims of the Duke of York, which rested entirely on his brother's consent. With the decease of Charles, any control of those lands would depend on the consent of a new king. Should that king end up being James, Penn's claims to the Lower Counties would be secure. But should James be denied the throne, Penn's claims would be far less secure, especially if challenged by a charter-bearing Lord Baltimore.

Although the likelihood of exclusion had faded, Penn remained profoundly anxious about the status of the Lower Counties. In April 1681, he issued a commission to his cousin William Markham to serve as Pennsylvania's de facto governor. Penn may have lacked the full range of palatinate powers, but he was still a sole, unitary proprietor, a role undifferentiated from governor, the colony's supreme magistrate.

Among Markham's first tasks after arriving in America would be to "settle bounds betwixt me & my Neighbours." By neighbors, Penn meant Maryland, and his concern was that without clarity about his colony's boundaries, Lower County colonists would believe they lived in Maryland or New York. Penn also instructed Markham to assemble a governor's council of nine leading Lower County colonists and to read before that council a letter informing them that "it hath pleased god In his providence to cast you within my Lott & Care." Penn assured his listeners he would be a benevolent and godly caretaker and would provide "wtever sober & free men can reasonably desire for the security & improvement of their own happiness," but "in the mean time, pray submit to the commands of my deputy so farr as they are consistent with the law, & pay him thos dues (that formerly you paid to the order of the Governour of new York)." It would be another year before Penn received his deeds to the region. But from the outset, his intentions were clear: whatever court politics might dictate, his colonizing would include the contested and vitally important Lower Counties.[13]

Governor Markham also carried a letter from Penn to the third Lord Baltimore, in Maryland to deal with new fiscal and political crises. Penn explained to his southern counterpart that "a great & prudent man, will always act Wth caution & obedience to the mind of his Prince," and as the current Lord Baltimore well knew, his prince, Charles II, had granted Penn a vast American estate. How appropriate, then, for Lord Baltimore to honor his king's will and "give my cousin & Deputy, all the dispatch possible in the business of the bounds, that observing our just limits in that & all other things we may begin & mantaine a Just & friendly intercourse." Penn's lobbying extended well beyond Lord Baltimore. Before he ever received any substantial response from the Maryland proprietor, Penn sent a letter to six prominent residents of Maryland's Cecil and Baltimore Counties noting that because they were "men of substance & reputation in that part of the bay, which I presume falls within my patent, I chose to take this opportunity to begin our acquaintance and by you with the rest of the people on yr side of my Country." Rest assured, Penn continued, "that I will be so farr from takeing any advantage to draw great profits to my selfe, that you shall find me & my govermt easy free & Just." Above all, Penn's new subjects would be freed from "any more Taxes . . . by any order or law of Maryland." The battle lines could not have been clearer. As far as

William Penn was concerned, Maryland's claims to the Lower Counties were null and void.[14]

Much like the English state, the Society of Friends, an extensive association of common believers, had (in no small measure because of William Penn's influence) come to understand its security and permanence as a function of its financial resources. From Quakerism's very beginning, Penn explained in a 1694 history of the Friends, its founding fathers, "not weary in well-doing," gave freely of their own financial resources, and did so "in large proportions, which they never brought to account, or desired should be known, much less restored to them, that none might want, nor any service be retarded or disappointed." One's personal finances and the Quaker church would be bound by mystic bonds rather than worldly credit and debt.[15]

Unfortunately, Penn's financial interests never fully aligned with his spiritual ones. In the month he received his charter, he wrote authorities in the Lower Counties with news that he would be embarking for America "if it please god." But it would be more than a year before Penn left England. The negotiations over the Lower Counties were protracted, and Penn's precarious finances demanded constant attention. Philip Ford, whom Penn employed to manage his business affairs, had extended thousands of pounds of credit to his master, loans that Penn secured with three hundred thousand acres of Pennsylvania land. Not surprisingly, given the disjunction between Penn's financial means and his commercial ambition, his relationship with Ford dissolved in acrimony. As Penn was about to sail for America, Ford alleged gross financial malfeasance. Penn, it seems, failed to post any kind of bond guaranteeing new loans Ford had underwritten.[16]

Shamed by financial scandal, as Penn prepared to leave England in August 1682, there would be no bold pronouncements about religious freedom or the future glories of Quaker America, just the cautious words of a deeply chastened man of God. Penn beseeched his wife, Gulielma, "to live low and sparingly, till my debts are paid." This was not a controlling husband demanding restraint from his free-spending spouse. To see that, Gulielma Penn had simply to "remember thy mothers example, when thy fathers public spiritedness had worst'd his estate." In Penn's case, that public-spiritedness was not really public. The Quaker church was a closed, corporate entity. But that had little impact on the sorrows of indebtedness. To be liberated to serve the Friends was to be liberated from worldly obligation: "I desire not riches: but to owe nothing and Truly that is wealth."

Further weighing on him, Penn's mother, Lady Margaret Penn, had just died, and Gulielma had begun suffering serious health troubles related to a difficult pregnancy. The only substantial indication of the toll these hardships took on Penn comes in his final letter to Gulielma and his children, perhaps the most heartfelt thing William Penn ever wrote, and one of his few remaining personal letters from the years of Pennsylvania's founding. In addition to its instructions for managing family affairs, and its profession to Gulielma, "the love of my youth and much [the] joy of my life," the letter instructs the Penn children to "be obedient to your dear mother," and if they marry during their father's absence, "mind neither beauty nor Riches, but the fear of the lord, and a sweet and amiable Disposition, such as you can love above all this world."[17] These are the words of a man who expected to be away for some time, possibly forever. The eldest of his three surviving children, a boy named Springett, was only seven as Penn prepared to leave.

On August 29, 1682, William Penn boarded the *Welcome* and two days later set sail for America.

CHAPTER 3

The Battle for Maryland's Far North

WILLIAM PETTY WROTE his dear friend William Penn on August 14, 1682. Petty had been student and secretary of the philosopher Thomas Hobbes and was former physician general of the English Army in Ireland. He was also responsible for the Down Survey, a comprehensive land survey undertaken by Cromwell's agents in Ireland. But his concern now was the value of five thousand acres he owned in Pennsylvania. As Penn prepared to leave for the colony, Petty offered his friend some final thoughts about the prospects for his American investment. Those thoughts were, in one sense, quite rosy: "Old Friend, My opinion is, that not onely Pensilvania, but all the habitable Land upon the Face of the Earth, will (within the next 1500 years) be as fully Peopled as England is now, That is to say, That there will bee a head for every Four acres of Land."

There was no avoiding the fundamental demographic fact that Pennsylvania would grow more populous. But Petty cautioned that these long-term trends offered very little reassurance about Pennsylvania's more immediate prospects. Settlers would surely come, but only with careful planning would settlement generate profit. Too much land and too few settlers would depress land values and rents. Too little land and too many settlers would have the opposite effect: land values would rise, but those higher values would drive settlers to lower-cost colonies.

To achieve the perfect balance, Petty suggested a ratio of population to land somewhere between that of the two royal domains he knew best, England and Ireland. If the former represented Pennsylvania's destiny, the latter, which Petty estimated possessed somewhere near one inhabitant for every ten acres, represented a much more immediate prospect, albeit not at the optimal ratio of land to persons—optimal at least in terms of potential income for Petty and his fellow investors. To secure that optimal ratio of land to colonist, Penn would have to survey his entire colony. This would require "a perfect Accompt of every Soule within yor Teritory and Jursidiction, and then, to sett out a peece of Land, conteyning 7 times that number in acres." A colony able to accommodate one person for every seven acres would afford much more space than was possible per Englishman in England and would result in land values substantially higher than in Ireland. As Pennsylvania's population grew and the quantity of land per capita fell, "I would then again number the Inhabtants and add to the first parcel, such an other parcel as might conteyne 7 times as many acres, as was the number of the Encrease of people." In time, even an estate managed according to Petty's formula would grow overcrowded, but for now, Petty was confident the plan would ensure optimal returns for Penn and his investors.[1]

Petty's scheme reflected his experiences in Ireland, where he lived for most of the years from 1653 until his death in 1687. Surveying Pennsylvania, even a portion of it, faced barriers—extensive mountain ranges, vast forests, broad rivers and bays—he never faced while working on the Down Survey. In addition, he had no sense of the legal complexities impinging on England's American claims. Ireland's indigenous population and its conquering population may have differed in religious allegiance but, by virtue of English reconquest, they were now subjects of the same governing order. And according to that order, plunder taken from Irish Catholic rebels now belonged to the English sovereign and could be conveyed accordingly.[2]

Other than the Lower Counties, which had been acquired by the English during the course of prolonged Anglo-Dutch hostilities, there had been no actual conquest in Penn's dominions—or at least none that generated legally sanctioned plunder. Neither the Dutch nor the Duke of York claimed control of the majority of Pennsylvania. Insofar as Europeans laid claim to any part of Pennsylvania, particularly the western extent of the Maryland-Pennsylvania borderlands, they did so not in the aftermath of clear military conquest but after decades of shifting Native-European alliance formation. Any existing claims to the lands adjoining Pennsylvania's southern boundary, in other words, were complex, negotiated ones. The rules of conquest and plunder had never applied, as they had in Petty's Ireland.

Confirmation of this important point can be found in William Penn's Indian diplomacy. Historians have tended to interpret Penn's relations with his colony's Native neighbors through his own words. In an early letter carried by his representatives to Delaware Valley Natives, Penn wrote that "the king of the Countrey where I live, hath given unto me a great Province therein, but I desire to enjoy it with your Love and Consent, that we may always live together as Neighbours and friends." Consent is the operative term here. Penn's Native neighbors would not be subjects, ruled by English lords, but consenting friends, living alongside English neighbors. Penn never justified his approach to existing territorial claims—whether Native or European—as a matter of conquest and plunder. Pennsylvania's lands would be secured through contract—treaties, deeds, and other legal mechanisms. This approach, Penn believed, contrasted sharply with that of his colonial predecessors in the Delaware Valley. "I am very Sensible of the unkindness and Injustice that hath been too much exercised towards you by the People of these Parts off the world," he explained to a Lenape delegation, "but I am not such a Man, as is well known in my . . . Country: I have great love and regard towards you, and I desire to Winn and gain your Love & friendship by a kind, just and peaceable life." In light of such careful diplomacy, it is hard not to see in Penn a unique figure, not just in colonial diplomacy but in English diplomacy more generally. In the words of historian John Smolenski, "Perhaps alone of all the founders of the British American colonies, William Penn resolved to treat the native peoples of North America with fairness and justice." The assessment echoes through decades of scholarship—William Penn, ever the peaceable Quaker, demonstrated uncommon respect for the property and culture of America's Indigenous peoples and, as a result, his colony has long stood out as a place of relative peace, at least until the middle of the eighteenth century.

There is much truth in this glorious tale. Pennsylvania, at least early in its history, was in fact relatively free from the sort of internecine Native-European conflict that plagued the southern Chesapeake and tore southern

New England apart in the 1670s. Pennsylvania's relatively peaceable rela-tions surely owed a great deal to Penn's acute sense of fairness and justice. But the law, as Penn employed it, also served other, less altruistic purposes.[3]

Between July 1682 and June 1684, William Penn concluded eleven sepa-rate land cession agreements with Native peoples living in southeastern Pennsylvania. The legality of these agreements was tenuous. Neither Penn nor his agents were ever entirely certain who had the authority among Na-tive leaders to cede Native land. But there is little doubt that Penn saw in these transfers a vital diplomatic instrument. They achieved little in terms of the fair distribution of resources, but they achieved much in affirming the fundamental point that Penn's colony was settled through good-faith dip-lomatic and legal process. In September 1681, Penn instructed several of his agents, sent to Pennsylvania to plot the colony's capital city, to let the Indians of the Delaware Valley know that "you are come to sit downe Lovingly among them . . . then present their Kings wth what [gifts] I send them, and make a friendship and League wth them." Conquest and plunder would have no role in the creation of Pennsylvania. The colony would, from its inception, be a legal construct, achieved through legal conveyance, treaty making, and royal writ.[4]

Except that, in fact, conquest and plunder would have a substantial role in the creation of Pennsylvania. Instead of serving as a direct justification for the seizure of Native lands, conquest and plunder would be the basis for Pennsylvania's legal claims to Maryland's far north. According to William Penn and, ultimately, the Lords of Trade, in failing to secure his colony's northern borderlands through conquest, Lord Baltimore had forfeited his claims to the territory. This argument, so profoundly at odds with the governing ideology of territorial acquisition in Pennsylvania, would prove William Penn's most effective weapon in his dispute with the third Lord Baltimore, a dispute that would overwhelm intercolonial diplomatic channels and force Penn and Lord Baltimore to present their case before a Crown court in London.

The creation of Pennsylvania was a stupendous achievement. In a po-litical climate racked with division, much of which harkened back to the chronic religious conflict of the age of Charles I, William Penn acquired title to a vast American estate. Under the best of circumstances, such royal dispensation would demand the shrewdest navigation of court politics. Penn achieved his primary political goal—and the chartering of a colony, whatever its economic and legal parameters, was a fundamentally political process. Penn's vigorous promotional activities, drawing investors and settlers from a Quaker network that stretched across the British Isles, were stunning in their success. Between December 1681 and December 1682, twenty-three ships bearing almost two thousand settlers arrived in Pennsylvania. Over the course of the next three years, the influx continued, and when it finally concluded, some ninety ships had brought about eight thousand settlers to the colony. The vast majority of these migrants were Quakers, mostly English, and mostly of middling socioeconomic status. They settled along the western shores of the Delaware, in the newly founded counties of Bucks, Philadelphia, and Chester. They were indentured servants, tradesmen, farmers, and shopkeepers, and many arrived with families, affording a level of demographic stability Maryland had only just begun to achieve.[5]

This migratory influx also brought new commercial vitality to the mid-Atlantic. Philadelphia, too modest even to host Pennsylvania's first colonial assembly in early December 1682, had grown to about eighty houses by 1683; by 1685, Philadelphians had built 357 houses. Many of these homes were occupied by artisans and small farmers, but it was the infusion of Quaker merchants that transformed Philadelphia from an idea in William Penn's imagination into a thriving Atlantic port. The earliest Philadelphians arrived from mercantile strongholds like London, Dublin, New York, and Barbados; drawing on the abundant resources of the new town's vast hinterlands and its advantageous riverine location, in just a few years they challenged New York's mid-Atlantic commercial primacy. Flush with money, a normally scarce commodity in the colonies, these Quakers invested in wharves, warehouses, and shops, and within a few years of the town's founding, ships, hailing from ports around the Atlantic littoral, were sailing up the Delaware to North America's newest city. Those ships brought axes, hoes, textiles, pork, beef, butter, cheese, and other goods; those goods they exchanged for furs, whale oil, and timber. The mid-Atlantic had never seen anything like it—a stunning commercial eruption in just a few years. Not only would all the commerce transform Philadelphia into the largest city in North America, but it would also transform the Delaware River into North America's first great commercial river. After

Quebec City, Philadelphia was North America's greatest river city, and remained so until the nineteenth century.[6]

Penn arrived in Pennsylvania in late October 1682, depleted after a brutal eight-week Atlantic passage. His political work could not await recovery. Most pressing was securing the allegiance of the Lower Counties. Penn's leases, unlike the charter for Pennsylvania, said nothing about the counties' governance; nor did they offer any clarity about his own governing authority over the settlements. For all his lobbying and legal maneuvering, until he gained control of the government of the Lower Counties, Penn's claims there would mean little. The remedy lay in constitutional union. Penn instructed the leading freeholders of the three Lower Counties to elect representatives to the first Pennsylvania colonial assembly, which met on December 4 at the former Dutch settlement of Upland, now known as Chester, in Pennsylvania.

Among the assembly's very first acts was formal approval of an Act of Union, binding the Lower Counties to Pennsylvania. The act, submitted to the assembly by eighteen of the Lower Counties' twenty-one representatives, sought "Incorporation in and with the province of Pennsylvania" and with that incorporation, "all the Rights & priviledges of the aforesaid province." The assembly also enacted a measure to ensure the allegiance of remaining Lower County Swedes. These colonists would be required to swear a solemn and godly oath of allegiance "to the king of Engld & his Heirs & Successrs, and fidelity and Lawfull obedience to Wm Penn Proprietary & Governr of the province of pensylvania & territories thereunto belonging & his heirs and Assigns." Penn's foreign subjects would have three months to pledge their allegiance and would be charged twenty shillings for the privilege of doing so. When it came to securing control over his colonial property, Penn was clearly a pragmatist. The Friends' hostility to oaths carried little weight in the English colonial outback, especially when applied to the Lower Counties, a place with few Quakers.[7]

The assembly complied with Penn's wishes when it came to political union, but in other matters it proved recalcitrant. It rejected Penn's Frame of Government, a constitutional document Penn and his advisors had labored over for most of the previous year but one that also sharply constrained the legislative branch. It also rejected a financial scheme essential to Penn's vision for his colony. Neither Penn himself nor the individual

Quaker merchants who began migrating to Pennsylvania would be enough to secure the colony's commercial future. For that, the colony would need the sorts of far-reaching trading networks engineered by Penn's commercial predecessors in the region, particularly the Dutch West India Company. In luring a fur-trading concern to Pennsylvania, the Free Society of Traders, Penn believed he could fill the void. As an independent joint-stock company, free to sell shares in itself, the Free Society would be able to finance the kind of trans-Atlantic commercial activity essential to Pennsylvania's long-term prospects. But there was a problem. For the company to be a licensed joint-stock entity, recognized by Pennsylvania authorities, it required a formal charter from the new colonial assembly. Unfortunately for Penn, the assembly refused to comply. Investors retreated, and with the Free Society unable to service its debts, the company's fortunes tumbled.[8]

The failure of the Free Society was much more than a financial failure for Penn. Because Pennsylvania incorporated preexisting European colonies, whatever political order William Penn established would evolve from some kind of federation of colonies. The rejection of the Free Society charter suggests that those colonies had no particular interest in the long-term financial viability of Pennsylvania. Individual traders would profit from Pennsylvania's abundant trading resources, but without a joint stock company whose fortunes were tied to the colony, Pennsylvania would lack something Virginia, Barbados, and to a lesser degree Massachusetts possessed: a cohort of interested investors willing to advance the colony's agenda at court. The absence of such potent advocates could become particularly costly should the question of control of the Lower Counties ever come before the king. Given how essential ocean access would be for Pennsylvania's commercial survival, merchant investors in London would surely grasp the importance of preserving the Pennsylvania–Lower Counties union. A William Penn lacking commercial advocates in London made for a weaker William Penn in Pennsylvania.

Penn's fixation on the Lower Counties has to be understood in the context of these economic and political challenges. The danger that colonial dissent would bring royal scrutiny was serious enough for Pennsylvania, but with no royal conveyance, secured by charter or patent, it was far more serious for the Lower Counties. There was very little to stop the king or his brother from reasserting control in this vital portion of Penn's estate. The best solution to this problem, Penn would conclude, was a formal charter for the Lower Counties. If Penn himself was not entitled to such an act of royal beneficence, surely his landlord, the Duke of York, was. Throughout his first year in the colonies, Penn's agents in London vigorously lobbied the crown on behalf of the duke, and in February 1683, Penn took up the cause. To Laurence Hyde, the Earl of Rochester, first lord of treasury, Penn wrote that his colony's success would depend upon Rochester, since it was up to him, a close friend who happened to have the king's ear, to advance the Duke of York's "Maryland Conveyance," as Penn called the Delaware charter. By the following March, it appeared Penn had been granted his wish. The Crown prepared a patent, granting the Duke of York rights to "all that Towne of Newcastle otherwise called Delaware and fort therein or there-unto belonging scituate lying and being between Maryland and New Jersey in America." Whether the patent was ever fully approved has never been established, but for Penn, the issue turned out to be moot: the Duke of York never issued him revised leases acknowledging that they rested on clear pro-prietary prerogative.[9]

In addition to what it says about the tenuousness of William Penn's Lower County claims, the fight over the lower Delaware is important for another reason. Penn's efforts, as he fully acknowledged to Rochester, were ulti-mately directed toward the annexation of the claims of another colonial proprietor. Given that the Duke of York claimed control of those lands, Penn could plausibly deny that his claims came at Lord Baltimore's expense. But there is little doubt he recognized the flimsiness of this pretext. Had his am-bitions been restricted to the Lower Counties, perhaps he would have taken a different tack—he could have simply hidden behind the tangled and opaque terms of the Duke of York's claims to those counties. But Penn was well aware that he also had designs on lands claimed by Lord Baltimore. There was no easy way to disentangle those claims from Penn's tangled Lower County claims.

Confusion over the proximity of New Castle to the fortieth parallel was emblematic. There was simply no way for the Lords of Trade to correct the error without either Pennsylvania's loss of its southern claims, including the Lower Counties, or Maryland's loss of its vast far north. For Penn, neither scenario was desirable. Any confirmation that New Castle was, in fact, well below the fortieth parallel was confirmation that it was within Maryland's original chartered bounds. And any confirmation of this was confirmation that the Lower Counties had been annexed from Maryland—likely a fatal blow to any effort to acquire a separate Lower Counties charter. The legal apparatus behind Penn's colonial enterprise had reached its limit, leaving the great Quaker few alternatives to conquest and plunder. In a letter to Augustine Herrman, who had volunteered to host negotiations between envoys of Penn and the third Lord Baltimore, Penn noted that he came "a man of peace yet" he feared not war. There was now little the Quaker empire builder would not do to secure the Lower Counties, and that meant, above all else, a defiant battle with his southern neighbor.[10]

Unlike his father, the second Lord Baltimore never saw America. Exhausted by the management of his English and Irish estates and lengthy battles with Virginia partisans, the journey proved impossible for him. This may have been just as well. Had he come to America, Lord Baltimore would have seen that his colonial fiefdom bore very little resemblance to the Catholic refuge he and his father envisioned. Although Maryland's several large manors were controlled by Catholic lords, the majority of the colony's land grants were held by Protestant freeholders. Lord Baltimore's considerable recruiting efforts had been mostly unsuccessful. As long as a tolerant Stuart monarch reigned, the promise of a colony that openly tolerated Catholicism, if not quite a Catholic colony, had little appeal to England's Roman Catholics— or at least those Catholics with the means to migrate to America. Even for Catholics who did leave for Maryland, only a very few did so with any real dedication to Lord Baltimore's religious vision. Far from a bold experiment in toleration, Maryland had become a place of incessant sectarian conflict, much like its southern neighbor, Virginia.

Maryland bore another and much more far-reaching similarity to Virginia. Its English settlers joined Virginia's planters in the Chesapeake's most profitable economic pursuit. In place of quiet manors, Protestant and Catholic tenants living together in peace, sustaining themselves and their lords with timber, hemp, flax, or the familiar agricultural fruits of the English countryside, Maryland was largely a place of independent landholders and staple agriculture. And the colony's chief staple would be what King James I, in an early indictment of tobacco's ill effects, called "a custome lothsome to the eye, hatefull to the Nose, harmefull to the braine, dangerous to the Lungs, and in the blacke stinking fume thereof, neerest resembling the horrible Stigian smoke of the pit that is bottomelesse."[11]

However exceptional the Lords Baltimore may have wanted their colony to be, and however different its anti-Catholic enemies expected it to be, staple agriculture meant that in practice the colony came to be nearly indistinguishable from Virginia. Traveling north from the mouth of the James River to the Potomac, a traveler would see nothing suggesting he had crossed from one colonial jurisdiction to another. However different Virginia and Maryland were in their respective inceptions, within a decade of the latter's founding, the two colonies came together as a single, largely undifferentiated Chesapeake plantation society. Perhaps the most readily visible expression of this fact was the pattern of settlement. This had little to do with the manorial prescriptions of the second Lord Baltimore and everything to do with locating advantageous tobacco plantations. Planters in Maryland "took up land in much the same way as in Virginia," James Horn observes, "considering first the quality of the soils, convenience of access for shipping, and proximity to other households." As Russell Menard and Lois Green Carr have written, from Maryland's very first settlement, much like in Virginia, plantations were "strung out along the river banks, on the necks of peninsulas between rivers, and on other navigable streams."[12] These waterways meant access to markets, and that access, above any other consideration dictated the distribution of Maryland's settlements.

By the middle of the seventeenth century, the frantic pursuit of tobacco profits meant that the banks of the major tributaries of the central and southern Chesapeake were being cultivated by planters with no particular allegiance to the colony in which they happened to reside. In part this was a function of the hydrography of the Chesapeake. With so many waterways and tributaries along which produce could be moved to ships in the deep-water Chesapeake, the region never developed any substantial market towns. Without these economic fulcrums, there was never any clear alliance of economic and political capital—an alliance that could have nurtured the sort of city-state politics that shaped other colonial regions. The West Indies had their Havana; New Netherlands, its New Amsterdam; New England, its Boston; New France, its Quebec City. But in the seventeenth century, no comparable urban market emerged in the Chesapeake. Planters did business directly with itinerant factors and ship captains, usually aboard ships anchored in the deeper waters of Chesapeake Bay. This further blurred the bounds between Maryland and Virginia. Had it not been for trade export duties imposed by colonial governments in the 1660s and 1670s, English and occasional Dutch factors would have been able to trade with utter indifference to the political geography of the English Chesapeake. Their pursuit was profit and, in collaboration with the toiling landholders of the Chesapeake, they did their part to create something of a tobacco juggernaut. In 1630, the Chesapeake Bay colonies produced around four hundred thousand pounds of tobacco.[13] Between 1640 and 1663, Chesapeake tobacco exports to the British Isles grew from about a million pounds annually to more than seven million. By the late 1680s, British imports had risen to nearly thirty million pounds. Far from alleviating Lord Baltimore's American problems, the tobacco boom appeared to make them worse.

In part because the Chesapeake colonies expanded into the Chesapeake's Eastern Shore, tobacco prices changed very little between 1660 and 1680. By the mid-1660s, they had fallen from a peak of around threepence per pound in 1640 to just half that. For most of the 1660s and 1670s, prices hovered above a penny per pound, and then in 1681 they fell to nine-tenths of a penny per pound. Because there was relatively little prime tobacco-growing soil on the Eastern Shore, and because that soil was generally in higher inland portions of the peninsula, prime tobacco produced there carried higher transport costs and slimmer margins. In areas with less fertile soil, lower-quality tobacco fetched lower prices.

Planters who settled the Eastern Shore in the late 1650s could thus expect substantially lower profits than their western shore predecessors, and lower profits meant that taxes consumed a higher percentage of plantation income—so a rise in taxes could be catastrophic. But this frightful scenario had become a certainty. Maryland's expansion had done little to increase proprietary income, let alone tax revenue, and costly new navigation acts imposed by Parliament left provincial authorities with few alternatives to new taxes.[14]

Having served both as Maryland's governor and proprietor, by the time William Penn established Pennsylvania, the third Lord Baltimore had become one of the most experienced colonial administrators anywhere in North America. His accomplishments included resolution of a boundary dispute with his colony's southern neighbor, Virginia; the survival of proprietary government through a series of insurgencies related to Bacon's Rebellion; and the maintenance of religious toleration. Given the persistence of anti-Catholicism following the restoration of Charles II, the latter was an especially remarkable achievement.

The price Lord Baltimore paid for sustaining his colony's toleration would be very steep, perhaps excessively so given the poor prospects of Anglicanism in the colonies. The Church of England was never able to provide enough clergy to establish itself as an influential presence in most of the mainland colonies. Although Anglicans constituted a majority of Maryland's population in its southern and western reaches, in 1676 there were only three Anglican ministers in the colony, and over the course of the next decade the situation for Anglicans would improve only marginally. In 1689, there were six active Anglican clergymen in Maryland. On the eve of the Pennsylvania boundary crisis, Lord Baltimore had no way of knowing how weak and fragmented his Anglican opponents were. But partly to counter a perceived Anglican menace, he tied his political fortunes to the former Whorekill region and its population of dissenting Protestants. In doing so, he tied his fortunes to the most economically fragile region of Maryland, and in the late 1670s that fragility, in conjunction with a fiscal crisis, would make for a nearly intractable political problem. Precisely as he confronted his expanding neighbor to the north, in other words, Lord Baltimore saw his political fortunes dim. Such was the context in which he undertook negotiation over his colony's northern boundary.[15]

Maryland's fiscal struggles stemmed from two related problems. First, internal, colonial taxes were paid almost entirely in tobacco. Those taxes came in two principal forms: quitrents, imposed directly by the proprietor on landed wealth, and poll or head taxes, imposed by the colony to support its administration. In both cases, stagnant tobacco prices took their toll. With no accurate way to forecast tobacco values, the colonial assembly, which set tax rates, had no accurate way to assess the value of the tobacco it took for tax payments. When it did assess that value, it usually did so at substantially inflated values. In 1662, the Maryland assembly set the rate at twopence per pound, or about a halfpenny above the actual market value; in 1669, it raised the rate to three and a half pence, more than three times the market value for a pound of Chesapeake tobacco. To compensate for the discounted tax rates, in 1671 the assembly granted the proprietor half of a new two-shilling export duty per hogshead of tobacco. This tax may have improved Lord Baltimore's financial fortunes, but with so little upward movement in tobacco prices, it also added to the burdens of his colony's Eastern Shore planters.

From the moment he assumed his colony's governorship, the third Lord Baltimore looked for ways to expand taxable commercial activity. Much of this quest centered on his father's push to establish port towns. St. Mary's City, the nominal capital of Maryland, was the initial focus of the governor's efforts. With the help of his uncle Philip Calvert, who had preceded him as governor and who was the young Charles's most trusted advisor, the new governor built a new statehouse and other public buildings as well as a Catholic chapel. Governor Calvert and his uncle also laid out the town to include space for the well-to-do private residents they hoped to attract. With these colonists' wealth would come commerce, and with that commerce would perhaps come the kind of transoceanic trade enjoyed by other colonial port towns. The quest for some kind of mercantile center proved increasingly urgent for Governor Calvert—too urgent to await the organic rise of St. Mary's City. Casting about for some alternative, in 1668 he selected sites for eleven additional port towns, but no substantial commercial capital town emerged in Maryland before Annapolis in the 1690s. Had tobacco prices not stagnated, Governor Calvert might have directed resources employed in his father's urbanization schemes toward a sustainable solution to the colony's northern problems.

Instead, not surprisingly, Maryland's revenue shortfalls continued, even as its population grew. Between 1681 and 1685, the price of Chesapeake tobacco fell below one penny a pound. Prices would creep back up, but as he confronted his northern antagonist, Maryland's proprietor had little reason to expect any substantial increase in tax revenue.[16]

As a means of preventing colonists from evading taxes by shipping tobacco directly to Europe, Parliament's 1673 Plantations Duty Act stipulated that duties on enumerated commodities such as tobacco would be paid in the colony where the shipment originated. Those duties would be collected by a corps of royal customs agents, officials over whom neither Calvert nor the Maryland assembly had any authority, at least as far as their revenue-collecting activities were concerned. Christopher Rousby, an agent known for fits of anti-Catholic vitriol, proved a particularly formidable challenge for the third Lord Baltimore. Rousby's ruthless and boorish pursuit of taxable goods infuriated colonists, and in 1681 he was accused by Lord

Baltimore of driving prosperous merchants and traders out of Maryland. In a letter to the Earl of Anglesey, lord of the privy seal, Lord Baltimore begged for Rousby's removal. His "seditious, and wicked" conduct "would dishonor the king, cheat his subjects and drive all manner of Trade out of my Province."

Rousby responded to Lord Baltimore's accusations with a charge of his own. He informed the Crown that Nicholas Badcock, another customs agent, had been wrongly accused by Maryland authorities of "debauchery and Lewdness." That the king's agents were allegedly men of such uniformly poor character, Rousby claimed, could only be explained as part of a conspiracy to "render us too infamous to be capable of our employments" and allow the proprietor to "get those offices . . . into the hands of his owne Creatures and Depend[ents]." The latter was an especially damning allegation, since customs agents were the only royal officials in Maryland. According to Rousby, Lord Baltimore was doing precisely what made proprietary authority a problem: he was placing his personal financial interests above the Crown's.[17] Rousby's gambit succeeded brilliantly. The customs commission refused to remove him and, in a harsh rebuke, informed the lord proprietor that any further grievances would have to be taken up with Rousby and his fellow customs collectors. In effect, when it came to matters of trade and customs, Rousby, Badcock, and any other customs agents in the colony stood equal to the proprietor.

Crown authorities were in general agreement: the problem in Maryland was not insolent and abusive tax collectors but a colonial proprietor who failed to grasp his responsibilities to the king and his empire. Unless that proprietor "do readily comply with the Acts of Trade and Navigation," the Lords of Trade warned, "His Maj[esty] Will call him to a further account and to direct a Quo Warranto to bee issued upon his Patent." A writ of quo warranto required the recipient to provide the Crown with a formal defense of any chartered privileges. Should a corporation prove sufficiently recalcitrant, the Crown could carry a writ of quo warranto to its logical conclusion. In the best-known such case, between 1681 and 1683 the Crown succeeded in revoking the municipal charter of the City of London. For the most part, these cases were used for political purposes—to reclaim seats in Parliament awarded as a privilege accompanying incorporation. In the case of a proprietary colony, the politics were much simpler. The Crown stood to gain no direct parliamentary power. It could, however, gain a new source of revenue and patronage, the latter in the form of all the new royal administrative offices a colony would yield.[18]

William Markham, Pennsylvania's governor, traveled to Maryland to meet with Lord Baltimore in August 1681. Markham carried a letter from Penn asking Baltimore to negotiate with "all the dispatch possible in the business of the bounds, that observing our just limits in that & all other things we may begin & maintain a Just & friendly intercourse." Penn's request yielded no resolution, only an agreement to locate in some definitive way the boundary separating Maryland and Pennsylvania, an imperative Baltimore had received directly from the king shortly after Penn's charter had been secured. Over the course of the following year, even that agreement fell apart. Lord Baltimore learned of Penn's efforts to gain the allegiance of prominent planters in Cecil and Baltimore Counties, including Augustine Herrman, in plain violation of "the Golden rule Mentioned in mr Penns Letter to me, *Doe to thy Neighbor as thou woulds he should doe to thee.*"[19]

With Penn's arrival in the colonies, diplomacy continued, and over the course of two years, from 1682 until Lord Baltimore and Penn returned to England in 1684, the proprietors sponsored four additional meetings. These resolved nothing. On two occasions, in December 1682 and May 1683, Penn and Baltimore met in the only face-to-face negotiations the men held. The two had met at least once previously, in 1677 in England, where they discussed the plight of Quakers in Maryland. The meeting had been initiated by Penn and focused on the Calverts' demands that the Quakers swear oaths of allegiance to the Maryland proprietor. While that particular issue remained unresolved, the meeting had been productive and cordial.

The same cannot be said of the two men's first American meeting. Penn pleaded with the third Lord Baltimore, claiming not only that a resolution of their mutual boundary was the king's will but also that he had no interest in annexing portions of Maryland. Penn's initial petition for an American colony, he explained, sought an enormous northern grant "not out of a covetous humour but only that I might reach the lake of Canada [Lake Ontario] for an inlett to my Province." The Lords of Trade assured him that he need not concern himself with such a distant inlet, since he would have access to the Delaware Bay. Penn took this to mean that the Crown was not interested in territory and its limits but rather in the "reasons of our

Pattents." And the reasons were to enhance English trade. "As for the Land in dispute," Penn reassured his counterpart, "I value it not but . . . for an inlet for the conveniency of my province." What mattered was commerce, and commerce depended on access to Atlantic sea lanes. Both colonies surely shared this object and thus should have "faire and amicable Correspondence . . . as between any united Provinces whatsoever." Lord Baltimore justifiably dismissed Penn's claims. After all, in a London meeting years earlier Penn had mentioned that he had been offered control of the Lower Counties but refused them because he had told Lord Baltimore "you knew it was mine." And now "I heare you have . . . possesst yourselfe of" those very lands. For Lord Baltimore, such territorial expansion, especially when so flagrantly contrary to the known interests of another proprietor, could not be explained as merely an outgrowth of the commercial spirit of Stuart empire.[20]

The following May, the two met again at New Castle. Penn, it seems, had decided to seek a compromise. In exchange for accepting the fortieth parallel as his colony's actual southern limit, he demanded a commercial corridor along the Susquehanna River, from the fortieth parallel to the Chesapeake Bay. That the lands constituting this proposed Susquehanna corridor were controlled by descendants of the original Susquehannock nation seems never to have entered the discussion. For the arrangement to work, Lord Baltimore would either have to transfer lands already ceded to the remaining Susquehannocks or buy back those lands. Since the Susquehannocks had become tributaries of the Iroquois, such a transfer would also depend on Iroquois consent, something Lord Baltimore was unlikely to receive given his clashes with New York authorities. Nonetheless, in a crafty bit of statesmanship, he accepted the proposal on the condition that Penn formally acknowledge Maryland's claim to the Lower Counties. After all, the third Lord Baltimore again reminded Penn, "*there was a time, when yo told me you knew I had a Right on delaware.*"[21] Given that Penn's control of the Lower Counties already rested on the flimsiest of legal grounds, the Maryland proprietor well knew his condition could not be met, but he also knew that should Penn acknowledge what he once had clearly believed—namely, that the Lower Counties were part of Maryland—Lord Baltimore would have firmer grounds for defending a boundary along the fortieth parallel. The circle around New Castle would now be in clear violation of the Maryland charter.

Penn seems never to have seriously considered the proposal, instead pursuing control of the Susquehanna by other means. In September and October 1683, through dubious arrangements with local Indians who may have been Lenapes or Susquehannocks, Penn acquired most of the eastern Susquehanna shore and a large portion of the western shore. Given that those land cessions included lands below the fortieth parallel, their legality, much like most of Penn's other Indian land purchases, would have depended on the resolution of the Maryland-Pennsylvania boundary problem.[22]

In September 1683, Lord Baltimore commissioned his cousin George Talbot to meet with Penn and again make plain the lord's demand: that Penn acknowledge Lord Baltimore's ownership of "all the Land Lyeing on the West side of Delaware River, and to the Southward of the fortieth degree of Northerly Lattitude."

What is notable about this mission is not that it failed or that it infuriated Penn, who was insulted that Lord Baltimore sent a lowly proxy to do his bidding, but that Penn had prepared a new defense of his claims, one grounded less in the intent of his royal patron than in the terms of Lord Baltimore's own charter. According to that solemn legal document, "the Ld Baltemore hath noe land given him by Patent, but what was unplanted of any, but sauvage nations, and this West Side of the Delaware before, and at the passing of his Pattent, was actually bought and possest by [the Dutch], a Civill and Christian State, in Amite with the Crown of England." By the very terms of Maryand's charter, which stipulated that the charter pertained only to "a Country hitherto uncultivated, in the Parts of America, and partly occupied by Savages, having no knowledge of the Divine Being," Charles I never intended to grant the Lords Baltimore lands conquered by another Protestant nation.[23] Although the grounds for palatinate powers had been precisely to fend off competing European colonizers, the Lords Baltimore failed in this as well. Though they tried, they never secured allegiance from the Lower County colonists. As Penn would explain to the Duke of York in early 1684, the second Lord Baltimore "never was in possession" of the northern portion of his grant, and "his neglect hath made his claim void." As every student of English law knew, neglect effectively meant an absence of government. Where there was no government there was no law, and "where there is no Law . . . there can be . . . no Title."[24]

Beyond casting doubt on the third Lord Baltimore's principal defense, which was that his claim to Maryland's far north had been secured by his colony's charter, Penn's newest argument had an additional legal benefit. The Delaware River valley had been settled by God-fearing Protestants well before Cecil Calvert received his colony's charter, and because those very same Protestants had been defeated by the forces of the Duke of York, their lands were now the equivalent of any wartime prize recovered by the Crown. "It is knowne," Penn explained to his interlocutors, "that if any of our English Merchants shipps be taken, & possest but 24 houres by an Enemy, if retaken by the Crown, they are prize; & this place was more than 24 years in the hands of the Dutch" before it was conquered by the Duke of York. Even if the Lower Counties had originally been taken from Lord Baltimore, they were now restored plunder, recovered by the king's brother who, in turn, distributed them as a prize to the Crown's loyal agents. That Lord Baltimore was a lord palatinate only reinforced the point. For as "he hath *regalia, Principality* . . . [and] is bound to keep his own dominions or else lose them; and if lost to a Forreigner, and taken by the soveraigne, the soveraigne hath the Right." Such was the law of nations, the *jus gentium*. As would be the case for any other state or principality, Maryland had no claim on lands conquered by another nation, including England, if those lands had never been rightfully conquered by Maryland.[25]

The fight over Maryland's far north had become a fight between conquering geopolitical entities—not quite nations or kingdoms, but expansive colonies whose territorial claims would rest on military conquest rather than feudal conveyance and legal title. The normal path for such entities to resolve territorial disputes was war.

In the late winter and spring of 1684, that was precisely the path the dispute began to take. The precipitating event was an attempt by agents from Maryland, led by George Talbot, to build a fort at Christina Bridge, just a few miles west of New Castle. In a letter to the Duke of York, Penn explained that Talbot had entered the area "to reduce the place by force" and that the Marylanders' conduct could be nothing other than a "Warlike invasion." William Welch, a Quaker merchant who had known Penn in London and who settled in New Castle, attempted to evict the intruders, but few locals heeded his posse comitatus.

Welch suspected that many, having earlier declared their allegiance to the Lords Baltimore and already in contact with Talbot and his men, "on purpose Absented themselves." With a force of just six or seven, Welch and his band did nothing to deter Talbot and his "riotous assembly" of militiamen.[26]

Penn pleaded for the Duke of York's intervention. Maryland had finally become the wayward, treasonous entity its early opponents had feared, and "if I am not mistaken I shall be able to make evident by Law, [the third Lord Baltimore] hath almost cancelled his Allegiance to the King herein, & exposed himself to his Mercy." As Penn prepared his brief, Lord Baltimore took actions of his own. In May 1684, just before Talbot's invasion, and just after commissioning his four-year-old son, Benedict Leonard, resident governor of Maryland, he set sail for England, intending to take his boundary case directly to the Crown. The move infuriated Penn, who saw it as a desperate attempt to preempt his own petition. "Such Arts," he wrote the Duke of York, "will never do," and as Colonel Talbot was rampaging through the Lower Counties threatening to expel "by violence [those who] would not submitt" to Maryland's new boy-lord, Penn was making urgent preparations to follow Lord Baltimore. On August 18, 1684, he sailed for England.[27]

A few months after Penn's return to England, Charles II died and his fifty-one-year-old brother James succeeded him to the throne. However the Maryland-Pennsylvania border dispute was to be resolved, it would be resolved by a Catholic king. Although himself a Catholic, Lord Baltimore would gain little by James's accession. Given the pervasiveness of anti-Catholicism and the near-calamity of the exclusion crisis, the last thing the Catholic James II needed was to appear to favor Catholic lords. What he did need were allies among dissenting Protestants, groups that would stand with him in the inevitable battle for religious toleration following the accession of a Catholic monarch. Lord Baltimore would now have to bide his time in the hope that controversy surrounding James's accession would dissipate and a loyal Catholic lord could once again enjoy the benefits of his Catholic majesty's favor. Unfortunately, time was something Lord Baltimore had very little of.

A few months after he left for England, his colony was rocked by a new customs scandal. The royal tax agent Christopher Rousby was murdered by George Talbot. During a drunken brawl aboard the *Quaker*, a customs patrol boat anchored in the Patuxet River, Talbot drew his carefully sharpened pocket dagger and fatally stabbed Rousby. Authorities arrested Talbot and took him to Jamestown in Virginia; given Rousby's habit of antagonizing Maryland's planters, and given Talbot's prominence, conviction in Maryland seemed unlikely. For Lord Baltimore the affair could not have come at a worse time. His swashbuckling cousin had done much to counter Pennsylvania's expansion, but now that same loyal servant was accused of murdering an agent of the Crown, an agent who had already notified Whitehall of Maryland's contempt for royal authority.

Another royal customs agent, Nehemiah Blakiston, reported to his superiors that Talbot's allies among Maryland's ruling elite continued to turn a blind eye to smuggling and other acts designed to "prevent our proceeding and just Executions of our Commissions in behalf of His Majesty." A colonial government capable of so defying the king's agents, Blakiston intimated, surely bore some responsibility for Rousby's murder. With Lord Baltimore's cooperation, Talbot was eventually convicted and sentenced to death by a Virginia jury. The sentence was commuted on condition that Talbot leave English dominions for five years. As a political matter, the Talbot affair cost Maryland's proprietor dearly. In addition to being Lord Baltimore's relative, Talbot had been young Benedict's closest advisor, effectively the colony's regent. As Lord Baltimore lobbied for the integrity of his original charter, his family's highest-ranking colonial agent languished in the custody of the Gloucester County sheriff, awaiting trial for murder of an agent of the king. If ever the Lords of Trade needed a reason to act against proprietary rule in Maryland, they surely had it now.[28]

To the Calvert family's great good fortune, fear of rebellion against the new king, James II, gripped London and slowed the workings of Whitehall, delaying for almost a year any consideration of the boundary conflict. At the end of the summer of 1685, the Lords of Trade agreed to hear the case. Through September and early October they gathered evidence and testimony, mostly from the proprietors themselves. By November 13 they had arrived at a partial decision. Maryland's proprietor, the lords decreed, had no right to the Lower Counties for precisely the reason Penn claimed: "the land in question was settled by Christians before Lord Baltimore's patent." The evidence Penn supplied left no doubt that the region's settlement predated the chartering of Maryland. One sixty-seven-year-old deponent, now residing in New York, recalled that in 1630, while working for the Dutch West India Company, he traveled to the company's Delaware River settlements, and there saw "a Trading house with 10 or 12 Servants" as well as a "Brikhouse belonging to the [Dutch] West India Company" and "3 or 4 familyes of Walloons." Lacking any clarity about the full scope of Dutch settlements and with a familiar disregard for the claims of the Lenapes, the lords imposed their own arbitrary boundary between Maryland and the Lower Counties. The great Delaware-Chesapeake peninsula would be divided "into two equal parts, From East to West, as far as Cape Henlopen, between the King and Lord Baltimore," with the king controlling the Cape's eastern side and Lord Baltimore retaining control of the western half.[29]

The lords' ruling obviously favored Penn, but as he had anticipated, in their efforts to address the Lower Counties problem they created new problems. In rejecting Lord Baltimore's Lower Counties claims, the lords affirmed the claims of the former Duke of York, now King James II. The Lower Counties had become a royal colony. The likelihood that the Crown would tolerate a reversion to proprietary rule, even in a relatively small and inconsequential colony, was practically nil.

The Lower Counties problem may have been foremost for William Penn, but for Lord Baltimore it was relevant primarily because it addressed the cartographic inconsistencies in Penn's charter. And those inconsistencies all unfolded from confusion over the location of the fortieth parallel of latitude. The Delaware peninsula was to be divided to the fortieth degree, which suggests the lords remained under the impression that this was roughly the latitude of New Castle. But after their various conferences in the colonies, both Lord Baltimore and Penn were clear that this was not the case. Lord Baltimore was also certain that questions over Maryland's northern boundary would prove immaterial to William Penn. With no firm decision by the Lords of Trade concerning Pennsylvania's southern boundary, there was nothing to temper Penn's territorial ambitions. In December 1685, Lord Baltimore thus made one final plea to the lords "that no more land shall be taken from my charter than what is actually cultivated in Delaware" and that the lords would "prevent Penn's people from making settlements near the heads and branches of the rivers that fall into Chesapeake Bay." Baltimore well knew that without a true resolution of the northern boundary problem, there was nothing to prevent William Penn from annexing more of Maryland. Soon settlers loyal to Penn would "break in upon the heads and branches of my rivers on the Eastern [shore]" of the Chesapeake and Maryland's far north would be lost.[30]

In the first half of the eighteenth century, Chester County, Pennsylvania, which included most of the easternmost territory annexed by Penn, and Lancaster County, whose western boundary was the Susquehanna, and whose southern boundary remained unresolved, would be Pennsylvania's fastest-growing counties. Pennsylvania's expansion into the disputed Maryland borderlands was not simply a reflection of organic westward movement. Penn's land transfer schemes encouraged migration to the region. In 1702, he established the township of Nottingham in the farthest southern reaches of Chester County. This tract, which Penn designated for Quaker settlers, was well below the fortieth parallel. Eight years later, Penn granted a group of Swiss Mennonites permission to settle along the Susquehanna in lands formerly controlled by the Susquehannocks—again, below the fortieth parallel. And as Scots-Irish and Quaker settlers pushed into the southern reaches of Lancaster and, later, York Counties, on either side of the Susquehanna, and below the fortieth parallel, the Penn family's agents did little to deter settlement in what remained disputed territory. The third Lord Baltimore struggled to counter Penn's advances with his own settlers.[31]

The combination of loosely allied settlers, jurisdictional ambiguity, and Native communities increasingly aggrieved by squatters' theft of their lands proved volatile, and by the middle of the eighteenth century, the Maryland-Pennsylvania borderlands would descend into repeated episodes of ruthless ethnic slaughter.

PART II

MARCHLANDS INTO BORDERLANDS

Unable to resolve their boundary dispute, the proprietors of Maryland and Pennsylvania struggled to secure income from their borderlands. Without jurisdictional clarity, the usual means for generating colonial revenue—taxation, rent, and land transfer fees—were unenforceable. Far from the rent-taking lords they aspired to be, the proprietors were, of necessity, active managers of their extensive American estates. For settlers, the steep costs of security would offset the benefits of limited taxation. As more Europeans moved into the Maryland-Pennsylvania borderlands, the region would become among the most violent in North America. While that violence initially involved clashes among colonists, the French and Indian War initiated a new and prolonged pattern of ethnocidal bloodshed. For the Native peoples of the Lower Susquehanna, the violence would have catastrophic results. For the proprietors of the colonies of Maryland and Pennsylvania, it greatly intensified pressure to resolve their long-standing boundary dispute. The arrival of English astronomers Charles Mason and Jeremiah Dixon in 1763 marked a new initiative to bring peace to the Maryland-Pennsylvania borderlands.

CHAPTER 4

The Squatters' Empire

THE PHRASE "SALUTARY NEGLECT" was made famous by the great par-liamentarian and polemicist Edmund Burke. Burke's reference, in a speech delivered in 1775, was to the British government's treatment of its American colonies, and it was meant to cast that treatment in the most benign possible light. Through Britain's "wise and salutary neglect . . . a generous nature has been suffered to take her own way to perfection." That perfection was the noble quietude long characteristic of relations between the colonies and the mother country. Like gentle but oblivious parents, a series of British monarchs and their fumbling but largely harmless ministers had given the colonies liberty to come of age under the lightest governing touch. That the colonies now rejected the British government's taxes and its various other exertions of punitive authority was only proof of the benefits of neglect. The people of America had become the most British of all Britons. In justified defiance, they rejected the violence the government of Prime Minister Frederick North inflicted on their funda-mental rights, and they did so in precisely the way their forebears had done: drawing on a deep and ancient reservoir of English constitutional principle, they staged a revolution in defense of a rightful constitutional order. Much like the ill-fated King James II, driven from the throne in late 1688, an irate and vengeful King George III would only incite more obstinacy from his liberty-loving subjects. The time had come for the king's head minister, Lord North, and his parliamentary enablers to step back from the brink and for the Crown, like a truly attentive parent, to reconcile with wayward children who were, after all, only exhibiting the values their parents professed. Burke's plea failed.

But the idea of salutary neglect, long detached from the immediate political context in which Burke spoke, has had remarkable persistence. Generations of historians understood the British government's treatment of its American provinces as a species of salutary neglect—albeit salutary not in the way Burke understood but in the sense that the neglect afforded space for the nurturing of a distinct and very American brand of politics. Government by consent and the supremacy of law, cornerstones of American republicanism, were born of the absence of government in British North America. Infused with notes of Frederick Jackson Turner's frontier and its generative democratic matrix of harsh wilderness and raw settlers, this theory of American political development assumed that the peculiarities of American government owed a great deal to the absence of British government. In recent decades the story has grown much bloodier, particularly when applied to the colonial American backcountry. Yes, the peripheral territories of the British Empire tended to exist beyond the reach of the British government and its various colonial proxies. But far from being a crucible of some common-man republic, that periphery was characterized above all by violence, sometimes of an ethnocidal character, and often of a chaotic, civil variety in which white settlers, detached from any meaningful imperial authority, resorted to vigilantism and outright terrorism, inflicting upon one another cruelties nearly as hideous as those they inflicted on their many Native neighbors.[1]

This localized vigilantism, so long identified with the various manifestations of politics out-of-doors—the riots and regulator movements that swept through parts of British North America in the decades before and during the Revolutionary War—has in the last half century seemed somehow defensible, despite its ethnocidal tendencies. For it may have produced death and destruction, but its reversion to violence was born of political necessity. Nowhere does this explanation for colonial politics apply more than in the Maryland-Pennsylvania borderlands. Both the Penns and the Calverts, eager to achieve through settlement what they could not through law, did little to control the chaotic movement of European migrants into the western reaches of their colonies. In addition to an open disregard for standing treaties and their Native signatories, this method of territorial assertion meant white settlers themselves faced grave legal uncertainty. Although in some cases they possessed title to lands they settled, the usual processes by which that title would be secured in law—the public registration of title and the payment of taxes—were erratic and incomplete when they existed at all. The neglect of a legal apparatus to control settlement meant that westerners often had no sense of where higher authority resided, a circumstance exacerbated by the halting and haphazard organization of reliable systems for addressing civil grievances.

By the early eighteenth century, the chaotic settlement of the western reaches of the Maryland-Pennsylvania borderlands presented colonial proprietors with a familiar dilemma. As William Penn's chief colonial land agent, the Quaker merchant and land speculator James Logan, explained to Penn's son John in 1727, the disorder along Pennsylvania's southern borderlands left the region effectively ungoverned. The problem was as old as the colony itself. With no jurisdictional clarity, the foundational transaction for establishing which government protected which population was impossible: "honest men cannot take people's money for a precarious title, and to refuse it is dangerous because it seems a tacit confession of the invalidity of your [family's] right or claim." The comment applied to the transfer of lands, but it could also have applied to taxation: to impose taxes where title was uncertain was, at best, dishonest, while not to do so was to acknowledge the absence of any legal claim to those taxes.[2]

Any observer of British North America would have recognized the danger in the combination of unregulated European settlement, jurisdictional confusion, and government impotence. As the members of Pennsylvania's Provincial Council put it in a 1722 communication to the colony's governor, "It is no new thing in America that Boundaries of two Countries should lie for many years undetermined." What was new, or at least unprecedented, the council noted, was "that Hostilities, or what amounts to them, were committed in such cases." The tit-for-tat border conflicts plaguing Maryland and Pennsylvania seemed destined to "throw both Provinces into a State of War." What is remarkable about this next chapter in the fight over the Maryland-Pennsylvania boundary is not that it brought war but that large-scale border war was averted for so long.[3]

Inclined toward the absolutist tendencies of the new king, James II, in November 1688 William Joseph, Maryland's new governor, stood before his first colonial assembly and, high-church-like, declared his fealty to God and king and demanded a host of new measures including a general day of thanksgiving and a solemn oath of fidelity. Joseph's tactics played very badly in a colony held together by a loose coalition of dissenting Protestants and ruling Catholics, and it provoked a rebellion by the colonial assembly that would drive him and all other Catholics from office.

For nearly three years, a coalition of Protestants would govern Maryland. Lord Baltimore, still in England, could do little. Finally, in the summer of 1690, following the Glorious Revolution and James II's flight, Crown authorities formally sided with the Protestant rebels and began the process of transforming Maryland into a royal colony. Although England's new Dutch king, William of Orange, never formally revoked the Maryland charter, in June 1691 he commissioned Lionel Copley, a distinguished Protestant military officer, as the colony's new royal governor. With the governor of Maryland now a Crown appointee, all the powers of governance the Lords Baltimore had enjoyed fell to the king's representative. Because the Crown chose not to completely vacate Lord Baltimore's charter, the Calverts remained Maryland's largest landowners, but the days of the Maryland palatinate were finished. In 1715, the year his father died, the Protestant convert Benedict Leonard, now the fourth Lord Baltimore, regained his family's proprietary rights in Maryland. Benedict died just a few weeks later, and his eldest son, Charles, would become Maryland's new lord proprietor.

Charles, the fifth Lord Baltimore, who was fifteen when King George I issued a new proprietary charter for Maryland, was in no position to resolve the old problems of his colony's far north. The young Lord Baltimore's guardian, Francis North, the 2nd Baron of Guilford, a privy councilor and former first lord of trade, retained Governor John Hart, who had been appointed by Queen Anne in 1714 during Maryland's time as a royal colony. Hart would remain in office until 1720. More interested in serving the Crown than in serving his young patron, Hart did little to address the boundary problem. This was unfortunate, since William Penn's position as a negotiator over colonial land claims had never been weaker.

Despite Pennsylvania's successes in achieving English control over vast swaths of the inland mid-Atlantic, Penn's personal financial circumstances had only worsened. Mounting debts, the largest owed to the family of his former business manager, Philip Ford, landed Penn in debtors' prison. After nine months' confinement, Penn had his debt to the Fords liquidated by a group of Quaker allies, and he was freed. But Penn's financial troubles persisted. His new creditors, who claimed Pennsylvania as collateral, gave him two years to fund the debt. Beholden to creditors and to a Protestant monarch with little interest in the allegiance of religious dissenters, Penn was in no position to achieve a favorable resolution of his southern boundary dispute. Penn's predicament was so serious that he spent years attempting to sell his colony to the Crown for £12,000, substantially less than the value of his original patent. The new rescue plan had been devised by James Logan as a way to satisfy Penn's creditors while allowing him and his employer to retain control of their American real estate interests. Queen Anne, the Protestant daughter of James and England's last Stuart monarch, actually approved the plan, but she died before it was finalized. Even had she lived to complete the transaction, her beneficence would have done little for William Penn. In December 1712, at age sixty-eight, Pennsylvania's founder suffered a crippling stroke.[4]

After continued physical decline, William Penn died on July 30, 1718. His sons from his second marriage to Hannah, John, Thomas, and Richard, gained control of the family's American holdings. The younger Penns would preserve their colony's religious tolerance, but they themselves possessed none of their father's dedication to the Society of Friends. One of them, Thomas Penn, would go to Pennsylvania in the early 1730s, but the brothers' interest in the colony and its governance never extended beyond a quest to restore the family's credit and secure its colonial income.

In June 1718, William Keith, who had been appointed by Hannah Penn to serve as deputy governor (the proprietor being the actual governor) on behalf of her ailing husband, received a report that "certain persons from Maryland had . . . lately Survey'd out Lands not far from Conestogo," the homeland of Conestoga, Shawnee, and Conoy Indians.[5] Ancestors of the Conoys and the Conestogas had fled the incessant violence and unrest of the Chesapeake, and the Shawnees had been driven from their Ohio Valley homelands by Iroquois raiders. Assured by the great William Penn and James Logan that with treaties came some degree of security, the lower Susquehanna Natives had long since discovered the fragility of Penn's promises. Keith was besieged with complaints about Marylanders invading Pennsylvania and stealing Native lands. His efforts to address the problem constituted an improvised patchwork of diplomatic exchanges and legal proceedings.

The pattern was reflected in Keith's response to a dispute over the manor of Nottingham, one of the few border areas directly controlled by the Penn family. When settlers there refused to pay quitrents and claimed to be living in Cecil County, Maryland, Keith appointed two local loyalists as magistrates and ordered them to assert the complete authority of the Chester County Court. An irate Governor Hart of Maryland dismissed Keith's gesture, noting that the inhabitants of Nottingham "had frequently been taxed by the magistrates of Cecil County" and were very happy to be taken "under the protection of my Lord Baltimores Government." The choice, Hart observed, was only a choice in theory. Legal reality demonstrated that Nottingham was "unquestionably within the Bounds of My Lords Grant from the Crown."

Keith's response to Governor Hart was effectively no response. He had assumed that with William Penn's death, the Penn family scheme to transform Pennsylvania into a royal colony would proceed and he would eventually enjoy the extensive emoluments of a royal governorship. Moreover, the restoration of Maryland's charter was an indication that Lord Baltimore had allies at court. A protracted legal battle would only give those allies reason to stand between Governor Keith and a royal governor's commission. Keith's best option was a plan for Nottingham that effectively preserved the status quo but allowed for some tax collection. Residents of Nottingham would be subject to the legal authority of whichever proprietor granted them rights to occupy the land. The scheme left it to local surveyors and magistrates to sort through the thicket of claims and counterclaims. Governor Hart never formally agreed to Keith's peacekeeping gambit, and the question of Nottingham remained one for local authorities.[6]

This policy of neglect prevailed across the borderlands, giving rise to the strange circumstance of taxation practices differing from property owner to property owner. Sometime in the late 1720s a Lower Counties colonist, deposed by attorneys representing Lord Baltimore, recalled that no "inhabitants of the said 3 lower Counties have ever paid any Quit-Rent to the Lord Baltimore or his Ancesters; and . . . several of the Inhabitants of the said three lower Counties say that they had never paid any Quit-Rent to [the Penns] or their ancestors." Another deponent recalled no "Quit-Rents being paid to the Proprietor of Maryland" but did recall hearing "that several of his Neighbors have paid Quit-Rents to the Proprietors of Pensilvania."[7] Although there is no comparable testimony for the western reaches of the borderlands, what evidence that does exist suggests similar patterns. After recovering taxes originally levied in Nottingham Manor by authorities from Cecil County, Maryland, authorities from Chester County, Pennsylvania, petitioned their colony's Provincial Council for due compensation. Governor Keith and the council dismissed the petition. The dispute, they had concluded, pertained to the "immediate service & security of the inhabitants of Chester County" rather than of the province as a whole. For Keith, dissatisfaction in Pennsylvania's southern and western provinces was preferable to conflict with an adjoining colony.[8]

A month later, Governor Keith would be confronted with border problems he could not so easily dismiss. Unlike the people of Chester County, the Conestogas and their fellow Natives were not subjects of the Penn family. They had treated with William Penn as sovereign states. For Keith to leave border conflict near Conestoga to local authorities was to risk the very alliances that had allowed Pennsylvania to avoid open ethnic warfare. But despite decades of reassurances from Penn, Logan, and their proxies, the Conestoga-area Natives were facing an onslaught of settlers, many from Maryland. Keith responded in the way any good colonial diplomat would: by extracting new treaty concessions. Pennsylvania would honor its commitments to the Conestogas and their lower Susquehanna Native neighbors. In exchange, those Natives would cede twenty thousand acres on the west side of the Susquehanna. Those lands would revert to the Penn family and would be called Springettsbury, named for William Penn's grandson Springett, who Keith mistakenly believed had been designated William's principal heir. Once Pennsylvania surveyors had plotted the tract, the Conestoga-area Natives would have exclusive settlement rights there. Although Springettsbury was a manor controlled by the Penns, in effect what Keith was proposing was an Indian reservation, secured from outside intrusion by the legal title of distant colonial proprietors.

Keith attempted to persuade Native leaders that by granting the Penn family title to Springettsbury, the Conestogas and their neighbors would secure it from Maryland's "Land Pyrates." Pennsylvania's lower Susquehanna Native allies saw things differently. Designations of ownership, established through land treaties, obviously had no meaning for settlers from Maryland, and as long as the borderlands remained disputed, they also had little meaning for Maryland colonial authorities. But the Conestogas had another reason to doubt Keith's plan. At least since the outbreak of the Tuscarora War in 1711, Iroquois warriors had been descending the Susquehanna on their way to Carolina to battle the Catawba and Cherokee enemies of their Tuscarora allies. The villages of the lower Susquehanna Natives had become vital way stations for these traveling warriors. They also became sources of additional young warriors, prepared to throw their lot in with the Iroquois. The informal alliances that followed affirmed the Conestogas' status as Iroquois tributaries. The lower Susquehanna Valley was now part of a vast Iroquois-controlled complex of tributaries; any new treaty concerning those lands would require Iroquois assent.[9]

Adding to Keith's problems was the murder of Sawantaeny, a Seneca fur trader married to a Shawnee and living several days southwest of Conestoga on the Monocacy River in northern Maryland. Sawantaeny had been trading with brothers John and Edmond Cartlidge, two factors employed by James Logan, when after a night of heavy drinking a dispute over payments devolved into a fight. By the end, the Seneca trader lay dead. The murderers would be apprehended by Pennsylvania authorities, but the subsequent proceedings, which never included a formal trial or conviction, did little to address damage done to Iroquois relations. Given the failure of Pennsylvania authorities to punish the killers, the Susquehanna-area Indians were well aware that further land cessions could provoke Iroquois retaliation, leaving them to choose between their longtime Pennsylvania allies and the region's dominant Native power. To ensure that Keith's Springettsbury scheme did not become a final and deadly provocation, the Conestogas' council insisted that as a condition for advancing the scheme, Governor Keith first establish treaty terms with the Iroquois.

In a truism of diplomacy, bilateralism was unlikely to be effective. Just as there could be no agreement between Pennsylvania and the Susquehanna Natives without considering the interests of a third party, the Iroquois, so Pennsylvania would have little hope of treating with the Iroquois without considering the interests of another third party, British North America's largest and wealthiest royal colony, Virginia. In an effort to stop Iroquois raids into Virginia and North Carolina, Virginia governor Alexander Spotswood, an old friend of Keith's, had petitioned the Pennsylvania governor to allow Virginia to treat directly with the Susquehanna Valley Indians.

In exchange, as allies of a powerful Virginia, they would be liberated from Iroquois influence. Keith justifiably feared that such an arrangement would force Pennsylvania into the kind of internecine ethnic conflicts that plagued other colonies. Should the Conestoga Indians become proxies for Virginia, war would almost certainly be unavoidable. To avoid catastrophe, Keith assured Spotswood that Pennsylvania authorities, through diplomacy and gifts, would limit Iroquois incursions. But Keith's overtures were no match for Iroquois hostility to their southern Indian enemies.

Faced with a choice between allowing Maryland to continue to annex portions of the western Pennsylvania borderlands, in violation of William Penn's treaties with the Susquehanna Indians, and infuriating authorities in Virginia with a new Pennsylvania-Iroquois alliance to secure Springettsbury, Keith took the latter path. Spotswood could be managed, but Maryland could not. As a means of placating the Virginia governor, Keith invited him to join negotiations with the Iroquois in the hope that, as part of an agreement regarding the lower Susquehanna, the Iroquois would agree to stop their incursions into Virginia.[10]

Governors Keith and Spotswood traveled to Albany to meet with Iroquois leaders in September 1722. They brought the marrow of North American diplomacy: gifts, including five casks of gunpowder and five hundred pounds of lead shot. Keith managed to persuade his friend to settle with the Iroquois despite the long-held view among Virginians that the Iroquois were inclined to "haughty Demands [that] all the King's Governours on this Continent dance many hundred of Miles to Albany to treat there upon every caprice of theirs."[11] As a condition of the Iroquois-Virginia treaty, Keith affirmed Iroquois control of territory west of the Susquehanna excluding Springettsbury Manor. In addition to Albany, Conestoga and Philadelphia would now be outlets for Iroquois trade goods, an advantageous arrangement precisely because it would allow Iroquois traders to play New York and Pennsylvania merchants against one another.

Although lower Susquehanna Indians had long contended with Iroquois power, any dependence had always been tempered by the assumption that, in accord with treaties fashioned by William Penn, Pennsylvania authorities would deal with them as autonomous treaty-making nations. Now, without consulting leaders of these communities, Keith traded Conestoga autonomy for license to settle Springettsbury Manor.

Shortly before the Albany conference, Isaac Taylor and Elisha Gatchel, two officials of Chester County, Pennsylvania, were ordered to appear in court in Cecil County, Maryland. The orders stemmed from an incident in June in which Taylor, the Chester County surveyor and a member of the Pennsylvania Assembly, was arrested by "a Party of men in Arms from Cecil County." Taylor, the Maryland magistrates claimed, was illegally surveying Cecil County land and demanding oaths of allegiance from residents, who assumed they lived in Maryland. Gatchel, Taylor's friend and a Chester County justice of the peace, followed Taylor to Cecil County to provide an alibi for his friend, but he also was arrested, accused by Maryland authorities of assisting in the annexation of Maryland territory. The two Pennsylvanians were released after a few days, but they were ordered to return to court in August 1722. Those proceedings resulted in further charges, and Taylor and Gatchel were brought before the provincial court at Annapolis.[12]

Governor Keith had been aware of the June arrests, but his priorities lay farther west. As long as the Taylor and Gatchel matter remained a local one, to be resolved by county officials through local county courts, it would do little to upset the fragile peace between Pennsylvania and Maryland. But as he prepared for the Albany conference, Keith was told that the two Pennsylvanians were now being held in Annapolis. The case against Taylor and Gatchel, plainly a consequence of the Maryland-Pennsylvania border dispute, had become a diplomatic one. Keith implored Maryland's governor, Captain Charles Calvert, a distant relative of the fifth Lord Baltimore, to resolve the matter through direct negotiations. Maryland authorities refused, and the case moved to trial.

According to depositions later taken by Maryland's executive council, Keith vastly understated the gravity of Gatchel's and Taylor's crimes. The two had been engaged in illegal acts of annexation, and those acts had been openly and explicitly sanctioned by the Pennsylvania governor. Accompanied by five other men, Taylor and Gatchel had issued an ultimatum to Marylanders residing near Nottingham: Pennsylvanians would seize the plantations of Samuel Brice, Charles Alleyn, Edward Lang, and Daniel Smith unless those four men swore oaths of allegiance to their rightful lords, the Penns. Such conduct, according to Maryland attorney general Daniel Dulany, represented a clear violation of Maryland's anti-riot law. Meeting in a group of three or more who intended to do "some degree of violence as beating a man or forcing him to quit his Lands or Goods," Dulany noted in a brief on the case, was precisely what Taylor, Gatchel, and their supporters had done.

Such a crime needed to be adjudicated in the Maryland provincial court because that court "has the same authority in Maryland that the Kings Bench has in England and we have instances enough in our Law Books that Riots and forcible Entries are frequently tried at the Kings Bench."[13] The position of Maryland's chief law enforcement officer pointed in an alarming direction. The long-standing if mostly tacit agreement that colonial boundary disputes would be a county matter, handled by local magistrates, seemed to have ended. Acting in lieu of the Crown courts, in an obvious escalation of the dispute, Maryland would turn to its own provincial court to settle the boundary problem, and if Pennsylvanians insisted on annexing Maryland, then Maryland's courts would treat those Pennsylvanians as the king's courts treated rioters and disturbers of the peace. Keith was left with no choice but to seek from his colony's executive council advice "for preventing the fatal Consequences of a General misunderstanding with such near Neighbours." Those fatal consequences included descent "into a state of war" and "the heavey Censures of his Majesty."[14] The dispute might well have erupted into open conflict had not the Cecil County sheriff allowed the two Pennsylvanians to escape to Philadelphia, where Pennsylvania's executive council confirmed that they were in no way subject to the jurisdiction of Maryland and "ought not by any means submit to any of their Courts or Orders, or acknowledge their Jurisdiction over them."[15]

This executive council order marked a new low point in Maryland-Pennsylvania relations. Keith's vain hope that somehow the two colonies' jurisdictional conflict could be worked out by local town and county courts was now entirely abandoned and, on direct orders from the Pennsylvania provincial government, Pennsylvanians living along the border were free to ignore whatever legal proceedings Maryland might attempt. Had Pennsylvania and Maryland been sovereign states, deteriorating relations would surely have pointed toward war. But the Penns and the Calverts had neither the political capital nor the constitutional authority to act as independent, sovereign entities, even of a quasi-independent palatinate variety.

Proprietorship in 1722 meant something very different than it had in 1632, let alone 1681.

Between 1720 and 1730, the Euro-American populations of Chester and Lancaster Counties, Pennsylvania's borderlands counties, grew from a few thousand to more than ten thousand. Most of the migrants who accounted for this massive population increase were Scots-Irish, or Ulster Scots, descendants of seventeenth-century Scottish settlers of Ulster, the northernmost province of Ireland. Encouraged by the Penn family and James Logan, who continued to manage the family's Pennsylvania business affairs, in 1717 the mostly Presbyterian Scots-Irish began migrating to America. By 1729, they occupied an arc of farmlands across Chester County west to a series of frontier settlements on the eastern banks of the Susquehanna. In addition, in 1727, the first of the so-called Pennsylvania Dutch began arriving at the port of Philadelphia. A small number of these migrants would also make their way to settlements near the eastern banks of the Susquehanna.

Across the southern border, Cecil County in Maryland experienced similar population growth. As of 1710, its population was slightly less than three thousand, with most living in the county's southern reaches, along the Chesapeake's Eastern Shore. By 1730, the combined population of Cecil, Chester, and Lancaster Counties was probably approaching fifteen thousand. There is no precise data on the population of Natives in the region, but the population of enslaved Africans was probably in the neighborhood of 10 percent of the total, with most of those residing near Cecil County's Chesapeake shoreline.[16] In their own version of salutary neglect, provincial authorities made few adjustments to the colony's legal code to accommodate its expanding population. For the most part, neglect succeeded. Aside from a constant din of cross-border legal action, locals lived in relative peace and the Crown remained oblivious. But in what must be characterized as an inevitable development given Pennsylvania's business model, population pressure on the east side of the Susquehanna began pushing settlers across the river to the lands reserved by Governor Keith for the Conestogas, Shawnees, and Conoys.

Much as the government of Lord Baltimore may have hoped settlement in the colony's far north would counter Pennsylvania's expansion, the reality remained that Maryland was above all a tobacco colony, its population focused on the coastal Chesapeake. Benedict Leonard Calvert, younger brother of the fifth Lord Baltimore and successor to his cousin Charles as Maryland's governor, faced this truth not long after his arrival in the colony. "Tobacco, as our staple, is our all, and Indeed leaves no room for anything Else," Benedict reminded his predecessor. The farther planters moved from the shores of the Chesapeake, the less profitable the tobacco trade. Whatever hopes his brother may have had of profiting from the colony's northern reaches, never mind countering an expanding Pennsylvania, would likely be dashed by the colony's overwhelming dependence on the tobacco trade.[17]

Ill health forced Governor Calvert from office in 1731, four years after his arrival and having made little progress in expanding Maryland's economy. His successor, former English calvary Captain Samuel Ogle, would have somewhat more success, but that success would be limited by an old and familiar nemesis. Ogle arrived with a new mandate to resolve Maryland's northern boundary problem. In an agreement signed and sealed in May of 1732, Lord Baltimore had agreed to a dividing line fifteen miles south of Philadelphia. He also relinquished any further claims to the Lower Counties.

As an act of diplomacy, the arrangement represented progress. It had been more than thirty-five years since the proprietors of Pennsylvania and Maryland had first attempted to resolve their border conflict. As an act of cartography, the agreement was a total failure. With little certainty about the precise location of a line fifteen miles south of Philadelphia, Governor Ogle feared manipulation by his counterparts—manipulation that could cost Lord Baltimore thousands of acres of prime farmland. In an effort to preempt any Maryland counterclaims, Thomas Penn, who was now in Pennsylvania to manage his family's affairs, commissioned a young Philadelphia printer, Benjamin Franklin, to print a pamphlet, *Articles of Agreement,* outlining his new accord with Lord Baltimore. The pamphlet, which included the first map printed in the English colonies south of New York City, may have persuaded Pennsylvanians that their lord acted in good faith. But it had no effect on Lord Baltimore, who ordered his colony's withdrawal from the new agreement. The Penn brothers, meanwhile, still struggling to satisfy their father's creditors, put Pennsylvania up for sale. At £60,000, the colony failed to find a buyer.[18]

A common assumption about Britain's mainland American colonies and their hinterlands has been the idea that dispute resolution through violence precedes formal institutions of governance. The Maryland-Pennsylvania borderlands suggest a somewhat different pattern. Far from alleviating the disorder and violence that characterized life in the lands between Maryland and Pennsylvania, the expansion of the institutional mechanisms of governance seems only to have made the problem worse. The incorporation of counties was, in Maryland and Pennsylvania, the first step in the formal incorporation of borderlands into the colonial legal system. Counties received representation in colonial assemblies and established jurisdiction, a necessary precondition for the functioning of local courts. In theory, having local courts was particularly important, since instead of traveling to the provincial capital or some distant county seat, litigants could resolve disputes before courts of their peers. In fact, however, these institutions did very little to alter the politics of the borderlands and may have even made them more prone to disorder and violence.

Consider the case of Lancaster County in Pennsylvania. After the influx of settlers along the eastern banks of the Susquehanna, the provincial court of Chester County, whose jurisdiction reached from the Delaware River, south of Philadelphia, to the Susquehanna, and then north to the Schuylkill River, was now more than a day's ride from the county's most remote settlements. In a 1729 petition, representatives of these settlements observed that the distance from the Chester County court left them vulnerable to theft and other crime, perpetrated by "idle and dissolute persons, who resort to the remote parts of the province, and by reason of the great distance from a court or prison, do frequently find means of making their escape." The petition was successful and the provincial government authorized a new county, bounded on the south and east by Octoraro Creek, on the west by the Susquehanna, and on the north by the Schuylkill. A new county seat, also called Lancaster, was established about ten miles east of the Susquehanna on lands owned by Andrew Hamilton, a former deputy governor and legal advisor to the Penn family. Within a few years of its founding, the neatly ordered town, with its central square and its jail and courthouse, had become a thriving provincial capital.[19]

The timing of Lancaster's creation speaks to the larger point. The tightening of institutional bonds did little to alleviate disorder precisely because that disorder was less a function of politics than it was of law. However much Pennsylvania's provincial authorities may have hoped that the institutionalization of government in the new Lancaster County would quiet the borderlands near the lower Susquehanna, jurisdictional uncertainty remained a barrier to these efforts. Lancaster County itself would not be a place of particular disorder, at least not for a few decades. But the western banks of the Susquehanna, across from the new county, would experience disorder, largely surrounding the insurgency of Lord Baltimore's most notorious proxy.

As a teenager, Thomas Cresap followed the path of so many other young Englishmen. He left his home in Yorkshire for the colonies, eventually settling in Maryland. Unlike so many of his countrymen, Cresap pursued opportunity not in the colony's tidewater areas but in its far north, a region settled more by Scots-Irish and Germans than by Englishmen. These facts suggest Cresap was something of an outlier, which he surely was. But other facts suggest that he was an outlier for reasons other than his frontier inclinations. Cresap struggled with financial misfortune and yet was able to acquire an extensive tract on the west banks of the Susquehanna, not far from a ferry landing controlled by the Quaker John Wright that would eventually bear the ferry proprietor's name as the town of Wrightsville. Cresap settled on his new homestead in 1729, shortly after he was commissioned justice of the peace and militia captain for Baltimore County. Far from simply an opportunistic English migrant—which Cresap surely was—he was an agent of Lord Baltimore, sent to the Susquehanna Valley to secure Maryland's claims to the valley's western reaches.[20]

For Pennsylvania authorities, there was never any doubt about Cresap's sponsorship. In late September 1731, as fall descended, the new justice of the peace for Lancaster County, Samuel Blunston, and his fellow magistrates rushed to complete the county's new courthouse. As they worked, they were approached by a familiar figure. Civility, known to his fellow Conestogas as Tagotolessa, approached the men in the company of an interpreter and presented a belt of wampum beads. The gesture indicated the gravity of Civility's concerns. It also confirmed that Civility spoke not for himself or his band of Conestogas but for all the Natives of the lower Susquehanna. Through his interpreter, Civility asked the Lancaster officials to send a message to the aged governor, Patrick Gordon, who had replaced Keith in 1726. In clear violation of agreements made with William Penn and former governor Keith, Pennsylvania had been unable to secure the western banks of the Susquehanna for the colony's Native allies.

Civility did not mention Springettsbury, but he did mention Conejohela, sometimes spelled Conegehally or Conojohela, the Native name for

Springettsbury. Civility had come to call these representatives of the Penn-sylvania colony to account. Action had been taken to implement gover-nance in the area formerly controlled by the Conestogas and their neigh-bors. Something equivalent needed to be done to secure the guarantees made by Governor Keith and Penn. Civility's community faced nothing so prosaic as rascals and crooks. Instead, foreign settlers from Maryland had begun intruding on their settlements. Among these intruders was "one Crissop," who was "very Abusive to them when they pass that way, And has Beat & wounded one of their women who went to Get Apples from their own Trees and took away her Apples."[21]

Blunston found Civility's visit alarming. He recognized that conflict be-tween the Conejohela Indians and a few Marylanders, particularly Marylanders as obtrusive and truculent as Cresap, put the entire region at risk. The Iro-quois and their historical enemies, the Virginians, would very likely be drawn into the conflict. Although the Penn family had drifted from its patriarch's Quakerism, the government of Pennsylvania was still dominated by Quakers. And although never uniform in their position on the matter, some form of pacifism had begun to take hold, making it very difficult for the government to provide material support for military action. Any war in the colony's west would most likely have to be fought by local militias with uncertain support from the provincial government.[22]

The danger of wider war was heightened by another problem. Iroquois warriors returning from raids against the Catawba and the Cherokee had discovered a new trade. For the most part, captives taken in these raids had been Native people, brought north and incorporated into Iroquois village life as slaves and servants. But as Virginia expanded westward, the Iroquois raiders traversed increasingly heavily settled lands and began taking captives of African descent. The exact origin of these captives is unknown. Most likely they were fugitives from plantation slavery. What is clear is that by the time the founders of Lancaster had begun establishing their county seat, this small vector in the transcontinental slave trade was firmly established. Blunston reported to Governor Gordon that Iroquois warriors had recently returned from southern raids with "three Negroes & a Mulatto," one of whom they sold to a Conoy Indian. The sale was il-legal. As a condition for Iroquois access to the warpath through western Virginia, the 1722 Albany Treaty had stipulated that Iroquois travelers would return runaway slaves for a bounty of one gun and two blankets.

Blunston's report suggests traveling warriors had begun finding more lucrative outlets for these captives.[23]

Pennsylvania may have been able to address intrusions from Maryland through diplomacy or legal action—although these methods had so far failed to stop squatters. But controlling the Iroquois slave trade would be more difficult, particularly if the border problem dragged on. The colony's alliance with the Conejohela Indians was now an alliance with Natives receiving what Virginia authorities viewed as stolen property. There is little evidence that the Iroquois were capturing runaways from Maryland, but there is evidence that Maryland runaways were finding their way to Shawnee villages in the colony's far western reaches. Were the Iroquois slave trade to expand, and were Maryland to find common cause with its southern neighbor over the issue of runaways, not only would it have new justification for laying claim to the borderlands, but it would have new justification for war against the Conejohela Indians.[24]

After several years of small-scale conflict, in late January 1734 Blunston finally issued a warrant for Cresap's arrest. The warrant was not for illegal squatting; Blunston recognized that Cresap had a powerful defense since he had been given title to his homestead by Lord Baltimore. Rather, Pennsylvania authorities had discovered that Samuel Chance, a member of Cresap's posse, was the runaway servant of Edmund Cartlidge, a Pennsylvania fur trader. A small detachment of Pennsylvania militiamen crossed the Susquehanna to arrest Cresap for harboring a runaway. This bold assertion of the Lancaster court's jurisdiction very quickly devolved into chaos. In the ensuing clash Knowles Daunt, a servant of John Emerson, the Lancaster County sheriff, was fatally wounded. Although eight of his associates were eventually arrested, Cresap escaped to a fortified compound defended by Maryland militiamen. Blunston and his men might have been prepared to arrest Cresap, but they had neither the will nor the capacity for siege warfare.

As an alternative, Blunston employed the original Euro-American instrument of territoriality. He began licensing Pennsylvania loyalists to settle the western shores of the Susquehanna. Although directly sanctioned by Thomas Penn, these grants lacked legal validity. They were nothing more than an attempt to reassert control over Conejohela, and were not particularly effective in doing that. By 1740, Blunston had issued four thousand licenses to survey Conejohela, but only about five hundred settlers registered with the Pennsylvania land office as having actually laid claim to plots in the area. Other than encouraging further settlement on Indian land, the measure's only discernible impact was to prompt a reaction by Maryland authorities. At Cresap's urging, they sent loyal surveyors, accompanied by a twenty-man guard, to begin plotting Maryland territory in the contested area. Cresap interpreted Maryland's actions as confirmation that his own claims were fully legal and began issuing title to lands, often already occupied by Pennsylvanians. Facing a choice between land payments to Cresap, sealed with declarations of allegiance to Lord Baltimore, or treatment by Maryland as "Rebels & Enemies to our Gracious Sovereign King George, to whom we have Sworn Allegiance," the mostly German settlers who had arrived at Blunston's invitation now faced eviction. Assuming Quaker Pennsylvania would avoid military conflict, Maryland governor Ogle ordered Baltimore County to muster a three-hundred-man militia to secure the southwestern Susquehanna Valley.[25]

After Lancaster responded with its own 150-man force, Ogle opted for a less truculent strategy. He offered to buy off German-speaking settlers by forgiving their debts to the Pennsylvania land office. The strategy failed, as German Protestants had no desire to abandon tolerant Pennsylvania for what was, effectively, an Anglican Maryland.[26] Ogle then turned to another group to advance Lord Baltimore's claims. Fully aware that the Conejohela Indians had been effectively abandoned by Pennsylvania provincial authorities and that Iroquois slaving had exacerbated tensions with Pennsylvania's erstwhile colonial ally Virginia, sometime in the early fall of 1736, he sent a message to the Iroquois Council offering to adjudicate Iroquois claims near the Susquehanna. The message, in fact, was nothing more than a pretext to draw the Board of Trade, the Privy Council body that replaced the old Lords of Trade, to intervene in the Maryland-Pennsylvania border dispute. An aggrieved Iroquois Confederacy, the governor and his envoys hoped, was much more likely to rouse the Crown to action than two privately controlled colonies. Unfortunately for Governor Ogle, this strategy failed as well. The Iroquois recognized that Marylanders had instigated the lower Susquehanna crisis; the burden of reconciliation would therefore lie not with Pennsylvania authorities or the Crown but with Governor Ogle and Lord Baltimore. James Logan, who had been acting governor since the death of

Governor Gordon in August, followed Ogle's overture with a diplomatic initiative of his own. Although the Treaty of 1722 acknowledged Iroquois control of western Pennsylvania, that acknowledgment rested on no binding land-cession treaty. A treaty that confirmed, once and for all, that the Conestogas, the Conoys, and the remaining Shawnees resided in Pennsylvania would effectively resolve the question of Conejohela.[27]

In what at first glance appears to be a stunning triumph for Logan and Thomas Penn, eighteen Iroquois headmen joined them for a council meeting at Philadelphia in early October 1736. The headmen represented the Cayugas, the Senecas, the Onondagas, the Oneidas, and the Tuscaroras, the last of whom were the Iroquois Confederacy's southern allies, formally admitted into the Iroquois League in the early 1720s. Penn and Logan hoped to gain major territorial cessions and secure Pennsylvania's control of the lower Susquehanna River and the Springettsbury area. Given how much Iroquois war making, captive taking, and now slave trading depended on the vital Susquehanna corridor, such a land cession would seem a distant hope. Negotiations dragged on for two weeks, a fact Pennsylvania diplomats attributed less to the scope of the colony's ambition than to the reckless sale of distilled spirits to their Native counterparts. With members of the Iroquois delegation "seen about the streets much disordered by Liquor, which 'tis believed they have been furnished . . . from some of the low Tippling Houses in this City," the Native diplomats were "rendered incapable of pursuing the Business for which they came." Logan managed to push a prohibition on liquor sales through the colony's assembly. Several days later the Iroquois headmen concluded an agreement to cede to the Penn family the entire Susquehanna River basin, with "all the lands lying on the West side of the said River to the setting of the Sun."[28]

In return, the headmen extracted from Thomas Penn a cache of goods including five hundred pounds of gunpowder, six hundred pounds of lead, forty-five guns, one hundred blankets, one hundred hatchets, five hundred knives, twenty-five gallons of rum, two hundred pounds of tobacco, one thousand tobacco pipes, one hundred shirts, forty hats, forty pairs of shoes with buckles, forty pairs of stockings, and hundreds of other items. For the Penns, it was all a very small price to pay and surely modest in comparison to additional Iroquois demands. Among those other demands were lower prices on trade goods, a condition Logan—negotiating on behalf of the Penns but also as acting governor and president of the colony's executive council—insisted he could not meet. They also asked for reduced liquor sales in the far west and a prohibition on further land transfers by the Susquehanna Indians and Delawares, now residing in the Lehigh River valley and the Wyoming Valley. Finally, they called on Pennsylvania authorities to protect Iroquois claims in far western Maryland and Virginia. Between the problem of runaway slaves and the growing threat from French-allied Indians in the Ohio country, neither Virginia nor Maryland was likely to give over control of its far west to a Native confederacy, even one so closely allied with the British. But more importantly, given that the entire 1736 treaty arose as a means of securing the western Maryland-Pennsylvania borderlands for Pennsylvania, gaining Maryland's assent to any aspect of the treaty would require stupendous diplomatic good fortune. In sum, as Iroquois negotiators surely recognized, most of their conditions would be difficult for Pennsylvania to meet, leaving the balance of diplomatic power in Iroquois hands. As Daniel K. Richter has noted, Iroquois transfer "of lands they never really possessed . . . to one Euro-American colony seeking to buttress its claims against another" had become a reliable means of maintaining the confederacy's position as the "dominant native political and military force in the Northeast."[29]

With proprietary authority over Conejohela nominally secured, Pennsylvania again attempted to arrest Thomas Cresap. Doing so now required no convoluted legal pretext. Cresap would be arrested and tried for the murder of Knowles Daunt. On November 25, a party of Scots-Irish militiamen approached Cresap's home, bearing a warrant for his arrest. Recent experience suggested a lengthy stand-off was a certainty. But shortly after the party's arrival, Cresap's pregnant wife went into labor. In the ensuing frenzy, the Cresap house caught fire. Cresap and some of his men attempted to flee but were apprehended, and Cresap was brought to Philadelphia to stand trial.

Maryland governor Ogle lost little time finding a new agent to lead the process of colony building in Conejohela. By Christmas Eve he had commissioned a new militia captain, Charles Higgenbotham, to secure what remained of Maryland's far north. Within a few days of his arrival, Higginbotham had begun harassing the mostly German-speaking Conejohela settlers, destroying their homes and arresting those who refused to declare

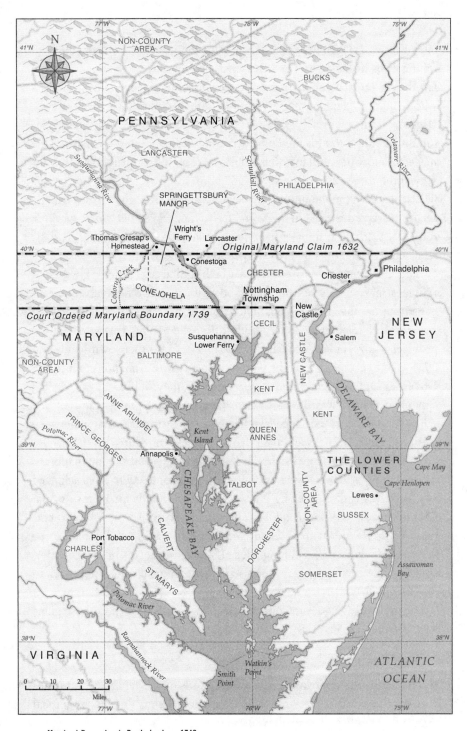

Maryland-Pennsylvania Borderlands, c. 1740

allegiance to the fifth Lord Baltimore. Blunston was forced to respond with militia raids of his own. The latest crisis abated only after Higgenbotham left the area to accompany prisoners to Annapolis. Members of his militia who remained "kept themselves shut up in their Guardhouse or Fortress." Higginbotham eventually returned, but with Lancaster deputy sheriff Salomon Jennings and his men now guarding the remaining settlements, he turned to more peaceful methods. These were no less extortionist—they involved the forced sale of Pennsylvania homesteads. Lancaster County officials, already complaining of financial hardships brought by the struggle across the river, now had to house and feed a new wave of German-speaking refugees. With little support from provincial authorities, Jennings and his men abandoned Conejohela to Higgenbotham.[30]

The Conejohela Germans, now a bedraggled and vulnerable mix of refugees and vassals of the Maryland colony, had effectively come to constitute another borderlands population abandoned by Pennsylvania's government. Lancaster County authorities, themselves frustrated by the provincial government's inaction, took matters into their own hands and concocted a scheme to send the Germans en masse to Annapolis to insist on Governor Ogle's intervention. The alternative, they were to tell Maryland's appointed leader, was direct Crown intervention. Nothing came of the scheme, but its very existence is indicative of the growing tension between western Pennsylvanians and their province's government.[31]

Even had Pennsylvania Germans had the means and the inclination to petition the Maryland governor, the scheme was unlikely to have achieved anything. Instead of securing the western borderlands for Pennsylvania, Cresap's arrest and the Iroquois-Pennsylvania treaty seemed only to embolden Maryland. Higgenbotham continued the work of colonizing the borderlands more or less unimpeded. If judged in terms of the colonies' abilities to secure territory through settlement, Pennsylvania's approach to the Maryland-Pennsylvania borderlands must be considered a failure.

Pennsylvania's losses may have been Maryland's gains, but those gains hardly came without cost.

Much as they had done in the days of the Lords of Trade, royal authorities viewed the conflict between Maryland and Pennsylvania as a local matter.[32] In August of 1737, they instructed:

> The governors of respective provinces of Maryland and
> Pensilvania for the Time being [to] not upon pain of incur-
> ring his majestys highest Displeasure permit or suffer any
> Tumults Riots or other Outragious Disorders to be com-
> mitted on the Borders of their respective Provinces . . .
> immediately put a Stop thereto and use their utmost En-
> deavours to preserve Peace and Good Order amongst all his
> Majesty's Subjects under their Governments inhabiting the
> Said Borders. And as a Means to preserve Peace and Tran-
> quillity on the said Borders, His Majsety doth hereby enjoyn
> the said Governors that they do not make Grants of any Part
> of the Lands in Contest between the Proprietors respectively
> nor of any part of the three Lower Counties.[33]

With no land transfers, there would be little chance of establishing territorial claims in the borderlands. And with no territorial claims there could be
no legal basis for taxation. The borderlands would remain at best a contested
squatters' empire, at worst a dangerous threat to regional security.

The following year, with continued complaints from the Penns and
their agents at court, the Board of Trade advised the king to issue a more
detailed proclamation concerning the boundary problem. In addition to
demanding that all prisoners, including Thomas Cresap, be repatriated,
the proclamation provided detailed guidance for addressing jurisdictional confusion. Given that the Lower Counties appeared settled in
their affiliation with the Penns, the Crown declared that the Penn family
could resume taxation and land transfers there. In settled portions of the
borderlands, from the Delaware River to the Susquehanna, the status quo
before Thomas Cresap's arrival would prevail. Jurisdiction would be determined according to original conveyances and tenancy agreements,
and the colonial proprietors would have no right to force individual tenants and landholders to alter jurisdictional affiliation. So-called vacant
lands, by which the lords meant Indian lands, would be bounded by a
temporary boundary line running along whatever line of latitude crossed
a point "fourteen miles and three Quarters of a mile south of the Latitude of the most Southern part of the City of Philadelphia," a slight
alteration of the original agreement in Maryland's favor. The resolution was "to be a Provisional and Temporary Order, to continue until the

Boundarys shall be finally settled, and be Declared to be without Prejudice to either party."[34]

Maryland and Pennsylvania assembled a new boundary commission to survey the temporary line. But with little clarity about the exact location of the boundary—the southern limits of Philadelphia proving almost as uncertain as the precise location of the fortieth parallel had proven fifty years before—the commissioners disputed nearly every aspect of the planned fifty-mile boundary survey, including the crucial matter of whether the calculation of the distance between Philadelphia and the line would account for the undulations in the countryside. Pushed along by the Pennsylvanians and the Crown, even after one of the Maryland commissioners had to return home because of his son's death, the commission nevertheless completed its work by the end of May 1739.

CHAPTER 5

An American Bloodlands

ON MONDAY, JUNE 18, 1744, the lawyer Witham Marshe set out from his home in Annapolis for Lancaster in Pennsylvania. Marshe traveled with Philip Thomas, a wealthy planter and prominent member of the governor's council, and the Reverend Thomas Craddock, an Anglican pastor and schoolmaster. The small party made its way north to the tiny outpost of Baltimore Town, at this point barely even deserving the designation of town. The following day, the travelers proceeded to the mouth of the Susquehanna and crossed the river into Cecil County at Lower Ferry, the Susquehanna's southernmost crossing. After spending the night at the house of Benjamin Chew, a justice of the peace for Cecil County, the party resumed its travels. Chew joined the travelers as guide. At the travelers' next destination, dismal Nottingham Township in Pennsylvania, Chew also became the party's official barber; the locals, most of whom were Quaker farmers attracted by Pennsylvania's lax tax laws, were too slovenly to provide such services.

After a night at a rude ordinary kept by the Quaker Thomas Hughes, the four men resumed their journey. They had been joined by four other travelers from Maryland: Edmund Jennings, another member of the governor's council; Colonel Thomas Colville, an assemblyman from Cecil County and the head of the county's militia; Colonel Robert King, an assemblyman from Somerset County, and another county militia leader; and Benedict Calvert, son of the fifth Lord Baltimore and also a member of the governor's council.

Continuing its journey northward, the party stopped to lunch and water its horses at a gristmill twenty miles from Nottingham. The travelers resumed their journey later that afternoon, passing through fertile Pennsylvania farm country. They reached Lancaster early that evening and took up residence at an inn owned by the Quaker Peter Worrall.

Marshe, ever the curious traveler and perceptive chronicler, spent the remaining hours of daylight studying his surroundings. In the company of Reverend Craddock and Benedict Calvert, he strolled to Lancaster's courthouse, an imposing two-story brick structure able to hold eight hundred in relative comfort. The visitors entered the building, observing its handsome and well-made furnishings, its carefully arranged antechambers, and its sturdy hearth. They ascended a ladder that led to the cupola atop the building. The view afforded an easy survey of the whole town, with its carefully plotted streets, its modest wooden houses, and its busy central market, but it also allowed Marshe and his companions to view Lancaster's extensive hinterlands and, at some distance looking west, the great Susquehanna River.

Lancaster must have struck Marshe as a very strange town. Unlike the Annapolis from which he came, or practically any other substantial American town, Lancaster had no port and was ten miles from the nearest major waterway. Though Lancaster was more like an English market town than any colonial city, in barely fifteen years its settlers nonetheless had fashioned an orderly and well-built county seat. For Marshe, more striking was the fact that Lancaster existed at the edge of civilized life. The main street was the chief artery connecting Pennsylvania's more settled eastern parts to its western backcountry, and the wild, untamed nature at the road's western end had not been entirely purged from the young town. Lancaster's inhabitants, who included a mongrel mixture of Germans, Scots-Irish, English, and a few "unbelieving Israelites," had failed to assimilate the "spirit of cleanliness" one might expect in an older, more civilized town. "In general," the people of Lancaster "are very great sluts and slovens." They rarely cleaned their homes, and when they did they left refuse outside, "which in the summer time, breeds an innumerable quantity of bugs, fleas, and vermin." It was no wonder that when Marshe returned to Worrall's inn and laid down his travel-weary head, he "was most fiercely attacked by the neighbouring Dutch fleas and bugs."[1]

Marshe was unable to dwell long on Lancaster's miseries. He and his fellow travelers came in an official capacity. They were Maryland's delegation to a momentous diplomatic meeting, assembling representatives from Maryland, Virginia, Pennsylvania, and the Six Nations of the Iroquois Confederacy. Marshe served as secretary to Maryland's delegation, whose official agents, commissioned by Governor Thomas Bladen, successor to Governor Ogle, were Jennings, Thomas, King, and Colville. The day after the delegation arrived in Lancaster, its Indian counterparts entered town. The Iroquois negotiators, in the company of their wives and children, led an Indian procession of 252 to the Lancaster courthouse. In addition to several Conoys and Shawnees, the delegation included thirteen Conestogas. They may have come from their nearby village, which, had he looked to the southwest, down Conestoga Creek, Marshe might have seen from the courthouse cupola. But Marshe showed no awareness of the Conestogas or their town. It was an ominous absence for a group that had long been the focal point of politics and trade in the lower Susquehanna.[2]

Witham Marshe's journey was above all a diplomatic mission. But it was also a journey through the Maryland-Pennsylvania borderlands, and it offers a glimpse of that disputed region during a period of relative calm. What is most striking in Marshe's account is the absence of any real sense of border crossing. At Nottingham, where he and his party crossed into Pennsylvania, Marshe observed that the predominantly Quaker population generally believed itself to live in Pennsylvania, but this was purely because of the "small taxes they are burthened with." In Maryland, in addition to quitrents and other fees and imposts, colonists were required to pay a clergy tax to support the colony's Anglican ministry. The tax amounted to forty pounds of tobacco per taxable member of the household. In declaring themselves Pennsylvanians, the Quaker residents of Nottingham Township also avoided subsidizing an established ministry, something Pennsylvania lacked. But Marshe made no effort to distinguish a matter of conscience from one of economy. Pennyslvania's attachment to religious toleration meant that settlers in the borderlands were more likely to accept Pennsylvania's dominion not because the colony tolerated religious dissenters and lacked an established clergy but because Maryland demanded a "most iniquitous tax."

The only other indication that Marshe and his party had crossed a border was the denomination of their payment to the Nottingham innkeeper, Thomas Hughes. Being prominent gentlemen and colonial officials, the delegation had the luxury of paying for room and board in hard currency. There would be no complex bills of exchange or book debt to cover the cost of the journey, and currency conversion would be a relatively simple matter. Hughes charged the travelers in Pennsylvania currency, which the travelers paid with silver coin, perhaps Spanish reals. The lodgers and their landlord, it seems, could readily exchange Maryland hard currency for services priced in Pennsylvania money. Currency denominations marked the transit from Maryland into Pennsylvania. But hard money coinage made this aspect of the border barely noticeable.[3]

This point—that there was little at all to suggest a meaningful geopolitical border in the Maryland-Pennsylvania borderlands—is not especially illuminating. For all the litigation and diplomatic haggling, by the mid-1740s a traveler of Witham Marshe's status could go between colonies more or less oblivious to their territorial limits. This also turns out to have been true for the many migrants who continued to make their way to the borderlands. Beyond what it meant for taxes, the boundary between Maryland and Pennsylvania did practically nothing to shape these people's movements. While the people of Nottingham Township identified themselves as Pennsylvanians for tax reasons, settlers west of the Susquehanna showed much less deference to matters of political economy and much more to a combination of hydrography and topography. What would become York and Cumberland Counties in Pennsylvania and Frederick and northern Baltimore Counties in Maryland were bounded on the east by the Susquehanna River, on the south by the Potomac, and on the north and west by the Appalachian range. Eighteenth-century settlers moving from eastern Pennsylvania across the Susquehanna either continued west toward the mountains or followed the many south-flowing waterways including the Monocacy River and the Antietam and Conococheague Creeks south toward the Potomac and into western Maryland and northern Virginia.[4]

The locations of rivers and mountains would have meant little had the borderlands not also possessed another vital natural feature. The roads that led west, through Chester and Lancaster Counties in Pennsylvania and northern Cecil County in Maryland and then into the new counties further west, also passed through some of the richest farmlands in North America. A combination of climate and fertile soil made the borderlands ideally suited for growing flax for linen makers and various cereals, including rye, wheat, barley, and oats. By the middle of the eighteenth century, immigrants had transformed the borderlands into America's first breadbasket to the world.[5]

By the early 1760s, farmers and grain brokers had built dozens of grist-mills, including the one Marshe and his traveling companions stopped at on their way to Lancaster. One estimate identifies sixty-three in Lancaster County alone. With immigration came innovation. The borderlands flour mills were as efficient as any in North America or Europe. The resulting decline in the cost of milling kept borderlands flour and bread competitive in global markets, and it meant that the export market remained vigorous through much of the eighteenth century. As farming expanded to the west, efficiencies in flour production compensated for higher transport costs. Lower production prices also transformed the chief outlet for borderlands flour, the city of Philadelphia, into the largest flour-exporting port in British America. The city accounted for over half of all flour shipped from the mainland colonies. New York City, Philadelphia's closest rival, exported less than half as much. By 1760, the city's fertile hinterlands allowed Philadelphia to surpass Boston as the largest port in North America, a distinction it would retain until the completion of the Erie Canal in 1825.[6]

The borderlands' agricultural boom and the territorial expansion it fed brought new strains to local government. The Cresap crisis had already stretched Lancaster County resources to their limits. Royal intervention did very little to alleviate the underlying problem. Through the 1740s, Lancaster County officials were still burdened with administering Pennsylvania law in the contested lands across the Susquehanna. By 1749, complaints about the resulting administrative difficulties prompted the Pennsylvania assembly to establish York County, contiguous with the former Conejohela. The following year, the assembly incorporated Cumberland County, to the west, with its county seat in Carlisle. Maryland's assembly also acted in these years, incorporating most of its far western reaches into the new Frederick County, with a county seat at Frederick Town on the Monocacy River. By 1750, Frederick County's seat would be the largest town in Maryland, with a population of about a thousand, several hundred more than lived in the colony's capital, Annapolis. That within three years provincial officials had formed three new counties in the borderlands is indicative of the overall demographics of the borderlands. According to one estimate, by 1760 more than fifty thousand German migrants had settled the borderlands counties.[7]

These booming new counties faced many of the same divisions that plagued their eastern predecessors. The most pronounced of these, at least among the European inhabitants, was that between English-speaking and German-speaking settlers. But there were abundant religious divisions within this larger constellation of Euro-American migrants. There were Scots-Irish Presbyterians, Irish and English Catholics, German Lutherans, German Reformed, Moravians, and assorted smaller German Pietistic sects. Racial division was also a fact of borderlands life. Territorial struggles between Natives and Europeans continued as a new racial divide emerged. The seasonal nature of grain production would make the region far more hospitable to contract and wage labor, but with so little surplus labor, farm families had begun to buy and rent slaves. By 1760, there were approximately three hundred slaves in Chester County and a hundred in Lancaster. The numbers in York and Cumberland Counties were much smaller, as was the total European population. Similar patterns can be seen in Maryland, with the relative numbers of slaves increasing through the middle of the eighteenth century, but the vast majority of the colony's slaves still inhabited prime tobacco-growing areas adjoining the Chesapeake.[8]

Within a generation of the 1736 Iroquois treaty the Native American population of the western borderlands had greatly declined. Of those few Conestogas, Shawnees, and Conoys who had accepted Governor Keith's invitation to relocate to Conejohela, most had abandoned the area by the time Marshe and the other delegates came to Lancaster. Some retreated to their original Conestoga villages, only to experience patterns of dependency and struggle common in many eastern Native towns. The continued decline of the eastern fur trade, the theft of productive agricultural lands, and overall population decline left the Conestogas dependent on wages from menial labor and small-scale trade. There is no detailed modern history of Conestoga, but all accounts suggest that by the middle of the eighteenth century it had become the poorest place in the lower Susquehanna Valley. The famous refrain, often repeated in eighteenth-century sources, that southern Pennsylvania was "the Best Poor Man's Country in the World" was typically race-blind.[9]

Most of the remaining Natives of the Conejohela area—Shawnees, and perhaps some Conestogas and Iroquois—had fled west across the northern Blue Ridge Mountains into the Appalachian Mountains and then down into the Monongahela, Ohio, and Allegheny River valleys. These borderlands refugees settled among bands of western Iroquois, or "Mingos," a group of dissident Senecas and Cayugas who, in defiance of the Iroquois Confederacy's council, had migrated to the region to take advantage of its relative abundance of game. Delaware descendants of the original Lenape had also migrated from northeastern Pennsylvania to the far-western Ohio country, as the area came to be known. The Ohio Delawares were refugees, driven west by shady land deals orchestrated by Thomas and John Penn. In less than a generation, these migrants made the Ohio country one of the most ethnically diverse and economically vibrant regions of British North America.[10]

By midcentury the borderlands had begun to acquire the ethnic and economic character that would define them for most of the next century: a mostly Protestant and European agricultural region, with a declining Native American population and a small population of African Americans. Insofar as there remained any Native peoples living along the Maryland-Pennsylvania borderlands, the majority remained concentrated in a single town. By the mid-1760s, even this concentrated settlement had been destroyed, leaving the borderlands' remaining Native Americans with only the loosest connections to any larger Native polity. The destruction of the settlement at Conestoga was one of American history's most notorious acts of ethnocide and among the worst episodes of ethnic violence in colonial Pennsylvania's history. It was also the final chapter of a story that had begun more than a century before and which completely recast the geopolitical character of the Maryland-Pennsylvania borderlands.

A patchwork of legally questionable land transfers along with a bewildering series of treaties meant the day-to-day matter of Indian-European relations, much like the problem of settlers' colonial affiliation, would be controlled at a local level. This localized diplomacy, if one can characterize the ad hoc patterns of relations between Natives and Euro-Americans in the borderlands as diplomacy, yielded acts of overt violence and vengeance, but far more prevalent were acts of tacit violence, inflicted through incremental dispossession and displacement. European migrants, destroying Native hunting grounds and farmlands and bringing distilled spirits and other trade goods, did most of the work. These pressures might have been reduced had the Iroquois shown more interest in the lower Susquehanna, but any hope for a change in Iroquois policy largely vanished with the 1736 Iroquois Treaty. From that point forward, the Iroquois Council would show itself more concerned with maintaining good relations with Pennsylvania than with the colony's Native inhabitants.

The best remaining prospect for the Conestogas and the few Shawnees and Conoys who remained in the Susquehanna Valley was some Iroquois reversal of fortune. Should the confederacy's economic and military resources diminish, there remained a possibility that its council would turn against Pennsylvania and, seeking to preserve free access to the Susquehanna River valley, attempt to rebuild its alliances with the Susquehanna Valley Indians. Although it would have been costly, by restoring economic relations between the Conestogas and the Iroquois such a development might have given the borderlands Indians a reprieve from the encroachments they had so long endured. Had Virginia turned against Pennsylvania, the shift in Iroquois fortunes might well have happened.

Instead, Virginia's diplomats at the Lancaster council meeting collaborated with their Pennsylvania counterparts to secure a truce with the Iroquois. At the center of that truce would be a number of colonial concessions, including compensation for four murdered Iroquois warriors. For the lower Susquehanna Indians, far more consequential was the chief Iroquois concession. As part of a dubious land cession to Virginia, their diplomats agreed to shift the Catawba warpath west, to the Appalachians. The Iroquois-Conestoga alliance, never very strong, was now dead and buried.

Frederick Calvert, the sixth Lord Baltimore and the last proprietor of Maryland, succeeded his father, Charles, upon the latter's death in 1751. With little interest in his American properties (Frederick never visited Maryland), the newest Lord Baltimore turned over management of the colony to a series of advisors, the most influential of whom was his uncle Cecilius. Aided by the officious Horatio Sharpe, the colony's longest-serving governor, Cecilius transformed Maryland into a cash cow for his nephew. The reliability of the proprietor's income was a function of the relative stability of Maryland's political order, itself the work of Governor Sharpe. Through the calculated distribution of patronage and the shrewd management of his patron's powers of remuneration, Sharpe built a potent power base with which to counter an increasingly independent and truculent Lower House of Assembly.[11]

Between 1748 and 1761 the Maryland proprietor's quitrent income alone nearly doubled from £4,333 to £8,383. The number is striking on its own terms, but when viewed alongside other aspects of proprietary land policy, it is truly extraordinary. Contrary to Witham Marshe's intimation that Maryland was the high-tax colony, Lord Baltimore continued his father's practice of suspending quitrents and other taxes for those willing to settle the colony's western reaches. Between 1748 and 1756, the practice drew nearly twenty-eight hundred settlers to the Monocacy River valley near Frederick Town. And yet, even accounting for the costs of these concessions, Lord Baltimore's midcentury Maryland income—which included quitrents, rent, and assorted land-transfer fees—was massive and increasing. From nearly £10,000 in 1748, it had risen to almost £16,000 by 1761. For the first time in the colony's history, Maryland's proprietor could consider himself a true rent taker: income flowed with very little active management by the lord proprietor himself.[12]

To historians of Maryland, the middle of the eighteenth century is often referred to as the colony's "golden age." As Lorena S. Walsh has observed, in terms of overall economic prosperity and political stability, the characterization may have some merit, but that prosperity and political stability were "rooted in a system of extraction of forced labor that depended on violent coercion and the maintenance of strict racial boundaries."[13] Slave labor accounts for the rise of Maryland's planter elite, and that planter elite controlled the colony's government. That planter elite was also concentrated in the most prolific tobacco-growing regions of the colony. The proprietor and the assembly, mostly owing to Sharpe's shrewd manipulations, were nonetheless able to find common ground over the colony's north and west. After the outbreak of war near the Ohio country in 1754, thousands of settlers abandoned the western reaches of Frederick County for the relative safety of eastern Maryland, a costly imposition on east-facing planters. To offset these new burdens on the colony's dominant political faction, the assembly extended a war-time supply bill that included a tax of twelve pence per hundred acres to all lands, including those owned by Lord Baltimore. This was a profound departure from a long-standing policy of exempting proprietary lands from colonial land taxes. Advised by Governor Sharpe that the cost would be modest in comparison to the loss of income brought by prolonged war, Lord Baltimore and the colony's planters agreed to this war-time expedient.[14]

Maryland's political stability would be tested during the course of the war as the assembly sought more support from the proprietor and his allies for the colony's modest military efforts. But because the prime theater of combat would center on the Ohio country and the Allegheny Mountains, Maryland's main military force was able to retreat to Fort Frederick on the Potomac and leave the colony's far northwest to hostile Indians and their French allies. Emptied of most of its settlers, western Frederick County demanded little in the way of defense and, with a tiny western frontier of just a few miles' breadth, bounded on one side by the Potomac and the other by the mountains of eastern Cumberland County, Maryland enjoyed the shortest and most easily defended western frontier of any colony in British North America. Adding to Maryland's wartime fiscal advantages, inaction on the Maryland-Pennsylvania border problem allowed the colony to evade defense costs in what the Penns and the Crown had determined to be part of Pennsylvania. For the first time in the history of its boundary conflict with Pennsylvania, Maryland was beginning to earn financial dividends from that conflict. Those dividends came in the form of the primary cost borne by colonial governments. As Maryland retreated from its peripheral areas, its neighbors, Virginia and Pennsylvania, would be left to bear security costs in those areas.

Maryland's actions also paid political dividends. With the conclusion of the French and Indian War in 1763, Thomas Penn, who would remain Pennsylvania's proprietor until the American Revolutionary War, faced much less certain financial prospects, in no small measure because of his colony's wartime expenses. The war had devastated large portions of the Pennsylvania borderlands, temporarily disrupting Pennsylvania's agricultural boom and reducing tax revenue needed to fund the colony's wartime debt. For the first time since William Penn's death, the Penn family faced the loss of its American colony.

Decades of declining proprietary power and the rising influence of the colony's assembly culminated in deep division over responsibility for the growing cost of security in Pennsylvania. Thomas Penn, who succeeded his elder brother John as senior proprietor upon the latter's death in 1746, struggled to find common ground with the colony's assembly. The group most akin to Maryland's planter elite were the prosperous merchants of Philadelphia, but a combination of fiscal politics and religion drove a deep and lasting wedge between them and the Penn family, producing a level of discord the Calvert family had not faced since the seventeenth century.

Before the French and Indian War, the colonial government had relied almost entirely on two sources of income: an excise tax on distilled spirits and interest paid on loans made by the colony's land office. During the war, the Crown and Pennsylvania's backwoods settlements, which bore the brunt of wartime violence, pushed the assembly to seek additional revenue. The most obvious source, given that war would likely disrupt seaborne trade, would be a new land tax, but as a political matter, few taxes would be more provocative. The Penn family's lands were excluded from land taxes—a policy that had been upheld in 1748 by the Board of Trade. Pennsylvania's many small freeholders, already bearing the costs of war, would surely bristle at a new colonial land tax that failed to address the exemption. Since the Penns had long relied on suspension of quitrents and land-transfer fees to incentivize settlement and land sales, the new tax would have very serious financial consequences, not just for the Penn family but also for the entire Pennsylvania economy. To pay the new tax, the Penns would need new revenue sources, most likely in the form of higher rents and more costly land. Without cheap land and all the various financial mechanisms James Logan and the Pennsylvania land office had long used to draw settlers to that land, migrants would go elsewhere, bringing their capital with them. Such concerns fell on deaf ears, and the General Assembly attempted to enact an equitable new land tax. Pitting proprietor against people, Governor Robert Hunter Morris vetoed the new tax.

An outraged Benjamin Franklin, writing on behalf of the General Assembly, laid bare the disfunctions of government in proprietary Pennsylvania:

> Vassals must *follow* their Lords to the Wars in Defence of their Lands; our Lord Proprietary, though a Subject like ourselves, would *send* us out to fight *for* him, while he keeps himself a thousand Leagues remote from Danger! Vassals fight at the Lords Expence, but our Lord would have us defend his Estate at our own Expence! This is not merely Vassalage, it is worse than any Vassalage we have heard of; it is even more slavish than slavery itself. . . . If [the Governor] can force us into this Law, the Liberty and Property, not only

of one Man, but of all the Men in the Province, will be invaded and taken away; and this to aggrandize our *intended Lord*, increase and secure his Estate at our Cost, and give him the glorious Privilege that no *British* nobleman enjoys, of having his Lands free from Taxes, and defended gratis.[15]

That Thomas Penn paid no taxes on his land partly because that land was rented and leased at highly discounted rates, a function of the Penn family's long policy of privileging long-term demographic expansion over short-term income, was of no moment to Franklin. Similarly, it also meant nothing that in large portions of the Penn family estate—the southern borderlands, for instance—the family had no effective means of guaranteeing the collection of rents and quitrents. In fact, unlike his English counterparts, Lord Thomas Penn was lord in name only, and the assembly's efforts to tax his properties suggested that even that was in doubt. But wartime optics remained atrocious. The perception, fueled by Franklin and others resentful of the perceived rent-taking ways of the Penn family, was that the proprietor gave little and took much.

This fight over fiscal fairness generated deep political division, but it is difficult to separate the immediate cause of that division from another, much older source of political discord. While the Penn family abandoned Quakerism, many of its colony's wealthiest families did not. Eighteenth-century government's principal justification for new revenue, war, carried no truck with this powerful faction and made it that much more difficult for Pennsylvania's wartime governors to address the colony's rapidly escalating security costs. Through a synchronous combination of religion and base fiscal politics, the Pennsylvania colony was thus uniquely ill-prepared to finance its own defense. Gottlieb Mittelberger, a German schoolmaster and organist who traveled to Pennsylvania in the early 1750s, observed with alarm, "There is nothing for which that country is less prepared than a war, especially because such a large number of Quakers live there who will not quarrel or fight with anyone. That is why magazines or stores of grain and provisions have never been set up." Mittelberger overstated Quaker opposition to war. Evidence of Quaker pacifism is ambiguous, but evidence for Quaker opposition to the Penn family's seeming fiscal intransigence is not. Mittleberer was most likely echoing the sentiments of neglected frontier settlers of German descent, many of whom conflated government paralysis with Quaker ethics. Nonetheless, there was a small but vocal and principled Quaker antiwar faction led by the "king of the Quakers," Israel Pemberton Jr. Pemberton and his brothers James and John opposed any measures, even defensive measures, that violated orthodox Quaker pacifism. Though they represented a minority, the Pembertons nonetheless fueled the popular perception that Quakerism was to blame for Pennsylvania's military problems.[16]

Beyond simply an inability or a refusal to pay for the arming and raising of militias, the building of forts, and the provisioning of British imperial troops sent to defend the colony, the Pennsylvania government faced an additional wartime difficulty. The jurisdictional confusion of the borderlands combined with the Penn family's lax titling and taxation practices unleashed a squatters' army throughout the colony. The result was a colony uniquely vulnerable to frontier violence. In a letter to the Quaker merchant Richard Partridge, one of the Pennsylvania assembly's agents in London, Franklin noted that the wartime sufferings of backwoods settlers were "a natural Consequence of the loose manner of Settling in these Colonies, picking here and there a good Piece of Land, and sitting down at such a distance from each other, as that a few Indians may destroy a Number of Familys one after the other, without their being even alarm'd or able to afford one another any Assistance." Whether because of Quaker ideals, the Penn family's parsimony, Pennsylvania's lax settlement regulations, or some combination of the three, Pennsylvania seemed destined for catastrophe.[17]

The same fertile lands, abundant game, wide flowing waterways, and Indian trade that had drawn Pennsylvania's Native refugees to the Ohio country drew fur traders from Pennsylvania. In the thirty years before the French and Indian War, fur exports from Philadelphia more than doubled, a direct result of the city's commercial reach into the colony's western borderlands. Unfortunately for Philadelphia's fur merchants, land speculators from Virginia had also come to the Ohio country. Seeking to take advantage of the terms of the 1744 Lancaster Treaty, which Virginians took as a total Iroquois retreat, a group of prominent Virginia planters and their associates, who included Thomas Cresap, formed an entity known as the Ohio Company for the purpose of establishing a new western colony. The company's commercial interests collided headlong with those of the Ohio country's fur traders. A flood of new settlers, enabled by the company's claims, now validated by the Crown and the colony of Virginia, would very likely achieve what European settlers had achieved in the lower Susquehanna and really every other eastern seaboard region whose game and whose Native populations endured the onslaught of slashing, fence-building European agriculturalists. For French fur traders and military personnel, who viewed the Ohio country as, at best, contested territory, the Ohio Company constituted an existential threat. To fend off this new Anglo-American menace, the French military and their Native allies constructed a chain of four forts stretching from the south shore of Lake Erie to the Forks of the Ohio. Fears that the southernmost of these forts, Fort Duquesne, would deter settlement on Ohio Company lands provoked the initial conflicts of the French and Indian War. In the most infamous of these early battles, George Washington, a Virginia militiaman whose half brother and father had been early Ohio Company investors, led several hundred men in a failed attempt to dislodge the enemy from putative Ohio Company lands. A little over a year later, another assault on Fort Duquesne led by British major general Edward Braddock left Braddock dead and his forces routed.[18]

Braddock's defeat, along with a series of ruthless Indian raids—some real but many entirely imaginary—led to the worst refugee crisis in the borderlands' history. In the summer of 1755, Cumberland County's able-bodied men numbered more than a thousand. By September 1756, fewer than one hundred remained, the rest having fled, abandoning the most abundant harvest "in the memory of Man." For York County officials, the fact that "the County of Cumberland is mostly evacuated" and that its harvest had been left behind meant that "the Enemy may easily enter and take Possession of Provisions sufficient to supply many thousand men, and be thereby enabled to carry their Hostilities even to the Metropolis" of Philadelphia. On the western banks of the Susquehanna, according to the newspaper Benjamin Franklin owned, the *Pennsylvania Gazette*, "for some Miles, the Woods were filled with poor Families, and their Cattle, who make Fires, and live like Savages." A Philadelphia merchant told a correspondent that many "women and children . . . in the greatest want of both Covering & Victuals" even managed to find their way back to the capital city, where they arrived "in a starving condition."[19]

In some ways, the stories the refugees told proved more consequential than the ordeals that drove them from their homesteads. Many had seen family members slaughtered, scalped, and butchered by furious and marauding Native warriors, but many more simply fled in panic, driven by rumors that similar terror awaited all who held out in the frontier regions of Pennsylvania, Maryland, and Virginia. Squabbling provincial authorities did little to end the crisis. In October 1755, rumors of impending French and Indian attacks swept through Lancaster. Edward Shippen, the local official charged with the town's defense, pleaded desperately with Governor Morris for reinforcements, and when none were forthcoming he took matters into his own hands. Fearful particularly for the town's women and children, Shippen reported to colonial authorities that the townsmen had constructed a safe house, surrounded by a moat and accessible only by drawbridge.[20]

The rumored Lancaster-area invasion never materialized, but isolated attacks throughout the region fed the tension and anxiety that were now hallmarks of borderlands social psychology. Pressured by the Crown, the Pennsylvania government did eventually direct resources toward defense, but the damage had been done. Years of neglect punctuated by the horrors of war, both real and rumored, did more to bring unity to the western borderlands than religion or ethnicity ever did. Desperate to mobilize their diverse and often antagonistic populations, officials fanned the flames, recognizing that, whether German, English, or Scots-Irish, the borderlands population would find common cause in its vague and generalized fear of the alleged instigators of terror, all of whom were said to be Indian proxies for vengeful French Catholics.

Exasperated by his province's hapless defenses, as a commander in the colonial militia, Franklin despaired of ever mobilizing frontier settlers, now "terrified out of their Senses." So pervasive was the fear that those few militiamen prepared to defend settlements along Pennsylvania's northeastern frontier found themselves abandoned by their kin, with no food, shelter, firewood, or other provisions. Franklin "threatn'd to disband or remove the Companies already posted for the Security of particular Townships, if the People would not stay on their places, behave like Men, do something for themselves, and assist the Province Soldiers."[21]

Military conflict in the Ohio country, meanwhile, only heightened the political acrimony surrounding military expenditure. In April 1756, Governor

Morris received news from Lancaster that a "great Body of the Inhabitants of the Back Counties" were preparing for a march to Philadelphia, "with design to force the Governor and Assembly to pass some Laws that they have prepared" to reinforce the defenses of Pennsylvania's frontier. In an effort to preempt such irregular politics, the governor issued a public declaration of war against the "Delaware tribe of Indians and others in Confederacy with them" who have "fallen upon this province and in a most cruel, savage, and perfidious Manner, killed and butchered great Numbers of the Inhabitants, and carried others into barbarous Captivity." Morris's was no formal proclamation of war by one nation against another. It was a clarion call for ethnocidal killing. Pennsylvania's Indian enemy was not merely an enemy nation but "Enemies, Rebels, and Traitors to His Most Sacred Majesty." With £60,000 from the Pennsylvania assembly, the governor offered a bounty of 150 Spanish dollars for each captive adult male Indian. "For the Scalp of every Male Indian Enemy above the age of Twelve Years, produced as Evidence of their being killed," the colony would pay 130 Spanish dollars.

Morris recognized the danger in his imperative. There remained Indians in Pennsylvania who understood themselves to be law-abiding subjects of the colonial government, and there would be no way to distinguish friends' scalps from enemies'. The governor's notice that "friendly Indians" were "expressly excepted out of this Declaration" was thus surely seen by the many Quaker and Native opponents of the declaration, not to mention other right-thinking Pennsylvanians, for exactly what it was: a limp attempt to disguise an invitation to ruthless racialized vigilantism.[22] Speaking on behalf of a group of friendly Indians, the Iroquois spokesman Scarouyady, an Oneida who had been living in the Ohio country, applauded the governor's declaration against hostile Delawares but cautioned, "Your people are foolish." Pennsylvania would have to protect friendly Indians. Shamokin, a northeastern Pennsylvania town of Indian allies, had been completely abandoned after its pleas for military assistance went unheeded. Now, Scarouyady explained, the Indians of Shamokin, "who are your friends, can be of no Service to you, having no Place to go to where they can promise themselves Protection." For "at present your People . . . think every Indian is against them" and the Shamokin refugees now faced unrestrained anti-Indian violence.[23]

Pennsylvanians may have been prepared to terrorize their colony's Indians, but it turned out they were little better at asymmetrical warfare than at more conventional methods. Governor Morris's attempt to harness racial anger achieved very little. No stampede of bounty hunters arrived at the statehouse; during the entirety of the colonial era, only eight scalp bounties were issued by the Pennsylvania government. Pennsylvania's enemies, fighting in small, fleet-footed raiding parties, a tactic honed over a century or more, made for elusive prey, and with few Indian allies, even Pennsylvania's small number of dedicated anti-Indian fighters provided a feeble counter to its attackers. This reality, in conjunction with pressure by Pemberton and his supporters, drove Governor Morris to undertake a parallel and more peaceful strategy.[24]

While initial attacks on the Pennsylvania backcountry came primarily from Ohio country Indians, by December 1755 the campaign against Pennsylvanians had taken an alarming turn. A group of Wyoming Valley Delawares began attacking settlements in Northampton County. Although displaced by shady land deals, much like their brethren who had migrated to the Ohio Valley, these so-called Eastern Delawares had hoped an Iroquois alliance would allow them to reclaim lands lost to Pennsylvania. But no such alliance materialized, and the Eastern Delawares elected to join their western kin in war against Pennsylvania. Prompted partly by Franklin's reports of the hopelessness of defending his colony's northern flanks, Morris decided to pursue a peace treaty. The Eastern Delaware headman, Teedyuscung, agreed to an initial council at Easton. Although the meeting achieved little, it did bring a period of relative quiet to Pennsylvania's northeastern frontier. This too might have saved some innocent lives, at least for a time. But over the following year the war in the west ground on, and Teedyuscung continued to push for restoration of Delaware lands. When violence resumed in the northeast, blame fell on the Quaker establishment, widely believed to support the Eastern Delawares.

The failure of Morris's initiative freed his successor, Governor William Denny, to assume a more militant foreign policy. But for that policy to succeed, British forces would need local Indian allies. The affirmation of Pennsylvania's Iroquois ties proved crucial: the Franco-Indian alliance in the West was showing signs of strain, and in negotiations with the Iroquois that affirmed their control of the western Allegheny Mountains, Denny offered a face-saving path for Ohio country Indians. Now they could effectively align themselves with the Iroquois, who, despite their declared neutrality in the recent war, recognized that should the fortunes of the war shift, the

British colonies would be best placed to advance Iroquois territorial and strategic aims. Once again, in linking their fortunes to the Iroquois League, Pennsylvania authorities demonstrated the colony's priorities. An alliance with the powerful Iroquois had far more strategic value than would one with Teedyuscung and the Wyoming Valley Delawares.

In theory, the arrangement left Pennsylvania's remaining eastern Indians subject to Iroquois rule, something the Wyoming Delaware assumed would strengthen their land claims. In fact, the Iroquois's habitual neglect of Pennsylvania's remaining Indian communities continued. In the hothouse of wartime Pennsylvania, and with a provincial government willing to authorize anti-Indian slaughter, Pennsylvania's remaining Native communities could hardly have been more vulnerable.

In the summer of 1758, British general John Forbes led a force of more than seven thousand British regulars and colonial troops west from Carlisle toward Fort Duquesne. Of the fifty-five hundred colonial soldiers, nearly half were from Pennsylvania. Slowly and methodically Forbes marched his army toward the French stronghold. Meanwhile, Western Delawares, encouraged by the Iroquois and by Governor Denny's assurances of new favorable trading policies, began abandoning their French allies. The French garrison at Fort Duquesne faced an increasingly desperate situation. Forced to choose between military defeat or a lengthy and uncertain winter siege, on November 24, 1758, the French abandoned their Ohio country stronghold. The war for Pennsylvania had now come to an end. Or at least the war had come to an end for the Euro-Americans of eastern North America. For the Indians of the Ohio country, the path to lasting peace was not so clear. British control of the region, secured by a giant new fortification at the Forks of the Ohio, called Fort Pitt in honor of William Pitt, the triumphant head of the British government, meant that four years of war had achieved very little. The European intrusions into this new Native homeland would continue, and the Native peoples of the Ohio country would face challenges to their survival very similar to those they had faced before the war.

Fort Pitt, built on the site of the old Fort Duquesne, dwarfed its French predecessor. Its massive walls, nearly sixty feet thick at their base, surrounded an extensive parade ground and barracks capable of housing as many as a thousand troops, roughly five times the number Fort Duquesne accommodated. The structure's size and permanence achieved precisely what British military officials hoped: it demonstrated—for all who cared to look—British intent in the Ohio country. The British Empire may have emerged as a global colossus following the Seven Years' War, as the French and Indian War was known in Europe, but military commanders recognized that inland North America, stretching from the western Great Lakes to the Appalachian Mountains, was British in name only. Native groups formerly allied with the French were unlikely to accept unconditional British rule, and the loyalty of those who had supported the British was far from certain.

Drawn across new roads constructed during the war, settlers flooded into the Ohio country. By summer 1761, the area around Fort Pitt had become a thriving village, with extensive farm fields, a coal mine, a sawmill, a stone quarry, and some 160 houses. From this new beachhead, squatters set out deeper into the countryside, establishing more farmsteads and further disrupting Native patterns of life. The fur-bearing game that had drawn Native peoples to the Ohio country was now suffering the same fate as the game that had once populated colonized areas to the east. With no alternative French outlet for Native trade goods, Native traders were unable to compensate for the scarcity of furs by seeking higher prices, leaving the Ohio country Indians facing a level of economic dislocation comparable to what they had faced during the war.

To these unhappy developments British military authorities added an additional insult. In the year after the fall of Montreal, General Jeffery Amherst, supreme commander of the British military in North America, ordered an end to the diplomatic practice of gift giving. To Amherst, the new policy was an obvious extension of Britain's postwar strategy: it allowed colonial officials to limit Indians' access to pernicious goods such as firearms and liquor, in turn easing the burden of preserving order across Britain's new continental empire. The same quest for order justified a series of additional British restrictions. Fur traders would no longer be able to establish independent trading posts or do business in Indian towns but would instead have to conduct all their trade at British military installations.

Amherst surely had little interest in exactly how Fort Pitt was perceived by the Native peoples of the Ohio Valley, but if he had, he would have understood British policies as ideally conceived to demonstrate that the British presence in Ohio country did little to protect Mingo, Delaware, and Shawnee territory and much to dispossess these communities of the very resources— game, trade goods, and land—that had drawn them to the region in the first place.[25]

That the peace lasted as long as it did is perhaps less surprising than the fact that there was ever a peace at all. British policy in the Ohio country did practically nothing to account for wartime deprivations, let alone the preceding decades of demographic change. By the spring of 1763, the apparently inevitable came to pass and the fragile postwar peace collapsed. Named for Pontiac, the Ottawa warrior and headman who led an attack on Fort Detroit, Pontiac's War drew together dozens of disparate Native groups throughout the Ohio country and the Great Lakes in a new battle against British authority. Although the war was named for an Ottawa, its impetus derived from a source much closer to the borderlands. Delaware religious leaders had long called for resistance to the liquor trade and Iroquois hegemony, both of which had facilitated Pennsylvania's appropriation of ancestral Lenape lands. During the war, Neolin, a prophet associated with the Western Delawares, began disseminating a similar message. Beyond abstention from liquor, Neolin urged a more general reformation of Indian ways. Any European trade, he explained to his followers, reinforced destructive patterns of dependence by weakening traditional Native modes of sustenance and survival. At a time when parsimonious British policy threw that dependence into stark relief, Neolin's message resonated throughout Indigenous eastern North America. As Neolin preached independence and abstinence, he also urged his followers to prepare for war. This message, too, found receptive audiences, and by the winter of 1763 it had inspired Pontiac and his militant followers to strike. When war erupted in late April, British authorities were utterly unprepared. Over the course of the next few months, they could only watch in horror as Native warriors captured smaller military outposts and laid siege to Forts Detroit and Pitt. By the end of the summer of 1763, the British army's entire inland complex of fortifications was either under siege or under direct Indian control.

With British forces trapped behind the walls of their new Ohio country fort and colonial regiments mostly disbanded, Pennsylvanians again sat helplessly as Shawnee and Western Delaware warriors prepared to return to wartime patterns of frontier violence. By October 1763, one report from Carlisle attributed some six hundred deaths to renewed Indian attacks. The numbers were horrific, but in a familiar pattern, actual attacks and rumored attacks combined to cast a vast halo of utter terror over the borderlands. Now, however, to the many frightened and newly displaced Euro-Americans were added hundreds of seasoned and well-armed fighters little inclined to defer to provincial authorities in matters of frontier security. Some organized themselves into new unofficial militias. John Armstrong, who had commanded Pennsylvania forces in the French and Indian War and now lived in Cumberland County, took charge of a three-hundred-man paramilitary force to fight Delaware incursions. Others organized themselves into smaller, less disciplined militias. Far more than at any other time in Pennsylvania's history, the colony faced an eruption of large-scale and ruthless ethnocidal vigilantism.[26]

That militarized frontier settlers were prepared to marshal their own defenses was a symptom of the persistent gulf separating frontier regions from Philadelphia and its Quaker-dominated government. The fiscal tensions that had stalled preparations for Pennsylvania's last war persisted, and with renewed violence, the colony's government proved no better prepared to defend its frontiers than it had been during the French and Indian War. One particularly embittered band of fighters from the town of Paxton in northern Lancaster County elected to direct its rage against the region's most vulnerable. In a scenario that had long been feared, frontier hatred of Indians turned on some of Pennsylvania's most loyal Indian residents. In early December 1763, the well-armed fighters from Paxton, subsequently dubbed "the Paxton Boys," a name reflective of the widespread sympathies these vigilantes generated, marched to the town of Conestoga, put the torch to its houses, and slaughtered five innocent residents. Among the dead was the elderly Sheehays, the Conestogas' last direct connection to William Penn.

While the attack on Conestoga was unjustified, it was not random—the Paxton Boys turned against these friendly Indians because they had long believed them to be traitors. Much of this assessment, it seems, rested on the reputation of a single man. Will Sock, a freewheeling Conestoga who had helped Pennsylvania provincial soldiers early in the French and Indian War, also traveled to Ohio country, raising suspicions that he was a Western Delaware sympathizer. Sock's alleged duplicitousness fed suspicions that the Conestogas could not be trusted. After the raids of Pontiac's War began, the Paxton fighters made unofficial incursions into Indian country. One of these, in late October, took them to the Wyoming Valley, abandoned by the

Eastern Delawares and now inhabited by settlers from New England. There, instead of hostile Indians, the Paxton party found the aftermath of slaughter. Ten New Englanders lay dead, their butchered and mutilated corpses displaying telltale signs of torture; the rest of the New Englanders had vanished, most likely taken captive by their Indian attackers. There was no indication that Will Sock or any other Conestogas had anything to do with the killings, but that meant little to the Paxton vigilantes.[27]

Pennsylvania's newest governor, John Penn, a nephew of Thomas who had arrived in Philadelphia just a few weeks before the slaughter at Conestoga, exhibited appropriate outrage and issued orders for the protection of the survivors. In response, Lancaster town leaders sequestered the survivors in the Lancaster workhouse, really just a jail that happened to be the town's most secure building. This turns out not to have meant much in the way of protection. Mid-eighteenth-century jails may have been able to contain captives, but they offered little to repel attackers. Several weeks after the initial Conestoga raid, a group of fifty or sixty anti-Indian fighters from Paxton, likely including the original raiders, stormed the workhouse and within minutes had dismembered, scalped, and mutilated fourteen Conestogas, including infants and children. Among the dead was Will Sock, indiscriminately murdered and tossed among the corpses of his wife and two young children. Not a single inhabitant of Conestoga is known to have survived the attack. The victims were not part of some alien band of anonymous refugees but neighbors with English names, living on lands granted them by William Penn well before Lancaster County existed.[28]

After learning of this latest murderous rampage, a flustered Governor Penn warned his fellow governor, New York's Cadwallader Colden, that "our back Inhabitants who have indeed suffered a great deal by the Indian War, have got it into their heads that one Indian should not be suffered to live among us." Every colony would feel reverberations, especially since the Paxton Boys would never be brought to justice.[29]

Displaying no remorse, the killers from Paxton submitted two formal lists of grievances to Pennsylvania's government. The documents detailed the sufferings of Pennsylvania's western Euro-American population and justified the Paxton Boys' rejection of any distinction between Indian friend and Indian enemy. The Conestogas were murdered, the petitioners insisted, not out of blood lust but because provincial authorities, in thrall to the naive and hypocritical altruism of deranged Quakers, elected to protect friendly Indians while ignoring the sufferings of white settlers: "The Hands that were closely shut, nor would grant his Majesty's General one single Farthing against a Savage Foe, have been liberally opened, and the publick Money lavishly prostituted to hire, at an exorbitant Rate, a mercenary Guard, to protect his Majesty's worst Enemies, those falsly pretended *Indian* friends, while at the same time hundreds of poor distressed Families of his Majesty's Subjects, obliged to abandon their Possessions, and flee for their Lives . . . in the most distressing Circumstances."[30]

So inept and intransigent had been Pennsylvania's government, it could not even direct requested funds to the British military, let alone the displaced populations of the colony's frontier. And yet it somehow found a way to direct tax revenue toward the protection of Indians. That the Penn family had for nearly a century assumed the role of protector of Pennsylvania's Native population, and had done so through formal legal transaction, obviously meant nothing to the petitioners. A government dominated by Quaker pacifists was a government for Quakers and nobody else.

In the years after the Paxton attacks, borderlands vigilantes—"banditti," as some government officials called them—continued to act with total disregard for virtually any legal authority, provincial or local. Shortly after their return from Philadelphia, a number of Paxton fighters attempted to annex the former Conestoga Manor, and although Lancaster County officials were able to evict the intruders, this momentary assertion of law and governance had little long-term impact. Indians unfortunate enough to find themselves in the borderlands were sure to face assorted abuses, including theft of their property. In 1766, a group of Tuscaroras traversing the old Susquehanna route from the south to Iroquois country were assaulted and robbed by residents of Paxton. The declining numbers of borderlands Indians did little to stem the fury of western Pennsylvanians. It did, however, force frontier fighters to redirect their rage.

In March 1765, a group of them, faces blackened and wearing Indian-like apparel, attacked a convoy of more than eighty pack horses en route to Fort Pitt. The attack occurred near Fort Loudon, west of the new border town of Chambersburg, and followed days of harassment as the horses and their handlers made their way west from Philadelphia. The attack was prompted by widespread belief that the pack train carried ammunition for Indians. In fact, the convoy carried gifts meant to help secure the peace after Pontiac's War. To British officials, the conduct of the "Black Boys," denoting the charcoal face paint worn by the attackers, was emblematic of the complete collapse of law and order on the Pennsylvania frontier. General Thomas Gage, who replaced Jeffery Amherst as commander of British forces in North America, offered his sympathies to Governor Penn for "the lawless Banditti on your Frontiers." The actions of these renegades had a sadly familiar source: "The Robberies and disturbance they have been guilty of with Impunity, emboldens them to every Act of Violence, whilst they flatter themselves that they are secure from Punishment." Pennsylvania's problems originated in the same sources identified by the Paxton Boys: a failure of governance. Neglect, it seemed, had finally proven itself to be anything but salutary.[31]

Nearly a century after its creation, the colony of Pennsylvania seemed uniquely ill-equipped to govern itself. In one of the many paradoxes of mid-eighteenth-century colonial politics, this problem brought a strange and troubling convergence of views among the people of Pennsylvania's borderlands and the British government agents charged with securing the welfare of Ohio country Indians. By late 1767, General Gage shared with Governor Penn his frustrations at the "obstinacy of the People who persist to Settle" on Indian lands in the Ohio country, despite assorted and kindly measures to stop them. At some point, Gage continued, as long as Pennsylvania's "Laws are defective, or the coercive Powers of Government are wanting," there was very little the British military could do to prevent renewed bloodshed. For "it is the *dread* that naturally follows the exemplary punishment of delinquents, that can only restrain such Lawless Banditti." Pennsylvania, Gage stressed, would have to find a way to enact and enforce such dread-inducing laws "before it is too late to prevent the Devastations, Cruelties and effusions of Blood."[32]

Much as the Paxton Boys themselves suggested, so General Gage concluded that Pennsylvania's problems lay with its government. Without the orderly administration of justice, there would be no peace in the borderlands. Benjamin Franklin, a relentless critic of Pennsylvania's frontier banditti, also identified the origins of Pennsylvania's problems in its inept Quaker-dominated government. But, after a decade struggling in vain to organize the colony's defenses, he came to believe that the colony's real problem was Pennsylvania's arcane constitution. Proprietary government simply could not govern an entity as extensive and diverse as Pennsylvania. Should there be any doubt, Franklin pointed to his province's "present . . . wretched situation":

> The Government that ought to keep all in Order, is itself weak, and has scarce Authority enough to keep the common Peace. Mobs assemble and kill (we scarce say *murder*) Numbers of innocent People in cold Blood, who were under the Protection of the Government. . . . Not a Magistrate dares wag a Finger towards discovering or apprehending the *Delinquents* (we must not call them *Murderers*). They assemble again, and with Arms in their Hands, approach the Capital. The Government truckles, condescends to cajole them, and drops all Prosecution of their Crimes; whilst honest Citizens, threatened in their Lives and Fortunes, flie the Province, as having no Confidence in the Publick Protection.

If Pennsylvanians, Indian or white, were ever to feel secure, a change of government was needed. Franklin's was not some early call to revolution but a bold call for royal government. In place of an executive branch beholden to a family of English rent takers, Franklin and his growing body of allies had concluded, Pennsylvania deserved to be governed by a representative of the Crown, "a gracious King . . . who has no Views but for the Good of the People."[33]

Even in the wake of recent mayhem, the scheme to reframe Pennsylvania's government faced fierce opposition. The Quaker lawyer and assemblyman John Dickinson saw no way to preserve Pennsylvania's religious liberties under royal government. As was the case with other royal colonies, a royal Pennsylvania would also be an Anglican Pennsylvania. Isaac Norris, the longtime Speaker of the assembly, feared royal government would achieve one of Thomas Penn's most-cherished aims: the weakening of the colony's assembly. But with so much venom directed at the colony's government, the assembly had concluded that some sort of action had to be taken and, short of accepting its own responsibility for the current crisis, the only other option was to attack the proprietors. With so influential and articulate an advocate as Franklin, this strategy acquired substantial momentum. After much debate and Norris's resignation, the assembly agreed to a formal request for royal government.

Although the push for a sweeping constitutional overhaul would ultimately fail, it prompted a lasting realignment of Pennsylvania politics. As part of its campaign to oust the Penns, the promoters of royal government had urged restraint in response to a new stamp tax, imposed by Parliament to help cover the costs of a British military presence in eastern North America. Pennsylvania's stamp distributor, John Hughes, a close friend and political ally of Franklin's, was the only stamp tax collector in all the mainland colonies not forced to resign and, unlike his counterparts, he suffered very little direct hostility—he was not, for instance, burned in effigy. So compliant was Pennsylvania's response to the new tax, British authorities grew suspicious. Surely the colony's conduct had some underlying political purpose. In response to the government's skepticism, Governor Penn shrewdly took credit for Pennsylvania's compliance with the stamp tax, and British ministers concluded that, whatever the previous decade had suggested and whatever Franklin may have claimed, Pennsylvania's government was perhaps the most functional in all of the mainland colonies. Before he was asked to form a government, the Member of Parliament for Banbury, Frederick, Lord North, rose on the floor of the House of Commons to express his high "regard for Pennsylvania, which had behaved so well in all the late Disturbances in America" over a new stamp tax, "and had shown such a dutiful Obedience to Parliament" in its compliance with a new Quartering Act, requiring colonists to house and supply British troops.[34] That perception may have pleased Thomas Penn and his nephew, but it meant very little to Pennsylvanians who remained deeply divided over the sources of their recent grief.[35]

It also did very little for the Penn family's principal concern: namely, the profitability of its American holdings. The years of war and bloodshed had barely dented the family's colonial income, but mostly this was because that income had been meager to begin with. A definitive southern boundary line would, at the very least, end the question of whether or not borderlands colonists could be taxed by the Penn family.

CHAPTER 6

The Science of Borders

IN MAY 1750, Lord Chancellor Philip Yorke, the 1st Earl of Hardwicke, issued the Court of Chancery's final decision on the Maryland-
Pennsylvania boundary dispute. It was, the noble jurist averred, an especially
difficult decision, "of a nature worthy the judicature of a *Roman* senate
rather than of a single judge." The lord chancellor's assessment was perhaps
inevitable, given that the case had dragged on for fifteen years, encompassing
the entirety of Lord Hardwicke's thirteen years on the bench. The wealthy
litigants and their teams of barristers had introduced an endless series of
motions and countermotions, some centering on the Chancery Court's
very jurisdiction in the case. Through all these proceedings, the evidence
accumulated—tedious depositions concerning taxation and the intent of colonial officials, along with a lengthy seventeenth-century paper trail. Sifting
through the mass of evidence and managing the onslaught of claims and
counterclaims had obviously taxed Lord Hardwicke. But he recognized the
case was also very typical of those decided by his court.

As a court of equity, the Chancery Court heard especially difficult and
complicated cases, normally settled through writs or injunctions. Had this
most contested of colonial boundary cases actually been about the validity
of specific territorial boundaries, acknowledged by Hardwicke to be "the
boundaries of two great provincial governments and three counties," the

case might well have fallen outside the court's jurisdiction. But the plaintiffs in this case, the Penn family, had not asked the court to settle the Maryland-Pennsylvania boundary. According to the Penns' lawyers, any questions about the location of that boundary had been settled in 1732, when the Penns and the fifth Lord Baltimore signed an agreement to establish a boundary commission. The issue was whether or not that contract remained valid. The case before the lord chancellor was entirely owing to the arbitrary and unjust decision by representatives of the fifth Lord Baltimore to withdraw from the commission—a clear violation of the 1732 settlement.[1]

In his defense, Lord Baltimore blamed the Penn family and its American representatives for the collapse of the commission. They had, he argued, deliberately and maliciously misrepresented the terms of the original agreement, making that agreement null and void and leaving the location of the Maryland-Pennsylvania boundary unresolved. For this reason, not only was the 1732 agreement invalid, the Penns' case also fell outside the Court of Chancery's jurisdiction. The resolution of colonial boundaries involved questions of "sovereign dominion" precisely because colonial territory was ultimately controlled by the Crown. The only court that could decide the case was the one court rightfully able to convey royal lands. That court was directly presided over by the highest magistrate, the king himself. Any agreement over colonial boundaries "amounts to an alienation, which these lords proprietors cannot do," since that was tantamount to "dismembering" the realm.

Lord Hardwicke dismissed the defense argument. In signing the 1732 agreement, the fifth Lord Baltimore consented to boundaries established by the boundary commission; there would be no question of dismembering the realm. In a decision marginally more beneficial to the plaintiffs, the judge thus ordered the Penns and Lord Baltimore to resume the work of delineating their American estates.

Lord Hardwicke's decision may have rested on the arcane legal matter of exactly what was at issue in the case brought by the Penn family—a contractual agreement concerning the creation of a commission charged with surveying an agreed-upon boundary. But he made no effort to conceal the far-reaching political issues underlying the decision. In "the settling and fixing of these boundaries in peace," the judge hoped to "prevent the disorder and mischief, which in remote countries, distant from the seat of government, are most likely to happen." The court's decision would thus be about ending, once and for all, chaos in the borderlands and affording the proper and rightful functioning of proprietary governance.[2] The lord chancellor was fully aware that securing a boundary according to terms now nearly two decades old would present serious problems for colonial authorities. Colonists long accustomed to neglect were unlikely to bow down to a distant imperial court's ruling, particularly when that ruling could bear on politically explosive matters such as taxation. In a somewhat shortsighted consideration of these facts, Lord Hardwicke nonetheless ordered the contesting parties to draft new or revised deeds and titles for privately held land in the borderlands. In theory, the process would correct errant proprietary claims and titling errors, all with an eye toward turning a lineal boundary between colonies from an abstraction into a legally sanctioned jurisdictional demarcation.[3]

Any lingering questions about the respective colonies' powers to grant title would now be moot. "Long possession and enjoyment, peopling and cultivating countries," Lord Hardwicke noted, "is one of the best evidence of title to lands . . . in *America*, that can be." Conquest had secured legal territorial right, and if there remained any question about the validity of that right, one had only to observe the state of the lands. The proprietors were given license to conquer their American plantations in order to improve "the navigation and the commerce" of England. That was precisely what had happened: "These two provinces have been improved [by] private families to a great degree to the advantage of the mother country." There could thus be no question about the proprietors' rightful claim to their colonies and, in turn, their territorial rights. Insofar as there were boundaries and those boundaries had been agreed to by the proprietors, they were valid. "In cases of this kind after an agreement," Hardwicke concluded, "it is not necessary for the court to resort to the original right of the parties." But this was precisely where the legal met the political. In 1750, nobody could have imagined that either Lord Baltimore or the Penns would somehow be able to force residents of the borderlands to abandon one putative political affiliation for another, especially if doing so involved a greater tax burden.[4]

Nor, in 1750, could observers have imagined that the true political consequences of the lord chancellor's decision would be unknown for more than a decade. The Chancery Court's ruling stipulated that the 1732 agreement be implemented within two years of the court's final decision. Although the new boundary commission eventually completed a portion of the boundary survey—the east-west line between Fenwick Island on the Delaware Bay and Taylors Island on the Chesapeake—incessant disagreements among the commissioners, foul weather, and the death of Charles Calvert, the fifth Lord Baltimore, in 1751 slowed the commission's work. The French and Indian War further delayed progress, and the actual work of implementing Lord Hardwicke's orders would not begin until July 1760, when Thomas and Richard Penn and Frederick Calvert, Charles's only legitimate heir and the sixth Lord Baltimore, signed a new agreement to establish another bipartisan boundary commission.

The political implications of a new colonial border may have remained uncertain a decade after the Chancery Court decision, but the law had finally done its work. It defined the boundary between the Lower Counties and Maryland and confirmed the location of the Maryland-Pennsylvania boundary. Nearly a century of jousting by proprietor grandees had finally come to an end, and with the end of the age-old territorial dispute would come an end to the jurisdictional confusion that had for so long plagued the borderlands.

The Penns and the Calverts had agreed on very little over the decades. But one point on which they now agreed was that, as the boundary commissioners struggled with their newest charge, some novel expedient would be needed to avert another collapse of the commission. The proprietors also came to agree on precisely what that new expedient would be. Where law and diplomacy had failed, the lords proprietors concluded, science would succeed. By the end of 1767, two experienced astronomers, assisted by a large surveying crew, had established the first-ever mutually sanctioned boundary between Maryland, Pennsylvania, and the Lower Counties. Science, it seemed, had succeeded where all else had failed.

Lord Hardwicke had suggested the new boundary commission begin its work with maps made in support of the original 1732 agreement. Even had those maps been accurate, the judge's advice was of little help to the boundary makers. As guides to actual colonial space, eighteenth-century maps were only marginally better than their mid-seventeenth-century counterparts. The main problem was that very little progress had been made establishing with any accuracy the relative locations of colonial landmarks. Part of the reason for this was simply the infancy of geodesy, the science of mapping the earth's surface. Users of the land, European or Indigenous, obviously had a certain mastery of the spaces they used. They knew distances, often by travel times; they recognized property markers; they understood the spatial relation of important landmarks. And they were able to translate that mastery into readily communicated form, whether in maps or in written text. What these forms of spatial knowledge did not accommodate was the principal tool of European geodesy—a system of terrestrial navigation using a grid formed by lines of latitude and longitude. Any effort to locate terrestrial coordinates in the mainland colonies very quickly collided with the harsh realities of the American countryside.[5]

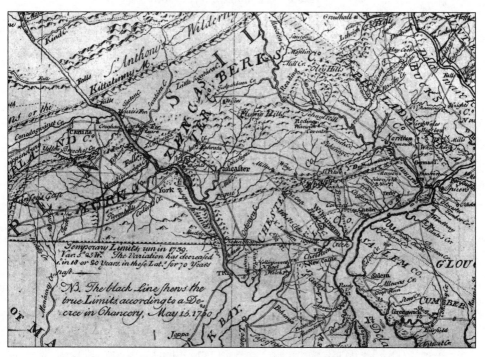

Detail from "A Map of Pensilvania, New-Jersey, New-York, and the three Delaware Counties," Lewis Evans, Philadelphia, 1752. The map shows two boundary lines, a dotted line corresponding to a temporary 1739 line and a solid line reflecting the Chancery Court decision on which Mason and Dixon would base their survey. Visible just above "York" is the faint remnant of "Cressop," removed from the 1749 original, perhaps at the request of Thomas Penn.
Library of Congress, Geography and Map Division.

European surveyors could use cathedral bell towers and features of the landscape to establish straight lines over long distances. But in America, wrote the cartographer Lewis Evans, there "are no Churches, Towers, Houses, or peaked Mountains to be seen from afar; no means of obtaining the Bearings or Distances of Places, by the compass." There were obviously mountains in North America, but there were so many that none stood out as a landmark. And when one stood atop them, to "look from these Hills into Lower Lands, is but, as it were, into an Ocean of Woods, swelled and depressed here and there, by little Inequalities, not to be distinguished one Part from another, any more than the Waves of a real Ocean."[6]

If the Maryland-Pennsylvania border was ever to reflect the intentions of the 1732 agreement, surveyors would have to overcome the barriers posed by the American countryside. For Lord Hardwicke and the proprietors, these problems were surely distant and manageable, but for the colonists charged with implementing the agreement, they seemed insurmountable. Governor Sharpe, who would organize and oversee Maryland's newest boundary commission, reported to his patron, Frederick Calvert, that the best cartographers and geometers "may not be apprized of all the Difficulties which will attend running Lines on the Surface of the Earth some thro a Forrest, some over Boggs & Marshes & others over a hilly or mountainous Country." Even should surveyors be able to overcome the barriers of climate and topography, additional problems remained. Lord Hardwicke's instructions contained profound ambiguities. What, after all, was a "due East & West Line"? Sharpe asked his patron. "Is it a parallel of Latitude? Or is any other Line . . . a due East & west Line?" Parallels of latitude and longitude curved in correspondence with the curvature of the earth. A straight east-west line, even if such a thing could be a scientific reality, would thus deviate from any line of latitude.

Governor Sharpe warned that unless this point was clear to the new commission, the Maryland-Pennsylvania boundary could drop far to the south, intersecting with the Potomac River at its northernmost bend and costing Lord Baltimore hundreds of square miles of territory. Other discrepancies over the precise location of the north-south meridian line dividing the Delmarva Peninsula might have allowed Lord Baltimore to regain "one way what was lost another," but this would depend on exactly how that line was established. The meridian line was to form a tangent line, running south from the westernmost radius of the Delaware Curve to a point at the middle of the Transpeninsular Line. The new commission's struggles to plot the meridian line had already failed, final proof that a straight line of more than eighty miles between two arbitrary points was beyond the ability of colonial American surveyors. Rather than ignite a new feud, Sharpe urged Lord Baltimore to seek the counsel of England's most "able Mathematicians."[7]

Lord Baltimore and the Penns, civilized and cosmopolitan Londoners, agreed with Sharpe. Where colonial surveyors would most likely fail, the most sophisticated mathematical and scientific minds might have some hope of success. Such minds were to be found among Britons consumed with the nature and movement of celestial bodies. None were more consumed with these matters than the staff of the best-funded and most advanced observatory in the English-speaking world, the Royal Observatory at Greenwich. Absorbed primarily with interpreting observations of the 1761 transit of Venus, a celestial event that allowed for the calculation of the earth's distance from the sun, the astronomer royal, James Bradley, had no particular interest in a distant colonial territorial dispute. But he did have an interest in demonstrating the superiority of astronomical methods for answering geodesical questions. In part, this was because Bradley and his protégé, and an eventual successor as astronomer royal, the Reverend Nevil Maskelyne, had become partisans in a high-stakes battle over the calculation of longitude.

For centuries navigators struggled in vain to calculate their location with respect to fixed points east and west, often with catastrophic consequences. To mistake one's longitude by even the smallest distance was to risk shipwreck. Calculating latitude was a much simpler matter. By measuring the height of specific stars above the horizon, seafarers could determine their latitude. The sun and other celestial bodies could also be used for this purpose, in conjunction with tables that allowed for the cross-referencing of the object's maximum height on a given day at a given latitude. But by the mid-eighteenth century, despite centuries of exploration and scientific experiment, no practical solution had been found to the much more difficult longitude problem. In 1714, seven years after four British naval vessels ran aground near England's southwestern coast, Parliament had acted to address the problem. The Longitude Act established a Board of Longitude and placed at the board's disposal a fortune of up to £20,000 in prize money (more than £1 million today) for whoever solved the longitude problem.

The Penn brothers and Lord Baltimore had been consulting with a number of mathematicians associated with the Royal Society, and these connections led them to Bradley and his associate, Maskelyne. The Reverend Nathaniel Bliss, who briefly succeeded the deceased Bradley as astronomer royal, picked up where his predecessor left off as advisor to the colonial propri-etors. Through this circle of mathematicians and astronomers, Thomas Penn learned of two astronomers who had recently returned from an expedition to the Cape of Good Hope, having traveled there to collect observations of the transit of Venus. Lord Baltimore lost little time in notifying his colony's governor that after "many Questions have been propounded & solved," he and the proprietors of Pennsylvania had agreed to share the cost of employing these experts. The two men, Lord Baltimore continued, were named "Dixon & Mason," and were "allowed by the best Judges here as Persons intirely accomplished & of good character." Charles Mason, the thirty-five-year-old assistant to Bradley at the Royal Observatory and an associate of Maskelyne's, was a well-known London astronomer. His as-sociate, an obscure Quaker astronomer named Jeremiah Dixon, five years his junior, had also assisted Bradley and had accompanied Mason to Africa. Mason, a recently widowed father of two boys, and his partner, the unattached thirty-year-old Dixon, would now travel to the American mid-Atlantic where they would apply cutting-edge science to the region's oldest, most in-tractable boundary dispute. For Lord Baltimore, the men were a godsend, equipped to "obviate all Doubts & settle & Determine all matters."[8]

It took practically no time for politics to intrude on Lord Baltimore's fantasy. By August 1763, just weeks after Mason and Dixon received their commissions, British officials had begun receiving accounts of Pontiac's Rebellion. Following their arrival in Philadelphia on November 15, Mason and Dixon proceeded with their preparations, largely oblivious to the un-rest raging in the American West. Instruments needed unpacking and fine-tuning, and the logistics of surveying more than 330 miles of boundary lines through forested backcountry needed tending to. Food, clothing, and shelter would all be needed—as would pay for the three dozen tradesmen and la-borers employed by the surveyors. Carpenters were needed to build obser-vation platforms; axemen would be needed to cut "vistos," enabling lines of sight through the dense woods; a steward, cooks, and tent keepers would provide camp support; chain carriers would haul and situate the cumbersome twenty-two-yard iron chains used for measuring distance between terrestrial points; and teamsters were necessary to move the astronomers' instruments, observation platforms, and limestone border markers imported from England. Forty years before Lewis and Clark, these obscure Englishmen organized the most ambitious scientific expedition in colonial American history.[9]

Judging from the journal they kept, Mason and Dixon deviated little from their commission. Although the survey would take most of four years, the journal's account offers little more than the most laconic details—coordinates, linear distances, astronomical observations, and the names of farm families whose lands were bisected by the newly situated boundary line. The astronomers themselves are mostly absent. This is as much a legal fact as a technical one. The two Englishmen were each, after all, promised substantial pay, along with travel expenses, and the journal demonstrated fealty to their employers' terms. For the parties to the Chancery Court case, any question about the "specific performance" required by the court could be addressed with the data assembled in the journals. Mason and Dixon may have been the most jocular and fun-loving of eighteenth-century Britons, but by design, none of that would have been evident in the official record. Careful reading, however, reveals—if not quite signs of campfire sociability or coffeehouse cheer—evidence that at least one of these Englishmen found it very difficult to conceal his occasional departures from the survey's objective.[10]

In the manner of a ship's log, the journals follow the daily progress of the survey and refer to the labors of both Mason and Dixon, but they were written by a single hand and are signed "C: Mason." For the most part, in keeping with the purposes of the journals, they are also written in the first-person plural, but occasionally they revert to the first person singular, describing activities and travels Mason undertook on his own. On the several occasions when the journals shift register, from surveyor's logbook to traveler's diary, Mason shows himself to have been a keen observer of the borderlands and their history. Dixon, unfortunately, remains something of a spectral presence. He may well have been the quiet Quaker, dutifully applying his mathematical genius to the thousands of calculations needed to ascertain the coordinates of the Line. Or he may have been a questing apostle of the Enlightenment, seeing everywhere in the heavens and on earth the work of some great divine clockmaker, work to which he, the English natural philosopher, had unique access. Or he may have merged toil and reverence, fashioning himself into some sort of high priest of science, bringing to all hearers the revealed mysteries of God's creation. There is no way to know.

Mason, the more easily ascertained of the two, still offers only occasional thoughts about the borderlands—and his observations were almost entirely confined to this portion of British North America. His reflections, or what remains of them, may have had something to do with his own ambitions for settling in America. Twenty years after he and Dixon completed their survey, Charles Mason and his family left England for the New World. Unfortunately, Mason fell ill at sea and died on October 25, 1786, about a month after returning to what had become the United States.

In late November 1764, after completing the meridian line dividing the Delmarva Peninsula, Mason and Dixon disbanded the surveying party and returned for the winter to their base of operations, John Harlan's farm, located near the forks of Brandywine Creek in Chester County. The previous winter the astronomers had set up an observatory on Harlan's property, now the location of what is locally known as the Star Gazers' Stone, the original benchmark stone placed by Mason and Dixon. According to the 1732 boundary agreement, the Maryland-Pennsylvania boundary, what the astronomers would call the West Line, was to lie exactly fifteen miles south of Philadelphia's southernmost limit. But since New Jersey lay fifteen miles due south of what the boundary commissioners determined to be that southern point (near the intersection of present-day South and Front Streets), Mason and Dixon looked due west for an accessible point from which to establish the latitude of the east-west boundary. That point happened to be on Harlan's property.

The farm had the advantage of being in an already deforested part of Pennsylvania, simplifying the measurement from the Harlan farm benchmark to a point fifteen miles due south, a point Mason and Dixon determined to lie at $39°43'17.4''$ north latitude. In locating the Line's latitude, Mason and Dixon made a scientific discovery that was of some importance for their surveying work but of potentially immense significance for the science of geodesy. Translating terrestrial distances into geodetic coordinates is not a simple matter. Degrees of longitude grow shorter as they move away from the equator, reaching zero at the poles. The terrestrial length of degrees of latitude remains uniform from the equator to the poles. But because the earth is not a perfect sphere, the distances between degrees of latitude are still not entirely uniform. Astronomers had assumed that, under perfect conditions,

The Original Star Gazers' Stone,
Harlan's Farm, Chester County,
Pennsylvania.
Courtesy of Stacey A. Rutledge.

a degree of latitude at the longitude of Harlan's farm would measure 69.5 miles. In fact, according to Mason and Dixon's calculations, in the lands south of Harlan's farm it measured 68.223 miles. The finding was of mostly theoretical value, but it did confirm what so many others had seen. Locating a boundary according to coordinates of longitude and latitude was astronomers' work. Although the calculation of a point of latitude remained a relatively simple matter, there could hardly be a more complex undertaking than establishing a terrestrial line of latitude, in effect knitting together many short straight lines to form a single curved whole. Doing so across the forested, mountainous terrain of the borderlands would be an undertaking of unprecedented magnitude in the history of North American land surveying.

If projecting a line of latitude was far more complex than identifying the latitude of any given point, for longitude the opposite was true. One could project a longitudinal line by following a line due north to the North Star. The problem was identifying the actual longitudinal coordinate of that line. Only complex astronomical calculations or a precise timekeeping instrument would allow an accurate plotting of a point of longitude. Mason and Dixon were forced to grapple with this problem because the only guidance the proprietors, the courts, and the surveyors had for determining the full length of the West Line was a provision in the Pennsylvania charter that identified Pennsylvania's western boundary as lying five degrees of longitude west of the Delaware River. In making the western limit of Pennsylvania a function of degrees of longitude, the Lords of Trade only made Mason and Dixon's work on the latitude of the West Line that much more critical. Because the length of a degree of longitude varies as a function of its proximity to the poles, even the slightest error could have had immense territorial consequences for Pennsylvania. Should the boundary line be located to the north of its proper location, the distance between degrees of longitude would be shortened, shortening the West Line and costing Pennsylvania territory at its western limit. Then there was the problem that, much like the length of a degree of latitude, the precise terrestrial length of degrees of longitude in the American mid-Atlantic had never been calculated.

These distances, of degrees of longitude and latitude, measured with more precision than had ever been attempted in North America, were not only important for locating the boundary line, as the astronomers recognized. They also made possible, for the first time, the accurate mapping of large portions of colonial North America. Building from the astronomers' observations, cartographers would be able to locate towns and geographic features with new regularity and precision. To observers who embraced the authority of a system of terrestrial coordinates, Mason and Dixon can be said to have transformed the American colonies. From a place where, quite literally, nobody ever knew where they were with respect to Western systems of terrestrial mapping, the borderlands would become the place in North America where human beings would have a more accurate sense of their place on the globe than anywhere else, with the exception of the last place Mason and Dixon had located before undertaking the Line. According to the *Nautical Almanac* of 1767, "it is probable that the Situation of few Places is better determined" than Cape Town, owing to Mason and

Dixon's labors. To that list of few places would soon be added the boundary line between Maryland and Pennsylvania.[11]

The astronomers began work on the West Line in March 1765 and for the next six months, they led their party toward Ohio country. Along the way, they marked the locations of important landmarks—towns, waterways, and mountaintops. They also measured the width of the Susquehanna at the Line: a little over eight-tenths of a mile. By October, the surveyors approached the Appalachian Mountains. As the weather turned, they began to retrace their earlier course eastward, securing boundary markers and rechecking coordinates. After another long winter, in April 1766, they resumed their westward trek. From a mountaintop 165 miles due west of the West Line's starting point, Mason gazed toward Ohio country. "The Lands on the Monaungahela and Ohio," he noted, "are allowed to be the best of any in the known parts of North America." It would be some time before settlers enjoyed the fruits of those lands. "At present," Mason wrote, "the Allegany Mountains is the Boundary between the Natives and strangers in these parts of his Britannic Majesties Collonies." Mason did not say exactly who he thought was native and who stranger, although common usage at the time saw the British as the natives and all foreigners—Indian and French in this case—as the strangers.[12]

The Appalachians would make for much slower surveying work than the hilly terrain to the east, and after only a few months the surveying party again began backtracking, along the way cutting an eight-yard-wide channel through the woods. For a brief period, perhaps a few years, until the channel was overgrown, travelers making their way between Maryland and Pennsylvania would have no doubt they were crossing a boundary line.

During the fall months, Mason and Dixon continued their astronomical observations and oversaw the placement of stone boundary markers along the north-south tangent line. They also established what they referred to as the East Line—the definitive distance between the Delaware River and the eastern end point of the West Line, now marking the northeast corner of the colony of Maryland. The distance was essential to the coming year's work, for Mason and Dixon would lead their party through the Alleghanies to the West Line's end point, but that end point could be known only if the surveyors also knew the exact longitude of a point on the Delaware River

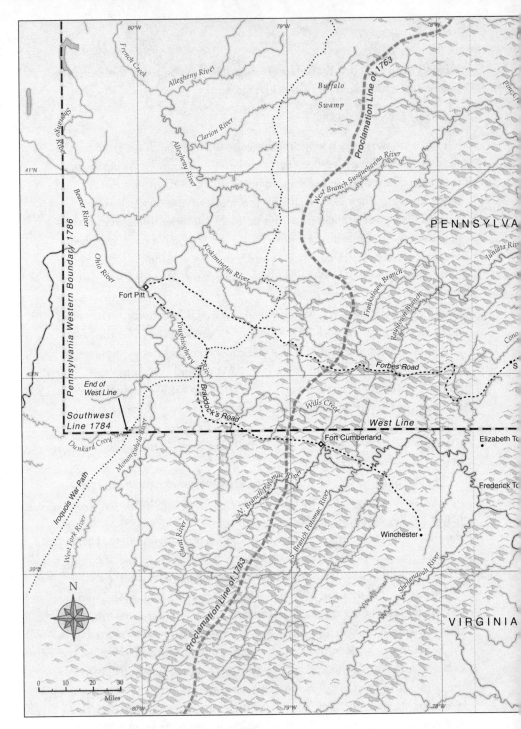

The Boundary Survey of Mason and Dixon, 1763–1767

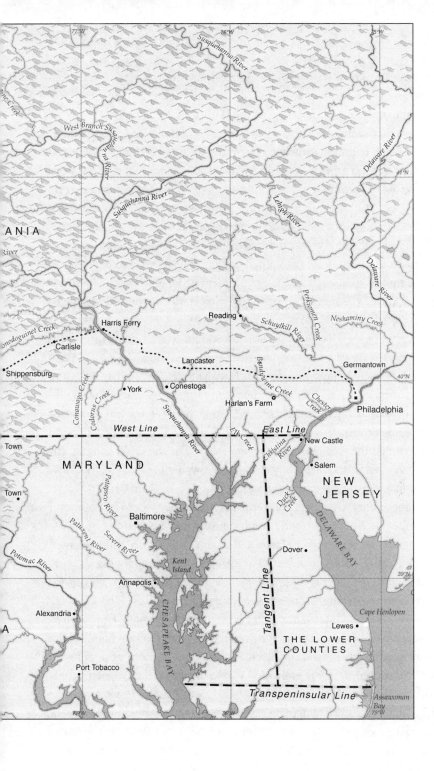

77°W

76°W

75°W

Susquehanna River

West Branch Susquehanna River

Delaware River

41°N

ne Creek

River

Susquehanna River

Lehigh River

Delaware River

ANIA

onodoguinet Creek

Harris Ferry

Reading

Schuylkill River

Perkiomen Creek

Neshaminy Creek

Carlisle

Shippensburg

Conewago Creek

Codorus Creek

York

Lancaster

Conestoga

Brandywine Creek

Harlan's Farm

Germantown

40°N

Chester Creek

Philadelphia

West Line

East Line

New Castle

Town

MARYLAND

Susquehanna River

Elk Creek

Christina River

Salem

Town

Patapsco River

Baltimore

Duck Creek

NEW
JERSEY

Patuxent River

Severn River

DELAWARE BAY

Potomac River

Kent
Island

Dover

Annapolis

39°N

Alexandria

Tangent Line

CHESAPEAKE BAY

Cape Henlopen

Lewes

THE LOWER
COUNTIES

A

Port Tobacco

Transpeninsular Line

Assawoman
Bay
75°W

77°W

76°W

at the exact latitude of the West Line. Once that point was established and a calculation of the length of a degree of longitude along the Line finalized, they established the exact location of the West Line's end point.

The astronomers spent the winter months of 1766 and 1767 back at Harlan's farm, continuing their work on the measurement of latitude and addressing queries from associates in England. By mid-April they were preparing to reassemble the surveying party for the final westward trek. But there would be a substantial delay. The Mason and Dixon survey had provoked a diplomatic crisis. As all parties recognized, the far western portion of the survey would cross lands controlled by Delawares, Shawnees, and dissident Iroquois, none of whom had any good reason to accommodate a surveying party sponsored by the government of Pennsylvania. These Indians recognized the survey for precisely what it was—the leading edge of colonial annexation.

To avert a new Indian war, authorities sought formal permission from the Iroquois to carry the Line to its western end. Governors Sharpe and Penn reassured the British superintendent for Indian affairs, Sir William Johnson, that their purpose was not to extend their lord proprietors' claims but simply "so that there may not hereafter be any Dispute between the Inhabitants of Pennsylvania & this Province [Maryland] about the Boundaries which has been too much the Case for many Years Past." For the Ohio country Indians, such assurances were likely to ring hollow, but for the Iroquois, now the designated overlords of the far west, they proved adequate.[13]

On June 3, the astronomers received news that they would be permitted to continue the West Line on the condition that they be escorted by an official Iroquois delegation. For Mason and Dixon's employers, this presented a new and very delicate problem. The delegation accompanying the surveying party would be traveling with men recruited from the growing population of wage-earning white workers (whether any of the laborers were of African, Native, or mestizo ancestry is unknown), normally employed to clear lands, build farmhouses and barns, move produce, and maintain the flour mills and ironworks that dotted the countryside—the same population responsible for recent ethnic violence. Fearing the worst, the boundary commissioners warned Mason and Dixon that "as the public Peace and your own Security may greatly depend on the good Usage and kind Treatment of these [Iroquois] Deputies, we commit them to your particular Care, and recommend it to you in the most earnest Manner not only to use them well yourselves but to be careful that they receive no Abuse or ill treatment from the Men you may employ." Among other measures, Mason and Dixon would have to limit the "spiritous Liquors to be given to the Indians . . . [to] small quantities mixed with water and delivered to them not more than three times every day." We are, once again, left with very little about the astronomers' reaction. But the course of the survey suggests that, for a time anyway, Mason and Dixon showed themselves to be astute leaders of their multiracial party. For most of the summer, the expedition, now including a fourteen-person Iroquois delegation and its interpreter, Pennsylvania fur trader Hugh Crawford, moved westward without incident.[14]

That would end on Saturday, September 12. After crossing the Cheat River, on what is now the West Virginia–Pennsylvania boundary, two Mohawk members of the Iroquois delegation demanded the survey be stopped. The journal gives no reason for the Mohawks' actions. They may have assumed the surveyors had exceeded their mandate. The Cheat River put Mason and Dixon's party about eleven miles west of Maryland's western boundary, first established in 1746 by a Virginia surveying party that included Peter Jefferson, father of Thomas. Given that the Iroquois had so frequently clashed with settlers claiming to be Virginians, the Mohawks may have assumed that in following the surveyors into Virginia, they placed themselves at grave personal risk.[15]

For unknown reasons the Mohawks were overruled, and the party continued its work until September 29, when the surveyors and their escorts prepared to cross the Monongahela River. Twenty-nine laborers and tradesmen refused to proceed across the river. They would not, they explained, enter country still controlled by Delawares and Shawnees. These laboring men feared that the official business of colonial governments, even with the sanction of the Six Nations, offered no protection in Indian country. Other than noting that he and Dixon managed to persuade fifteen axemen to remain with the party, Mason says nothing more of the episode, but it was a clear indication that, at the farthest western reaches of the Line, the colonial proprietors' plan to partition large swaths of the North American continent was beginning to fray.

A few weeks after crossing the Monongahela, the remaining members of the party approached Dunkard Creek, named for a nearby village destroyed during an Indian raid in 1755. The warpath established by the 1744 Lancaster Treaty (and replacing the Susquehanna Valley as the Iroquois's primary southerly route) ran along the east side of the creek. The surveyors pressed on for another day until a leader of the Iroquois delegation informed them that the Six Nations Council had identified the warpath as the surveying party's western terminus—a point the boundary commissioners seem to have missed. The survey would go no further, and on October 10, 1767, at the West Line's 232nd mile, thirty-one miles short of its intended end point, Mason and Dixon completed their boundary survey. This end point now lies just off present-day I-79 between Morgantown, West Virginia, and Waynesburg, Pennsylvania.[16]

Mason and Dixon led their party back toward the eastern seaboard, spending the next month building stone and earth mounds to secure the wooden mileposts marking the mountainous western reaches of the Line. The eastern portion of the Line, to milepost 135, near Sideling Creek and west of present-day Hancock, Maryland, had been marked with limestone monuments imported from England and placed at two-mile intervals. Most

Original Crown Stone, showing the Calvert family crest. 1907 photo.
Image 5072, Box 4, Records Relating to Commonwealth Boundaries (Series #17.394), RG-17, Records of the Land Office, Pennsylvania State Archives, Harrisburg.

Original Crown Stone, showing the Penn family crest. 1907 photo.
Image 4555, Box 4, Records Relating to Commonwealth Boundaries (Series #17.394), RG-17, Records of the Land Office; Pennsylvania State Archives, Harrisburg.

of the stones bore a simple "M" on one side and a "P" on the opposite; at five-mile intervals the surveyors placed more elaborate crown stones, bearing the Penn family crest on the Pennsylvania and Delaware sides, the Calvert family crest on the Maryland side. The stones were too cumbersome to haul deep into the mountains, but for the rest of Mason and Dixon's lines, they would stand, English-made monuments to the astronomers and laborers who cut their way through the mid-Atlantic woodlands.[17]

The Proclamation of 1763, issued by King George III in October, must be regarded as among the most futile and ill-conceived royal decrees ever issued by a British monarch. The partition it established had been designed to separate Britain's new continental empire into an eastern half, occupied primarily by Euro-American colonists, and a western half, to be the domain of Native peoples—separating the natives and strangers of Charles Mason's

British America. Colonists would be allowed to travel to the west side of that line, but only as merchants and fur traders. Land purchases and settlement would be permitted only when conducted under the auspices of British imperial and military officials, a group far more concerned with maintaining peace in Indian country than with satisfying settlers' appetite for new lands.

The trans-Appalachian west would in effect become a new kind of royal colony, secured by British military personnel and freed from the internecine racial violence of the borderlands. The British government may have hoped Ohio country Indians would see in this gesture an act of goodwill, worthy of a great and benevolent king. But colonists would ensure that any hope for such an outcome proved stunningly naive.

During the years Mason and Dixon made their way west, the futility of the proclamation had become clear to all. Settlers paid little attention to the king's partition, and colonial officials, charged with securing Ohio country Indians against the settlers' onslaught, threw their hands up in exasperation. The chief British agent for Ohio country (and William Johnson's deputy), a fur trader named George Croghan, complained to Franklin in a 1768 letter that the hunting grounds of the Ohio country Indians had been "shamefully encroached on, and no notice has been taken of the *Agreement*" establishing the line. What could Ohio country Natives conclude but that, "as we [Britons] have conquered the French, we intend to . . . possess their Country, without paying them for it?" Croghan was well aware that Franklin, then serving as Pennsylvania's chief lobbyist to the British government, could do little to stop the westward flow of settlers, "but thus much give me leave to assure you, that if the Natives cannot be convinced of the Justice of the [British] Nation, by immediately confirming the Boundary with them, we shall soon be involved in the most general and distressing War with them, that America has ever felt."[18] Far from bringing peace, the Proclamation Line seemed certain to bring war. As the Iroquois delegation clearly recognized, the same was so for the Mason-Dixon Line. Most likely they also recognized that the danger of war was only heightened by the fact that these two newest British-imposed boundaries worked at profound cross-purposes. Mason and Dixon's line established that the Proclamation Line bisected the chartered claims of the colony of Pennsylvania. But according to the 1763 proclamation, this newly delineated Pennsylvania territory was in fact Crown territory, reserved for the king's Native subjects. Lord Hardwicke did not anticipate that his decision, addressing one jurisdictional conflict, would give rise to another, but that is precisely what happened. In a predictable turn of events, colonial officials found themselves groping for solutions to a new boundary problem. And once again those solutions involved forced relocations and the political manipulation of legal land claims.

A few weeks after Mason and Dixon established Pennsylvania's claims to the western Alleghany watershed, British officials asserted royal supremacy in the region and demanded that Governor Penn act against Pennsylvanians illegally living west of the Proclamation Line. The very fact that the settlers in question could be identified as Pennsylvanians was entirely a function of Mason and Dixon's work. Until the survey was completed, these settlers understood themselves to be Virginians, entitled to their lands under Virginia law. For royal officials, Mason and Dixon's line settled this jurisdictional question. Whatever the loyalties of the western settlers, they were now subject to the laws of Pennsylvania, and those laws obligated Pennsylvanians to adhere to British imperial law. By the terms of that law, these former Virginians were illegally living in Indian country.

In early January 1768, Governor Penn carried out his duty to ensure that all Pennsylvanians complied with Crown law. He asked the colonial assembly to endorse the removal of Pennsylvanians living near the convergence of the Monongahela and Cheat Rivers, an area through which Mason and Dixon's surveying party had passed a few months earlier. The action would be a bitter pill, but there was no alternative. "I must inform you," Penn explained to Pennsylvania's lawmakers, "those Settlements upon the Indian Lands to the Westward of the Alleghany Mountains, now appear, by the Line lately Run between Pennsylvania and Maryland, to be within the Bounds of this Province."[19]

In exchange for its support of the governor's plan, the assembly demanded that the Penns take bold action to secure peace in the west. Pennsylvania desperately needed a restoration of "the Government to its former Power and Dignity, lately so insolently trampled on," by those charged with, among other things, bringing the Paxton Boys to justice. For "should Crimes of the first Rank, of the deepest Dye, remain unpunished, Wicked men will never be wanting in any Country to take Advantage of the Times and the Debility of Government, to commit the like or other Crimes." As guardians of the

"Laws upon which the Honour and Dignity of the Government depend," the assemblymen explained to Governor Penn and his executive council, "we are pressed by the Strongest Motives to take this opportunity of earnestly intreating your Honour that diligent and Speedy Inquisition be made after those atrocious offenders who have stained the Land with innocent Blood and bid defiance to the Laws of their Country." What prompted this plea, beyond simmering frustration over the inept response to the massacres of the Conestogas, was news "that a Number of Senecas has been lately killed on the Frontiers of this and the neighboring Provinces." While the assembly still had few details, it was clear that the killers were settlers, probably residing in territory known to fall under the jurisdiction of Pennsylvania. As details of the murders trickled east, the province would discover that it now confronted a second murderous rampage worthy of the Paxton Boys. Governor Penn had failed to apprehend one band of murderers, an obvious insult to the colony's Native neighbors. He could not now repeat that grave error.[20]

On this, the assembly and the governor were in agreement. Something needed to be done to bring order to the far western borderlands. As to how the problem was to be addressed, there was very little agreement. Until governance could be established in Pennsylvania's borderlands—and for the assembly, governance meant above all the proper punishment of murderous Indian haters—the forcible removal of illegal settlers would accomplish little. Governor Penn, meanwhile, pressured by Johnson and the British general Thomas Gage and legally bound by the king's recent Proclamation Line, could see no option but removal, even if removal of illegal settlers further impeded any quest to bring frontier vigilantes to justice.

A few days after Governor Penn presented the assembly with his removal plan, the colony's executive council received news of yet another massacre in far northern Cumberland County. Frederick Stump, a German settler, and his servant Hans Eisenhauer, known locally as John Ironcutter, had murdered ten Natives, including several children. The circumstances of the killings were familiar enough: Stump, already well known for his theft of Indian lands, received six Indian visitors, including Cornelius, locally known as the White Mingo. There was much drinking, and Stump, who claimed the party grew belligerent and refused to leave his home, turned on his guests. He dumped the six bodies in a nearby creek. Fearing that news of the murders would provoke retaliations, Stump and Ironcutter traveled fourteen miles to the Indians' village. They found two cabins occupied by one woman, two girls, and a very young child, perhaps a baby; the two Pennsylvanians murdered them all and burned the village.[21]

Penn's government would have to act decisively if it had any hope of retaining credibility with the assembly, with Gage and Johnson, and with an Iroquois Confederacy that remained, for the moment, the colony's only Native ally. William Patterson, a former militia captain responsible for the murder of three innocent Moravian Indians, apprehended Stump and Ironcutter, earning himself a £200 bounty and buying the government some time. Hoping that an old pattern could be reversed and Indian-killers would finally be punished, authorities requested that Stump and Ironcutter be transferred from Carlisle to Philadelphia, but John Armstrong, the local magistrate, rejected the request, claiming extradition would endanger the prisoners' escorts. In fact, Armstrong feared the political consequences of acting against Stump and Ironcutter. For locals, sympathy clearly rested with the accused. While Armstrong fought the murderers' extradition, a group of eighty westerners, reportedly including some of the original Paxton Boys, freed the Indian-killers.

Governor Penn now found himself with precisely the political problem he sought to avoid. New reassurances meant little to his colony's Native neighbors without condolence payments—£2,500 paid to the Six Nations, the Delawares, and the Shawnees—but those payments, precisely the kinds of gifts the Paxton Boys and other frontier rebels decried, only exacerbated the alienation of his colony's western settlers. The Quaker-dominated assembly had little compunction about exploiting the governor's predicament, lambasting him not only for his inability to bring Stump and Ironcutter to justice but also, he reported, "for neglecting the Duties of my Station, relative to the Murders committed" at Lancaster.[22]

Johnson and his Ohio country deputy Croghan reassured Penn that his gifts calmed the fears of the Iroquois and the Ohio country Indians, at least for the moment. But in an ominous coda, Johnson noted that "to remove their discontent totally, when we consider the Nature and Number of their Grievances, was more than could possibly be done." The reality, as Johnson surely recognized, was that whatever the intent of Governor Penn's diplomacy, Pennsylvania's far western borderlands remained almost completely detached from the colony's central governing authority. Penn's western agents, the county magistrates, the sheriffs, justices of the peace, and others loyal to the government were no match for the overwhelming frustrations of western settlers. And now some of those same settlers faced the prospect of forced relocation.[23]

By late February 1768, Penn managed to extract from his colony's assembly begrudging approval of a proclamation that "any Person or Persons, settled upon any Lands within the Boundaries of this Province, not purchased of the Indians by the Proprietaries thereof," who failed to permanently vacate those lands within thirty days, "shall suffer Death without the Benefit of Clergy." Western officials were no more willing or able to enforce the Governor's order than to bring Indian-killers to justice. But what stunned colonial authorities was the reaction of local Indians. On April 2, after visiting the illegal Pennsylvania settlements, totaling about 150 families, western officials reported that local Natives viewed expulsion of the settlers as preparation for Indian war.[24]

An Iroquois delegation sent to Fort Pitt refused to intervene on Governor Penn's behalf. The expulsion of white settlers, they explained to Penn's representatives, "was a Matter which no Indians could with any satisfaction be concerned in." It was "for the English themselves to compel their own people to remove from Indian Lands." In fact, the delegation's position was more subtle than this summary suggested. The problem, according to Keyashuta, a leader of the Six Nations delegation, was that the Iroquois had as little faith in the power of Pennsylvania's government as did white frontier settlers. Even if illegal settlements could be removed, the removal would surely be temporary. Pennsylvania's government would eventually conclude treaty arrangements allowing the exiles to return, and a government unable to bring Indian-killers to justice would be unable to contain any residual hatred resulting from Iroquois participation in settler expulsion.[25]

The whole affair was yet one more fiasco for the proprietary government and one more demonstration of the futility of boundary making in the borderlands. Although the impetus for relocating settlers was established by Mason and Dixon's line, efforts to implement policy confirmed that, in fact, the Line meant very little to those living along it.

In October 1768, Governor Penn sent a delegation to meet with the council of the Iroquois League at Fort Stanwix in New York. After lengthy negotiations and a payment of £10,000, the delegation persuaded the council to deed to the Penn brothers all remaining Iroquois lands within the bounds of Pennsylvania. For Governor Penn, the land transfer was an enormous victory, not because it afforded his family free access to tens of thousands of acres of new land but because it resolved the conundrum of his colony's far-western settlers. The Fort Stanwix Treaty moved the boundary between Indian country and Pennsylvania west to the Ohio River. The squatters and their Indian allies at the far western end of Mason and Dixon's line were now fully and unambiguously subject to the laws of Pennsylvania, at least as far as the Iroquois and the British government were concerned. Removing illegal settlers, and the political costs that would have entailed, would be something Governor Penn could consign to the policy dustbin. But with this great gift came a new crisis.

As part of the transfer of territory, the Iroquois ceded to Pennsylvania the former Delaware lands in the Wyoming Valley, along the North Branch of the Susquehanna River. The region had long been contested, not only by its former Lenape inhabitants but also by Connecticut land speculators who believed that, according to Connecticut's 1662 charter and a 1754 Albany Treaty, those lands were Connecticut lands. Aware that these speculators had, with the blessing of the Connecticut assembly, organized themselves into the Susquehanna Company for the purpose of claiming the Wyoming Valley, Governor Penn took urgent countermeasures. By December 1768, he had authorized the creation of a series of new proprietary manors. Through the usual combination of favorable leases and tax deferrals, the governor and his land agent, James Tilghman, tried to do in the Wyoming Valley what their predecessors had done in the Maryland-Pennsylvania borderlands: stop foreign settlers by offering steeply discounted lands to Penn family loyalists.

As a fiscal matter, the scheme failed in familiar ways. Tax breaks and lax leasing policies meant that, for all the expense of surveying and distributing the new lands, the Penn family would earn very little to defray the costs of security in the area. As a political matter, the scheme also failed in familiar ways. Rushing to counter the danger from Connecticut, Tilghman sold enormous tracts, too spread out to support flour mills, let alone the kinds of market and mill towns that could muster a reasonable defense of sparse frontier settlements. A tax collector who traveled to the area warned Governor Penn's uncle Thomas, co-proprietor along with the governor's father, that, finding an absence of towns in which to market their produce and find refuge

in the event of renewed frontier violence, settlers would surely abandon the region for "Virginia, first converting their Effects into Money and carrying that with them, thereby promoting the present scarcity of Money and impoverishment" in Pennsylvania. So infuriated were westerners with the absence of commercial and governmental resources that some allied themselves with the Susquehanna Company. Governor Penn begged Gage to intervene, but the British general feared losing his force to colonial civil war. Encouraged by disgruntled Pennsylvania frontiersmen, by 1774 some two thousand Connecticut-sponsored settlers claimed Wyoming Valley lands under the auspices of the Susquehanna Company. What the Penns gained along the Line they lost in the Wyoming Valley.[26]

Mason and Dixon spent their final winter in Pennsylvania making astronomical observations, mostly to verify their measurements of the terrestrial length of latitude. They also prepared a map of their Line for the Reverend Richard Peters, secretary of Governor Penn. The manuscript map was made in two large

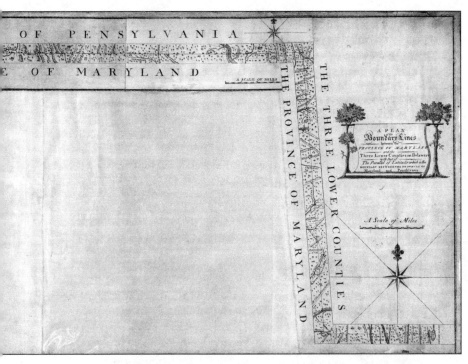

"A plan of the west line or parallel of latitude, which is the boundary between the provinces of Maryland and Pensylvania: a plan of the boundary lines between the province of Maryland and the Three Lower Counties on Delaware with part of the parallel of latitude which is the boundary between the provinces of Maryland and Pennsylvania," James Smither and Robert Kennedy, from Charles Mason and Jeremiah Dixon, Philadelphia, 1768. Assembled here as a single map, the 1768 engraving of Mason and Dixon's strip map was printed on two sheets, the eastern portion on one and the West Line, in three parts, on another. The map's western edge leaves little doubt that Mason and Dixon's work remained unfinished.
Library of Congress, Geography and Map Division.

sheets, one showing the West Line, the other the Maryland, Pennsylvania, and Delaware boundaries. The West Line section consists of six sheets of rag paper, six and a half feet in length and six and three-quarters inches in width. The map's eastern portion, depicting the meridian line and the Transpeninsular Line, is roughly two feet by one and a half feet; both are carefully titled, with delicate cartouches and the signatures of the map makers, "Cha: Mason Jere: Dixon." Not long after the maps were finished, Philadelphia engraver James Smither and Printer Robert Kennedy produced printed versions.

The maps are remarkable in a number of ways—their detail, their evident accuracy, the painstaking mapping of geodesic findings. But perhaps the maps' most unusual quality is their overall form. Mason and Dixon confined their cartography to the three miles on either side of the boundary. Theirs was, in the narrowest sense, a map of the Lower Counties–Maryland–Pennsylvania borderlands. The map shows that Maryland had been fully delineated from the Lower Counties and Pennsylvania; it shows a small portion of the curve that separated the Lower Counties from Pennsylvania, but that had not been part of the astronomers' commission. And it places the end of the West Line just across a bend in Dunkard Creek, at mile 230, two miles east of where the surveying party ended its work. The map's detail ends at Dunkard Creek, but Mason and Dixon carried the edges of their six-mile-wide map to the end of the paper, leaving an unmistakable void where the survey ended.[27]

In the months after finishing the map the astronomers finalized their American measurements, and in early September they returned to England. After presenting their American astronomical findings to the Royal Society, Britain's premier scientific organization, Mason and Dixon accepted new commissions to gather observations for a second transit of Venus. Mason was sent to Londonderry and Dixon, in the company of William Bayley, assistant to Astronomer Royal Nevil Maskelyne, traveled to North Cape at what is now the far northern tip of Norway.

After completing his observations, Jeremiah Dixon returned to the place of his birth, Durham County, to work as a surveyor, mostly in the employ of John Edgerton, lord bishop and lord palatine of Durham. Dixon appears never to have married and died at Cockfield, County Durham, in January 1779, aged forty-six. He was buried at the Society of Friends Burial Ground in Staindrop, Durham County.

Charles Mason continued to work as an astronomer. During the 1770s, he worked for the Royal Society, exploring variations in gravitational force on the earth's surface. But most of his time was spent working for Maskelyne and the Board of Longitude, producing standardized lunar tables and star maps for calculating longitude. Mason's work for the board appeared in Maskelyne's *Nautical Almanac*, first published in 1765, but continuing in print to the present day. For thirty years after its initial publication, the *Almanac*'s acknowledgments recognized Mason's contributions, but during his lifetime Mason's earnings from the tables totaled only £850, nowhere near what he needed to support his growing family.

After the American Revolutionary War, Mason took a post surveying loyalist land grants near Halifax, Nova Scotia. In September 1786, with his second wife, Mary, seven sons, and a daughter, he and the family left Halifax for Philadelphia, home to two influential acquaintances of Mason's, Benjamin Franklin and the instrument maker and astronomer David Rittenhouse. Mason died a month after his arrival and was buried at the Christ Church burial ground in Philadelphia. Mason's widow and their children remained in Philadelphia for several years, destitute and longing to return to England. In 1790, Mary petitioned the new American president, George Washington, "through humanity, and respect for the memory of a good man, who spent his life-time in promoting useful knowledge," to provide financial aid for the devoted astronomer's struggling widow and children. There is no evidence Washington responded, but the family was eventually able to return to England, where Mary lived off Mason's meager back pay from the Board of Longitude.[28]

PART III

A BORDER EMERGES

Mason and Dixon's work brought an end to the Maryland-Pennsylvania boundary dispute, but it hardly brought an end to conflict in the Line's borderlands. Anti-Indian violence continued into the 1790s. For settlers along the Line, the continued unrest was of a piece with government's continued failure. Continuity in borderlands politics did not accompany continuity in the region's economy. The rise of a new, more accessible market in Baltimore transformed the Mason-Dixon Line borderlands into one of the most productive agricultural regions in the world. That agricultural productivity generated collateral investment in manufacturing and infrastructure, and by the 1820s, greater Baltimore was among the most heavily industrialized regions of the United States. Although the transformation of the regional economy gave the Line the appearance of an innocuous boundary between states, by the early nineteenth century few Americans of African descent would view the Line that way.

CHAPTER 7

The Making of States, Free and Slave

AS WAR RAGED TO THE WEST, John Woolman, a Quaker shop owner, tailor, scrivener, and antislavery activist from West Jersey, began a tour of the southern colonies. Woolman's purpose was to reinforce a message he had begun propagating among American Friends more than a decade earlier: the holding of human beings in bondage could not be justified by scripture or any spiritual tenet of Quakerism. Woolman would bring his message to Quakers in Maryland, Virginia, and North Carolina. Among Friends in West Jersey and Pennsylvania, Woolman's views were well known, and many had begun embracing his antislavery message. But southern Friends remained to be converted. Earlier trips south, in 1746 and 1748, met mostly with indifference, although some Friends accepted an evangelical call to treat slaveholding as a path to Christian conversion. But of the southern slaveholding Quakers, very few had been prepared to challenge the morality of slavery, let alone give up their own human property.

Woolman had assembled his views on slavery as *Some Considerations on the Keeping of Negroes* and eventually published the tract under the auspices of the Philadelphia Friends Yearly Meeting. The timing was not ideal. Woolman had no way to know this when he submitted his manuscript to the Friends in 1754, but the pamphlet would appear during some of the most violent years of the French and Indian War. As Pennsylvanians turned on the colony's Quaker elite, a Friend's righteous condemnation of slavery would find few proponents beyond the small circle of antislavery Friends. For Woolman, neither the war nor the views of Pennsylvanians were material. What mattered was the fact that his fellow religionists kept human beings in bondage. So long as that was the case, so long as Quakers themselves tolerated the horrid trade in enslaved human beings, the biblical under-pinnings of the Society of Friends would be at risk. There was simply no way the Friends could claim any kind of unifying, common doctrine when so many members sanctioned a clear outrage against that doctrine.

As the war continued its bloody march through the lives of western Penn-sylvanians, Woolman took his antislavery message south. Traveling along some of the same roads Witham Marshe had traveled thirteen years earlier, Woolman and his brother Uriah, who was traveling south for business, crossed the Susquehanna River to its western shore at Lower Susquehanna Ferry, now Havre de Grace, Maryland. Although Woolman's purpose was to save southern Friends for true Quakerism, his crossing of the Pennsylvania-Maryland boundary reminded him—in the starkest terms—of just how daunting that task would be. The objects of his message lived in a society so far gone, so morally desiccated, and so entwined with the corrupting insti-tution of chattel slavery that liberating them from the effects of unchristian bondage would require redemption on a scale far greater than that afforded even by the abolition of slavery. "Soon after I entered this province [of Maryland]," Woolman recalled, "a deep and painful exercise came upon me." The source of the feeling, Woolman explained, was the fact that "the people in this and the Southern Provinces live much on the labor of slaves, many of whom are used hardly." With heart and voice "of the true Shepard," Woolman intended to bring to meetings of southern Friends the message that "conduct is more convincing than language, and where people, by their actions, manifest that the slave-trade is not so disagreeable to their princi-ples but that it may be encouraged, there is not a sound uniting with some Friends who visit them." Between Maryland's slaveholding Quakers and their nonslaveholding coreligionists, in other words, the normal silence of quietist Quakerism suggested something very different from the enveloping spirit of divinity. It suggested deep and troubling doctrinal division.

Woolman found this state of affairs overwhelming and struggled to pre-serve his own inner godliness. As a wandering apostle, traveling with little more than a message of Christian charity, he depended on his Quaker hosts for room and board, but in Maryland this practice, so ordinary a part of

Quaker charity, fed a deep sense of dread. Woolman could not rightfully take gifts of food and shelter from the owners of slaves, but neither could he fulfill his apostolic plan without relying on the network of southern Quakers who provided for him during his travels. A man of worldly affairs as much as a man of faith, Woolman settled on a simple material solution to this deep and perplexing spiritual conundrum. He resolved to leave his slave-owning hosts prized silver coins, to be given to "such of their negroes as they believed would make the best use of them."

As a means of easing his conscience, Woolman confided in his journal, the paying of slaves, especially through their often wealthy and indolent masters, "was a trial to both me" and the slaves' masters, who, confronted with Woolman's strange payments, bristled at so obvious a violation of the laws of slavery. "But the fear of the Lord so covered me at times that my way was made easier than I expected; and few, if any," of Woolman's slaveholding hosts "manifested any resentment at the offer, and most of them, after some conversation, accepted." Money may have eased the moral burdens of travel in Maryland, but it hardly erased them. For that, Woolman still needed his faith. "From the time of my entering Maryland," he noted, "I have been much under sorrow, which of late so increased upon me that my mind was almost overwhelmed, and I may say with the Psalmist, 'In my distress I called upon the Lord, and cried to my God,' who, in infinite goodness, looked upon my affliction, and in my private retirement sent the Comforter for my relief, for which I humbly bless his holy name."[1] The payment of slaveholders in the hope they would pay their slaves, Woolman was telling his reader, was a small price for the very worthy aim of saving the Society of Friends from its pact with slavery.

That Woolman, the Jerseyan who entered Maryland by way of Pennsylvania, should have been thrown into such profound moral consternation by crossing into an adjoining colony is important, but perhaps not for the reason he suggests. Woolman would have us believe that when he entered Maryland, the specter of slavery hung over him in the way it would decades later, as whites and African Americans traversed the Mason-Dixon Line. But whatever Woolman may have felt about the boundary between Maryland and Pennsylvania, the reality was in fact very different. Nowhere in the lands adjoining the boundary were there any substantial restrictions on the owning of enslaved human beings. The provinces of Maryland, Pennsylvania, and the Lower Counties all tolerated slavery and the slave trade, and while slavery may have been the foundation of Maryland's extensive tidewater economy, that fact did little to differentiate its borderlands from those of its northern neighbor.

··

By 1750, Pennsylvania and the Lower Counties were home to more than eight thousand slaves, more than two-thirds of whom lived in the Lower Counties. (Woolman's own Jerseys were home to well over five thousand.) In Maryland, the numbers were much higher. In 1750, more than forty thousand slaves lived in the colony, but the vast majority remained in southern tidewater counties, where 40 to 50 percent of the population was enslaved. In the Lower Counties, where slaves constituted a much higher percentage of the population than in Pennsylvania, they still were only 20 percent of the total.[2]

Woolman knew there were slaves in Pennsylvania, not to mention in his home province of West Jersey; he surely knew that compared to tidewater Maryland, there were many fewer slaves in northern and western Maryland. He also surely knew there remained slave owners among the Friends of the Delaware Valley. What is important about Woolman's account, then, is not its intimations about a boundary between slavery and freedom but the fact that it presumes any clear boundary between Maryland and Pennsylvania at all.[3]

Woolman's sense of the boundary was not unique. For decades, travelers had remarked on the stark contrast between Maryland and the provinces to the north. Dr. Alexander Hamilton, a Scottish physician who migrated to Annapolis in 1739, traveled to New Castle in the Lower Counties, which he understood to be a town in Pennsylvania—and he was, technically, correct. While enjoying the comforts of Curtis's, an inn and ordinary, Hamilton met three Pennsylvanians returning to their homes after conducting some business at the Maryland land office in Annapolis. What Hamilton learned was for Woolman an inviolable truth: Maryland was very different. The problem was not slavery but something more general and ambient, something about the social order of the colony. One could not cross from Pennsylvania or its consort colony, the Lower Counties, without an acute sense of descending the scale of civility. As they ambled through their chatty breakfast with Hamilton, one of the Pennsylvanians, offended by the landlady's mistaking him for a common laborer, replaced his woolen nightcap with a clean linen one and announced that now "I'm upon the borders of Pensylvania and must look like a gentleman; 'tother was good enough for Maryland, and damn my blood if ever I come into that rascally province again." This Pennsylvanian's perspective was shared by his fellow travelers. Maryland was, they all agreed, a place of "immorality, drunkenness, rudeness and immoderate swearing." In Pennsylvania "no such vices were to be found." Hamilton did not disagree. He knew this characterization of Marylanders' manners "was pretty true," although he had little knowledge of Pennsylvanians beyond his encounter with a few of them at New Castle. When the discussion turned to matters economic, Hamilton had to dissent. The Pennsylvanians believed the soil in their province was "far more productive of pasturage and grain." This Hamilton dismissed; he well knew the boundary between the two colonies corresponded to no natural or topographical divide. Whether Marylanders' manners differed from those of Pennsylvanians, the doctor could not say. But what was clear was that Maryland elicited disdain from its northern visitors.[4]

Given the starkness of the transition—the sudden onset of dread and foreboding with the crossing from Pennsylvania into Maryland—it is hard not to conclude that Woolman's reaction reflected this kind of age-old chauvinism. An intuitive eighteenth-century social science allowed Woolman to conclude that whatever was wrong with Maryland was attributable to an especially evil form of unfree labor. This meant that, for him, there was no separating the moral entanglements of slavery from the society that sanctioned those entanglements. Woolman's perspective afforded no nuance. To cross from Pennsylvania into the deeply corrupted Maryland was to experience, in a weird and metaphysical kind of way, the dark specter of slavery.

The point is that well before Mason and Dixon had accurately mapped the Maryland-Pennsylvania boundary, it carried deep significance as a dividing line—despite almost a century of evidence that in fact the Maryland-Pennsylvania borderlands were far more united than they were divided. As Hamilton seemed to sense, whatever it was that divided Maryland from Pennsylvania would have been difficult to discern until one descended past the mouth of the Susquehanna River to the complex of waterways through which colonial North America's tobacco crop made its way to market.

Neither the French and Indian War nor the Mason-Dixon Line did much to alter these demographic and economic facts. By the mid-1770s, the distribution of enslaved populations had changed very little, although the total numbers of slaves had risen, more or less proportionately, throughout the mid-Atlantic and upper southern colonies. The borderlands remained the breadbasket of British America, a place of family farms, where sons, daughters, wives, and mothers labored alongside servants and the occasional slave, but the region was not shaped in any obvious way by the institution of slavery. In the terms formulated by historian Ira Berlin, the borderlands were societies with slaves, but they were not slave societies.[5]

Beginning in the mid-1770s, the perception that the crossing of the Mason-Dixon Line involved much more than the transit from one British province to another would receive new and far-reaching credence. The campaign begun by Woolman and his coreligionists would accelerate, as radical proponents of constitutional reform adopted fundamental tenets of Quaker antislavery doctrine. These tenets would become settled law when, in 1780, the Pennsylvania House of Representatives passed the Act for the Gradual Abolition of Slavery, the Western world's first statutory act of abolition.[6] For the first time, the boundary line created by Charles Mason and Jeremiah Dixon came to resemble in law what the likes of Woolman long claimed it to be: a line between slavery and freedom. But, as with just about every assumption related to the Mason-Dixon Line or any other geopolitical demarcation, even this one demands qualification.

The Gradual Abolition Act's passage did not abolish slavery in Pennsylvania, nor did it alter the nature of slavery in the borderlands. Insofar as the act transformed Pennsylvania into a "free" state, it did so slowly and haltingly. Decades would pass before a traveler, otherwise uninformed, would have reason to conclude that in crossing the Line she crossed from a free state to a slave state. If anything, the Revolutionary War and subsequent economic change did far more to unify the borderlands than to divide them. Nonetheless, if Pennsylvania's Act for the Gradual Abolition of Slavery did not quite transform the Line into a boundary between freedom and slavery, it did transform the Line into a boundary between a legal regime largely tolerant of the enslavement of human beings and one that, at least by statute, was the least tolerant of human bondage of all the new American states. For this reason, any understanding of exactly how the Line came to be a line between slavery and freedom must begin with the story of why Pennsylvania enacted such a law and why Maryland and the state of Delaware, as the Lower Counties declared themselves after independence, did not.

While there is no denying the relative radicalism of Pennsylvania's Gradual Abolition Act, the other border states' failure to enact comparable antislavery legislation suggests a legal and political divide far more reflective of hindsight than historical reality. Although Quaker antislavery activists and their non-Quaker allies enacted a sweeping antislavery law, what separated Pennsylvania from Delaware and Maryland was not antislavery sentiment. Quaker activists, including Woolman and Delaware antislavery crusader Warner Mifflin, made great strides in both Maryland and Delaware. By the mid-1780s, they had placed gradual abolition bills before both states' legislatures. Neither bill was ultimately enacted, but support for both extended well beyond Quaker antislavery circles. Within a few years of these legislative initiatives, both Maryland and Delaware had become home to influential nondenominational abolition societies.[7]

Further, insofar as antislavery sentiment along the Line had any persistence, it did so as much because of the growth of Quaker altruism as because that altruism aligned with the economic interests of the colonies' wealthiest merchants and planters. This was as evident in Pennsylvania as it was in Maryland and Delaware. Antislavery reform was a dynamic and powerful political force in the borderlands; so too was proslavery opposition to that reform. In some sense, the terms "antislavery" and "proslavery" suggest a clearer and more readily definable set of public positions than partisans in debates over slavery actually assumed. Supporters of measures designed to curtail or even eliminate slavery did not necessarily support a Quaker-like absolute moral condemnation of slavery, just as opponents of those measures were not necessarily indifferent to the immorality of slavery. But a brief survey of so complex a topic necessitates a bit of shorthand. Imperfect though the terms are, "antislavery" and "proslavery" are more or less in line with convention: the one denoting ideals and advocacy directed toward the constraint and ending of slavery, the other directed toward the preservation of a status quo more than any sort of coherent ideological defense of the institution of slavery. The limits of terminology aside, what is clear is that in the half century following the completion of the Line, antislavery and proslavery sentiment coexisted in roughly equal measure throughout the Mason-Dixon borderlands.

Delaware was perhaps most emblematic of this coexistence of antislavery and proslavery sentiment. Before the general surge of antislavery activism swept state legislatures during and after the Revolutionary War, the Lower Counties had begun following their Quaker minority. In late March 1775, a few weeks before the outbreak of war at Lexington Green, the assembly passed a bill banning the importation of slaves. The gesture was, on its face, modest. In prohibiting the introduction of new slaves, it secured the value of existing slaves. Similar restrictions had been attempted in other colonies, mostly through the imposition of prohibitive duties on slave imports, but some colonies also attempted more sweeping statutory prohibitions. In 1760, South Carolina's assembly banned slave imports, more out of fear of slave rebellion than any principled opposition to slavery. Political allies of British slave traders ultimately forced South Carolina's governor to veto the measure. In the early 1770s, driven by similar imperial policy, royal governors also vetoed antislavery measures in Massachusetts and New York.

For Pennsylvania's governor, John Penn, still the governor of the former Lower Counties, the Delaware Assembly's prohibition raised some very difficult political questions. Hoping for reconciliation between the revolting colonies and the mother country, a prospect that also meant the preservation of his family's American income, Penn had no interest in a measure that would needlessly provoke British authorities. For the same reason, he had no interest in a legislative act that would strengthen the hand of Pennsylvania's growing antislavery movement, a movement whose push for duties on slave imports had succeeded in raising a prohibitive duty of £10 per imported slave (enacted in 1761) to £20 in 1773 (though the Board of Trade rejected the new duty). Penn's veto of the Lower Counties' slave trade prohibition was thus pure politics, but it had the effect of suppressing antislavery legislation. In a familiar pattern, lawmakers in colonies and states with proslavery governors and significant proslavery populations made great show of their support for antislavery measures that had practically no chance of passage. In the Lower Counties, however, the assembly's 1775 prohibition cannot be written off as mere political theater.

With the Revolutionary collapse of proprietary governance, Delaware lost no time overturning Penn's veto. Its new state constitution, which also instituted the name of "the Delaware State" and was ratified in 1776, banned the importation of slaves for commercial purposes. Immigrants could still bring their enslaved property into the state and, technically, citizens of the state could sell slaves to one another. But "no person hereafter imported into this State from Africa ought to be held in slavery . . . and no negro, Indian, or Mulatto slave ought to be brought into this State, for sale, from any part of the world." In 1787, Delaware enacted a series of additional antislavery laws meant to further restrict the importation and exportation of slaves. Anyone who brought a slave into the state, no matter the slave's origins, for the purpose of selling that slave, would face a substantial fine, and the slave would be deemed free. The export of slaves for sale required the approval of three justices of the peace, later increased to five. Any violation of the law brought a £100 penalty. Perhaps most important, the new laws liberalized manumission regulations by abolishing the requirement that any slave owner provide county governments a £60 bond of indemnity for any manumitted slave between the ages of eighteen and thirty-five. Slave owners would now bear no statutory cost for freeing working-age slaves.[8]

While slavery remained legal in Delaware, the effect of these measures was to substantially weaken the institution. Between 1770 and 1810, the number of Blacks in the state declined by 75 percent. By 1810, a higher percentage of Delaware's remaining Black population was free than was the case in either New Jersey or New York, both of which had by that time passed acts for the gradual abolition of slavery. A combination of seasonal agriculture and the absence of a dominant slave-trading mercantile interest accounts for the lack of sustained opposition to the restriction of the slave trade and the liberalization of manumission laws. Age-old proslavery claims that, in freeing enslaved people, slave owners shifted the burden of care to the public, or that they impinged on public safety by freeing a population inclined to incite rebellion among the still enslaved, carried little weight in a state whose economy relied so little on slave labor. Between 1790 and 1810, the proportion of enslaved people in Delaware's total population fell from 15 percent to 5 percent, while the population of free Blacks more than tripled, from 3,899 to 13,136. In short, although antislavery activists failed to abolish slavery in Delaware, they succeeded in vastly reducing the numbers of enslaved Delawareans. That reduction, at least in terms of the numbers, looked very much like the decline of slavery in states with gradual abolition laws. "In the absence of state-mandated abolition," historian Patience Essah notes, "Delaware slave owners voluntarily fashioned a successful gradual abolition system." The long-term result of these actions was that "by the Civil War slavery in Delaware was a totally defunct institution."[9]

The story of antislavery legislation in Maryland was very similar, if the economic backdrop was very different. In 1771, the colony raised the long-standing tax on imported slaves to a prohibitive £9 per slave, and in 1783, the new state legislature enacted a full ban on the importation of slaves. In 1790, the Maryland legislature overturned a 1752 statute that had strictly limited voluntary manumissions. Now, slave owners could free slaves in their last will and testament, provided there were no liens on the estate and the formerly enslaved were still able-bodied and of a laboring age. The provision, it should be said, was hardly a great act of altruism. Echoing long-made claims that manumission was used by slave owners to offload the burden of caring for old or infirm slaves onto the public, Maryland prohibited manumission of older slaves or slaves otherwise unable to labor, much like Delaware.

In addition, in 1796, the state enacted laws sanctioning the long-standing practice of deeded manumission, which turned enslaved persons into so-called term slaves: it guaranteed future manumission, provided an array of stringent conditions were met. The latter included full compliance with masters and the payment of various fees—in effect, the return of earnings to the master. In theory, the laws were meant to limit the expense of manumission while allowing slaves to purchase their own freedom. In practice, they resulted in a cruel new form of bound labor. The terms of the deeds and the conditions that made them legally binding—the deeds had to be notarized by two witnesses and a justice of the peace and had to be registered with county courts within six months of their activation—were cumbersome and provided plenty of opportunity for abuse by corrupt officials or financially strapped slave owners. Because the terms of the contracts depended on good behavior and productivity, both of which would be determined mostly by the slave's master, the lure of freedom became an effective means of maximizing labor output while minimizing the various financial risks associated with slavery, including the flight of slave property and resistance to slave labor regimes, either of which would violate the terms of the deed.[10]

Despite the exploitation enabled by term slavery, the liberalization of Maryland's manumission laws had the effect of greatly expanding the number of free Blacks in the state. In 1790, Frederick County was home to nearly four thousand Blacks; only 213 of them were free. By 1850, the total number of Blacks in the county had more than doubled and 50 percent were free.[11] The numbers for the rest of the state show a similar pattern. Between 1790 and 1810, Maryland's free Black population grew fourfold, while the state's enslaved population grew by only about 1 percent. In 1790, Maryland's population of free Blacks was second-highest in the country, trailing only

Virginia. By 1810, there were more free Blacks in Maryland than in any other state—a ranking the state would retain until the Civil War. By 1850, of all states in which slavery remained legal, Maryland followed only Delaware in the percentage of its Black population who were free, although the gap in total percentage in the two states was substantial. More than half of Marylanders of African descent remained enslaved, while in Delaware the number was only slightly over 11 percent—totals of 90,368 and 2,290, respectively. In Virginia, nearly 90 percent of the Black population—almost 500,000 people—remained enslaved.[12]

These numbers point to Maryland's slow and incomplete detachment from the plantation economy of the Chesapeake. From 90 percent of Maryland's total agricultural production in 1747, tobacco fell to 14 percent by the eve of the Civil War. With these agricultural changes came familiar changes in the labor market. Wage and contract labor remained dominant in the state's expanding grain-producing regions. For reasons historians still do not fully understand, Maryland's southernmost counties, meanwhile, remained dependent on enslaved laborers. These areas did continue to produce tobacco, but in ever smaller amounts and with ever narrower margins. During the War for Independence and the French Revolutionary Wars in the 1790s, tobacco exports declined to almost zero, forcing many of even the most intrepid tidewater planters to turn to less lucrative but also less labor-intensive crops. And yet slavery persisted on tidewater plantations.

Part of the reason may lie in the relative concentration of enslaved African Americans—a far higher concentration than elsewhere in Maryland, and a ready rationale for the common refrain that manumissions would encourage rebellion or expand the ranks of the indigent. Exploiting these tired canards, state representatives from Maryland's southern counties could be expected to oppose most antislavery legislation. This politically driven opposition to antislavery laws took on a new life after the conclusion of the War of 1812. The market value of Maryland's enslaved population increased with the rise of the nineteenth-century internal slave trade and the forced removal of tens of thousands of enslaved African Americans from the Upper South to the Cotton Belt. In sum, although slavery persisted in Maryland, it did so at the margins of what would become one of the most economically dynamic states in the Union. In the words of Barbara Jeanne Fields, "In southern Maryland and on the Eastern Shore, slavery shambled along in the lengthening shadow of isolation."[13]

That a slave state could also be a state in which slavery occupied an increasingly marginal part of the labor economy is illustrated by the views of Luther Martin, a graduate of the College of New Jersey (later Princeton University) who had moved to Maryland to practice law. An ardent patriot and long-serving attorney general of Maryland, Martin was also elected to the state's delegation to the national Constitutional Convention in Philadelphia. He possessed none of the qualities that would mark him as a partisan in debates over slavery. He was not Quaker, and although he was known to have owned as many as six slaves in 1790, he was not a tidewater planter. He lived in Baltimore Town, and what agricultural land he owned was mostly in northern Baltimore and Anne Arundel Counties. Though the racial politics of the mid-Atlantic provided for endless and fascinating alignments, there was no necessary connection between opponents of slavery and opponents of other kinds of racialized brutality. Nonetheless, it is worth observing that Martin was related by marriage to Maryland's most famous Indian-haters. His wife, Elizabeth, was the granddaughter of Thomas Cresap and the daughter of Cresap's son Michael, known mostly for his role in the barbarous 1774 massacre of the family of Logan, a Mingo headman and trader. Martin was not an Indian-hater, but he was Maryland's most prominent opponent of a new federal constitution, partly on the grounds that it was a fundamentally proslavery charter.

Weeks of debate over the issue of representation in a new federal congress concluded in the summer of 1787 with the infamous three-fifths compromise. In exchange for the right to include three-fifths of their enslaved populations when determining total population for apportionment of seats in the House of Representatives, southerners agreed to allow Congress to end the transatlantic slave trade after 1808. A furious and dejected Martin condemned the compromise as "*a solemn mockery of,* and *insult to . . . God*" and an insult that gave the slave trade "a *national sanction* and *encouragement.*" Those who endorsed the proposed federal charter did so "to the *displeasure* and *vengeance of Him,* who is equally Lord of all, and who views with equal eye the poor *African slave* and his *American master.*"[14] Ultimately, though, the problem was more political than moral. Early in the Constitutional Convention, Martin had called for a constitutional ban on slave imports, but he was rebuked by John Rutledge of South Carolina and several northern delegates fearful of alienating the most pro-slavery state. Northerners' political cravenness, in Martin's view, was emblematic of a problem the Constitution would enshrine in law.

Summarizing his concerns for the assemblymen of his home state, Martin noted that whatever the status of Maryland's slaves, representation proportional to population favored "the states which have large and extensive territory . . . Since it is the states of extensive territory, who will most speedily increase the number of their inhabitants . . . and will therefore, most speedily procure an increase to the number of their delegates." Maryland and other states with no vague western easement would suffer, while the expansive southern states of "Virginia, North Carolina, or Georgia, by obtaining one hundred and twenty thousand additional inhabitants, will be entitled to four additional delegates." That these states would soon eclipse Maryland, confined as it was by its old colonial boundaries, was all the more galling because slave imports would bring expanded legislative representation. The whole arrangement was a political outrage and an affront to good conscience. In words worthy of John Woolman, Martin implored his colleagues in the Maryland legislature to recognize that their state had been presented with a new federal compact in which "those states who have restrained or prohibited the importation of slaves" will now be unwitting parties "to that detestable and iniquitous traffic" precisely because they were prepared to be signatories to a national compact that clearly and obviously encouraged the importation of slaves. Self-interested Marylanders would surely be "desirous to share in the benefits arising from [the slave trade] and the odium attending it will be greatly effaced by the sanction which is given to it by the general government." The new federal Constitution would be an unqualified disaster for Maryland.

Martin's crusade was ultimately unsuccessful. Maryland became the seventh state to ratify the new US Constitution. Martin may have been sincere in his hatred of slavery and the slave trade, but in a state with a substantial Quaker population and an economy ever more reliant on free labor, opposition to the slave trade represented the politically expedient position. To oppose the slave trade was to appease opponents of slavery without alienating slave owners, who long presumed an inverse correlation of supply and price when it came to slaves. Opposition to the slave trade carried the added benefit of its association with American patriotism. Because Britain and its merchants were routinely accused by patriot propagandists of controlling the transatlantic slave trade, opposition to the trade was akin to opposing trade in tea, textiles, and assorted other British goods. For Martin to oppose the new federal Constitution because it sanctioned the slave trade was thus a politically shrewd posture, precisely because it could draw the support of both antislavery and proslavery Marylanders. Other than the fact that, for all his moral outrage, he was a slave owner, there is little to suggest Martin was engaged in such subterfuge. But, much as was the case throughout the borderlands, the coexistence of pro- and antislavery views among white Marylanders makes it difficult to separate the purely political from the righteously moral. Opposition to the institution mingled with political and economic expediency to create an ideological synthesis that often looks more like neglect and indifference than the sort of outright partisanship exemplified by Martin. That indifference was entirely compatible with an institution in obvious but slow and halting decline.[15]

John Woolman's second antislavery mission to the southern colonies occurred after the outbreak of the French and Indian War, a period that witnessed the most significant expansion of borderlands slavery to date. Farmers, servants, and laborers joined local and colonial militias, forcing farm owners and other producers to seek an alternative labor source. Many turned to slavery. Between 1750 and 1760, Pennsylvania's slave population grew by more than 50 percent, or about 1,500 individual bondspeople. Between 1760 and 1770, it grew by another 28 percent or about 1,200, to a total enslaved population of 5,561. As an overall percentage of Pennsylvania's population, these numbers marked no substantial change. Between 1750 and 1780, Pennsylvania's slave population never exceeded 2.4 percent of the state's total, a paltry number compared to Delaware's, which had a higher number of slaves overall, and whose slave population was almost 20 percent of the state's total population in 1780. Nonetheless, 1762 represented the apex of the African slave trade to Pennsylvania. As a percentage of Pennsylvania's overall population, the number of slaves imported into the colony had been higher earlier in the eighteenth century. But in terms of total numbers of Pennsylvania slaves, the early 1760s were the unquestionable peak. In 1762, more than five hundred African-born slaves were brought up the Delaware River, most to be disembarked in the Philadelphia area.[16]

The growth of slavery in Pennsylvania would slow to a trickle during the Revolutionary War and end forever in 1780, but given new prohibitive import duties and the collapse of much transoceanic trade, there is no way to know how much of the slowdown was due to ideology and how much to economic reality. Most likely both were factors, but neither suggests the ultimate triumph that would come in 1780. In fact, along with the growth of antislavery sentiment, the Revolutionary War years still saw growth in the number of enslaved Pennsylvanians—albeit at a much slower rate than during Pennsylvania's previous war. Natural growth in conjunction with a small number of slaves brought into the state raised the number from fewer than six thousand in 1770 to nearly seven thousand in 1780, an increase in the state's slave population of about 23 percent. Had Pennsylvania remained loyal to King George III, as a powerful and perhaps even predominant part of its population had hoped it would, and had its farmers and merchants been able to continue the importation of enslaved Africans, the number would surely have been much higher.

Perhaps more illuminating than Pennsylvania's overall slave numbers are shifts in the geography of slavery. While the state's slave population grew between 1775 and 1780, the number of slaves in Philadelphia fell by 25 percent, from 728 to 539. The number of free Blacks in the city, meanwhile, more than doubled, from 114 to 241. Some of this change may be attributable to continued pressure from within the Society of Friends, pressure that coalesced after the Philadelphia Yearly Meeting formally required any remaining slaveholding members to free their human property. The number of Philadelphia's Quaker manumitters during the Revolutionary War years far exceeded the numbers of manumitters from all other denominations combined. But Quaker manumissions come nowhere near accounting for the full decline in Philadelphia's slave population. For that, the labor market provides a better answer. A prohibitive duty on imported slaves combined with a wartime reduction in the number of ships calling at Philadelphia would mean only one thing for the price of enslaved Africans. As Philadelphia's existing slave population aged, died, was sold, or ran away (some finding refuge with the British military as enlistees or protected loyalists), the city's former slave owners turned to alternative labor sources. Despite this rapid decline of slavery in Philadelphia, the overall slave population of Pennsylvania grew. During the years of the Revolutionary War, Pennsylvania slavery acquired a distinctly rural cast.[17]

Data compiled by Gary B. Nash and Jean R. Soderlund show exactly this shift. Before the war, about a fourth of Pennsylvania's slaves lived in Philadelphia; by 1780, fewer than 10 percent lived there. In Chester and Philadelphia

Counties, in the eastern part of the state, slave populations declined, although at a significantly slower rate than in the city of Philadelphia. But in counties farther west, especially those counties along the West Line, the story is very different. Lancaster County experienced an eightfold increase between 1759 and 1780. In York County, the exact number of slaves in the decade before the war is unknown, but what evidence there is suggests the number was very small, if not negligible. By 1780, the county's slave population was approaching eight hundred. Slavery's shift from urban to rural and from eastern to western Pennsylvania would continue in the decades after the Revolutionary War. By 1810, insofar as slavery existed in Pennsylvania, it was a decidedly rural and western institution. It was also a decidedly borderlands institution. As Nash and Soderlund have written, "Slaveowners in western Chester, Lancaster, York, Cumberland, Westmoreland, and Washington counties—all located along the border with Maryland and Virginia—held their slaves most persistently." By 1790, well after Pennsylvania mandated gradual abolition, these counties accounted for about 44 percent of Pennsylvania's total population, but they accounted for about three-fourths of the state's slaves, or around twenty-eight hundred bondspeople.[18]

This geographic trend—slavery's move from a predominantly urban institution to a predominantly rural and western one—does not reveal the full story of slavery's distribution in Revolutionary Pennsylvania. Although the period saw an expansion of slavery in the borderlands counties, that expansion is notable only in comparison to trends elsewhere in Pennsylvania. In both absolute numbers and as a percentage of the region's total population, slavery's borderlands presence remained negligible, and grew more so in the latter decades of the eighteenth century. By 1790, barely more than 1 percent of the populations of Lancaster and York Counties, or about a thousand people, were enslaved; by 1810, that number had fallen by 80 percent, to about two hundred individuals. In those two original western borderlands counties, slavery's demographic profile was not all that different from what prevailed in Pennsylvania's eastern counties. There was growth, but it was minimal, and with gradual abolition that growth very quickly turned to decline. But here again, the numbers do not capture the full story in Pennsylvania's borderlands. The relative stasis of slavery in Pennsylvania's Susquehanna counties was not replicated in the state's newest counties, particularly in the far southwestern corner, an area that until 1780 was still claimed by Virginia. During and immediately after the Revolutionary War, as migrants from Virginia settled in what became Washington, Fayette, Westmoreland, and Allegheny Counties, the slave population grew dramatically. By 1780, 1,140 slaves lived in these far southwestern borderlands counties, most brought from Virginia. As Pennsylvania's gradual abolition law took hold, the numbers declined, and by 1790, 834 lived there. But the western slave population remained significant. It constituted about 22 percent of Pennsylvania's total slave population and around 1.3 percent of the region's total population.[19]

Changes in the distribution of the state's slaves do not change the overall story of slavery in Revolutionary Pennsylvania. Much as in Delaware and northern Maryland, it was very much an institution in decline. And while that decline owed much to wartime trade interruptions and Pennsylvania's prohibitive antislavery import duties, developments in the state's far west suggest that interstate migration explains why that decline was not more precipitous. Following the passage of the Gradual Abolition Act and the completion of the westernmost end of the Line in 1784, far southwestern Pennsylvania came to look more or less like the rest of the borderlands, at least as far as slavery was concerned. Freedom for enslaved Pennsylvanians did not arrive without struggle, whatever the law said. Insofar as Pennsylvania's slave owners paid any fealty to the law, they did so in the loosest and most self-interested possible manner, devising a host of favorable forms of term servitude that effectively allowed them to retain the labor of their bondspeople, often for decades. The absence of slavery in the borderlands did not mean the absence of unfree labor.[20]

Much as in Delaware and Maryland, the population of free Blacks in Pennsylvania grew exponentially during the second half of the eighteenth century, with most of the growth coming after 1780. Between 1775 and 1790, Philadelphia's free Black population increased by a factor of sixteen. By 1800, free Blacks constituted almost 9 percent of the city's total population, a fourfold increase after 1780. The eastern countryside experienced similar demographic shifts. Thirty-six free Blacks lived in Chester County in 1765. By 1780, the number had risen to 137, and by the turn of the century it had risen to nearly 1800, or about 4 percent of the county's total population.[21]

This overview suggests an institution in decline well before the passage of Pennsylvania's abolition act. But it does not suggest an institution nearing extinction. The Act for the Gradual Abolition of Slavery took aim at a weakened and increasingly isolated segment of Pennsylvania's labor market. It did this in a state where slaves had always represented a tiny percentage of the state's overall labor force—tinier by a substantial margin than even in neighboring northern states New York and New Jersey. In 1780, New York's slave population was nearly three times Pennsylvania's; New Jersey, which had less than half Pennsylvania's total population, had a slave population about 30 percent larger than Pennsylvania's. In this sense, then, it is not surprising that of the three borderlands states, Pennsylvania enacted gradual abolition. Unlike Delaware and Maryland, it was home to very few heavily invested slave owners, and those who remained were too few in relative numbers to constitute a substantial political threat to gradual abolition. There were Pennsylvanians opposed to abolition, some slave owners, some not, much as there were proslavery Delawareans and Marylanders, not to mention New Yorkers and New Jerseyans. And in all of these other states, proslavery voices coalesced to defeat early calls for abolition. New York, which saw potent calls for abolition as early as 1777, failed to enact gradual abolition until 1799; New Jersey, long home to a vocal antislavery movement, only passed a gradual abolition act in 1804.[22]

Of the three states adjoining the Mason-Dixon Line, and perhaps even of all the new American states outside of New England, in sum, the political economy of slavery made Pennsylvania uniquely hospitable to abolitionism. Given the zeal of its Quaker antislavery activists—in 1776, the Philadelphia Yearly Meeting issued directives to all Delaware Valley Quaker meetings requiring them to follow its example in banning slave owners from membership—and the weakness of the institution they attacked, slavery seemed destined to fall in Pennsylvania. And yet, after independence, it took four years for Pennsylvania to make the ideal of gradual abolition into law. As would be the case through slavery's long history, the politics of the matter developed a kind of life of its own. Far from a direct path to abolition, that politics followed a crooked route through Pennsylvania's revolution, a route that made abolition, even of the cautious, incremental sort Pennsylvania eventually enacted, anything but a foregone conclusion. In a typical and frustrating paradox of Pennsylvania politics, the developments that account for abolition's slow progress were the same ones that ultimately made gradual abolition at all feasible. The politics of slavery in Revolutionary Pennsylvania is a story of steps forward and back, and it is a story driven as much by antislavery sentiment as by strenuously persistent pro-slavery sentiment.

....

The path to gradual abolition began with the reconstitution of Pennsylvania's government. Owing to a radical faction of pro-independence partisans, Pennsylvania's first state constitution, enacted in September 1776, was by far the most democratic of Revolutionary America's new state constitutions. Never before or since would Abraham Lincoln's glorious Gettysburg Address phrase "government of the people, by the people, for the people" be more aptly applied to an American frame of government. To a degree seen in no other state, the popularly elected representative branch of Pennsylvania's government was to be predominant. The new state of Pennsylvania would have a unicameral assembly, with no meaningful checks on its lawmaking powers. A supreme Executive Council would have twelve elected members, one of whom would be selected to serve as the council's president. The council would have assorted executive powers to appoint civil and military officers, enforce law, conduct interstate diplomacy, engage in judicial proceedings, and initiate legislation. But the new frame of government denied this upper chamber veto power, the executive's age-old legislative tool. Other states also abolished executive veto, but only in Pennsylvania was that assault on executive power combined with unicameralism, the abolition of property qualifications for officeholding, and some of revolutionary America's least restrictive voting requirements.[23]

Gone from the Pennsylvania constitution was any vestige of the old Anglo-American mixed constitutionalism, with some version of king, people, and landed aristocracy coming together as a balanced and glorious governing whole. To its defenders, the new charter was a model for the American republic. In doing away with the outrageous humbug that was mixed government, the framers of Pennsylvania's constitution had done away with governing interests "separate and distinct from, and inconsistent with, the general welfare of the people." In the words of Thomas Paine, a recent English immigrant to Pennsylvania who, more than any other, popularized the theoretical underpinnings for Pennsylvania's radical constitutionalism, in place of the unitary and independent executive office, the lawmaking branch of government should be "managed by a select number chosen from the whole body, who are supposed to have the same concerns at stake which those have who appointed them, and will act in the same manner as the whole body would act were they present." Powerful executives and quasi-aristocratic upper houses merely distorted this fundamental form of good government and contradicted nature's maxim that "the more simple any thing is, the less liable it is to be disordered, and the easier repaired when disordered."[24]

In the eyes of its many critics, including such ardent champions of independence as John Adams of Massachusetts, Pennsylvania's constitution represented a monstrous perversion of the most basic principles of good governance. Paine's idea of republican government, Adams noted in his *Autobiography*, was "without any restraint or even an Attempt at any Equilibrium, or Counterpoise," and would surely produce nothing but "confusion and every Evil Work." Reducing government to a single elected tribunal simply promoted, in Adams's view, "systems of anarchy." In the view of one appalled observer, Pennsylvania's new frame of government represented nothing but "an execrable democracy—a beast without a head." No government "with only one legislative branch," another wrote, "yet failed to end in tyranny." As defenders and critics acknowledged, with so much power concentrated in one branch of government, by design those factions who controlled the new state assembly controlled the state. Should that faction coalesce around any particular reform, it was thus very likely to be enacted.[25]

In addition to elevating to supremacy a single representative branch of government, Pennsylvania's constitution required annual elections, imposed term limits on assemblymen, established provisions for the public review of all assembly business, and broadened Pennsylvania's franchise to include all tax-paying men over twenty-one years of age. Since virtually any male head of household would be required to pay at least a poll tax and since adult sons of taxpayers retained voting rights but were exempted from the poll tax, of the state's adult men only apprentices, slaves (free Blacks who met the qualification could in fact vote), and paupers would be denied the vote. That women, the enslaved, the destitute, and anyone who refused to pledge allegiance to the new government were denied the vote in an eighteenth-century polity is not particularly surprising. More striking is the fact that the new charter would offer only the most modest correction for another disenfranchised group, western Pennsylvanians.[26]

As had been the case before independence, this regional political imbalance was entirely by design. With independence, the intention was not so much to preserve the power of a heavily urban Quaker-mercantile elite and their eastern English-speaking allies.[27] Rather, the intention was to preserve the power of a new patriot coalition, also mostly urban and eastern, led by a core group of Philadelphia mechanics, artisans, and professionals, many of whom had been introduced to popular politics through their service in assorted public safety committees and militias. In addition to their ardent patriotism and their conviction that military service justified a voice in government, what unified this new Revolutionary governing faction were two articles of faith: first, an abiding hostility to an old order dominated alternately by wealthy Quaker merchants and by a fickle, shapeshifting pro-proprietary faction; and, second, a deep hostility to the old feudal maxim that land is power. These two precepts were obviously closely aligned. In an early draft of the declaration of rights to be prepended to the state's new constitution, the framers asserted that "an enormous Proportion of Property vested in a few Individuals is dangerous to the Rights, and destructive of the Common Happiness, of Mankind." Republican government, at least as it was construed by the mostly urban radicals who claimed control of Pennsylvania in the Revolution's early days, would have no place for those vestiges of landed privilege so long defended by the Penns and their court enablers. Any quasi-aristocratic upper house or executive agent of some rent-taking British lord would be forever banished. In addition to those old and familiar targets, in its hostility to the representation of property, urban republicanism also took aim at those independent yeoman farmers immortalized in Thomas Jefferson's celebrated agrarian republicanism. Urban producers as much as rural farmers, the makers and sellers of things along with the originators and sellers of agricultural produce, would have equal standing in the new republic of Pennsylvania.[28]

In drawing power away from its traditional landed custodians and affirming the citizenship of Philadelphia's urban artisans and professionals, Pennsylvania's republican government may have been designed to achieve a fairer distribution of governing authority, but in the frenzied push for constitutional reform, this high-minded ambition meant that Pennsylvania's new and very different governing order ended up looking very much like the old in at least one critical respect.

The 1776 state constitution apportioned six representatives each to Pennsylvania's eleven counties and the city of Philadelphia. After a regular census, the first of which would be conducted two years after the adoption of the new charter, counties would adjust the number of representatives to reflect their respective populations. The constitution's framers left to the assembly the details of precisely how this was to be done. But the implications of a system based on proportional representation were unmistakable. With Pennsylvania's taxpaying population still concentrated in eastern counties, including the city of Philadelphia, the state's most populous regions would be its most powerful—much as had been the case in the colonial era. By 1780, of the seventy-two House members, forty-nine hailed from counties east of the Susquehanna. Of those forty-nine, five came from Philadelphia alone; another nine from the surrounding county. Bedford and Westmoreland, the farthest western counties, sent two and three representatives, respectively. Furthermore, because it apportioned representatives in proportion to the number of taxable inhabitants, and because slaves paid no tax, Pennsylvania's new constitution ensured that slavery and political power would never align, especially since the state's remaining slaveholders were so heavily concentrated in its sparsely settled western borderlands.[29]

A constitution favorable to antislavery interests was far from an antislavery constitution. The framers of the Pennsylvania constitution included no provisions to abolish or further restrict slavery in the state. Exactly why this is so, given the prevalence of antislavery activism and the close alliance of urban republican and antislavery interests, may have been just another price to be paid for jurisdictional confusion. While the constitution's framers were surely aware that slavery was an increasingly western phenomenon, they had no way of knowing the full extent of slavery's westward drift. Because Mason and Dixon had been unable to complete the Western Line, much of Westmoreland County, an area increasingly populated by Virginians and their slaves, remained unincorporated. The framers of Pennsylvania's constitution could never have known that this sparsely settled and distant area, eventually incorporated as Washington and Fayette Counties, would have some of Pennsylvania's highest concentrations of bondspeople. That Pennsylvania's constitution says nothing about slavery, in other words, may simply reflect the framers' assumption that the aims of Pennsylvania's antislavery activists were already being fulfilled. By all accounts, slavery in Pennsylvania was in decline.

Almost two years passed after ratification of the new state constitution before the first bill for gradual abolition came before the state assembly. That measure went nowhere. A second bill, proposed in November 1778, received slightly more attention, and the following year the House established a committee to draft a gradual abolition bill. After a series of preliminary votes, the bill became law on March 1, 1780.

The absence of any antislavery language in the state's constitution and the nearly four years it took to pass sweeping antislavery legislation suggest that even after the creation of a governing system ideally designed to facilitate the statutory end of slavery, abolition still faced formidable political barriers. The precise nature of those barriers is not entirely clear. The best available evidence for lawmakers' position on abolition remains their votes on the gradual abolition bill. These indicate a great deal of division over the act, but beyond that, they say very little. Thirty-four assembly members voted in favor; twenty-one were opposed. There is some indication that opponents included antislavery representatives who found the final bill too weak, but otherwise there is little to suggest a clear pattern among opponents of the bill. Some but not all opponents were slaveholders; some but not all came from areas with relatively large concentrations of slaves. The same held true for the bill's supporters. A personal connection to slavery seems to indicate nothing about a lawmaker's position on the bill. Even the expected east-west separation is difficult to discern. Although most of the opposition to the bill came from western representatives, the majority of representatives from Berks County, in the east, opposed the bill, as did nearly half of those from Philadelphia County. Similarly, the representatives from the west's Bedford County supported the bill, while those from Westmoreland County did not.[30]

One possible explanation for some of the haphazardness in voting is that, as would be the case with any initiative requiring intervention from local magistrates, this bill created an immediate vested interest that had nothing to do with slavery. Local court clerks would be entitled to charge fees to slaveholders who, under the new act, were required to register their human property. For a western magistrate such as John Agnew, clerk of the Court of Sessions for Cumberland County, the profiteering could be substantial. Agnew registered dozens of slaves, and profited accordingly. Such venality surely violated Pennsylvania's constitution and its prohibition on profiting from public office. Income from any office that "through an increase of fees or otherwise becomes so profitable as to occasion many to apply for it" was to be reviewed by the state assembly. Opponents of the act may thus have rejected it not because they were proponents of slavery but because some of the act's provisions appeared contrary to the republican spirit of the 1776 constitution.[31]

The absence of any clear demarcation between opponents and supporters of the act may have also been a reflection of the aims of the act. It was, un-questionably, an antislavery measure—the most forceful passed by any state to date. But in comparison to what the most ardent antislavery activists sought, it was an astonishingly limp gesture. As Nash and Soderlund observe, "the law freed not a single slave" and the "total abolition of slavery would not come to Pennsylvania . . . until 1847." Not unlike the antislavery pro-visions enacted by Maryland and Delaware, Pennsylvania's celebrated act was sufficiently weak to provide coverage for advocates on both sides of Pennsylvania's slavery debate. For slavery's opponents, the act included a rousing call to relieve "the sorrows of those who have lived in undeserved bondage." It prohibited the importation and sale of slaves within the state, and it granted freedom—after a twenty-eight-year term of indentured servitude—to all children born to a slave mother after the act's passage.

As a means of distinguishing between those children born before the act's passage and those born after, slave owners were required to register all slaves with local authorities such as Agnew. Those who failed to comply within eight months of the act's passage would forfeit their enslaved prop-erty. The act also granted all African American Pennsylvanians, slave or free, nearly full recognition in the state's courts, with one notable exception: enslaved Pennsylvanians would still be unable to testify against whites—a near universal provision of colonial slave codes. In some ways, granting Blacks access to the courts was the act's most important antislavery provi-sion. In the decades after the act's passage, dozens of Black Pennsylvanians now illegally held in bondage successfully sued for their freedom.[32]

At the same time, and in near total deference to the property rights of slave owners, the act avoided any intimation of forced manumissions. Children born to enslaved mothers before the date of the act's passage would remain enslaved, whether they were born decades earlier or the day before the act's passage, and those born after would still be given no right to the fruits of their own labor until well into adulthood. These measures would mean the persistence of slavery in Pennsylvania for the better part of two generations and ensured that children of slaves became a lower caste. Insofar as the act involved any forced manumissions, it did so only as a negative sanction, directed at those slaveholders who failed to comply with new registration requirements. While the courts were often sympathetic to slaves who claimed their freedom on the basis of masters' noncompliance, enforcement of the registration requirement was lax and slave owners routinely evaded the law by transferring ownership of slaves to relatives and business associates in other states.

In addition, the act offered no help for sojourning slaves brought into the state by travelers, seafarers, foreign diplomats, or delegates to Congress, which normally met in Philadelphia. As long as these slaves were not sold or held in Pennsylvania for more than six months, the state would fully acknowledge their owners' rights to property in human beings. For those enslaved Americans crossing the Line from Maryland or Delaware into Pennsylvania, in other words, the act changed nothing. Movement among the border states would be as it had always been: mostly unregulated and indifferent to the institution of slavery. What would be true for slaves legally transported across the Line would also be true for those illegally transported.

Should a slave from an adjoining state seek refuge in antislavery Pennsylvania, she would find no such thing: "this act or any thing in it contained shall not give any relief or shelter to any absconding or runaway Negro or Mulatto slave or servant," and the owner of any runaway "shall have like right and aid to demand, claim and take away his slave or servant, as he might have had in case this act had not been made." The same logic applied to runaways from Pennsylvania, seafaring slaves, or any other slave who, for some extenuating reason, had not been registered with authorities. Absence would not confer freedom. As long as these enslaved Pennsylvanians were registered within five years, their status would be unchanged.

In sum, as bold a gesture as gradual abolition was, for enslaved Pennsylvanians and their children the act changed very little at all, at least in the short term. In the longer term, the act had far-reaching consequences, the most important of which was the expansion of Pennsylvania's antislavery movement. Although the movement remained a heavily Quaker one, new political fights elicited by the act drew an important new constituency to the movement: Pennsylvania's growing free Black community.[33]

Among the most important of these new fights centered on the act's sole provision for forced manumissions—namely, that slave owners who failed to register slave property would forfeit that property. The act's opponents argued that registering enslaved property was often difficult if not impossible, especially for some of Pennsylvania's most remote slave owners. Their proposed solution was an extension of the registration deadline and the reenslavement of bondspeople unfairly and precipitously manumitted under the terms of the initial act. The ensuing campaign for these amendments became a call to action for free Blacks. One, writing in the Philadelphia *Freeman's Journal* under the pen name "Cato," a reference to the incorruptible Roman general and senator who stood in celebrated defiance of the dictatorial Julius Caesar, warned the state's lawmakers that "a law to hang us all, would be 'merciful,' when compared with" reenslavement, which would be the inevitable result of the reversal of forced manumission. "For many of our masters," Cato warned, "would treat us with unheard barbarity, for daring to take advantage (as we have done) of the law made in our favor." Cato's plea represents the leading edge of what would become a driving force in Philadelphia's antislavery coalition. Antislavery activism in Pennsylvania would henceforth be an unmistakably multiracial campaign. It would also be a far better organized, better funded, and more influential campaign than it had ever been, counting among its first victories defeat of the anti-forced-manumissions initiative.[34]

The institutional center of Pennsylvania's antislavery movement was the revitalized Society for the Relief of Free Negroes Unlawfully Held in Bondage, eventually renamed the Pennsylvania Society for Promoting the Abolition of Slavery (PAS). The PAS provided legal support for Black Pennsylvanians seeking liberation from enslavement and pushed for new laws to strengthen the original 1780 act. Its efforts were rewarded in 1788 when the state assembly enacted a series of additional antislavery measures. These represented an unalloyed victory for Pennsylvania's antislavery campaigners, perhaps more unalloyed than even gradual abolition itself. Slave owners intending to reside in the state would no longer be given a six-month grace period to determine what to do with their enslaved property. Their slaves would be freed immediately upon the owner's assumption of residency. In addition, there would be a mandatory £75 fine for anyone attempting to remove any Black Pennsylvanian with the intention of selling her into slavery or term servitude elsewhere. For the forcible kidnapping of free Black Pennsylvanians with the intention of selling them into slavery, the new law imposed a stiffer £100 penalty. To further curtail the illegal export of Black children, it imposed new registration requirements for all Black children born after the passage of the 1780 act. Local authorities would henceforth have no doubt about the status of these children and, with their names and ages officially linked to masters, authorities would be equipped to monitor the movement of children and better enforce prohibitions on child smuggling. As a further means of discouraging the sale and export of slaves and term slaves, the act outlawed any transaction that separated family members by more than ten miles. The law also prohibited what had become one of the most pernicious practices under the original act: the transportation of pregnant slaves to proslavery states as a means of securing ownership of slaves' newborns.

Finally, after members of the PAS discovered that a Philadelphia shipyard had outfitted a ship for the slave trade, the society undertook a petition drive in support of legislation banning Pennsylvania shipbuilders from serving the trade. More than just closing loopholes in the 1780 act, this initiative represented a new front in the antislavery battle. The PAS was advocating direct sanctions on businesses with even a secondary connection to the slave trade. The campaign was a success. As stated in the 1788 amendment:

> If any person or persons shall build, fit, equip, man, or otherwise prepare any ship or vessel, within any port of this state, or shall cause any ship or other vessel to sail from any port of this state, for the purpose of carrying on a trade or traffic in slaves, to, from, or between Europe, Asia, Africa or America, or any places or countries whatever, or of transporting slaves to or from one port or place to another, in any part or parts of the world, such ship or vessel, her tackle, furniture, apparel, and other appurtenances, shall be forfeited to the commonwealth, and shall be liable to be seized and prosecuted.[35]

It is difficult to say how much the extension of Pennsylvania's antislavery law owed to Philadelphia's Black population. But pamphleteers such as Cato and well-known African American antislavery activists such as the Reverend Richard Allen, founder of the African Methodist Episcopal Church,

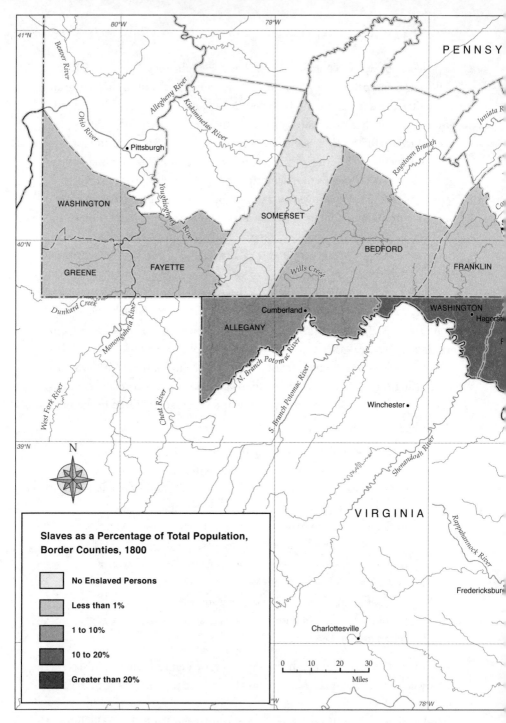

Slaves as a Percentage of Total Populations, Border Counties, 1800

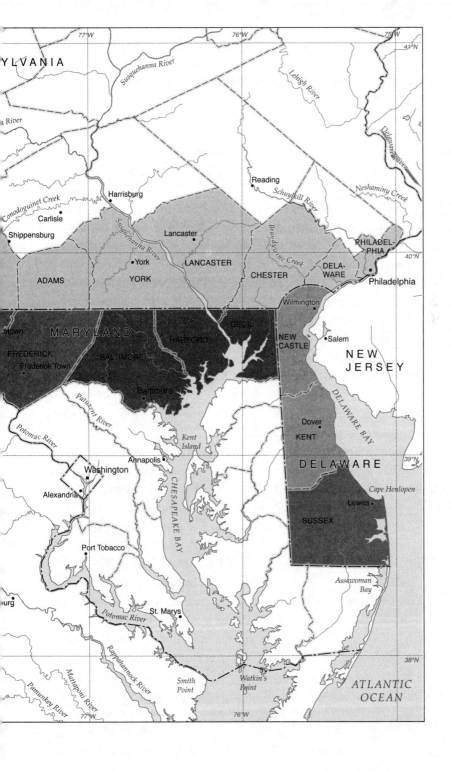

were only a few of the most vocal members of a growing Black antislavery movement.[36]

By 1790, a fifth of Pennsylvania's Black population lived in Philadelphia, still home to less than a tenth of the state's white population. The population of borderlands Blacks, meanwhile, changed very little. By 1820, the Black population had risen above 6 percent of total population in only the eastern-most border counties of Chester, Delaware, and Philadelphia. In the rest of Pennsylvania's border counties, the Black population grew at roughly the rate of the overall population and nowhere near the rate of the Black popula-tion of Philadelphia and its immediate environs. The growth of Philadelphia's Black population was partly a function of the urban migration of free Blacks and self-manumitted slaves. For some of these migrants, the Line between Maryland and Pennsylvania may have been seen as a line between slavery and freedom. But there is also abundant evidence that for many this was not the case—that Black migration near the Line had more to do with economic opportunity than with assumptions about Pennsylvania's antislavery legal order. Although Philadelphia was America's largest city until eclipsed by New York, Baltimore was the nation's fastest-growing. For colonial travelers, from Hamilton to Marshe and Woolman, Baltimore barely merited any com-ment at all. The town was nothing more than a clutch of shacks, "a scattered group of houses." By 1770, however, six thousand people lived there, nearly as many as lived in Newport, Rhode Island. By 1810, Baltimore had become the third-largest city in the United States; only Philadelphia and New York were larger.[37]

With Baltimore's overall growth came a commensurate growth in its Black population. In 1790, almost 1,600 of the city's 13,503 residents were Black. The vast majority of those—about 75 percent—were enslaved. By 1810, the city's Black population had reached more than ten thousand, and more than half were now free. Following the overall pattern of Maryland, Baltimore's slave population fell substantially as its population of free Blacks grew. Between 1810 and 1830, the city's free Black population nearly tripled, while its population of slaves fell by about 12 percent. By 1820, more than ten thousand free Blacks lived in Baltimore, only a few thousand fewer than lived in Philadelphia. When the free Black population is combined with the 4,357 slaves still living in the city, Baltimore's total Black population exceeded

Philadelphia's by about 10 percent, or more than a thousand people. Much as was the case in Pennsylvania, free Blacks seeking community and economic opportunity flocked to Maryland's most dynamic urban economy. And much as was the case in Philadelphia, the vast majority of those urban migrants came from the surrounding countryside. Although the number of slaves in rural Maryland counties declined at a much slower rate than in Pennsylvania, the number of free Blacks in those counties changed very little, while the number of free Blacks in Baltimore rose by a factor of more than six between 1800 and 1840.[38]

Baltimore's Blacks, both free and slave, faced a decidedly less egalitarian and just future than did their counterparts in Philadelphia. But in the late eighteenth and early nineteenth centuries, the fundamental legal differences between the two cities had only a marginal effect on the movement of Maryland's free Blacks. Many of them no doubt went north to Philadelphia, but many more chose to stay and make their way in a state where slavery remained legal. Much of the reason for this was family and kinship. Freed people often preferred to stay in a state and city where slavery remained legal than to leave close kin who remained enslaved. But of equal importance was economic opportunity. As free Black Marylanders weighed their economic prospects, many determined that the benefits offered by the booming city of Baltimore outweighed the many disadvantages of remaining in a slave state. Leaving the borderlands for the city, these Americans played a central role in the shaping of the Line. Not only did their migrations limit the growth of Black populations in Maryland's border counties, but they also enabled the primary development in the early nineteenth-century borderlands economy. Their labor contributed to Baltimore's emergence as the Upper South's primary port city. As much as Philadelphia had done in the prior century, Baltimore's rise would fuel new and unprecedented growth in the borderlands.

CHAPTER 8

Borderlands as Heartland

ALTHOUGH HE ALLIED himself with Philadelphia's antislavery partisans and may have had a hand in drafting the 1780 abolition act, the pamphleteer and revolutionary Thomas Paine did little to advance the cause of abolition. He was far more concerned for the survival of republican government itself. Without a firm constitutional foundation, one that secured in perpetuity the people's sovereign power, Paine believed, the achievements of the American Revolution would be for naught. Although Pennsylvania's unique governing structure did much to fend off enemies of republicanism, the new republican states still faced threats from landed interests, monied interests, and clerical interests. As the Revolution progressed, these threats revealed a new and very troubling truth. The very people on whom representative government depended appeared vulnerable to the manipulations of malignant antirepublican interests. If voters and their representatives could be deceived into thinking their interests were also those of self-serving elites, American republicanism's demise would be certain. Without institutional mechanisms to prevent destructive manipulations of the popular mind, the people would be lulled into complacency, and an old order of monarchs and empires, courtiers and placeholders, would rise again.

This hazard was endemic to all republics, but Paine's particular interpretation was nurtured in his adopted home province of Pennsylvania. He spent most of the war years in and around Philadelphia, and with the war's end, he continued his involvement in public affairs, mostly as a promoter of the fiscal policies of Robert Morris, superintendent of finance for the Continental Congress. As he and Morris surveyed the tumultuous financial landscape left by the Revolutionary War, Paine came to believe that perceptions of that landscape were dangerously divergent. He and Morris assumed that the survival of the republic of Pennsylvania, let alone the United States, would depend on Congress's ability to fund its wartime debt. But they also assumed that addressing that debt would mean a species of eighteenth-century austerity: to lower government borrowing costs, and perhaps even begin to retire public debt, Congress and the states would need to generate revenue through taxation.

Following prevailing monetary theory, Paine and Morris assumed taxes would have the desired effect on the costs of government debt only if they generated substantial hard money reserves. For the plan to work, in other words, the new republican governments of the United States would have to do precisely what the hated government of Great Britain had done for so long. They would have to require at least some tax payment to come in the form of gold and silver coinage, commodities that had only grown scarcer during the war years. In addition to expanding their hard money reserves through taxation, the new post-Revolutionary governments would have to ensure the stability of those reserves by controlling war-time inflation. With so much of the war financed by paper money, this would mean, above all, reducing the supply of often-depreciated paper currencies.[1]

One politician's anti-inflationary fiscal responsibility is another's austerity politics. The measures Morris and Paine promoted might have brought lower borrowing costs for the American states and Congress, but those same measures would raise borrowing costs for American farmers, mechanics, and other artisan manufacturers. A smaller money supply overall combined with a scarcity of hard money coinage would do what it had always done in the American colonies: it would push interest rates higher, apparently enriching creditors and leaving already struggling American borrowers facing compounding economic hardships. Having asked Americans to sacrifice so much on behalf of a war against unjust taxes, authorities could hardly ask them to bear a new, increased tax burden, especially as their creditors appeared to benefit from the fiscal effects of that tax burden. Traveling to Lancaster in 1783, German botanist and physician Johann David Schoepf encountered "much complaining over the burden of taxes"; in Frederick Town,

Maryland, "as everywhere, there is much and loud complaint over the scarcity of hard money and the publick imposts. . . . Many people absolutely cannot pay taxes, and still more have no desire to, until they are rigorously compelled."[2] With no means of rigorous compulsion, Morris and Paine had limited success in their attempts to correct the new nation's fiscal problems, but the basic tension their policy proposals revealed—between debtors, or those who saw anti-inflationary austerity as unjust, and creditors, or those who favored tighter fiscal control and anti-inflationary hard-money monetary policies—would be the single most important political divide facing the new United States. Congress's attempts to address its fiscal troubles without exacerbating that divide would lie behind a host of national reforms, from the Northwest Ordinance of 1787 to the eventual replacement of the Articles of Confederation with a new federal Constitution in 1789.

For Paine, political division born of fiscal policy remained, above all, a local problem, one that Pennsylvania's unique system of government only seemed to make worse. "Instead of that tranquility which [Pennsylvania] might have enjoyed, and instead of that internal prosperity which her independent situation put her in the power to possess," Paine explained to a friend in 1786, "she has suffered herself to be rent into factions." Paine had little hope that the state's current system of government would afford a way past the division. "The proceedings of the Legislature for these two years past," he continued, "are marked with such vehemence of party spirit and rancorous prejudice, that it is impossible any country can thrive or flourish under such manifest misconduct."

This rancorousness was partly a function of economic austerity. Pennsylvania's farmers and their representatives were no more amenable to higher taxes and costlier credit than their colonial predecessors had been. But to that source of disenchantment was added Pennsylvania's old east-west divide. For much of the eighteenth century, the prime driver of that sectionalism had been the belief that Pennsylvania's eastern interests placed their particular political and financial aims above westerners' security. During the course of the Revolutionary War, that east-west divide acquired a new and especially troubling source. Western Pennsylvanians had begun taking their business south to the region's fastest-growing city, with grave political consequences: "They are not only beyond the reach and circle of that commercial intercourse which takes place between all the counties on [the east side of] the Susquehanna and Philadelphia, but they are entirely within the circle of commerce belonging to another state, that of Balti-more." In Paine's America, there was no separating the political from the commercial. Could it be any wonder that Pennsylvanians "not affected by matters which operate within the old settled parts of the state" so readily dismissed the fiscal strictures propounded by the likes of the Philadelphians Thomas Paine and Robert Morris? Western Pennsylvanians' commercial prospects now depended on merchants with no interest in the welfare of the commonwealth of Pennsylvania. And in Paine's view, such a misalign-ment of commercial and political interests represented a profound threat to good government.

Although the story of Anglo-American government in eighteenth-century Pennsylvania had long been punctuated by backcountry disap-pointment, there was no question about the locus of that government. Like all empires, the empire of Pennsylvania had an imperial center, albeit one with few of the architectural trappings commonly associated with a great imperial city. Philadelphia had become precisely what William Penn had hoped it would become: the city through which the mid-Atlantic's trade flowed, and from which its government exercised even a very limited au-thority over an expanding hinterland. In the minds of liberal republicans such as Paine, that limited authority depended above all on the commercial links that tied Philadelphia's hinterlands to the city. But now the city's commer-cial primacy was being challenged. Although Pennsylvania's backcountry remained nominally governed from Philadelphia, its trade was moving to Baltimore. For Paine, the development could mean only one thing. Instead of bearing debts to Philadelphians, western Pennsylvanians would be in-debted to Baltimoreans, leaving them beholden to creditors with no interest in the welfare of the republic of Pennsylvania. Could it be any wonder that these western farmers had little interest in the prosperity of their eastern brethren, let alone the republic of Pennsylvania as a whole?[3]

Paine discovered this flaw in his state's political economy during a fu-rious fight over the chartering of the Bank of North America, a semipri-vate entity intended to help Congress restructure its finances. To western Pennsylvanians, the proposed bank was a fraud perpetrated by eastern Pennsylvanians at the expense of their western brethren. William Findley, an Irish immigrant and legislator from far western Westmoreland County and one of the bank's most vocal opponents, spoke for many of his con-stituents when he reminded Pennsylvanians that "the government of

Pennsylvania being a democracy, the bank is inconsistent with the Bill of Rights thereof, which says that government is not instituted for the emolument of any man, family, or set of men." These were principles that Paine, of all Americans, could hardly dispute. But in Paine's view, Findley set his sights on the wrong target. In attacking the bank, Findley and his allies were in fact attacking the fundamental political fabric of republican Pennsylvania. Not only did their overblown hostility to a largely benign financial institution fuel westerners' alienation from the eastern part of the state, but it also invited manipulations by out-of-state malefactors happy to exploit old divisions for financial gain. "By attacking the bank," Paine explained, the bank's political opponents "have caused a considerable part of its cash to be drawn out and removed to Baltimore." For Pennsylvanians doing business in Baltimore, the short-term benefits of this capital flight were unquestionable. More money in Baltimore meant cheaper credit, but at what political cost?[4]

"Would not the politician be considered a madman in England," Paine asked, "who should propose to break up the bank in that nation, and send away to Holland and other countries the money which those foreigners have deposited with them?" Such, in effect, was what the bank's opponents proposed, leaving all Pennsylvanians with no choice but to establish credit with hostile outside interests. Western Pennsylvanians' total inability to act for the republic's common welfare offered a frightening glimpse of the state's future. A republic with so little unity in its economic interests could never be unified in its political ones. For some, the solution to the problem was obvious. "Happy would it be for Pennsylvania," wrote one newspaper correspondent in 1787, "if her boundaries were comprised by the Susquehanna; we should be more compact and more united." Paine hoped for a less radical solution. By facilitating communication between the state's contesting sections, internal improvements in the form of turnpikes, canals, and bridges would restore Pennsylvania's commercial unity, and from that commercial unity would follow political unity.[5]

Reflecting very similar thinking, the Pennsylvania state government initiated a sweeping program to enhance westerners' access to eastern markets. In the spring of 1786, the state's Executive Council empaneled an internal improvements committee to consult with similar committees in Delaware and Maryland. Its purpose was to construct a canal between the Delaware and Chesapeake Bays. But the committee's charge proved largely hopeless.

As Executive Council president Benjamin Franklin warned, the states were unlikely to have common interests, with Maryland likely to "press more particularly on the subject of the Susquehanna navigation," while Pennsylvania and Delaware would be most interested in a canal across the Delmarva Peninsula. Recognizing that what was in the interest of Pennsylvania would not necessarily serve Maryland, Franklin saw little hope of success "unless a spirit of mutual concession take place among the negotiators." The committee exhibited very little of that spirit, forcing western Pennsylvanians to take matters into their own hands. In October 1789, representatives from Lancaster, York, Cumberland, Northumberland, Dauphin, Huntingdon, and Mifflin Counties met to initiate their own program for internal improvements. They would begin accepting voluntary subscriptions for the purpose of clearing "the Navigation of the River Susquehanna, as far South as Wright's Ferry." This effort was unlikely to do much for Pennsylvania's political fortunes. Easier movement of goods down the Susquehanna was as likely to reinforce backcountry ties to Baltimore as to Philadelphia.[6]

Over the course of the next decade Pennsylvania's east-west sectional division would grow more pronounced, and some of that division would be fed by the very internal improvements Paine championed. Much as western Pennsylvanians had opposed the Bank of North America, they opposed the many private companies chartered by the state legislature to build and manage internal improvements. The idea that entities such as the Schuylkill Permanent Bridge Company would profit from the trade of hardworking farmers was so repugnant to western Pennsylvanians that when the state drafted a new constitution in 1790, two westerners proposed a sweeping constitutional reform abolishing the state's power to grant monopoly privilege to banks, bridges, turnpikes, canals, and other government-chartered enterprises. The proposal was defeated along mostly sectional lines: of the forty-four delegates to oppose the ban, thirty came from eastern counties. Ten of twelve supporters of the ban came from western counties.[7]

Paine's solution to Pennsylvania's political problems may have been doomed to failure, but his diagnosis of the problem was correct. Pennsylvania did indeed have a western problem—a problem as old as Pennsylvania itself. What now divided western Pennsylvanians from those in the state's eastern half was less security and war than it was commerce and credit. And so long as Pennsylvania's new government appeared unwilling to support farmers' demands for cheap credit and easy market access, Pennsylvania's sectional divide would persist. With state governments no better than their colonial predecessors at asserting taxation authority, the borderlands' political economy would be shaped by other forces, largely independent of the influence of those governments. In terms of ethnicity, in terms of trade, and in terms of politics, the commercial basin lying between the Susquehanna watershed and the Appalachian Mountains, and stretching south from the Pennsylvania borderlands to the Potomac River, and then east through Frederick Town to Baltimore, would have far more to unify it than would the states demarcated by the Line.

Even the problem of slavery would have little impact in this greater Baltimore. This is not because the region's economy made slavery irrelevant. Self-manumitted slaves from Delaware, Maryland, and Virginia would seek passage across the Line in ever-increasing numbers, eliciting the fundamental legal fact of the Line: the problem of fugitives from slavery. Nothing would do more to transform the Line from a jurisdictional divide into a political one than the flight of the enslaved. But that transformation would be slow and halting. In the half century after the passage of Pennsylvania's abolition act, the borderlands would acquire their own unofficial legal regime—one far less hostile to the institution of slavery than to the eastern, urban interests that championed its abolition. On the north side of the Line, this would mean a politics largely indifferent to the moral injunctions emanating from the eastern reaches of Pennsylvania. On the south side of the Line, it would mean a politics with little connection to either the proslavery politics of the tidewater Chesapeake or the antislavery politics of eastern Pennsylvania. Insofar as those politics, north and south of the Line, converged on the issue of slavery, they would do so not out of principled opposition to slavery but out of a common interest in commercial expansion. Family labor and wage labor would dominate in the grain-producing borderlands. As long as the politicians in the region ignored the problem of slavery, their constituents were happy to do so as well.

Thomas Paine may have understood the sectional tensions dividing Pennsylvanians. He may even have correctly diagnosed the problem as one exacerbated by commercial interests from an adjoining state. But he had practically no grasp of the historical forces behind Pennsylvania's sectionalism. The commercial basin encompassing most of the borderlands would have looked very different had not Pennsylvanians driven from their state most of its Native population. An accurate sense of the actual numbers of Native Americans in Pennsylvania after the Revolutionary War is very difficult to ascertain. The US census, begun in 1790, did not include Indians, assuming them to be subjects of sovereign but dependent nations. The prevailing opinion among historians is that in the aftermath of the midcentury anti-Indian warfare and its resurgence during the Revolutionary War, the numbers were very small. Aware that one of the patriots' grievances with Britain was its attempt to limit Euro-American squatting on Native lands, many Indian communities aligned themselves with British and loyalist forces. In western regions, those forces were often isolated and poorly provisioned, leaving their Indian allies vulnerable to fierce retribution. Those Natives who attempted to remain neutral suffered the fate of many similarly inclined Native groups throughout the colonial and Revolutionary eras. Buffeted by pro-British Indians and anti-British Euro-Americans, they suffered reprisals at the hands of both. The pattern repeated itself in countless acts of barbarous slaughter during the course of the Revolutionary War, including an especially ruthless episode perpetrated by Pennsylvanians beyond the state's western boundary.[8]

Christianized Delawares living among Moravian missionaries at the town of Gnadenütten on the Muskingum River in the Ohio country had spent the war defending themselves against accusations of treachery. Ohio-area Indians accused them of allying with American patriots, responsible for the theft of Indian lands. White American settlers claimed they gave refuge to pro-British Native warriors bent on avenging the theft of those lands. Until very late in the war, Moravian and Delaware diplomacy had succeeded in providing a modicum of security for the Gnadenütten Indians. But that diplomacy finally failed in the winter of 1782, after a band of western Pennsylvanians concluded that warriors responsible for recent captures and killings near Fort Pitt had been given refuge in Gnadenütten.

In early March, more than 150 Pennsylvania militiamen descended on the town and slaughtered ninety-six men, women, and children. Shortly after the Gnadenütten massacre, militiamen attacked a group of pro-patriot Indians living on an island adjoining Fort Pitt. The attackers killed four and forced the survivors to seek refuge with the Continental troops remaining at the fort. One of those refugees was Killbuck, a well-known pro-American Delaware leader. The spirit of the Paxton Boys was alive and well. No matter how peaceful, no matter how accommodating of Euro-American religious and economic habits, no matter how committed to the patriot cause, Indians were unlikely to find safety or justice in western Pennsylvania. By 1790, only a single group of Seneca Indians, living along the Allegheny River in the state's northeastern corner, permanently resided in Pennsylvania.[9]

Settlement and Indian-killing had achieved their expected ends, but the absence of a perceived Indian threat did nothing to diminish the alienation of western populations; on this point, the observations of Paine and countless others are hard to dispute. In addition to freeing formerly Native lands for Euro-American farming, mining, and logging, the destruction and displacement of the region's Native populations freed its inhabitants from any meaningful dependence on their new state governments. With the clearer sense of taxation jurisdiction brought by the Mason-Dixon Line, the states of Maryland and Pennsylvania could in theory demand more revenue from the borderlands. But the political justification for that taxation had mostly vanished.

Few developments better illustrate the economic consequences of ethnocide than the rise of the port city through which much borderlands produce passed. In addition to the British-American appropriation of Native lands, Baltimore's growth was a function of three related advantages. First, as the northernmost deep-water port in the western Chesapeake Bay, Baltimore was the ideal destination for produce shipped east from Frederick and south down the Susquehanna and its many tributaries. The city's location was advantageous for more distant borderlands farms and towns as well. Higher transport costs for goods shipped from York, Carlisle, and other communities east and south of the far northern Blue Ridge Mountains could be offset with other advantages. In shipping goods to markets in Baltimore, producers avoided a costly ferry crossing of the Susquehanna or the dangerous portage required to move goods through shoals and rapids in the Susquehanna's southern reaches. "What they need of foreign, particularly the indispensable West Indian goods," one visitor wrote of the town of York, "such as rum, sugar, mollasses, coffee & c., they fetch from Baltimore in Maryland; not because that city is nearer to them or offers better market for their flour, grain, and cattle, but on account of the disagreeable and uncertain ferriage over the Susquehanna."[10]

Second, Baltimore fared far better than its rival ports during the Revolutionary War. In 1788, French journalist and traveler Jacques Pierre Brissot de Warville noted that Baltimore "was but a village before the war; but during that period, a considerable portion of the commerce of Philadelphia was removed to this place."[11] Unlike Boston, Philadelphia, and New York, Baltimore was never occupied by enemy troops, and unlike other port cities—Charleston, Savannah, and Norfolk—it never endured a lengthy British naval blockade. This meant that although their ships still faced wartime risks, the city's merchants could otherwise continue their work more or less unimpeded; it also meant that Baltimore's merchants were well positioned to supply foodstuffs to the Continental Army, although as the war approached its final years, few of them did so eagerly, with often profoundly disruptive consequences. Neither Congress nor the state of Maryland was prepared to pay market prices, inflated as a result of wartime scarcity. In early 1780, a period of particular desperation for Continental Army forces, commissioners appointed by the governor of Maryland to seize food stores in Baltimore complained of "a great clamour among the people that we will starve them by seizing their provisions." The source of this erroneous fear, the commissioners believed, was a distressed Baltimore grain and flour broker. The protesters failed and Baltimore's commissioners were able to send hundreds of barrels of flour out of the city, much of it north, to Philadelphia and the New York area.[12]

Not only was Baltimore spared the direct impositions of British forces, but its hinterlands fared much better than the farmlands near Philadelphia and New York, areas trampled and ransacked by American and British troops during the early phases of the war. Flour and grain merchants in Baltimore thus enjoyed a mostly uninterrupted supply of produce, and between the needs of militias and the Continental Army, as well as continued vigor in their export markets, they also enjoyed far less disruption in their ability to dispose of American agricultural produce. Even an embargo on grain exports imposed by the Continental Congress and the state of Maryland between 1778 and 1780 had only marginal impact on Baltimore's trade. Merchants who defied the embargo by shipping produce to French forces in the West Indies found high prices and handsome profits.[13]

Third, and by far the most important of Baltimore's advantages, was the demand for its primary exports, flour and bread. Throughout the war, Baltimore's flour merchants supplied Cuba, the French West Indies, Jamaica,

Barbados, and other British West Indian colonies, often shipping their products aboard schooners specially designed to evade British blockades. Because
humidity accelerated the perishability of flour and bread, West Indian merchants and planters could hold only very limited stocks, ensuring consistent
demand for Baltimore's flour. Baltimore's location at the southern edge of
North America's most productive grain-producing region gave its merchants an additional advantage. The city was closer to the West Indies than
any Delaware River port; more importantly, passage through the lengthy
Chesapeake afforded extended shelter from the hazards of the open ocean.
These navigational advantages ultimately meant comparatively lower shipping costs for Baltimore's merchants.

Following the war, the lower transportation costs of Baltimore's West Indies trade allowed the city's merchants to offset some of the benefits long
enjoyed by their competitors in Philadelphia, generally thought to export
higher-quality grain and flour, and by the late 1780s, Baltimore's merchants
were able to build on these advantages and expand into European markets.
Disastrous European harvests sent European grain prices skyward. Between
1788 and 1789, the price of American flour and bread in France rose by a
factor of ten. For Baltimore's merchants, these price increases fueled further investment and commercial expansion. From roughly 10 percent of the
city's flour exports at the end of the Revolutionary War, Europe accounted
for 44 percent by 1789. The growth of Baltimore's European trade is an indication that the city's merchants were also becoming less reliant on the
West Indies trade, something that would be beneficial during the 1790s when
that trade was interrupted by the Haitian and French Revolutionary Wars.
By 1793, Baltimore was exporting more than two hundred thousand barrels
of flour annually, or roughly five times its prewar annual flour exports. By
1793, Maryland had become the third-largest American exporter among the
states, and Baltimore accounted for more than 84 percent of that trade. By
1795, it accounted for more than 95 percent of Maryland's exports, and most
of what it exported was grown and processed in the Maryland-Pennsylvania
borderlands.[14]

Baltimore's wartime boom rippled through the borderlands. Frederick
County saw a 300 percent increase in wheat production between 1770 and
1800. That most of the wheat made its way to market in Baltimore is suggested by the equally explosive growth in the number of flour mills. Because
mills had to be built along streams and creeks and because flour, being more

compact, was cheaper to transport than grain, mills tended to be built in the countryside near the sources of their grist. Between 1798 and 1810, the number of mills in Frederick County rose from 80 to 101. By 1810, Washington County, Maryland, west of Frederick County, had fifty-two mills producing more than eighty-six thousand barrels of flour per year, a slightly higher output than its parent county, Frederick. Although wheat and flour dominated the economy of the borderlands, farmers produced all kinds of other commodities for export, including animal hides, butter, timber products, and livestock. The constant quest to control transportation costs, particularly from the farthest western reaches of the borderlands, compelled many farmers to convert grain to spirits and livestock, both far more mobile commodities, although livestock added to the transportation woes of greater Baltimore, as roads became clogged with pigs and cows en route to Baltimore's slaughterhouses.[15]

While most of the borderlands' economic dynamism rested on agriculture, it was not exclusively so. Abundant timber for charcoal fuel, waterways and roads for transport, mineral resources, accumulating capital, entrepreneurial energy, and technical know-how—the latter three brought by the continued influx of European immigrants—gave the region an important role in a nascent industrial revolution. The early American iron industry occupied an arc from New York City and northern New Jersey south through eastern Pennsylvania and across the Susquehanna into the borderlands. On the eve of the Revolutionary War, Maryland and Pennsylvania were the leading colonial exporters of iron and iron products. As early as 1759, a Swedish visitor to Lancaster County observed that the pig iron produced in the region's foundries was not taken to Philadelphia's markets but was "carried to the Susquehanna River, thence to Maryland, and finally to England." According to one survey, in 1786 the area around Lancaster was home to seventeen ironworks and sixteen sawmills. Much of what those facilities produced was exported through Baltimore.

With the growth of manufacturing came the growth of other kinds of small-scale artisanal industry. In 1786, Lancaster, accurately described by one traveler as the "largest inland town in the United States," was home to "fourteen hatters, thirty-six shoemakers, four tanners, seventeen saddlers, twenty-five tailors, twenty-five weavers of woolen, linen, and cotton cloth, three stocking weavers, twenty-five white [pewter and tin] and black smiths, six wheel wrights, eleven coopers, six clock and watchmakers, six tobacco and snuff manufacturers, four dyers, seven gun smiths, five rope makers, four tinners, two brass founders, three skin dressers, one brush maker, seven turners, seven nail makers, five silver smiths, three potters, three brewers, three copper smiths, and two printers in English and German." By the early 1790s, Hagerstown (known at the time as Elizabeth Town), northwest of Frederick Town, just a few miles below the Line, and just above the Potomac, was home to a nail manufactory, a textile dyeing works, a tannery, a printer, a hatter, a tailor, dry goods and grocery sellers, and a coppersmith from York, who established a shop in Hagerstown "for the convenience of the inhabitants of the back part of this county." By 1807, Frederick County contained two smelting furnaces, two iron forges, and two glassworks. By 1810, a survey of Pennsylvania's economy found that 20 percent of the state's manufactured goods came from borderlands counties—Lancaster, Dauphin, Cumberland, York, Adams, and Franklin.[16]

Had the combination of commercial growth and jurisdictional clarity brought by the Mason-Dixon Line solved the primary problem the Line was meant to solve, the Maryland-Pennsylvania borderlands would constitute a strange utopian exception to the familiar patterns of American fiscal politics. In fact, of course, there was nothing at all utopian about the Line and its borderlands. Economic growth in the borderlands was accompanied not by a greasing of the proverbial wheels of state revenue but by political fragmentation that only reinforced long-standing resistance to taxation. To the farmers and manufacturers living near the Line, state fiscal policy was no more tolerable than colonial policy had been, and federal taxation was no more tolerable than British taxation. These borderlands political realities would erupt into a sweeping rejection of a federal excise tax on distilled spirits in 1794. Far from enabling taxation in the borderlands, broad-based commercial growth only made fiscal policy more fraught.

The history of taxation in the borderlands is not easy to write. With no centralized tax-collecting bureaucracy to assemble and record tax receipts, only a very fragmentary record remains to document the actual practice of taxation. The bulk of that record is divided into two parts: bills passed by state legislatures, and the records of court action to punish tax evaders. Since the states relied on a species of tax farming, where appointed tax collectors were responsible for assessing and collecting taxes, much of the actual business of taxation was an entirely personal matter: neighbors making deals with neighbors. Given the pervasiveness of debt and the scarcity of hard money, those deals often involved complex credit arrangements where taxpayers were forced to borrow from collectors, and collectors often leveraged those debts to cover their own debts, the latter frequently assumed to cover tax quotas owed to the states. With so much of the eighteenth-century revenue system entombed in the personal account books of local tax agents, sorting through the tangle of personal debt and credit obligations and finding any kind of direct line to state coffers is nearly impossible. But what is clear is that this cumbersome system, entangled with local politics, not to mention local hostility to distant taxing authorities, was susceptible to widespread corruption.

As long as tax collectors were able to use taxpayer debts as collateral, they were able to cover state quotas and allow their neighbors the luxury of deferred payment. But these arrangements often came to grief. Probate courts charged with liquidating the debts of deceased tax collectors routinely discovered that those debts far exceeded the value of the collectors' assets. In other cases, corruption was far more overt. After creditors sued John Ward Veazey, tax collector for Cecil County in Maryland, the state discovered that Veazey had paid practically nothing into the state's coffers. He was arrested and imprisoned, but the taxpayers would find no relief. To pay Veazey's creditors and compensate the state for lost revenue, Maryland's governor appointed a new tax collector and charged him with recovering all monies Veazey was supposed to have collected. To avert further corruption, the new tax collector, Peter Lawson, was required to post a £5,000 bond and to make his account books public. Measures of this kind may have helped counter corruption on the part of tax collectors, but they did very little to facilitate tax collection. If anything, tighter legal controls only elicited new forms of tax resistance.[17]

At times that resistance took the form of direct verbal and physical abuse of tax collectors. In 1784, a Fayette County tax collector was severely beaten, and in April 1786, a crowd forced a Washington County tax collector to walk from town to town bearing "many . . . marks of Ignominy" and exposed "to every insult, and mockery that [the crowd's] invention could contrive." More commonly, resistance took subtler forms. Building on experience from the days of the 1765 stamp tax crisis, local folk often banded together and formed no-bid pacts to thwart the public auctioning of the property of insolvent tax-payers. In some cases, local citizens were prepared to go even further. An official from York reported in December 1786 that after failing to find bid-ders for seized property, a tax collector from a neighboring county had re-located the auction to York's county seat. But "on the day of [the] sale, a number as I supposed of about 200 men . . . came into town some armed with guns, others with Clubs," intending to stop the auction. "Being told that . . . the consequences" of their attempts "to obstruct the execution of the Laws, might prove fatal to some of them . . . had no effect." Only after local magistrates issued arrest warrants was the tax collector able to proceed with the auction.[18]

So chronic would Pennsylvania's tax collecting woes become that in July 1789, Charles Biddle, secretary of the state's Executive Council, issued a desperate plea to the state's county tax commissioners, reminding them that "the great neglect in Collecting the State Taxes has furnish'd just cause of complaint to the Public Creditors who cannot receive their Interest," bringing the devastating depreciation of the state's paper currency. Biddle implored the commissioners "to take the most Vigorous & effectual mea-sures for the Collection of the Public Taxes . . . without delay." Such pleas reflected years of experience, especially with counties west of the Susque-hanna, where local officials, more concerned with their reputations at home than in far-off Philadelphia, freely manipulated the revenue system to shield friends and neighbors from state taxes. In 1786, the treasurer of Franklin County reported to Philadelphia officials that local magistrates charged with enforcing tax law "would threaten the people as much as possible but not proceed against them." And in cases where the courts were able to steel themselves for a tax fight, locals found creative methods to inhibit proceed-ings, including the obstruction of roads leading to county courthouses. In cases that actually made it before a court, local juries often showed them-selves more sympathetic to taxpayers than to the state, and even in cases where juries voted to convict tax evaders, local sheriffs and constables found a host of methods for deflecting and delaying final court judgments ranging from the failure to execute arrest warrants to the rigging of property auc-tions in favor of tax delinquents.[19]

As the Veazey case suggests, Maryland's ability to collect taxes was little better than its northern neighbor's, but Maryland's lawmakers, less inhibited by sectional tensions, instituted a more forgiving tax policy. Christopher Edelen, tax collector for Frederick County, routinely extended credit in lieu of direct tax payment and then leveraged those debts to finance a growing personal debt. Upon Edelen's death, his creditors looked to his estate for the recovery of that personal debt. Since, in effect, Edelen's debts had become public debt, his creditors would be collecting tax revenue owed the state. For the state to recover those taxes, it would have to either liquidate Edelen's estate, leaving his family destitute, or demand payment from Frederick's indebted taxpayers. It chose a middle path, ordering executors of Edelen's estate to collect balances due him from taxpayers, but providing nine months for those taxpayers to find new lines of credit.

In May 1789, citizens from Harford County petitioned the Governor's Council to intervene after tax collectors began selling seized property "at so low a price as must occasion the ruin of many citizens." So advantageous to purchasers, normally associates of tax collectors, the corrupt sales generated nowhere near enough to cover tax bills, bankrupting taxpayers. To avoid widespread financial ruin, the Governor's Council ordered local collectors to cease the sale of debtors' property, to prevent the corrupt dumping of taxpayer property, and to provide a full accounting of all property acquired in payment of taxes.[20] These sorts of concessions to taxpayers were common; less common but no less emblematic were concessions with a clear and obvious commercial purpose. Shortages of hard money, natural disasters, and business failure could all be brought to bear in seeking tax relief. John Frederick Amelung, the celebrated German glassmaker in Frederick County, petitioned the state assembly in 1788 to invest in a new glass manufactory. Amelung requested a cash advance of £10,000 and "an immunity from taxes for six years." Maryland's assembly readily obliged. Amelung had, after all, already invested £20,000 of his own money in an enterprise that employed 342 Marylanders.[21]

That the Maryland side of the Line seemed more prepared to sacrifice state revenue for commercial growth and political harmony suggests a boundary line between two different political economies, one more committed to austerity, the other to cheap credit. As a political matter, this difference would, as Paine predicted, perpetuate sectionalism in Pennsylvania. Seeking cheaper credit, producers in greater Baltimore would remain dependent on the region's most accessible commercial center. But nothing did more to unite the Maryland-Pennsylvania borderlands than federal tax policy.

Albert Gallatin is an unlikely partisan in the fiscal politics of the Maryland-Pennsylvania borderlands. Born in 1761 to an aristocratic family in Geneva, Switzerland, and a graduate of the famous Geneva Academy, founded in 1559 by disciples of John Calvin, Gallatin emigrated to the United States in 1780. After a brief stint teaching French at Harvard College, he worked as an interpreter and business associate for a French merchant. In 1785 he established a dry goods store and began acquiring farmland a few miles north of the Line on the eastern bank of the Monongahela River in Fayette County, Pennsylvania. Gallatin was surely the best-educated settler in the far western borderlands. Americans had long revered the Geneva Academy. Henry Laurens, a former president of the Continental Congress and one of South Carolina's wealthiest planters, sent his sons to the academy, and Franklin's grandson Benjamin Franklin Bache had also been a student there. In addition to so exclusive a formal education, Gallatin had known Voltaire, a friend of his grandmother's, and as a teenager he'd read the works of Geneva's most celebrated contemporary, Jean-Jacques Rousseau. Having been educated in one of Europe's oldest republics, Gallatin would also have been justified in counting himself among the westerners best equipped to judge the fealty Pennsylvania's government showed to republican principles. In 1789, when that government undertook to revise its constitution, Fayette County sent Gallatin as its representative to a state constitutional convention. Although Gallatin supported the push to replace the 1776 constitution with one more akin to the new federal Constitution, he was among the convention's most democratic voices. He advocated more proportional representation in the House, direct election of senators (as opposed to election by electors), a freer press, and a further broadening of the franchise.

Fayette County subsequently elected Gallatin for three years running to the state assembly, where he championed penal reform, immediate abolition, and internal improvement. Gallatin was also the assembly's most astute and influential fiscal mind. His 1791 report for the Ways and Means Committee showed him firmly in the hard money, fiscal conservative camp, as did his support for a new Bank of Pennsylvania, an institution Gallatin later claimed would allow Pennsylvania to defray "all the expenses of government without any direct tax during the forty ensuing years."[22] With dividends from the state's portion of the bank's shares, Gallatin believed, not only would Pennsylvania liquidate its debts, but it would also free itself from contentious taxes.

Although he embraced tenets of hard money fiscal policy, Gallatin was not another champion of austerity in the tradition of Morris and Paine. His support for fiscal discipline in his home state and his advocacy of public financial innovation rested on a kind of city-state political economy of precisely the sort Paine and Morris advocated—with Philadelphia's financial fortunes, so, all these political economists assumed, went the political fortunes of the republic of Pennsylvania. But unlike his Pennsylvania progenitors, Gallatin saw federal fiscal policy as a barrier to state policy, especially if that policy involved new taxes. For this reason, Gallatin sponsored a series of resolutions condemning a new federal tax on distilled spirits. The resolution had no effect on federal tax policy, and several years later, after Gallatin had been excluded from a seat in the US Senate for allegedly failing to meet its residency requirement, his home county joined the far western borderlands in a rebellion against the federal government's new whiskey tax.

For President Washington and his cabinet, the western tax rebellion erupted at an extremely inauspicious moment. The country's leaders had been looking across the Atlantic to another revolutionary republic as its quest for sweeping constitutional reform collapsed in a frenzy of hideous judicial murder known as the Terror. Any sense on the part of antitax partisans that they were simply continuing unfinished patriot business by opposing unjust taxes faced a cacophonous press, happy to associate the rebels' actions with the horrors of France's disastrous revolution. Western Pennsylvanians, following the model established during the stamp tax protests, had organized themselves into committees of correspondence, described by their critics as radical French "Jacobin" or "insurgent" clubs bent on inciting the American apostles of Robespierre, the "Sans Coulotte's of Pittsburgh," those bloodthirsty "vipers who would overturn all order, government, and laws." Although there was practically nothing French about the western borderlands, and although the tax rebellion far transcended this small and remote backcountry enclave, Federalist supporters of the president's tax policies claimed that it had become "a center of terrorism under the guiding hand of Albert Gallatin."[23]

As part of his own efforts to address the financial problems of the federal government, in 1791, George Washington's dashing treasury secretary Alexander Hamilton persuaded Congress to enact the tax on distilled spirits. With very few exceptions, Americans had mostly known taxes in the form of poll taxes, property taxes, and trade imposts. None of these constituted taxes on domestic manufactured goods. Such "internal" or excise taxes were commonplace in Britain—Thomas Paine had worked for the king's Excise Service before migrating to Pennsylvania. But after the catastrophe of Parliament's stamp tax, essentially an excise tax on printed paper goods, few national politicians were prepared to consider taxes on American-made goods. Given that the states and other localities already relied on direct poll and property taxes, and given the high costs of assessing these taxes, not to mention their widespread unpopularity, there was little thought in the Washington administration of adding new federal poll or property taxes. This left imposts on goods.

Americans had long known and tolerated import and export tariffs, and given that they could be assessed by federal customs agents, stationed at a relatively small number of deep-water ports, these were far less costly to collect than almost any other kind of tax. On the propitious date of July 4, 1789, before the Washington administration had even created the office of the Treasury, Congress enacted a tariff on a variety of enumerated imported goods including cheese, shoes, candles, soap, and carriages. But not long after taking office, the nation's first treasury secretary, Hamilton, made known his belief that the tariff was inadequate, in part because it would be vulnerable to the inevitable wartime interruptions of trade. At precisely the moment the federal government would be most in need of revenue, it would be least able to generate that revenue. And if the Revolutionary War had demonstrated anything, it was that national security was the only politically viable grounds for federal taxation. Hamilton thus proposed what had long been regarded as the least politically costly form of internal taxation: a sort of sin tax on distilled spirits. The federal government had already imposed levies on imported spirits, but these were defended in part as a means of protecting the New England rum industry. Now, Hamilton had concluded, since the government was in need of additional revenue, an excise tax was the only reasonable option and a tax on distilled spirits would be the least objectionable such tax. Since 1700, the colony of Pennsylvania had periodically taxed internal liquor sales. Virginia and Delaware had imposed similar internal taxes.[24] As an administrative matter, a tax on spirits could also be much more readily administered than one on assorted other manufactured goods. Measuring liquid volume required no cumbersome mechanical scales or complex mathematical calculations of volume.

The initial bill establishing the tax was enacted in 1791 with little fanfare, but by the summer of 1794, no American politician could doubt the political cost of the new federal tax. Seven thousand aggrieved western Pennsylvanians marched on Pittsburgh and the home of the region's despised federal excise collector, John Neville. Similar demonstrations erupted elsewhere in the region, from Carlisle south to Hagerstown and Frederick Town.[25]

Hamilton had long been troubled by tax resistance in Pennsylvania, partly because the federal government had relocated from New York City back to Philadelphia, but also because he recognized the dangers of sectionalism. Not only did it divide the states themselves, but now it threatened to tear the whole country apart. Since 1776, frontier regions of the new United States had begun addressing their age-old disenfranchisement with calls for new states. Vermont is the best-known of these. It seceded from New York shortly after independence, fourteen years before the United States granted it statehood. But there were a number of others, including Transylvania, south of the Ohio River, and Westsylvania, encompassing the border region between Virginia and Pennsylvania. With the Revolutionary War's end and the new partisanship following the ratification of the Constitution, citizens in some of these regions began agitating for true independence, as separate countries. Few of these separatist movements ever amounted to much, but they excited profound and not entirely unwarranted concerns from supporters of the new United States government.

The threat of British war against Spain, a tottering presence in Florida and the trans-Mississippi West, prompted Secretary of State Thomas Jefferson to warn President Washington that without prompt action, Britain might "encircle us completely, by these possessions on our landboard, and her fleets on our sea-board." This was Jefferson's worst nightmare. British control of the trans-Mississippi West would give America's prime international rival control the Mississippi River, a crucial outlet for western produce. Were that territorial control to yield new British colonies, British planters would also imperil American supremacy in the production of vital exports: "tobacco, rice, indigo, bread, lumber, naval stores, [and] furs" would pour forth from Britain's new American colonies, destroying whatever commercial advantages the young United States enjoyed.[26]

Feeding fears of secessionist movements and foreign annexation, the federal government had already discovered the limits of its authority in the West. In the new state of Kentucky, the Washington administration was unable to find anyone prepared to risk life and limb to collect the whiskey tax. A similar failure seemed to prevail in far western Virginia and North Carolina. With a substantial federal arsenal and military installation at Fort Pitt, a loyal tax collector in John Neville, and a relatively functional court system, western Pennsylvania was the best equipped of all the renegade western regions to enforce the new law, yet even here federal authority was unable to contain the crisis. But if federal law was to be enforced, the tax rebels had to be suppressed. Hamilton concluded that "there was no choice but . . . prosecuting with vigour delinquents and Offenders" in the one rebellious province where prosecution seemed at all practicable.[27]

In Albert Gallatin, Hamilton had a true rival. In many ways, the two were unlikely political opponents. Both were generally sympathetic to hard money fiscal policies, and both were refined men who, among other things, shared a revulsion toward slavery. Their differences centered on arcane constitutional principles. Hamilton, fearful of the centripetal forces pulling against the American Union, saw in the federal government's power the Union's best hope for survival. Gallatin, the product of the city-state-republic of Geneva, embraced the view, so frequently expressed by Antifederalist opponents of the 1789 US Constitution, that republics became empires at their peril. Small polities, where the governing class could have sympathy, born of common experience, with ordinary citizens, were the only republics of any duration. In Pennsylvania, Gallatin witnessed the dangers empire posed for republican government. Factionalism and paralysis were chronic. On a larger, national scale, such hazards would surely assume more menacing form.

A 1792 petition to Congress drafted by Gallatin on behalf of fellow western Pennsylvanians noted that the new tax law was, on its face, "dangerous to liberty . . . and incompatible with the free enjoyment of domestic peace and private property." How could it have been otherwise when that tax appeared to target the one commodity sustaining the economy of the far western borderlands? The "peculiar situation" of western Pennsylvanians, the petition explained, made the tax cruelly "unequal and oppressive." The reason should have been obvious: "Distant from a permanent market, and separate from the eastern coast by mountains which render the communication difficult and almost impracticable, we have no means of bringing the produce of our lands to sale either in grain or in meal. We are therefore distillers through necessity, not choice, that we may comprehend the greatest value in the smallest size and weight." The impost on distilled spirits, in other words, punished those farmers already at greatest commercial disadvantage. Any savings in transportation costs brought by transforming grain into spirits would now be negated by "a high duty."[28]

In the summer of 1794, following federal military intervention, Gallatin went to great pains to distance himself from "any criminal excesses into which the people, or any part of the people, may have fallen." But he pulled no punches when justifying their grievances. The following year, as the state House acted to punish Gallatin and other elected representatives from the rebellious Westmoreland, Washington, Fayette, and Allegheny Counties, Gallatin stood before his fellow assemblymen to reiterate what, at the end of the day, was the fundamental problem animating the tax rebels. Western Pennsylvanians were one of a number of constituencies to reject the new federal tax, and yet they and their representatives were targeted as the rebellion's sole and ultimate originators. Gallatin's fellow state assemblymen knew this as well as anyone. For, he reminded them, "on the 22d January, 1791, the House of Representatives of this State, upon the motion of two members from the city [of Philadelphia], adopted, by a large majority, resolutions" condemning the new excise tax as "the horror of all free states." Now, several years later, that same house felt it necessary to punish only those members hailing from the counties that acted against so obvious an outrage. "Was it more criminal," Gallatin asked, "in the inhabitants of the western country than in this House to circulate their opinions?"[29]

Gallatin's argument suggests deep sympathy for at least one aspect of the tax rebels' complaints—their abiding sense of disenfranchisement. The far western portion of the Line had only been surveyed in 1784, and Pennsylvania authorities struggled to collect revenue even in portions of the borderlands where the boundary had been settled for much longer. In some sense, Gallatin's willingness to represent western Pennsylvanians in their grievance against the federal government had more to do with that government's utter inability to assimilate a foundational principle of republican government—namely, that government demonstrate a capacity to represent the interests of all citizens. In imposing a tax on a population already frustrated by government's age-old failures, the administration of President Washington demonstrated a damning insensitivity to this basic mandate and appeared bent on fashioning the new federal government into a British-style imperial regime, driven by the politics of the capital and utterly unable to accommodate the politics of the distant backcountry. Efforts to suppress the unrest provided no reason to think otherwise.

Washington's secretary of war, Henry Knox, and attorney general, William Bradford, advised the president that the tax rebellion demanded a decisive military response. Only direct and forceful intervention, Bradford insisted, would suppress "hope of successful resistance" and induce "early submission to the Laws." The President ultimately assented and on September 30, he and Hamilton personally met the northern branch of a nearly fourteen-thousand-man expeditionary force at Carlisle. A few weeks later, after appointing General "Light Horse" Harry Lee commander of the northern force, the president left for Fort Cumberland in Maryland, where he reviewed militiamen sent by Maryland and Virginia. With his new federal army, half the size of the Continental Army at its peak, prepared to put down the tax rebels, President Washington returned to the nation's capital at Philadelphia. By the time the military arrived in Pittsburgh, its primary antagonists had been the weather and the Appalachian Mountains.

Bent on justifying their long march, troops nonetheless set about punishing the tax rebels. Finding few obvious ringleaders, they rounded up dozens of random unarmed frontiersmen. The closest Lee and his army came to the rebellion's putative leaders was Hugh Henry Brackenridge, a lawyer, a novelist, and a state representative for Westmoreland County. Although he had been a vocal opponent of the excise tax, Brackenridge had no role in the rebellion. After two days of interrogation, he was released. In the end, US government operations yielded around twenty arrests, mostly simple laborers and small farmers, unlikely ever to have produced much whiskey, let alone threaten federal authority. Of this group, only two were actually convicted of treason: John Mitchell, a country farmer and debtor fighting the loss of his remaining property, and Philip Vigol, a common laborer who apparently owned nothing at all. President Washington eventually pardoned both men.[30]

The bulk of the federal troops headed back east in November, leaving behind a fifteen-hundred-man occupation force. With no clear military mission and little discipline, the troops turned to the familiar occupiers' practices of drunken rampages, destruction of property, and looting. Although Brackenridge obtained some justice for clients who lost property in the federal operation, the political damage had been done. "The temper of the country was greatly ruffled at these indignities," and the damage was only getting worse. Brackenridge had learned that his efforts to get justice for westerners made him a marked man. During routine trips to Pittsburgh, he heard "threats of assassination" from federal soldiers who seemed to believe "that the government considered me as a man that might justifiably be murdered."[31]

The famed tax on spirits might never have had anything to do with the Line and its borderlands had the Washington administration elected to enforce the law elsewhere. But the very fact that the president and his advisors came to see in Pennsylvania's brand of insurrection a variety of resistance at once menacing and manageable was a reflection of work the Line was intended to do. Unlike Kentucky or western North Carolina, western Pennsylvania had a well-functioning court system with clearly delineated jurisdiction, partly enabled by the Line. Because of Fort Pitt, it also had well-trodden roads over which federal troops could travel. But those very advantages rested on age-old political fissures. Much like successive governments of Pennsylvania, the federal government inserted itself in the politics of the borderlands at its peril.

The legacy of the western borderlands tax revolt went far beyond politics. Military personnel brought hard money to the region, among the most specie-poor parts of the country. With new financial leverage, farmers and laborers bought land, driving up property prices—which proved hugely advantageous when former members of the federal force returned to the fertile, resource-rich countryside to acquire homesteads of their own. In 1795, the *Pittsburgh Gazette* reported that "the emigration to this country this fall surpasses that of any other season," with the result that "land that two or three years since was sold for ten shillings per acre, will now bring upwards of three pounds."[32] What the western borderlands lacked in market access was now being addressed through an infusion of new capital.

In the short run, the Whiskey Rebellion may have failed to repeal the excise tax, but it made the rebels wealthier. In the long run, however, the rebellion would set the terms of federal tax policy. Albert Gallatin, serving as treasury secretary for President Jefferson, oversaw a far-reaching revision of the federal tax code, a process that involved a repeal of all federal internal taxes, including the one on distilled spirits.

The Louisiana purchase, for all intents and purposes, put an end to the dangers of western secession. The Mississippi River and the port of New Orleans were now controlled by the United States. Of course this geopolitical triumph brought political dangers as old as the American republic itself. With no communications between new western territory and the mercantile capitals on the East Coast, there was little to prevent Louisiana or the Ohio country from doing to the cities of the East Coast what Baltimore's commercial hinterlands had done to Philadelphia. The problem seemed at bottom one of internal improvement. In an 1802 letter to Senator William Branch Giles, a member of Virginia's House delegation, Secretary Gallatin described it succinctly: roads and canals linking the far west to the Atlantic states "will contribute towards cementing the bonds of the union between those parts of the United States whose local interests have been considered as most dissimilar."[33]

Gallatin would later conclude the United States had been woefully slow to create such obviously vital public works. The problem now was not politics but money. The normal financial mechanisms for such costly improvements were failing. Private companies, chartered primarily by the states, proved unable to generate sufficient capital to cover the costs of constructing canals and turnpikes of the scope needed by an expanding United States. In England and Europe, such internal improvements could be relatively short and still attract enough traffic to generate returns for private investors. In the United States, distances between mills, provincial towns, and major ports were vast, exceeding the financial resources of private investors. Given the size of the United States and the likelihood that any truly profitable canal or turnpike would have to reach adjoining states, many public works "remain unattempted, because their ultimate productiveness depends on other improvements, too extensive or too distant to be embraced by" any single group of investors, particularly if those investors were also interested in the prosperity of Philadelphia or Baltimore or New York City. There was really only one solution to this problem: "the early and efficient aid of the *federal* government."[34]

As early as 1802, Congress authorized funds for a new National Road linking the Ohio country to the Atlantic coast, but only in 1806 could any consensus be achieved about the best location for such a road. The road would travel west, from Cumberland, Maryland, through far southwest Pennsylvania. When its first leg was finally completed in 1818, it reached the small settlement at Wheeling, Virginia, on the Ohio River a few miles west of Pennsylvania's western boundary. The road's eastern leg linked it to Hagerstown and a network of roads connecting the western borderlands to Baltimore. Eventually the National Road, also known as the Cumberland Road, would be extended farther west, into Illinois country, and in the twentieth century, as US Highway 40, it reached San Francisco. Beyond linking the Atlantic states to Ohio (which became a state in 1803), in the 1820s, the Cumberland Road briefly transformed Baltimore into America's second city. Until the completion of the Erie Canal in 1825, the road would be the primary commercial link between Ohio and the East Coast.

In the years after the Whiskey Rebellion, Pennsylvanians attempted to do on a state level what the United States did on a national level. They broke the ancient imperial matrix of trade and government by moving the state's capital from its commercial center of Philadelphia, first to Lancaster in 1799, and then in 1812 to Harrisburg. In part, the relocation of Pennsylvania's capital reflected political pressures in most of the original American states, as disenfranchised westerners imposed their will on government by relocating its locus inland from old, eastern capitals. In Pennsylvania, this political change was unlikely to alter economic reality. The great commercial basin straddling the Line from the shores of the Susquehanna Valley to the Appalachian Mountains remained oriented south, toward Baltimore.

After journeying west through York to Chambersburg in lower Franklin County, in 1809 a traveler from Philadelphia noted that "the roads from Baltimore are numerous so that the whole produce of this country goes direct to that town & not to Philadelphia." The southerly orientation of western Pennsylvania confirmed "the zeal with which the Marylanders are improving the carriage from this State [so] that the produce of this part of it will undoubtedly center in Baltimore." Other commentators were not so naive. Maryland had nowhere near the wealth of Pennsylvania, and yet it clearly outpaced its northern neighbor in facilitating its own commercial development. This was not simply a matter of markets; it was one of politics and policy. One outraged correspondent writing in the *Aurora,* a Philadelphia newspaper founded by Benjamin Franklin's grandson Benjamin Franklin Bache, complained about the "wayward and mistaken policy of Pennsylvania," which failed to promote "the extension of her own internal commerce, by the improvement of the great natural resources which she possess—but, in fact, this policy is perverting the benefits which providence has kindly bestowed upon her . . . by directing them, so as to promote the interests of another state, and the foreign commerce of a rival capital." That state was Maryland and that rival capital Baltimore, the state's commercial capital.[35]

Greater Baltimore's commercial boom continued through the early nineteenth century, fueled by the arrival of hundreds of Irish and English road builders. Pennsylvania's borderlands would be less connected to the state's eastern metropolis than they had ever been. Had technology not intervened in the late 1830s, western Pennsylvania might well have gone the way of Vermont or West Virginia, eventually becoming its own state. But railroads and canals would transform the towns of the borderlands from outposts of a greater Baltimore into commercial and manufacturing hubs in their own right, Baltimore one among several markets competing for their trade. Greater Baltimore would persist, but now as an integrated trading and manufacturing region rather than the hinterland of a single commercial capital.[36]

CHAPTER 9

Fugitive Diplomacy

THE WORK OF Mason and Dixon did little to stem ethnic violence in the western borderlands. But the post-Revolutionary years witnessed a change in the nature of the violence. Until the 1780s, little borderlands conflict intersected directly with the institution of slavery. Anti-Indian violence did have a great deal to do with the rise of commercial agriculture in the borderlands, and the rise of commercial agriculture had much to do with the extension of slavery inland along the Line, particularly on its southern side. Borderlands violence also long had a connection to the Indian slave trade. The Iroquois quest to secure southern warpaths was partly a quest to secure access to Native captives and, increasingly, fugitives from slavery, which in turn fed anti-Indian sentiment among borderlands slave owners. But beyond these important exceptions, there had been very little to link slavery to ethnic violence in the borderlands. Few people of African descent had ever been implicated in the violence, and few of the security concerns of Euro-American settlers had any direct connection to slavery. In the Line's history, anti-Indian violence and slavery occupy very different parts of the story: the former a matter mostly for the colonial era, the latter for the Line's nineteenth-century history. This separation is, in the end, a narrative conceit. In fact, in the year 1791, the colonial and nineteenth-century histories of the Line collided with far-reaching national consequences.

Mason and Dixon's inability to complete the final western portion of the
Line prepared the way for almost twenty years of haggling between Pennsylvania and Virginia over Pennsylvania's western boundary. Although it
took nearly a century for the dispute to emerge, its origins were familiar.
The Pennsylvania charter stipulated that the colony's western limit would
lie five degrees of longitude west of the Delaware River from the point where
the colony's southern boundary abutted the river. The colony's founding
charter said nothing about the precise nature of the actual boundary. Would
it be a straight meridian line, running north from the West Line's western
terminus? Or would it simply follow the course of the Delaware River at
five degrees' distance? The matter was of no small consequence since it
would determine the extent of two eastern states' claims in the resource-rich
Ohio country.

Pennsylvania authorities long feared that a boundary tracking the
Delaware River would leave Fort Pitt in Virginia, costing Pennsylvania's
western economy a vital center for trade. To compensate for this potential
loss, Governor Penn sought clear title to a contested western tract constituting most of the northeast of present-day West Virginia. After five years
of negotiations, Pennsylvania's Executive Committee agreed to abandon
these southwestern lands to Virginia in exchange for an agreement that secured Pennsylvania's claims to Fort Pitt. Instead of dropping south to the
thirty-ninth parallel, as the additional tract would have required, Pennsylvania's southern boundary would continue along the line initially plotted by
Mason and Dixon, and the state's western boundary would follow a meridian line running north from the end point of the West Line.[1]

The five commissioners appointed to survey the newly established boundaries included the Virginian James Madison and the Philadelphia mechanic
and scientific instrument maker David Rittenhouse. In an early use of the
name by which the Line would come to be so well known, the Virginia
assembly ordered its commissioners to extend "the line commonly called
Mason's and Dixon's line" due west, "on condition that the private property
and rights of all persons acquired under, founded on, or recognized by the
laws of either Country previous to the date hereof be saved and confirmed."
All deeds, bills of sale, and other property transfers, that is, were to remain
in force, in accord with the law of whichever state (referred to here as

"Country") sanctioned those transactions. Pennsylvanians found to reside in Virginia would retain property rights established under Pennsylvania law. Virginians who discovered themselves living in Pennsylvania would retain their property as guaranteed by the laws of Virginia.

These instructions might be interpreted as a brazen act to protect Virginians' property in slaves, but there is little evidence for this. A resolution affirming Virginia's newest boundary provisions, drafted by the Virginia state assembly and endorsed by the state's full legislature, says nothing about slaves but does make plain Virginia's intent to secure revenue from land sales. Irrespective of which state a title holder was found to be living in, he would remain responsible for payments to the land office of whichever state had granted the initial title. Payments made for lands acquired following the Declaration of Independence but now found to be improperly titled would be returned to the state in which the landholder was found to reside. Although taxpayers who had taken advantage of jurisdictional ambiguity to avoid payment would not be punished (there would be no charge for taxes in arrears), upon completion of the new survey, tax collection would begin in earnest. In other words, while lawmakers made much of landholders' property rights, their actions made much more of land office payments and tax revenue. That Virginia's lawmakers had so little to say about slave property may simply have been a matter of timing. The full implications of Pennsylvania's Gradual Abolition Act, which became law a few months before the Virginia assembly issued its western borderlands resolution, were still unknown.[2]

By the time the Line's newest boundary commission completed its work in the fall of 1784, thousands had migrated into the borderlands adjoining the far western limit of the Line, many assuming they had settled in pro-slavery Virginia.

David Davis and his family migrated there from Maryland in 1780. Davis purchased a homestead from Charles Stewart, who had obtained the land from the state of Virginia. According to the bill of sale, Davis and his family, which included a young slave named John, lived in Ohio County, Virginia. The Davises were able to plant and harvest one crop on their new farm before frontier warfare drove them back to Cumberland, Maryland, where they stayed for the next few years. The Davis family returned to its Virginia homestead to discover that their land had been bisected by the now-completed Mason-Dixon Line and that the family would be subject to

Pennsylvania law. According to that law, because David Davis had never registered John, the young slave was now entitled to his freedom, but Davis refused to comply, later claiming that since John had only known the Davis family, Davis acted in his slave's best interest. To conceal the infraction, Davis rented John to citizens firmly residing in Ohio County. Davis may have hoped to evade Pennsylvania law, but John had other ideas. While rented out to Virginian James Miller, he fled north, across the Line, and into Washington County, Pennsylvania.

Rather than bear the costs of retrieving John, Davis traded rights to the now runaway slave for another slave whom he promptly sold to Virginian Thomas McGuire. There would be no question about whether the slaveholder David Davis complied with Pennsylvania law. The slave catcher Baldwin Parsons, meanwhile, purchased John, intending to recapture the boy and carry him back to Virginia, where he expected to sell him at a substantial profit. It was all very predictable in its complete disregard for John's well-being and its high regard for the financial interests of the parties engaged in this illicit trade.[3]

Davis's actions, routine among the slave owners in the western borderlands, would be lost to history had it not been for eleven prominent citizens of Washington County, Pennsylvania. In February 1789, these men—lawyers, storekeepers, and merchants—formally assembled themselves into the Washington Society for the Relief of Free Negroes and Others Unlawfully Held in Bondage. Although it was affiliated with the PAS, the group had an unmistakable identity of its own. In addition to eschewing the term "abolition," its membership included no known Quakers and it employed extralegal tactics rejected by the PAS.[4]

In 1791, two Virginia officials testified that Virginians traveling west to Kentucky by way of Fayette County in Pennsylvania had been repeatedly ambushed by members of the society. The tactics, according to this testimony, involved waylaying travelers with a friendly dram and then persuading the accompanying slaves to remain in Pennsylvania as free Blacks. In one case, the society liberated three slaves and informed the owner he could recover his slaves at a later date and only if he guaranteed their eventual liberty. The slave owner, Samuel Bailey, complied, but when he next passed through the area, he "was informed that his negroes were free, and that he could not expect to get them." These sorts of tactics may account for the society's short life. Quaker abolitionists in Fayette County refused to join, and with its static membership and provocative tactics, by 1794 the Washington Society was no more. But in the years before its demise, it managed to make one of its chief objectives, the liberation of John Davis, an issue of national prominence.[5]

To the Ohio County Virginians, John's escape was clearly the work of the "Negroe club," as they called the Washington Society. In fact, the society had not yet been formally chartered when John liberated himself. Conflating the terms of Pennsylvania's gradual abolition law with the financial interests of the society's members, Virginians also accused the society of imposing a six- or seven-year indenture term on John "as a *compensation* to themselves for their *humanity*." Although it is unlikely that John's rescue was, as the Virginians implied, simply a gambit to kidnap a slave and force him into another kind of servitude, the accusation likely had some merit. Pennsylvania law stipulated that children of slaves remain servants until adulthood. The PAS itself endorsed a similar program of freedom by degrees. Rather than permit self-manumitted former slaves to remain as free Pennsylvanians, the PAS routinely returned them to slavery on condition that their owners accept them as term slaves. The Washington Society invited John to remain in Pennsylvania, as a free Black. But this hardly meant the society had any expectation John would live as a free Pennsylvanian.[6]

John's age is unknown, but as a young man, well under twenty-four, he would have been subject to laws against vagrancy and pauperage. To prevent young Blacks from becoming a public charge, the laws required them to be bound out as indentured servants until reaching adulthood. Such laws, which existed in most American states and which dated back to at least 1726 in Pennsylvania, had long been justified by the familiar claim that freed Blacks posed a special danger to white society. Pennsylvania law as it would have been applied in John's case was no accidental survival of early Georgian legal principle. On December 6, 1790, Alexander Addison, secretary of the Washington Society, wrote his correspondents at the PAS in Philadelphia to explain the society's resistance to fully freeing its rescued clients: "Removing the fear of a master, the only restraint of which their debased and untutored minds were conscious, without being able to fix upon them the check of honour, the Laws or Religion; we loose them to unprincipled licentiousness, idleness and every concomitant vice . . . for we in freeing these unfortunate men from their human masters, seem to deliver them up to the control of Satan and their own Lusts and make them more the children of Hell, than before they were of misery."[7] The message here was unmistakable: freed people were better off remaining in some form of bondage.

Whether this accounted for the society's treatment of rescued former slaves is unknown, but the general pattern of dismissing Black freedom and embracing forms of bondage short of slavery is as old as the opposition to slavery itself and almost surely left Virginians wondering how their neighbors across the Line could be so confident in the morality of their antislavery laws. In the case of the Washington Society, in sum, there is no separating the humanitarian opposition to illegal enslavement from the racist embrace of bondage for freed Blacks.

It must nonetheless be recognized that the society's efforts on John's behalf initiated sixty years of state and national wrangling over fugitives from slavery. Those efforts began when Baldwin Parsons set out to retrieve John Davis. According to Ohio County assemblymen William McMachen and Benjamin Biggs, "Mr. McGuire, Mr. Parsons and Mr. Wells, gentlemen of the most unexceptionable characters, of great respectability and of independent property, roused with indignation at the nefarious practices of this negroe club," traveled to Pennsylvania to recapture John. With no due process, in May 1788 the posse kidnapped the boy, carried him back to Virginia, and sold him. John's Washington County advocates hired a Virginia lawyer to sue for John's freedom, but the case went nowhere. Recognizing that kidnapping was a crime in its own right, these western antislavery activists took a new tack. Instead of seeking John's return to Pennsylvania, they would seek the extradition of his kidnappers. Perhaps, even if John could not be liberated, Virginians could be deterred from pursuing other runaways.[8]

The Washington County Court of Oyer and Terminer accepted the argument of the Washington Society and, in November of 1788, indicted three Virginia slave catchers for the crime of kidnapping. To initiate the extradition process, Pennsylvania's governor would have to do what the comity clause of the United States Constitution required of him: request from his counterpart in Virginia the extradition of John's kidnappers. With no direct access to the governor, the Washington Society forwarded an extradition request to the PAS—the society did this just as it declared its formal affiliation with the PAS, suggesting that the affiliation was mostly a function of John's case. The Washington Society assumed that their Philadelphia affiliate would pursue the case and demand urgent action. Instead, the PAS advised the Washington Society to encourage John to flee back to Pennsylvania. The westerners complained that this advice "had it been pursued and unsuccessful, as it probably would have been, would have drawn upon the poor soul an aggravated repetition of his past sufferings and might have hurried him beyond our reach forever."[9]

It would be two and a half years before the PAS forwarded the original Washington Society extradition request to Pennsylvania governor Thomas Mifflin. What finally prompted the PAS to act was another extradition request, this one also prompted by a western border crisis, but one of much more familiar origins.

On March 9, 1791, twenty-five armed white men from Virginia attacked a small Delaware encampment on the west side of Beaver Creek (now known as Beaver River), a northern tributary of the Ohio River, near Pittsburgh. According to fur traders who witnessed the attack, the victims had been intoxicated, probably with spirits acquired from the traders themselves. The attackers killed three men and one woman and then "stripped and plundered" the camp, taking nine horses, three rifles, and other recently acquired goods. Fur trader William Wilson, one of the witnesses, begged the Virginians to have mercy. Their victims were well-known peaceful and civil trading partners. In response to Wilson's pleas, the Virginians offered the familiar racist refrain of generations of borderlands Indian-killers: even "if these people had not done any mischief," no matter, for "others had, and they were all alike."[10]

Wilson was able to rescue a young boy from the attackers and bring him to Pittsburgh, where he was adopted by Cornplanter a Seneca ally who had served Pennsylvania in the Revolutionary War. Appalled by the attack, shocked by the arrival of the orphaned boy, and skeptical of the powers of interstate diplomacy, on March 17, a little more than a week after the massacre, Cornplanter and three other local Native leaders, New Arrow, Half Town, and Big Tree, wrote the authority responsible for the protection of independent Native peoples, the new United States president, George Washington: "Father!—We hope you will not suffer all the good people to be kill'd, but your People are killing them as fast as they can." There was no equivocation or ambiguity in the Indians' message: the internecine frontier violence that plagued the borderlands and the Ohio country for so many decades would return unless something was done to bring the Beaver Creek murderers to justice. And when it did, American fighters would find few remaining Indian allies.

Washington turned the matter over to his secretary of war, Henry Knox, who, after some investigation, confirmed the accuracy of the Indians' account. Writing to Pennsylvania governor Mifflin, Knox made the all-too-familiar observation that "if such crimes as the murder of friendly Indians should be suffered to pass . . . with impunity, the endeavours of the United States to establish peace on terms of Justice and humanity will be in vain. A General Indian War will be ex[c]ited."[11] Unfortunately for Governor Mifflin, Knox saw no way for the federal government to intervene. The alleged crimes, like most such crimes committed within incorporated states of the United States, were subject to state law. Governor Mifflin would have to bring the perpetrators to justice—and since the perpetrators had returned to Virginia, Virginia governor Randolph would have to extradite them.

Initially Governor Mifflin's communications with Randolph seemed to follow the path laid out in the comity clause of the Constitution: along with his request for the extradition of the murderers, Mifflin submitted assorted legal documents, including affidavits describing the massacre and identifying two of the perpetrators, Ohio County militia captains Samuel Brady and Francis McGuire. Upon receiving the documents, Randolph followed the letter of the law. He immediately issued a proclamation offering a $300 reward for the apprehension of either of the identified murderers, along with general orders for all magistrates to use every expedient to apprehend them. "Up to this point," the historian William R. Leslie wrote of the case in an early study, "there was not even a ripple of discord between Pennsylvania and Virginia." In coming months, though, the limits of the Constitution's provisions for comity would be laid bare.[12]

Trouble began very soon after Randolph received the extradition request. The chief magistrate of Ohio County, Colonel David Sheppard, sent the governor a very different account of the massacre. Sheppard explained to Randolph that Captain Brady and his men had in fact attacked the murderers of Virginians, clearly demonstrated by a fact conveniently excluded from Governor Mifflin's communications. A nearby blockhouse had been occupied by "a Wilson & Co., who was Notoriously known to supply . . . ammunition and arms of all kinds." With those arms, twenty-nine Virginians "have been most cruelly murdered." On the basis of this testimony, Randolph denied Mifflin's extradition request. He also sent clear signals that his government held Pennsylvania responsible for the Virginians' murders and would seek redress through federal law. Trade at the Beaver Creek block-house had, after all, involved the sale of arms and ammunition to Indians, a clear violation of the 1790 federal Act to Regulate Trade and Intercourse with Indian Tribes.[13]

Pressured by the Washington administration to punish the Beaver Creek killers while facing the perennial western problem of all Pennsylvania governors, Mifflin found himself between hammer and anvil. Action was likely to exacerbate tensions with an adjoining state. Not to act was to risk renewed Indian war.

In a radical change of tactics, Mifflin sent Governor Randolph a new and more concise extradition request, including a simple petition submitted to him by John McCree and William Rogers, secretary and vice president of the Pennsylvania Abolition Society. The petition requested the extradition of John Davis's kidnappers. Historians have been unable to identify any clear link between this request and the Beaver Creek request other than the fact that one of Davis's kidnappers, Francis McGuire, had also been indicted for the Beaver Creek murders. But the timing of Mifflin's communication suggests a deeper link. Given the pressures Mifflin faced to bring the Beaver Creek murderers to justice, there is little reason to think he would have risked another rebuke from Governor Randolph unless he thought doing so would advance the Beaver Creek case. The PAS also very likely had something to do with the timing of this new request. Although it had been more than two years since John's kidnappers were indicted, the PAS chose to communicate the extradition request to Governor Mifflin on May 30, the day he received a letter from Secretary Knox outlining the administration's position on criminal extradition.[14]

As Mifflin and the PAS no doubt expected he would, Randolph rejected this newest extradition request. In what may well have been his intention from the outset, Mifflin then turned to President Washington. The only possible resolution of the impasse was direct federal intervention. Washington turned the matter over to Secretary of State Jefferson, who in turn forwarded a dossier on the conflict to Attorney General Edmund Randolph, former governor of Virginia and cousin of the state's governor. Once again, however, the Washington administration pushed the matter back to the states. "*Now* to interfere," Randolph advised the president, "would establish a precedent for assuming the agency in every embryo dispute between States."[15]

Washington shared his attorney general's assessment with Governors Mifflin and Randolph. Mifflin complied with the suggestion that he submit more evidence to the Virginians, but to no avail. Governor Randolph refused to contradict the testimony of the representatives from Ohio County, and by 1792 he still had done nothing with Mifflin's request. For reasons that have never been explained, President Washington broke with his attorney general and elected to intervene. In late October 1791, Washington asked Congress for a bill clarifying states' responsibilities for interstate fugitives from both justice and slavery or servitude. On November 15, Theodore Sedgwick, congressman from Massachusetts and chair of the committee charged with drafting the new legislation, presented an extradition and rendition bill to the House.

A year passed with no further action. The Senate, meanwhile, authorized the drafting of its own bill, which contained one clear concession to slave owners: now, anyone known to be interfering with the rendition of fugitives from slavery would be subject to a very substantial $500 fine, payable to the slave's owner. The provision was a clear and unalloyed attempt to thwart the Washington Society and any other would-be abolitionists. In addition to penalizing anyone who "shall harbor or conceal" known fugitives from slavery, the fine would apply to anyone who "shall knowingly and willingly obstruct or hinder" the recovery of runaways. In early 1793, the Senate passed the bill, which received overwhelming approval in the House. It was signed into law by President Washington on February 12, 1793, and for fifty-seven years would remain the sole federal statute concerning fugitives from slavery.[16]

In spirit, the law followed the comity clause, Article IV, Section 2, of the United States Constitution. Comity would apply in cases of criminal extradition, while the recovery of alleged fugitives from servitude and slavery would follow the old common-law principle of caption, entitling property owners to recover lost or stolen property without court intervention. Long applied to livestock, in the colonies caption had also been applied in cases of runaway servants and slaves. Under the federal constitution, the same basic principle had applied, leaving fugitives from servitude and slavery a local, civil matter. In forcing slave catchers to demonstrate the validity of claims on alleged runaways, the new law did empower local magistrates to prevent illegal kidnappings, but it also effectively forced judges and other local law enforcement officials to license slave catchers. Over the course of the next few decades, as more and more judges north of the Line found themselves forced to apply a federal statute enabling southern slave catchers, the distinct legal cultures across the Line would grow more pronounced. The eventual passage of personal liberty laws in Pennsylvania and other northern states was, in part, a reflection of this growing divide. But in 1793, the legal conflicts surrounding fugitives from slavery remained a problem for antislavery partisans, a distinct minority in the borderlands.

By the time the 1793 law was enacted, John Davis had been illegally enslaved for almost five years and the Washington Society was on the verge of dissolution. Davis would gain nothing from the law, and with his primary advocates unable to sustain their organized campaign for his liberation, his case drifted into the historical shadows. The best the society could do was recover damages from Davis's former owner, David Davis. The arrangement, brokered by one of the society's attorneys, David Bradford, required Davis to compensate the society for the costs of pursuing John's kidnappers. Davis turned over a horse and a promissory note he had been given in payment for John. In effect, society members received profits from the trade in slaves to compensate themselves for legal action taken on behalf of a man illegally forced into slavery. These sorts of moral inconsistencies were not exceptions in the history of the Line. In a booming borderlands, with an ever-expanding market for cheap labor, altruism often represented only the thinnest of veils for white antislavery partisans.

McGuire, meanwhile, was never extradited to Pennsylvania for the kidnapping of John Davis. Virginia's new governor, Henry Lee, reverted to the same argument made by his predecessor—that Pennsylvania authorities failed to justify extradition. Nor was McGuire, or anyone else, ever punished for the Beaver Creek murders. Hugh Henry Brackenridge pursued the case against the murderers, but again Governor Lee stonewalled. For the victims of any cross-border crime, the new 1793 federal Fugitive Slave Law achieved practically nothing. For the state magistrates charged with prosecuting that crime, it also changed very little. The pursuit of fugitives from criminal proceedings would remain a diplomatic matter, to be worked out by state governors and their representatives; for the legal problem of fugitives from slavery, a patchwork of local legal precedent, state law, and interstate diplomacy would remain the primary means of redress. And for much of the next half century, as federal lawmakers framed one compromise after another to keep national sectionalism at bay, ever more fugitives from slavery, taking advantage of the laws' many loopholes, crossed the Line into antislavery Pennsylvania.[17]

Until the federal government assumed control of the fugitive slave problem with the passage of a second Fugitive Slave Act in 1850, legal action related to fugitives from slavery was a near constant burden for the courts of the states adjoining the Line. Occasionally court action or inaction would lead to statutory revision of state law, but for the most part the pattern was one of judicial and legislative restraint. In part, the states' behavior seems to have been driven by a jurisprudence of historical necessity—the belief that, whatever the Constitution actually said about the matter, the spirit of comity had to shape fugitive slave law. A state might have antislavery laws, but as long as there were proslavery states, it could not have antislavery law. The survival of the Union depended on judges' abilities to walk this fine line. As William Tilghman, chief justice of the Pennsylvania Supreme Court, noted in an 1819 decision, "Whatever may be our private opinions on the subject of slavery, it is well known that our southern brethren would not have consented to become parties to a constitution . . . unless their property in slaves had been secured."[18]

The pattern can be seen in *Commonwealth v. Holloway*, an 1816 Pennsylvania case brought by the PAS on behalf of Eliza, the daughter of Mary, a fugitive slave from Maryland. Eliza had been born several years after Mary arrived in Philadelphia. Mary's owner, James Corse, captured both Mary and her daughter and had them imprisoned in a Philadelphia jail to await rendition. The PAS then successfully petitioned the state supreme court for a writ of habeas corpus, forcing the court to confront the question of whether or not children of alleged fugitives born in Pennsylvania would be subject to Pennsylvania law. According to that law, the children of enslaved mothers born after the passage of the 1780 abolition act could not be enslaved. But Corse's lawyer argued that according to Maryland law, Eliza's status followed her mother's, who was a fugitive from slavery. Comity would therefore dictate that Pennsylvania follow Maryland law. The Pennsylvania Supreme Court disagreed. Writing for the court, Chief Justice Tilghman's opinion followed a half century of legal precedent established with the ruling of Lord Mansfield, chief justice of the King's Bench, in the landmark British case *Somerset v. Steuart*. The case concerned James Somerset, a former slave who sought his freedom in Britain on the grounds that his former owner, Charles Steuart, had no right to recapture him as long as Somerset resided in Britain. Lord Mansfield ruled in Somerset's favor on the grounds that to do otherwise would be to exceed his judicial powers. Since no law formally legalized slavery in Britain, to rule against Somerset would, in effect, create such law—a clear violation of the judiciary's constitutional authority. Tilghman followed similar reasoning in his *Holloway* decision. With no law concerning the children of alleged runaway slaves, the court was left to employ existing law, and that law granted freedom to children of slaves residing in Pennsylvania. Corse appealed the decision, but a US district judge upheld it, again following Lord Mansfield's principles of judicial restraint.[19]

The decision infuriated Maryland slave owners, and in an effort to address their frustrations, in December 1816 that state's assembly issued a resolution denouncing Pennsylvanians' disdain for the rules of comity and federal fugitive slave law. The resolution, a political palliative for the wounded pocketbooks of Marylanders, went nowhere, as did a series of subsequent attempts at new national fugitive slave legislation. In Pennsylvania, meanwhile, outrage over the kidnapping of free Blacks continued to grow until 1820 when, infuriated by the Pennsylvania high court's refusal to grant an accused fugitive trial by jury, the PAS lobbied for the country's first far-reaching personal liberty law. The law, enacted in March 1820, clearly stated that kidnapping was a felony, punishable by steep fines and imprisonment. As a means of preventing corrupt bargains between petty officials and slave catchers, the law also imposed financial penalties on any local alderman or justice of the peace who, without authorization from higher officials, heard claims to alleged fugitives from slavery—a direct challenge to the 1793 federal Fugitive Slave Act.[20]

The case of John Read suggests Pennsylvania's new law did much to harden the legal divide the Line had become. Read was alleged to have fled slavery in Baltimore and settled in Chester County, where he supported his family as a common laborer. On a December night in 1820, Samuel Griffith of Baltimore, who claimed to own John, traveled to Read's home intending to capture him. Read, who had long feared kidnappers, was known to have been armed. In the fight to secure his home, Read killed Griffith and mortally wounded another man. Marylanders expected murder charges, but a local Pennsylvania jury convicted Read of the lesser charge of manslaughter, another pointed rejection of comity.[21]

To arrest the growing legal divide between their state and antislavery Pennsylvania, the Maryland legislature petitioned Congress for a new Fugitive Slave Act. A proposed bill was debated but never enacted. In a final, desperate bid to resurrect comity, the 1822 Maryland legislature convened a joint committee of senators and House members to negotiate directly with Pennsylvania governor Joseph Heister, and although the governor was sympathetic to the Marylanders' pleas, the Pennsylvania legislature proved much less receptive. With few alternatives, Maryland continued to pursue a diplomatic solution to the problem of fugitives from slavery. In January 1826, a legislative delegation led by Senator Ezekiel F. Chambers and Assemblymen Archibald Lee and Robert H. Goldsborough traveled north to the capitals of Delaware, New Jersey, and Pennsylvania. The delegation's object, again, was redress for "the immense losses sustained by the citizens of this state by the absconding of their slaves, and the great difficulties experienced in recovering them." There was none of that eighteenth-century habit of euphemism. The issue was now unequivocally about runaway slaves and the Maryland legislature's "solemn appeal to the government of those states, in which the greatest portion of such fugitives are known to seek refuge."

The delegates never made it to New Jersey, but in Delaware they were rewarded with the passage of a new fugitive slave law. The law was not everything Maryland's legislature wanted—it formally prohibited slave catchers from capturing alleged fugitives, but it did authorize claimants to petition local magistrates, who could then issue arrest warrants for the accused runaways. Antislavery activists found to be assisting fugitives would be subject to a mandatory $500 fine, on top of the rarely imposed federal fine, and a prison sentence of between three and twelve months. Finally, the law stipulated that any free Blacks found to be helping fugitives travel by water would be subject to either fine and imprisonment or thirty-nine lashes.[22]

The delegation's successes in Delaware were modest but promising. The new law affirmed the principle of comity, although it placed the burden of arresting and remanding alleged fugitives on local magistrates and left the claimants with a substantial evidentiary burden. As had been the case with fugitive slave law from its inception, the accused had no rights. The only legal question, the legitimacy of the claim to the alleged fugitive, was to be decided on the basis of the claimant's ability to document that claim. A perhaps more unalloyed victory for the delegation was a new Delaware law. "Any suspicious colored person" was required to carry the equivalent of a passport, "approved and renewed by some Justice of the Peace in the parts through which such a person hath traveled." Failure to comply was grounds for arrest and treatment as a presumed runaway slave.

Americans of African descent had long been obligated to carry papers proving their status. But now Delaware law, in an extension of the pass system widely implemented in nearly every other slave state, burdened all Blacks with the obligation to track and document their movements. The law effectively extended Maryland's system for controlling the movement of free and enslaved Blacks across the entire Delmarva Peninsula. In Maryland, at least since 1715 when the colony's assembly formalized long-standing practice in the Chesapeake, any slave traveling outside the county where her owner resided was required to carry a formal pass. Freed Blacks were required to carry free papers or freedom certificates. Widespread counterfeiting and the use of stolen certificates by alleged runaways prompted the state to revise the laws in 1805. The freedom certificates would now include a physical description of the bearer. Although state slave codes had formalized some of what would come to be known as the "pass system," the requirement that all free Blacks also be prepared to prove their identity was a sign of things to come. Under the guise of protection from illegal kidnapping, free African Americans living near the Line would bear an ever heavier burden for defending their liberty, a burden unknown to whites on both sides of the Line.[23]

During its 1826 mission, the Maryland legislative delegation found in Pennsylvania a strange welcome. Governor John Andrew Shulze received the lawmakers at his residence in Harrisburg on a cold day in early February. Schulze had taken office in 1823 as the fugitive slave problem was entering its most tumultuous period since the early 1790s—particularly tumultuous, at least, for the governments of the states adjoining the Line, if not for the many victims of illicit and licit kidnappings. In a note accompanying the delegation's credentials, the governor affirmed his hope that the delegates would be received by Pennsylvania's lawmakers "in that friendly and conciliatory spirit due to the representatives of a sister state." Unfortunately for Maryland's slaveowners, the state's delegation proved no match for the PAS and its allies. Alerted by antislavery activists in Delaware, the PAS had already begun lobbying the legislature when the Marylanders arrived in Harrisburg. In a stunning rebuke, far from appeasing Maryland's slaveowners, Pennsylvania's lawmakers passed a new personal liberty law.

Enacted in March 1826, the law was a masterpiece of antislavery politics. Turning the Maryland mission on its head, instead of addressing the fugitive slave problem the law addressed Pennsylvania's kidnapping problem. To recover their property, slaveowners would first have to present a local magistrate with extensive documentation, including a sworn and notarized affidavit from the claimant's home state attesting to the legitimacy of the claim (formerly an oath of truthfulness from the claimant or his agent would have sufficed). If local magistrates judged sufficient compliance with these conditions, a warrant for the arrest of the alleged fugitive could be issued and executed by a sheriff or town constable.

Upon her or his arrest, the alleged runaway would have the right to habeas corpus. And as with any criminal proceeding, the accused would be entitled to present evidence for a defense. If the accused runaway had to be jailed, this was to be done with clear deference to constitutional prohibitions on undue and prolonged imprisonment. Imprisonment would also be done at the expense of the claimant.[24]

As a political gesture, the law's meaning was unmistakable. Free and freed Blacks were entitled to due process and a level of personal liberty—above all liberty from kidnapping—similar to that enjoyed by white Pennsylvanians. These protections came at a high cost. Although slave catchers would have to work through Pennsylvania courts, all Blacks would be subject to a legal process that, for all intents and purposes, criminalized skin color. Black Pennsylvanians might now have some confidence that they would not be forced into slavery. But whether legally free or fugitives from slavery, these Pennsylvanians would live under fear of unjust arrest and imprisonment by the very state authorities charged with protecting them from the illegal slave trade.

That the new law had mixed results should come as no surprise. For decades, an illicit trade in slaves had been transporting Pennsylvanians across the Line into lifelong bondage. This "other underground railroad," as historian Julie Winch has characterized it, bore many hallmarks of the more familiar Underground Railroad. It relied on both Black and white smugglers; it employed safe houses; and it made ready use of forged documents. If there remained any doubts that the Line was being transformed from a jurisdictional boundary into a true border, they were not to be found among the various conductors and traffickers behind the illicit movement of people of African descent back and forth across the Line.

The rise and fall of the borderlands' most infamous man-stealing ring offer a vivid illustration of the challenges state governments faced in their efforts to control human trafficking. The Cannon-Johnson gang, named for Jesse Cannon and his son-in-law Joe Johnson but controlled by Jesse's wife, Patty, operated on the Delmarva Peninsula, along the Maryland-Delaware border. The kidnapping ring appears to have emerged around 1815 and continued to operate through 1829, when Patty was finally arrested and charged by Delaware authorities with murder.[25]

The audacity of the Cannon-Johnson gang remains stunning. Using various agents, including women, children, Blacks, and whites, gang members lured unsuspecting Blacks, most often children, frequently orphans, and forced them onto boats plying the Delaware Bay. The captives were carried south for sale into bondage. The gang's most audacious act came to light the year Pennsylvania enacted its boldest personal liberty law—and probably had something to do with the law's passage. Almost two dozen children were victimized by an orchestrated scheme to transport captives from Pennsylvania and Delaware to plantations in Mississippi. Most of the victims were young boys who had been working as apprentices and indentured servants, but the kidnappers also targeted girls, one of whom was collecting firewood in Delaware and was abducted after straying across the state line near Elkton, Maryland. A number of the victims had been working on Philadelphia's commercial docks and were lured onto ships, forced below deck and bound. The captives were then taken to the Johnson-Cannon homestead on the far southern Maryland-Delaware border, where they were shackled for days. Their southward journey most likely began by boat, down the nearby Nanticoke River and out into the Chesapeake Bay, where a group of shackled children would have aroused little suspicion. After disembarking, most likely near Mobile, Alabama, the captives were forced to march, chain-gang-like, to Mississippi, where they were sold through a network of illegal slave dealers.

After learning of the rash of kidnappings, Philadelphia's mayor, Joseph Watson, initiated an investigation of "the mazes of this infernal plot, by means of which, a great number of free-born children, during several years past, have been seduced away and kidnapped, principally, and almost wholly as I believe, by a gang of desperadoes, whose haunts and headquarters are now known to have been, on the dividing line between the states of Delaware and Maryland."[26] Using reward money from the City Council and employing a Mississippi lawyer, Duncan Walker, Watson managed to locate most of the children and initiate legal proceedings against the Johnsons and Cannons. Even though he had cooperation from authorities in the states in which the ring operated, an ancient prohibition on slave testimony against whites made Pennsylvania's kidnapping case impossible to prosecute. What ultimately brought down the Cannon-Johnson ring was a discovery of human remains on Patty Cannon's farm. Local police established that the family had murdered a Georgia slave trader, the daughter of a slave owned by the Cannons, and two other children, probably born to slaves on the Cannon farm.

In April 1829, Patty Cannon was arrested for these crimes. She died while awaiting trial in the Georgetown, Delaware, jail. Before her death, Patty confessed to at least twelve other murders, including that of her late husband. Patty and her accomplices were tried and convicted of murder in absentia. Only one member of the ring was ever convicted for the kidnappings. John Purnell, an African American responsible for the initial kidnapping of many of the Cannon-Johnson captives, was arrested in Boston in the summer of 1827 and extradited to face charges in Philadelphia, where he was convicted on two counts of kidnapping, sentenced to forty-two years in prison, and fined $4,000.[27]

Despite Pennsylvania's laws, man-stealing along the Line persisted, and free Blacks lived as foreigners within, obliged to demonstrate their status both in the ordinary course of travel and before magistrates charged with administering Pennsylvania's personal liberty laws. Where the law did change was in the matter of comity and the fugitive diplomacy on which it had so long depended. Pennsylvania's personal liberty laws would eventually come before the United States Supreme Court as *Prigg v. Pennsylvania*, a case that initiated the effective removal of the fugitive slave problem from the Constitution's comity clause, among the most far-reaching constitutional changes in American history.

The federal government's efforts to resolve the fugitive slave conflict reflected the growing political divide between antislavery Pennsylvania and proslavery Maryland and Delaware. But, as always in the history of the Line, politics cannot be separated from trade, agriculture, and industry. It is not coincidental that as the fugitive slave issue divided the states along the Line, that division was reflected in profound shifts in the political economies of the states along the Line. Greater Baltimore had, for decades, brought a fragile unity to states otherwise divided over the issue of slavery. But with the fulfillment of a dream articulated long before by the likes of Thomas Paine, even that seemingly immovable commercial block would collapse, leaving the producers of central and western Pennsylvania with little reason to do business in Baltimore. Canals and railroads would, for a time, resurrect greater Philadelphia, and with that resurrection came a total transformation of the political economy of the borderlands.

CHAPTER 10

The Fall of Greater Baltimore

"I LABOURED UNDER only one peculiar disadvantage that I am aware of," recalled the English political economist and travel writer Harriet Martineau. Among the many Europeans to write about the young United States, few were women, but this was a matter of little consequence for Martineau. Her status as an English-born lady offset any barriers her sex may have imposed between her and her American subjects. Martineau's disadvantage was that she was nearly completely deaf. She had suffered progressive hearing loss over the course of her thirty-two years. Martineau's two-volume 1837 masterwork, *Society in America,* thus required a disclaimer. Readers deserved to know that Martineau's disability did not "endanger the accuracy" of her account. To the contrary, "because I carry a trumpet of remarkable fidelity," an instrument that afforded a great deal more intimacy "than is given to people who hear general conversation," Martineau enjoyed the sorts of candid exchanges only possible with the "ease and privacy in conversing with a deaf person."[1]

These intimate exchanges revealed a deeply troubled nation. For all of the new country's idealism, for all its high-minded republicanism, its common-man politics, dark currents coursed through the American soul. Martineau applauded American democracy—its unique capacity to extend the franchise to property-owning men and its assertions of equality of condition for white male citizens. Much like her liberal progenitors, who included Thomas Paine and the feminist Mary Wollstonecraft, Martineau was a political radical—she advocated expansion of the franchise, equal rights for women, and the immediate and unconditional abolition of slavery. Although her travels through the United States and its western territories brought her into contact with plenty of like-minded Americans, she also encountered an America where the disenfranchisement of women and the enslavement of Americans of African descent coexisted with a crass, morally bankrupt greed. That this troubling America flourished in the American South, assiduously concealed behind a veneer of assumed gentility, made it all the more pernicious. But the problem was not limited to Americans south of the Line. It seemed endemic to whatever it was the American experiment had achieved. One needed look no further than the many Americans who shared Martineau's antipathy toward slavery but somehow believed the problem best addressed by another horrible cruelty. Among "men of earnest philanthropy," and "well-meaning and thoroughly persuaded persons," Martineau encountered advocates of that "miserable abortion—the colonization scheme."[2]

Colonization dated back some decades, to well before the 1817 chartering of the American Colonization Society, but as the political struggle over slavery grew, so too did the commitment of the movement's growing ranks. In transporting freed people to a West African colony, colonizationists believed they overcame the chief barrier to manumission, the slaveholders' perennial fear that freed people would fall into vagrancy or incite slave rebellion. Whatever its many genteel, middle-class advocates professed, Martineau saw in colonization a cruel act of self-deception perpetrated by "the clergy, public lecturers, members of legislatures, religious societies, and charitable individuals both North and South," all of whom "believe themselves to be laboring on behalf of slaves." In fact, colonizationists had been "opiated into a false sleep." The answer to America's slavery problem was plain: "the abolition of slavery . . . complete and immediate."[3]

The absurdity of colonization was, for Martineau, a reflection of a kind of willful economic and demographic illiteracy. This breed of antislavery activist ignored a fundamental trait of the very booming economy that enriched them. In a nod to one of her political economist progenitors, the English population theorist Thomas Malthus, Martineau pointed out that America's relentless territorial expansion fed a growing demand for agricultural labor, which, in turn, fed the expanding markets for that labor's produce. Far from becoming rebels, freed people would be readily absorbed by an

ever-expanding wage-earning workforce. The "bald fiction" of colonization was borne out by the raw numbers. For all its financial resources, for
all its popularity among America's wealthiest and most progressive class, the
American Colonization Society had only managed to transport a few thousand people to West Africa. Meanwhile, tens of thousands of Americans of
African descent had been forcibly removed to the ever-expanding southern
and western reaches of the country.[4]

At the heart of Martineau's critique of colonization was her recognition
that the American economy, with or without slavery, was astonishingly dynamic. That dynamism may have driven a demand for slave labor, but it also
drove the demand for laborers paid a living wage. America's chronic fugitive slave problem illustrated precisely this point: "Everybody who has been
in America is familiar with the little newspaper picture of a black man, hiking
with his stick and bundle, which is prefixed to the advertisements for
runaways." Precisely what drove Black Americans to flee slavery would be
concealed as long as southerners and their enablers in the colonization movement feared the discovery that fugitives from slavery were as self-interested
as any other American. If permitted to dispose of their labor freely, they
would go to extraordinary lengths to maximize the remuneration to which
they were justly entitled.[5]

That same self-interest was evident in the South's economy and its relentless demand for bound labor; it was also evident in the industrial growth
of the Upper South and the North. Migrants from Ireland, refugees from
southern slavery, young women from rural America—all flooded into Baltimore, Philadelphia, New York, Boston, and countless smaller industrializing
villages and towns, in search of wages. Many wage earners found employment, albeit under often brutal conditions, in a rapidly expanding sector of
the American economy: the construction of bridges, canals, and railroads.
By the time Martineau visited the United States, the country was in the
midst of one of history's greatest-ever infrastructure booms. "It is very
comprehensible to the traveler why this new country so far transcends others
of the same age in markets and means of transport," Martineau observed.
To be sure, there were vast regions, particularly in the Deep South, where
"the mail roads are still extremely bad." But those problems were being
remedied, even in the country's remotest regions. With the rise of the great
technological marvel of the age, the railroad, the country's internal improvement boom would only accelerate. In Pennsylvania, New York, Rhode

Island, and Massachusetts, railroads already abounded and "have succeeded so admirably, that there is no doubt of the establishment of this means of communication over nearly the whole of the United States, within a few years, as by-ways to the great high-ways which Nature has made to run through this vast country." By the time Martineau passed through the borderlands adjoining the Mason-Dixon Line, the effects of that internal improvement boom were unmistakable.[6]

The French travelers and social scientists Gustave de Beaumont and Alexis de Tocqueville had traveled from Philadelphia to Pittsburgh in 1831. Beaumont remembered the three-day trip as "one of the most arduous that I have taken." Traveling night and day over roads that had changed little since the French and Indian War, Beaumont took no particular note of the natural glories of the western borderlands, for "one is necessarily a cold admirer when freezing." Just a few years later, Harriet Martineau covered much of the same ground, traveling from west to east. Although it took her four days, she traveled almost entirely by canal and railroad, along Pennsylvania's new Main Line. "This ungainly combination of railroads and canals, with 174 locks, three tunnels, and a unique inclined plane for lifting segmented boats over the Allegheny Ridge," writes the historian John Lauritz Larson, "anchored a statewide system of lateral canals and other public works that totaled 637 miles in 1835." For Martineau, the Main Line was more than a fleeting expression of Pennsylvania's ingenuity—never mind its politicians' financial prowess. This internal improvement and others like it accounted for the incredible "bustle of the great northern markets." Americans had overcome the tyranny of distance, and soon the benefits would be known even in the country's remotest corners. It would be a matter not of decades but of years before "the spread of comfort and luxury will be as great as that of industry is now," and "by a vast augmentation of the means of transport, markets will be opened wherever the soil is peculiarly rich, the mines remarkably productive." Soon there would be no backcountry, no frontier, nothing at all to distinguish the distant interior of America from its booming Atlantic coast. Internal improvement would effectively make the United States one giant Pennsylvania. In Martineau's view, that expansion would be driven by the same labor system that drove Britain's industrial revolution. Wage labor, not slave labor, harnessed a natural human craving for self-betterment, and that craving, rather than the coercive instruments of the slave driver, would drive American economic expansion.[7]

For a liberal English political economist, the twin obsessions of slavery and economic growth were fully compatible. The latter was an entirely familiar development in England. The former, at least from the vantage of the British Isles, was the great anomaly. Technological innovation and wage labor were the engines of Britain's industrial growth, according to Martineau's liberal explanation for that growth. That much of the produce that fed England's textile industry, the world's largest and most advanced, was the result of American slave labor was lost on few British political economists, but where abolition failed, simple economics would prevail, and slavery would vanish before a global tide of wage labor.

Several years before arriving in America, Martineau made precisely this point in her first major work, *Illustrations on Political Economy*. The book assembled a series of fictional tales for the purpose of introducing working people to the basic principles of political economy. One of the stories, "Demerara," follows Alfred Bruce, the son of a wealthy Guianan sugar planter, who returns to the family plantation with his sister Mary after completing his schooling in England. Alfred had fully assimilated liberal, free-market doctrine, and after listening to his father's complaints about the insecurities of West Indian wealth, he initiates a prolonged dialogue about the structural flaws of the plantation complex. To demonstrate his central claim—namely, that slavery is fundamentally inefficient—Alfred undertakes repairs to an irrigation dam on the condition that he be allowed to pay the enslaved dam builders. Not surprisingly, the project progressed in record time. The lesson was obvious, Alfred explained to his deluded father: "Labor is the product of mind as much as of body; and, to secure that product, we must sway the mind by the natural means,—by motives." A wage is the most basic such motivation, because it is the most basic recognition of self-interest, and "laboring against self-interest is what nobody ought to expect of white men,—much less of slaves."[8]

For Harriet Martineau, in other words, in addition to being an inhumane abomination, slavery had become an economic anachronism. Its survival was purely a function of politics—decisions by southerners and weak northern activists to allow the persistence of an inefficient and unnatural form of labor. As a social scientist, Martineau was very much of her time, whether decrying colonization or defending the inevitability of free labor. Her methods were impressionistic. She made no effort to digest, in any kind of comprehensive way, American data on labor and its relative productivity. Had she done so, she might have found evidence that, as a pure matter of labor costs, American slavery was not so inefficient—the question remains a source of historical debate.[9] But had she spent more time in the Line's borderlands, her impressions would surely have been confirmed. Free labor was clearly displacing slave labor.

Martineau's labor theory is also consistent with another change in the borderlands labor market. Beginning in the 1790s, state legislatures and courts imposed a growing array of restrictions on white servitude. In 1793, the Pennsylvania Supreme Court effectively banned the indenturing of native-born minors. Twenty-five years later, the Maryland State Assembly enacted a series of reforms designed to weaken its indenture system, including limits on terms of servitude and the requirement that ships' masters release immigrants after sixty days, a fatal blow to the servant trade. Unable to hold out for optimal prices, recruiters could no longer expect to cover the costs of the transatlantic transit, let alone generate a profit.[10]

Although the decline was most precipitous among white indentured servants, it was also evident in the case of Black servants. By the 1830s the many children of slaves or former slaves who indentured themselves as part of the PAS path to emancipation had either reached their majorities or been released from their contracts. The recovery of the European economy after the Napoleonic Wars and efforts by European governments to prevent the flight of skilled and unskilled labor, meanwhile, vastly reduced the number of Europeans prepared to cover the cost of migration by indenturing themselves to Americans. But perhaps the single most important reason for the decline of contract labor was precisely what Martineau would have assumed. A relentlessly expanding market for unskilled labor made the enforcement of labor contracts increasingly difficult. The development can be seen in the labor problems of an early borderlands industrial concern, the Chesapeake and Ohio Canal Company.

The company was a classic public-private partnership chartered by the states of Maryland and Virginia, as well as the District of Columbia and the United States Congress. With legal sanction by all the region's largest political entities—states, the District of Columbia, and the federal government—the private enterprise acquired the right to build and operate a series of inter- and intrastate canals linking the Potomac and Ohio Rivers. By 1850, twenty-five years after the company was chartered, Cumberland, Maryland, remained the Chesapeake and Ohio Canal's terminus. In 1852, the Baltimore and Ohio Railroad reached the Ohio at Wheeling, Virginia. One of the problems the canal builders confronted was the absence of an adequate labor supply. The company's directors expected to use British labor recruiters to attract a thousand canal workers. The colonial pattern of exchanging passage across the Atlantic for five, six, or seven years of bound labor had long since disappeared. An expanding British industrial economy provided workers with plenty of alternatives to servitude. But a downturn in the British economy made a brief return to the old mode appear feasible. In fact, however, what labor recruiters were able to extract from prospective migrants bore very little resemblance to colonial indenture contracts. Instead of years of service, the canal workers would be indentured for only a few months—long enough to cover the costs of transatlantic passage. After their indentures expired, they would commit to an additional year as wage laborers. Between August and October 1829, recruiters sent some five hundred British men to work on the canal.[11]

The company had little power to enforce its recruitment contracts, and workers deserted by the dozens, some just a few days after arriving in America. Maryland's arcane colonial servant laws entitled the company to recover the runaways and gain compensation for unfulfilled contracts, but the courts had little appetite for a resurrected contract labor system. One federal judge who ruled in favor of the canal company noted that he did so reluctantly, since indentured servitude was now "opposed to the principles of our free institutions." Other judges proved far harsher, ruling against the company and affirming the general repugnance elicited by any form of contract labor. The proprietors of the new Baltimore and Ohio Railroad, meanwhile, were all too happy to employ the runaways. Had the courts and the general public been prepared to do to the canal workers what it had routinely done to African Americans, the indenture scheme might have worked. Similarly, had the company not been competing for laborers with the Baltimore and Ohio Railroad, its owners might have been able to control wages and retain its workers. But competition for labor and a legal order sympathetic to free white labor left the canal company's labor scheme a shambles. What was true for the Chesapeake and Ohio Canal Company would be true for all employers in the

Mason and Dixon borderlands. And those same forces, market forces and moral forces, would account for an acceleration in the long decline of slavery along the Line.[12]

By 1840, there were no slaves in the Pennsylvania borderlands. The number of free Blacks in the region, meanwhile, continued to rise, although the rate of increase was nearly the same as that of the population at large. While some of those free Blacks were very likely servants or apprentices—census takers made no distinction between servants and wage laborers—the trend was clear. By this period, most servants and apprentices were young; agricultural laborers tended to be older and male, and the overwhelming majority of those men worked for wages. In Delaware, the pattern was similar. By 1840, there remained 2,605 slaves in the state, a little more than half the number of twenty years earlier. Sixty percent of those slaves resided in the state's southernmost county, Essex. Meanwhile, in this overwhelmingly rural state, the free Black population grew by about a fourth between 1820 and 1840. In New Castle and Kent Counties, that population outnumbered enslaved Delawareans by 12.5 and 13.6 times, respectively. In southern Sussex County, there were more than two and a half times as many free as enslaved Blacks. The vast majority of these Blacks, along with countless white laborers, worked for wages.

Even in Maryland, the borderland state with the largest slave population, the border counties reveal patterns very similar to those of Pennsylvania and Delaware. With no statutory prohibitions on slavery in Maryland, the causes of its decline in that state's counties along the Line lie elsewhere. The simplest explanation is proximity to the antislavery North. But the evidence points in a different direction. Although the number of enslaved Marylanders living in the border counties declined in the 1830s and 1840s, the rate of decline hardly suggests an exodus. Almost 4,500 slaves remained in Frederick and Baltimore Counties. To be sure, many Americans of African descent freed themselves and made the high-risk journey north. But those slaves living near the Line faced an array of barriers others living further south would not have faced—they were often well known to local whites highly attuned to the potential for unlawful flight. Greater surveillance made flight nearly as difficult for the enslaved living near the Line as for those living further south. As we have seen, slave owners near the Line routinely addressed the problem of slave flight by simply disposing of their enslaved property

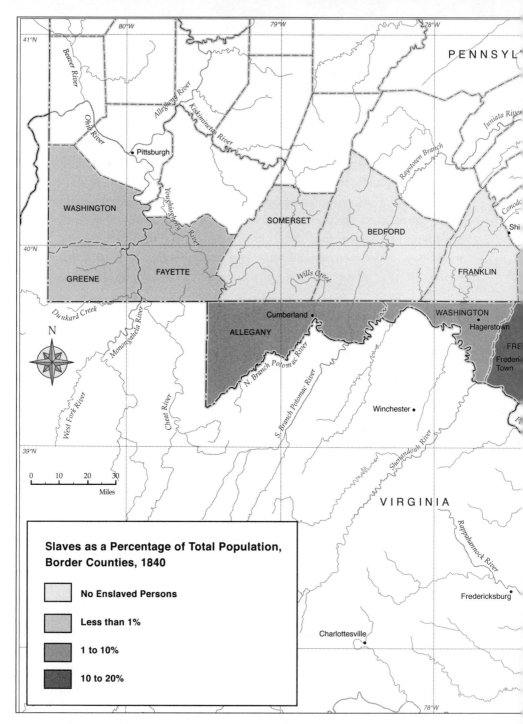

Slaves as a Percentage of Total Populations, Border Counties, 1840

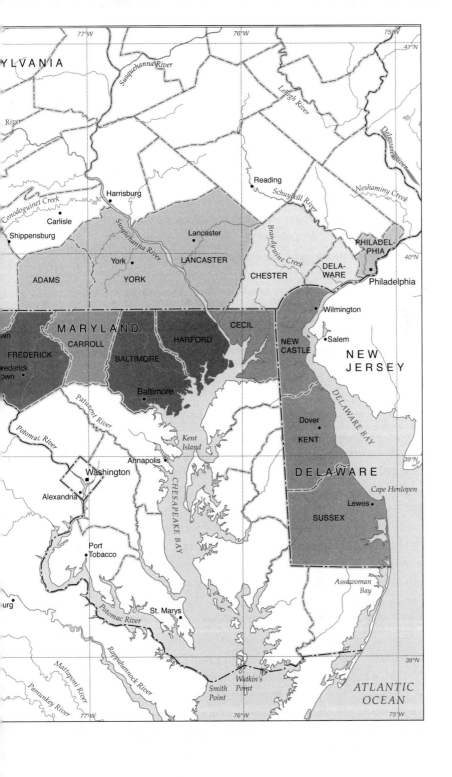

through the ever-expanding internal slave trade. For many, then, remaining enslaved near the Line may have been preferable to the risk of capture and sale downriver to the Cotton South. The dilemma was nowhere better articulated than in the autobiographical writings of the most famous of all of Maryland's runaways, the abolitionist Frederick Douglass:

> To look at the map and observe the proximity of Eastern shore, Maryland, to Delaware and Pennsylvania, it may seem to the reader quite absurd to regard the proposed escape as a formidable undertaking. But to *understand,* some one has said, a man must *stand under* . . . for the nearer were the lines of a slave state to the borders of a free state the greater was the trouble. Hired kidnappers infested the borders. . . . At every gate through which we had to pass we saw a watchman; at every ferry a guard; on every bridge a sentinel, and in every wood a patrol or slave-hunter. We were hemmed in on every side.[13]

None of this is to suggest that the enslaved were not responsible for the decline of slavery in the borderlands. While many may have been reluctant to free themselves, many, including Douglass, did do so. But in accounting for the decline of slavery in the Maryland borderlands, it is difficult to separate active slave resistance from other economic variables.

The whipsaw movements of nineteenth-century agricultural markets meant that ever fewer borderlands farmers could afford to hold capital assets such as slaves. While slaves and land could serve as collateral, the former was the more readily liquidated asset—especially with the expansion of the internal slave trade. The 1819 financial panic, the first of a series of far-reaching financial meltdowns, brought a devastating contraction in credit markets, leaving farmers with the perfect storm of inadequate credit and shrinking markets. Between 1819 and 1828, grain prices in Philadelphia's markets fell by almost 30 percent. In Maryland, the collapse was roughly the same: from a high of $14 per barrel in 1817, flour prices plummeted to less than $4 by 1821.

On the heels of the decline in grain and flour prices followed a decline in land values. Although cotton prices also fell during the panic, cotton producers had profited so spectacularly in the previous years that there was little decline in their demand for slave labor. By 1820, cotton represented 32 percent of all American exports, a more than fifteen-fold increase since the mid-1790s. With so much of the nation's capital flowing to the cotton belt, farmers in Maryland's borderlands had one obvious mechanism for addressing market volatility. Following the panic of 1819 and the collapse of Baltimore's grain markets, the slave population of the most populous borderlands counties plummeted. One study of Frederick County found a more than two-hundred-fold increase in interstate slave sales, accounting for a 12 percent fall in the county's slave population. Similar patterns replicated themselves across northern Maryland. In cases where farmers did not sell slaves, many turned to an alternative means of monetizing this asset. In 1816, only a few of Frederick County's slaveowners took out mortgages on their enslaved property. Between 1820 and 1825, what had once been a rarity became commonplace. County property records show sixty to eighty new mortgages on slaves each year. It seems very unlikely that those loans were used to purchase more slaves. In addition to the declining numbers of slaves, Maryland experienced a far-reaching fall in wages. The collapse of grain and flour prices, so devastating to the export economy of Baltimore, brought a flood of wage laborers to the countryside. In the aftermath of the panic, one resident of Washington County, Maryland, reported that in just a couple of months, the wages of farm workers fell by almost 30 percent.[14]

What remained of the borderlands' unfree labor economy after the Panic of 1819 would be further eroded in the summer of 1836. The Hessian fly, thought to have been brought to North America by German Hessian soldiers during the Revolutionary War, destroyed the mid-Atlantic wheat crop. Those farmers who had recovered from the crisis of 1819 found new financial peril and did what many of them had done after the 1819 panic. The slave population of most of Maryland's borderlands counties fell again. Between 1830 and 1840, Baltimore and Frederick Counties, which accounted for the vast majority of the slaves remaining in the borderlands, saw their slave populations decline by about 30 percent.

Among the weaknesses of liberal political economy was a kind of labor market fundamentalism—demand, so the reasoning went, would sustain living wages. Between 1800 and 1850, agricultural wages in the borderlands changed very little.[15] In Maryland, monthly wages fluctuated between $10 and $12. For other workers, a boom-and-bust economy meant that real earnings were also stagnant. The wages of canal workers varied substantially in the 1820s and '30s but rarely kept pace with inflation. During the 1830s, when the canal-building boom reached its zenith, higher wages began colliding with declining investment capital. Canal companies across the region collapsed and, with the Panic of 1837 and the subsequent depression, wages plummeted. "The pattern," labor historian Peter Way has written, "was thus one of a period of stable wage rates during small-scale construction, followed by steady growth as the number of projects expanded, then contraction as work dropped off during the depression that followed."

The volatility of wages and the challenges laborers faced in achieving a reasonable standard of living accounts for a new form of borderlands political discord. From the time its construction began in 1828, the Chesapeake and Ohio Canal experienced at least ten major episodes of labor unrest. So bad were the canal's labor problems that on five separate occasions between 1834 and 1840, the Maryland state militia intervened. Similar patterns were evident north of the Line. Of sixty-five incidents of American labor unrest associated with canal construction between 1780 and 1860, nineteen occurred in Maryland and thirteen in Pennsylvania.[16]

For some northern Marylanders, the changing labor market aroused predictable forms of anger and hostility. In a memoir about her childhood, Asia Booth Clarke, the sister of Abraham Lincoln's assassin, recalled life on the family farm in rural Harford County, northeast of Baltimore. Junius Brutus Booth, the father of Asia and John Wilkes, an intensely bookish, frustrated actor, prone to episodes of alcohol-induced insanity, was also a religious progressive and opponent of slavery. The elder Booth was not so opposed to slavery that he eschewed it entirely. Rented slaves worked the family farm, but the bulk of the labor on the Booth farm was provided by wage-earning Irish immigrants. For young John Wilkes Booth, the presence of these men was a source of acute distress. Asia recalled that "it was the custom for members of the family to dine and sup with the white men who did the harvesting." Enamored of a southern hauteur that "fences off familiarity and its concomitant evils" and that rejected northern democratic pretense for a world of southern masters and mistresses, John viewed this sort of proletarian mingling as a total assault on propriety and demanded that his mother and sisters avoid meals with these "ignorant menials." Not surprisingly, the farmworkers came to despise the Booth family for its "dirty British blood," made dirtier by its "southern ideas," only feeding young John's antipathy. While still a teenager, he would begin attending clandestine meetings organized by the anti-Catholic, anti-immigrant network of conspiracy theorists whose members hid their affiliation by responding to interlocutors' questions with a simple "I know nothing."[17]

Booth's hatred of immigrant labor was closely related to his admiration of a highly idealized white South. Not only did that world of ladies and gentlemen affirm the masters' superiority to the laboring servant or slave, not only did it enforce separate spheres for gentle ladies and laboring men, but it was also orderly and disciplined. Of course, this was an entirely mythical perception, resting on the appallingly dishonest depictions of proslavery propagandists. But it explains how someone like John Wilkes Booth could see immigrant labor and the slave regime of the deep South as somehow antithetical.

The raw nativism and the paternalism of John Wilkes Booth were commonplace among those Marylanders who saw in their state's economic transformation a symptom of moral decay. But the hostility to immigrants, which was fundamentally a hostility to free labor, could hardly be embraced by Marylanders who favored the state's rapid industrial growth. For those capitalists and their many allies who saw in a competitive labor market a source of Maryland's economic expansion, Know-Nothingism had little appeal. Immigration's economic benefits far outweighed its social costs, and even the latter could be addressed by reforming the laborers themselves. For some, this meant religious reform—drawing Catholic workers into Protestant churches—but for many more the place to begin was with ruinous drink. For what, in the end, made the Irish so undisciplined, what brought on their immoral and carousing habits, but the penchant for beer and spirits? A Protestant Republic simply could not afford to be overrun by inebriated Catholic laborers. Religious reform, let alone the quiet discipline of a Protestant ethic, was an impossibility as long as alcohol clouded the minds of the targets of that reform. "The Holy Spirit," noted one contemporary temperance pamphlet, "will not visit, much less dwell with him who is under the polluting, debasing effects of intoxicating drink."[18]

There was nothing coincidental about the concurrent rise of free labor and temperance. In addition to attracting large numbers of young immigrant men habituated to the pleasures of drink, turnpikes, canals, and railroads only improved market access for western distillers and brewers by lowering the cost of the transportation of their produce. With limited licensing restrictions, retailers happily exploited the convergence of supply and demand. Grog shops proliferated along rail lines and canals, providing teetotalers an easy explanation for growing labor unrest. The directors of the Chesapeake and Ohio Canal expelled grog sellers from its work sites and banished subcontractors who engaged in the common practice of supplementing wages with alcohol. The company also petitioned the Maryland Assembly to prohibit licensed liquor sales within a few miles of the canal. The petition failed, and the company's many other measures proved no match for its employees' taste for drink.[19]

On the north side of the Line, the push for temperance was every bit as fierce. In 1827, a group of temperance advocates founded the Pennsylvania Society for Discouraging the Use of Ardent Spirits. The society shortened its name to the Pennsylvania Temperance Society in 1834, by which time it could claim almost 150 chapters across the state. The part of the state responsible for much of Pennsylvania's liquor production experienced an absolute stampede of temperance activity. By 1834, Washington County alone was home to thirty-six separate chapters of the state temperance society. Lobbying by these groups forced the closure of 40 of the county's 113 distilleries. Over the course of the next decade, the movement only grew. By 1843, the Pennsylvania Temperance Society boasted a membership of almost thirty-five thousand. Although their success was mixed, temperance crusaders persuaded many employers to stop awarding liquor allowances. But such measures would obviously be ineffective if employers simply turned liquor allowances into wages, which could be used to purchase liquor. Temperance crusaders thus showered the state legislature with petitions for alcohol-free zones around factories, mines, iron foundries, and other industrial concerns. As was the case in Maryland, these initiatives met with very limited success. Distilleries and breweries provided crucial outlets for Pennsylvania's grain producers, and politicians were reluctant to excite the ire of the state's rural population. Memories of the Whiskey Rebellion were still fresh for some, particularly those from the western part of the state.

Political resistance to temperance would only grow with the ratification of Pennsylvania's 1838 constitution. The new state charter reduced the residency requirement for white male citizenship from two years to one. Now it was not just liquor producers who inhibited temperance legislation; the state's politicians had to confront the plain truth that to deny workers their drink was to risk alienating a massively expanding constituency.[20]

Much as Martineau wanted it to be otherwise, the decline of slavery and contract labor brought only marginal improvements in the lives of Black Americans, in large part because these economic changes rested on a very old politics of white supremacy. The pass system had long limited opportunity for free Black workers, but as politicians began competing for white workingmen's votes, additional restrictions began entering the law books. An 1832 Maryland law, for example, imposed ruinous fines on any nonresident free Black who stayed in the state for more than ten days. Although the law was proffered as a measure to prevent free Blacks from inciting slave rebellion, its economic significance is unmistakable. Free Blacks from Pennsylvania would be unable to compete for work in booming Maryland. In 1840, the legislature prohibited free Blacks from entering the state entirely. Not only could free African Americans from Pennsylvania no longer seek work in Maryland, they could visit kin only at great risk—risk that included, for those unable to pay fines, possible sale into slavery. Revised manumission laws further restricted freed Blacks' mobility. As part of the 1832 Black Code, freed people were required to leave the state, either voluntarily or under the auspices of the Maryland Colonization Society. Any who chose to remain—and there were many—would have to acquire formal authorization or risk reenslavement. The state even created a Board of Managers for the Removal of Colored People to oversee the state's collaboration with the Colonization Society.[21]

Restrictions on the movement of free and freed Blacks surely had something to do with the continued urbanization of the borderlands' Black population. Between 1830 and 1850, the number of free Blacks in Baltimore rose by two-thirds to more than twenty-five thousand. By 1850, 34 percent of Maryland's free Black population resided in Baltimore. The pattern replicated itself throughout the state, with free Blacks substantially more concentrated in larger towns than in the surrounding counties. In Frederick County, free Blacks constituted less than 10 percent of the population. In Frederick Town, their numbers approached 14 percent of the total. In Washington County, formerly part of western Frederick County, 6 percent of the population were free Blacks, while in Hagerstown the number was over 11 percent. The shift was less pronounced in Pennsylvania and Delaware, but a move to the cities was still evident. Between 1830 and 1850, Philadelphia County's free Black population rose by a third to almost twenty thousand. And New Castle County, Delaware, by a wide margin the state's most populous county, experienced a nearly 25 percent increase. In all the more rural borderlands counties of Maryland, free Blacks as a percentage of the population barely increased, while slave populations declined substantially. In Pennsylvania there was far less variation, but still, five of twelve border counties experienced declines in the relative size of their Black populations. The same was the case in Philadelphia County, where overall population growth was around 100 percent. The county's free Black population came nowhere near that rate of growth, but it nonetheless did grow, and by 1850 around four times as many free Blacks lived there as lived in Chester, the county with the next-highest free Black population. Prohibited from competing for wages in adjoining states, free Blacks chose kin and community in urban Black enclaves.[22]

Harriet Martineau's liberal social science has had remarkable staying power. As late as the 1950s, historian Louis Hartz interpreted the nineteenth-century political economy of Pennsylvania through a similar theoretical frame. Much like Martineau, Hartz saw in early nineteenth-century Pennsylvania a place of extraordinary economic dynamism. And like Martineau, he saw Pennsylvanians as essentially self-interested—markets would prevail over morals. But Hartz also offered a crucial qualification to his nineteenth-century classical liberal forebears. Early American capitalism was not laissez-faire capitalism. To assume otherwise was, for Hartz, only to embrace the tired frontier myth that the lightly governed American outback was uniquely fertile ground for unfettered market forces. For Hartz, politics, driven by regional commercial interests, generated policy designed to sustain and subsidize sectional commercial interests. And nowhere, in Hartz's view, was this distinctly American version of state-managed capitalism more evident than in Pennsylvania, where "government assumed the job of shaping decisively the contours of economic life," and usually did so at the behest of specific interests. Much like the influential mid-twentieth-century Hungarian political economist Karl Polanyi, Hartz sought to put the lie to the classical liberal ideal championed by latter-day inheritors of Martineau and other proponents of free market doctrine. Far from being the market's enemy, government—the liberal democratic variety as much as the authoritarian variety—facilitated the movement of goods and capital. Such thinking would clearly be anathema, if not to Martineau and her political economist contemporaries, then at least to their latter-day free-market inheritors. But still, Hartz's understanding of political economy in Pennsylvania, both as an ideological matter and as an actual economic one, assumes a frame largely compatible with that of the classical liberals. Interests rather than ideals, profits rather than ideology, regional jealousies, and a kind of economic nationalism, rather than any commitment to abstractions, even of the free market variety, drove Pennsylvania's political economy.[23] In Hartz's view, much as in Martineau's, constitutional mechanisms such as state boundaries ultimately had very little meaning. Commercial interests, using the levers of government, shaped economies and did so with far more regard for themselves than for any legal or constitutional barriers.

Much as opponents of slavery and, *pace* Hartz, Philadelphia's commercial leaders struggled to have it otherwise, the white population of the borderlands continued to behave as if there were no Mason-Dixon Line. Capital, labor, goods—all flowed freely, mostly to the great advantage of the city of Baltimore and its commercial classes. Interests, not constitutional impositions on those interests, were what ultimately shaped the political economy of the region adjoining the Mason-Dixon Line. But those same interests—embodied, for Hartz, in the persons of financiers, merchants, and other capitalists who dominated Pennsylvania's politics—would ultimately be responsible for making the Line into something more than an innocuous vestige of colonial property disputes. Internal improvements, financed by the public-private partnerships Hartz so brilliantly illuminated, would ultimately bring an end to greater Baltimore. Canals had some role in this change, but it was the railroads that sealed greater Baltimore's fate.

Pennsylvania Governor Joseph Ritner, elected as the candidate of the Anti-Mason Party and a product of far western Washington County, declared in his 1836 state of the state speech that next to the Freemasons and other secret societies, the "great malady of the times is that desire . . . of acquiring wealth without labor." As long as some Pennsylvanians embraced the "doctrine that money is power," the state would be overwhelmed by "a gambling spirit of speculation." This truism sat awkwardly with greater investment in transportation infrastructure, a pillar of Ritner's economic platform but one likely to enrich the eastern financial interests he decried. Those interests, as far as Ritner's overwhelmingly western, rural constituency was concerned, only seemed to be growing more powerful. Pennsylvania's state debt had ballooned during the internal improvements boom, a boon to creditors. The problem was less a financial one than a political one. In an exceptional rhetorical maneuver, Ritner noted the ever-mounting costs of canals and railroads, "sad proof of the selfishness of sectional jealousy and of log-rolling legislation." Pennsylvanians could agree that speculative investment had pernicious effects on ordinary Pennsylvanians. Internal improvements, in contrast, benefited all. Such, in essence, had long been the fundamental political dilemma of the borderlands: how to serve the commonwealth without moving capital from the countryside to the city?[24]

This perennial question found new prominence at the constitutional convention of 1837, in a debate over whether both the city and the county of Philadelphia deserved representation in the state assembly. Delegates from greater Baltimore complained that the fifteen legislators from the city and the county routinely aligned against improvements benefiting the western part of the state. One delegate from Franklin County noted that when "the citizens of York . . . applied to the Legislature for liberty to make a railroad with their own money to the Maryland line, ever many in the city and county of Philadelphia opposed the application." Thaddeus Stevens, a convention delegate from Gettysburg, complained that nothing, not political party, not the well-being of the state's economy, not benevolence, intruded on Philadelphia's predilection to vote its narrow financial interests. "When it became necessary to build up a system of internal improvements for the benefit of that great metropolis," Stevens recalled, "we find the [assemblymen] from the city and county of Philadelphia . . . almost voting to make it a penal offence to clear a channel in [the Susquehanna], for fear that some persons would prefer carrying their produce down it to Baltimore, in preference to carrying it . . . on horseback to Philadelphia."[25]

Although Maryland's sectional divisions were never as pronounced as Pennsylvania's, they did exist, usually dividing the state's tidewater from its western and northern counties. To avoid the inevitable sectional fights over public works most clearly benefiting greater Baltimore, proprietors of the state's growing network of canals and railroads settled on a frothy mix of patriotism and pomp. Accordingly, July 4, 1828, was a very busy day for the builders of Maryland's new arteries of commerce. John Quincy Adams, in the final year of his only term as president, would preside over proceedings in Georgetown, still a small river village in the District of Columbia. Before nearly a thousand spectators, the president would break ground for the new Chesapeake and Ohio Canal. Forty miles to the northeast, another ceremony was under way. This one involved setting a cornerstone commemorating the start of construction of the primary rival to the Chesapeake and Ohio Canal, the Baltimore and Ohio Railroad. Presiding was Charles Carroll, the ninety-year-old scion of one of colonial Maryland's wealthiest families and one of the few surviving links to Maryland's Catholic colonial past. In addition to being an investor in the railroad, Carroll had the added and far more important distinction of being the only surviving signer of the Declaration of Independence. The ceremony took place on former Carroll family land, sold to the railroad by Carroll's cousin James Carroll and now adjoining Mount Clare, James Carroll's estate and the former Carroll family summer residence. The elderly Carroll followed his labors with a sip of water and seems to have suffered no ill effects from the day's performance. President Adams, just a few days shy of his fifty-ninth birthday, meanwhile, reported that the ceremony and the ensuing celebrations left him so "exhausted and fatigued . . . that I was disqualified for thought or action the remainder of the day."[26]

Two years later, Carroll, now ninety-two, was the first passenger on the new railroad. He rode aboard a horse-drawn car, traveling thirteen miles to Ellicott's Mills. By 1834 the railroad had reached Harpers Ferry on the Potomac, and by 1835 a southern branch reached Washington. The completion of a railroad bridge across the Potomac in January 1837 unleashed the true potential of the Baltimore and Ohio. Five years later it reached Cumberland, in far western Maryland, a major junction on the National Road. The new railroad fueled the latest phase of Baltimore's rise. In 1848, the railroad carried 66,000 tons of coal to Baltimore, 13,000 tons of livestock, 7,000 tons of iron, 6,000 tons of stone, and 5,000 tons of tobacco. The Baltimore and Ohio railroad brought this cargo to Baltimore at higher speed than had ever before been possible, and although canals moved cargo more cheaply, railroads did so at between a third and half the price per ton per mile of other forms of overland transport.[27]

The same internal improvements boom that served Baltimore also served Philadelphia. For greater Baltimore, that meant only one thing: rural producers and regional market towns that had overwhelmingly depended on the markets of Baltimore would become ever less dependent on those markets. Railroads meant that parts of the borderlands long detached from Pennsylvania's commercial capital now had cheap and speedy ways of accessing Philadelphia's markets. The railroad boom also meant that those borderlands producers who had relied so heavily on Baltimore for credit could exploit the robust credit markets of Philadelphia.

York, Pennsylvania, was among the many borderlands towns transformed by the railroads. The Baltimore and Susquehanna, completed in 1838, secured York's ties to Baltimore, but a new railroad bridge at the old Wright's Ferry landing, now the town of Wrightsville, afforded the town easy access to Lancaster and Philadelphia. As a borderlands rail hub, York saw its industrial growth accelerate, and it emerged as a regional manufacturer of leather goods, farm implements, railroad cars, and all sorts of iron goods, from steamboats and steam locomotives to assorted consumer goods such as stoves, tools, and griddles. York's first iron foundry, established by Phineas Davis and Israel Gardner, had become so proficient that when the Baltimore and Ohio railroad commissioned the building of its first steam locomotive, called the York, it turned to Davis and Gardner. While most of York's trade remained oriented toward the much closer city of Baltimore, more of the town's trade was being directed to Philadelphia. For fine goods, particularly goods imported from Britain and Europe, Philadelphia was the preferred supplier. This only made sense. Although Baltimore had boomed over the course of the previous half century, most of that boom rested on trade with the growing American South and the West Indies. Philadelphia and its merchants remained, as they had been in the colonial era, the mid-Atlantic's chief importers of European-made goods. During the course of the nineteenth century, Philadelphians' knowledge of those goods and the continued influx of European migrants also made Philadelphia a center for the manufacture of consumer goods. Clothing, shoes, hats, pianos, windows, furs, and watches came to York mostly from Philadelphia. More than a satellite of Baltimore, York was now a manufacturing and transportation hub in its own right, a development made possible by the extension of Philadelphia's hinterlands across the Susquehanna into the western borderlands.[28]

A similar pattern appears in the growing towns and cities of Lancaster County. The newer town of Columbia, located at the old Wright's Ferry landing on the east bank of the Susquehanna, eleven miles west of Lancaster, was transformed by internal improvements into a dynamic transit point for goods moving to and from both Baltimore and Philadelphia. In 1829, the opening of a fourteen-mile canal linking the Chesapeake and Delaware Bays offered Columbia ready waterborne access to Philadelphia's markets— readier, that is, than the slow and hazardous sixty-six-mile Philadelphia-Lancaster turnpike. By 1834, a rail line linked Philadelphia to Columbia by way of Lancaster. With the completion of the Wrightsville Bridge across the Susquehanna, the town was also connected to Baltimore by rail. In addition to serving as a transit point for goods and produce, Columbia evolved into a regional industrial center. Through its river port it had ready access to timber and coal, both used as fuel for iron smelting. In the decade after 1844, ten coal-fired smelting furnaces were established near Columbia. By 1850, production of the new furnaces had reached 18,600 tons.[29]

Greater Baltimore of the 1830s and '40s would be a victim of its own commercial growth. York, Hagerstown, Frederick, Columbia, Lancaster, Carlisle, Chambersburg, Gettysburg, and dozens of other towns and cities across the Mason-Dixon borderlands prospered and grew—and all became less dependent on any single market. While this was the beginning of the end for greater Baltimore the commercial basin, greater Baltimore as a political region would change more slowly. Continued competition for wages generated some familiar struggles. Those struggles can be seen with particular clarity in Columbia, a town founded by antislavery Quakers, and long a home to slaves manumitted by Quaker planters in Maryland and Virginia.[30]

The 1830 federal "census" identified about 20 percent of Columbia's population as Black. That percentage changed very little over the next two decades. In 1850, there were 873 people of African descent living in Columbia. Most of these were wage laborers, but some were middle-class property owners. What is perhaps most important about Columbia's Black population is that over half had been born in Maryland and Virginia, most likely as slaves. Columbia's lumber mills, iron foundries, rail yards, and docks had

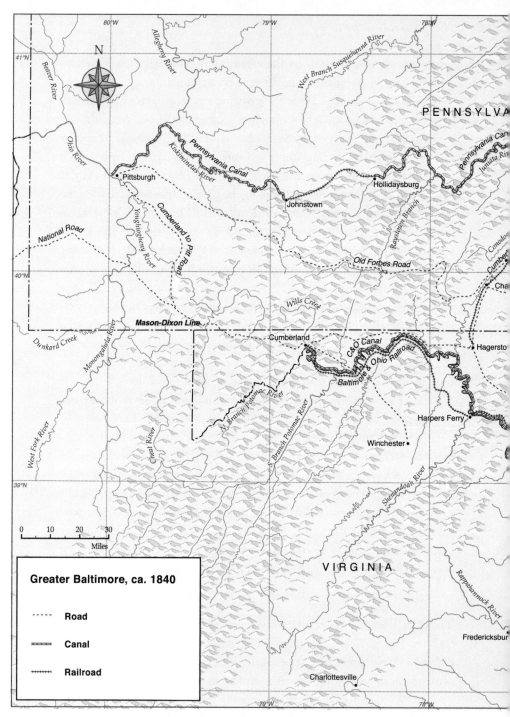

Greater Baltimore, c. 1840

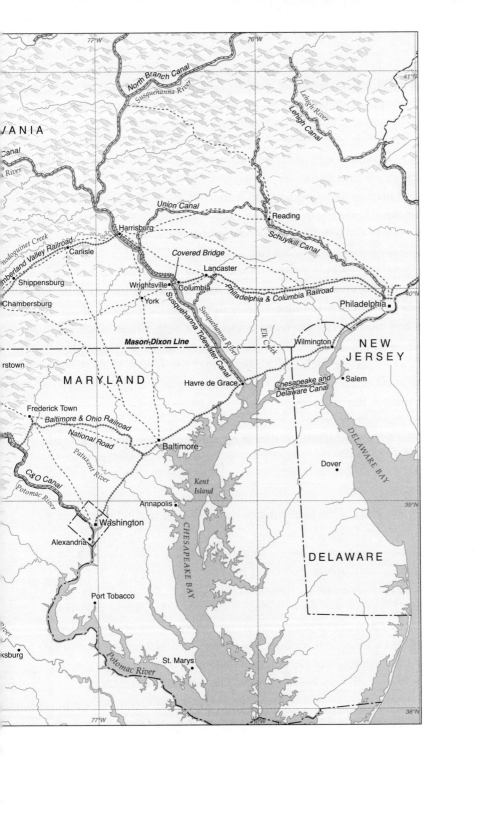

provided employment for freed people. The exact proportion of this southern-born Black population is unknown, but the evidence suggests it would have been substantial. Contemporary testimony identifies Columbia as a busy way station on the Underground Railroad. While conductors urged runaways to continue their flight north, these pleas were often ignored. William Whipper, an African American Underground Railroad conductor and lumberyard manager, recalled passing "hundreds to the land of freedom" in the late 1840s, but many others, "induced by high wages, and the feeling they were safe in Columbia, worked in the lumber and coal yards."[31]

The towns on the Pennsylvania side of the Mason-Dixon Line imposed a terrible devil's bargain on their free Black citizens. They could flee farther north, far from kin, or accept the many hazards of remaining near the Line. The gravity of the decision hinged only in part on the dangers of kidnapping and reenslavement. Wage competition with whites often left free Blacks with lower wages or forced them into cities and towns where the Black population constituted a much larger proportion of the labor force—and thus one somewhat less vulnerable to racists' attempts to control the labor market. But in the booming industrial towns of greater Baltimore, even in towns with substantial Black populations such as Columbia, the competition for wages and the politics of race often defeated the benefits of urbanization.

The year 1834 marked the beginning of a twenty-year rise in the number of riot complaints heard by Lancaster County's courts. The surge in accusations coincided with episodes of urban unrest that swept through the largest mid-Atlantic towns and cities between 1834 and 1836. Between 1832 and 1849, Philadelphia experienced five distinct periods of violent, destructive urban unrest. In Baltimore, in August 1835, anger over the failure of the Bank of Maryland erupted into several days of rioting that destroyed much of the city's center. Order was only restored after a militia under the command of General Samuel Smith, an aged military hero from the War of 1812, stormed the city. This unrest and similar riots in other American cities unleashed fears that every gathering was prelude to riotous upheaval, accounting, at least in part, for the Lancaster courts' rise in riot cases.[32]

While historians continue to debate the reasons for the surge in actual urban unrest, questions of race and slavery were rarely far from the surface. Mobs opposed to abolition routinely attacked abolitionist meetings and the homes of prominent abolitionists. In October 1835, an antiabolitionist mob in Boston nearly killed the nation's leading white abolitionist, William Lloyd Garrison, and in 1837, the abolitionist newspaper editor Elijah P. Lovejoy was shot and killed while defending his Alton, Illinois, press from a pro-slavery mob. This popular unrest was primarily the work of white men, but over the 1830s the nature of the mobs began to shift. From political demonstrations against what their organizers regarded as pernicious and radical abolitionism, they devolved into raw race riots, taking more or less random aim at African Americans, African American property, and anything else that could be associated with urban America's Black population.

In the summer of 1834, mobs of mostly white workingmen attacked Philadelphia's Black community. Stephen James, a hardworking family man, was murdered in the violence, and the homes of prominent Philadelphia Black families were attacked. The rampage was driven by familiar economic grievances—white laborers' resentment over wage competition from Black workers. A citizens' committee, charged with identifying the causes of the rioting, urged Black leaders to inform the city's Blacks of "the necessity, as well as the propriety, of behaving themselves inoffensively and with civility at all times and upon all occasions; taking care, as they pass along the streets, or assemble together, not to be obtrusive."[33] The contagion of anti-Black rioting reached Columbia the same month it erupted in Philadelphia. A mob of white men, mostly laborers and petty tradesmen, tore through Columbia's Black district, sparing lives but not property—especially that of Columbia's well-established Black middle class.

Rather than face more destruction by the white mob, Stephen Smith, Columbia's most prosperous Black resident, chose to liquidate his flourishing lumberyard. Columbia's middle-class white residents, meanwhile, blamed abolitionists within the Black community for inciting the attacks. This canard was given the lie by the rioters' own testimony. The problem was not abolitionism but wage competition. As reported by the *Columbia Spy,* the rioters expressed long-pent-up frustrations over "the practice of others in employing the negroes to do that labour which was formerly done entirely by whites." Not only did this give the town's Blacks an advantage in employment, in the view of the rioters, but it also allowed some of them to enter the middle class. Meanwhile, in words emblematic of so much white grievance in the borderlands, "poor whites may gradually sink into the degraded condition of the negroes," enduring similar and "disgusting servility to their employers and their unbearable insolence to the working class."[34]

Attacks on Columbia's Black community continued for another year. The dynamics differed little from those behind the initial outrage—white work-ingmen attacking the property of free Blacks. Although race riots are the most readily identified acts of racial violence directed at working and middle-class Blacks, they barely begin to capture the full range of racial abuse Amer-icans of African descent endured in the years of free labor's expansion. In some cases the assaults on working free Blacks were planned as orderly paramilitary acts—an indication of how untroubled urban whites were by blatantly discriminatory assaults on Black economic freedoms. In 1828, for instance, the white cartmen of Baltimore petitioned the state legislature for a ban on Black cartmen. The campaign failed; Baltimore's merchants initi-ated a countercampaign, not out of sympathy for the plight of Baltimore's Black cartmen but out of a desire to keep wages low.[35]

Perhaps the best-known instance of white workers terrorizing Black labor appears in Frederick Douglass's autobiography. Though Douglass was still enslaved, his master hired him out to a Baltimore shipyard. After eight months working as a caulker alongside white and free Black ship's carpen-ters and apprentices, the yard's white carpenters struck. "Their reason for this," Douglass recalled, "was, that if free colored carpenters were encour-aged, they would soon take the trade into their own hands, and poor white men would be thrown out of employment." Although the owner of the ship-yard acceded to the demands of the white carpenters, he continued to em-ploy the slave Douglass, who was attacked and beaten by white apprentices "in sight of not less than fifty white ship-carpenters."[36] "Every arrival from Europe," Baltimore lawyer and historian John H. B. Latrobe noted, was a warning to the area's free Blacks. These immigrants "enter into competition with the black man in all the avenues of labor." The consequences of this unrelenting flood of white labor were plain: "In Baltimore, my home town, ten years since, the shipping at Fell's Point was loaded by free colored ste-vedores. The labor at the coal yards was free colored labor. In the rural districts around Baltimore . . . free colored laborers, ten years since, got in the harvest, worked the mine banks, made the fences, and, indeed, supplied, to a great extent, all agricultural wants in this respect. Now all this is changed. The white man stands in the black man's shoes." Racial animus was hardly the only difficulty Black wage earners confronted.[37]

In addition to the pass system and other restrictions on Black movement, Maryland's free Blacks faced a host of other restrictive injunctions. Free Blacks were required to secure formal license to own a gun, purchase ammunition, own a dog, or purchase liquor. In order to sell produce, including bacon, pork, beef, mutton, corn, wheat, tobacco, rye, or oats, a justice of the peace, along with two "respectable" witnesses, would have to vouch for the legality of the goods, the presumption being that, if sold by Blacks, they were likely stolen. Free Blacks could not operate boats without white supervision, and in most Maryland counties they could enter taverns and shops only during limited hours. Most of these regulations were justified as necessary for curtailing theft and slave flight. But their primary effect was to limit the economic prospects of free Blacks, driving ever larger numbers to Baltimore and north across the border to Pennsylvania.[38]

In conjunction with restrictions on Black movement, these laws had a chilling effect on the labor markets of greater Baltimore. Black laborers simply could not follow work and wages in the way whites could. One Pennsylvania farmer who lived near the Line recalled that "the colored men employed as farmhands could not be sent across the line, even with a team, lest they would be claimed as slaves."[39] Although greater Baltimore was the most economically expansive portion of the borderlands, competition for labor existed elsewhere along the Line, particularly on Maryland's Eastern Shore and in Delaware. Decades of rising labor costs, owing mostly to the departure of free Blacks, prompted Delaware to implement its own Black Code, although with an intent opposite that of its neighbor state. To prevent the state's free Blacks from seeking higher wages out of state, Delaware imposed a residency requirement. Those who left the state for more than six months would lose their residency status and be vulnerable to assorted vagrancy statutes in adjoining states, some carrying the punishment of reenslavement. To address an apparent "habit of leaving the State during the most important working seasons, when their labor is most necessary to the white population," in 1849 the state revised its vagrancy code. Free Blacks who returned to the state after an absence of more than sixty days would face prosecution under the revised vagrancy laws. Now, any kind of migratory quest for better wages carried the risk of imprisonment and re-enslavement. White farmers could, effectively, keep free Blacks as wage slaves.[40]

During the first half of the nineteenth century, the laws of slavery did very little to overcome the forces of the market along the Line. Farmers, petty merchants, manufacturers, and laborers all moved and traded freely in the borderlands, with little particular connection to any state or its financial and commercial capital. Labor, goods, and capital moved back and forth across the Line just as any good liberal would have expected. The one exception to this pattern was the labor of African Americans. For enslaved laborers, though ever fewer in number, the restrictions were obvious and familiar. But for free Blacks, legal restrictions in conjunction with illegal cross-border kid-napping and intimidation by free white laborers and their antiabolitionist al-lies converged to impose a new kind of servitude. Insofar as the Mason-Dixon Line had any economic significance in early nineteenth-century America, it did so primarily because it had significance in the lives of Black Americans.

Another Harriet, the self-manumitted slave and Underground Railroad conductor Harriet Tubman, spent much of her youth struggling to grasp the Line's meaning. Tubman was born in the early 1820s on Maryland's Eastern Shore, in Dorchester County. The timing of her birth was inauspicious. The internal slave trade was particularly active on the Eastern Shore, and Har-riet watched siblings, cousins, and other family members shipped off to the Deep South. Harriet was spared this fate but endured her own horrid trials. Beginning at age five, her owner hired her out, first as a domestic, then as a field hand. She endured long separation from her mother and endured much physical abuse. Harriet eventually married John Tubman, a free Black also from Dorchester County. Around 1849 she began hearing rumors that her owner—who a local lawyer had discovered was maintaining a claim to ownership of Harriet in violation of the will of Harriet's mother's former owner—intended to send her downriver to cover debts. As did so many other enslaved Americans living near the Line, Harriet abandoned every-thing and gave herself over to conductors on the Underground Railroad, eventually making her way to Philadelphia.

In 1869, Tubman collaborated with the writer Sarah Hopkins Bradford on the autobiographical *Scenes in the Life of Harriet Tubman*. Tubman describes a series of visions, in one of which, she explained to Bradford, "I seemed to see a line, and on the other side of that line were green fields, and lovely flowers, and beautiful white ladies, who stretched out their arms to me over the line, but I couldn't reach them no how. I always fell before I got to the line." That line, it later became clear, was the Line separating slave states from free. Tubman does not say that those states were Maryland, Delaware, and Pennsylvania. As was the case for enslaved Americans everywhere, it did not much matter where the Line ran or what states abutted it. What mattered was that there was such a line—a metaphoric river Jordan. "When I found I had crossed that line," Tubman recalled, "I looked at my hands to see if I was the same person. There was such glory over every thing; the sun came like gold through the trees, and over the fields, and I felt like I was in Heaven. . . . I had crossed the line. I was free." Of course, the glory that came over Tubman was not unqualified. With freedom came a clear sense of loss: "My home, after all, was down in Maryland; because my father, my mother, my brothers, and sisters, and friends were there." As a conductor on the Underground Railroad, Tubman would do all she could to bring family members and other bondspeople across the Line.[41]

Her efforts, and those of countless other freed people, would prompt the federal government to seek the most far-reaching legal transformation in the Line's history. From a boundary between states, given legal legitimacy by the laws of those states, the Line would become an instrument of federal law, used by the federal government to arrest the flow of fugitives from slavery. Not only would those efforts fail, but they would reinforce for white Americans what had been so clear to Americans of African descent for at least two generations.

PART IV

THE AGE OF THE MASON-DIXON LINE

By the 1850s, two Mason-Dixon Lines had emerged. One, a largely innocuous jurisdictional limit with little meaning for white Americans, including the legions of recently arrived immigrants who populated the borderlands. The other, long familiar to Black Americans, was a quasi-international border regulated by a legal apparatus that now included federal law enforcement agents. By 1860, these two Lines had begun to merge into one as Black Americans, through their flight from slavery and efforts on behalf of those fleeing slavery, forced northerners to confront the reality that southern slave power had become national slave power. The borderlands began to show signs that now, for white Americans, the Line was far more than an innocuous jurisdictional boundary. For the first time in its history, political division along the Line would reflect the nation's larger sectional divide. With the eruption of war in 1861, few borderlands whites would doubt the Line's profound significance. Even though Maryland remained in the Union, it did so reluctantly and not out of a desire to join a crusade against slavery. For Confederate military commanders, the Line remained what it had long been for Black Americans: the border between North and South, making Maryland a vital object of Confederate conquest. But it was clear to Confederate general Robert E. Lee that securing Maryland would be impossible without securing what remained of greater Baltimore. For the first time since the mid-eighteenth century, the borderlands experienced the destructive force of large-scale military conflict.

CHAPTER 11

The Second Fugitive Slave Act

THE PHILADELPHIA PHYSICIAN, revolutionary, and evangelical Benjamin Rush founded Dickinson College, in Carlisle, the capital of Cumberland County, the same year the Treaty of Paris ended the Revolutionary War. Sons of the borderlands, some of whom were raised in German-speaking households, would learn the refinements of the English language, Latin and Greek, moral philosophy, and Christian theology. Some would elect to serve as ministers of God's word in the war-weary borderlands. To facilitate the formal sanction that would allow the college to incorporate, Rush and his associates named it for John Dickinson, a former member of the Delaware colonial assembly, Pennsylvania's most esteemed jurist, and, as president of the Pennsylvania Supreme Executive Council, presiding magistrate for the state's formal chartering of the college.

Rush was an astute physician and a skilled propagandist for the various revolutionary causes he championed—which, beyond the independence of the United States, included the abolition of slavery and new treatments for disorders of the mind—but as a political economist, he was decidedly out of his element. He had very little sense that as greater Baltimore's leading institution of higher education, Dickinson was unlikely to attract the sort of grave and duty-bound backwoods Pennsylvanians he hoped for. Within a few decades of Dickinson's founding, the college had been absorbed into the maw of greater Baltimore and now sat nowhere near the western edge of

Pennsylvania's Euro-American settlement. Its students were far more likely to be young men on the make, hailing from America's first great commercial heartland, than Rush's untutored sons of a fictive American frontier.

Among the college's early graduates were two products of the Line's borderlands, Roger B. Taney and James Buchanan, both of whom became prominent lawyers, and both of whom would serve in two of the highest offices of the land—one as chief justice of the United States Supreme Court, the other as president of the United States. Both also followed a similar path in their political allegiance. They began their public careers as members of the old Federalist Party of Alexander Hamilton and John Adams, but migrated to Andrew Jackson's Democratic Party and eventually attached themselves to the most proslavery wing of that party. Insofar as any two men could have been responsible for the catastrophe that carried the United States into civil war, these two are as likely as any to warrant blame. But their place in the Line's history lies less with the collapse of the Union than with their paths to political prominence.

Taney moved from the executive branch to the nation's highest court, and James Buchanan, as much a fixture in Washington as in his home county of Lancaster, rose primarily through electoral politics. The two men's political paths would converge on March 4, 1857, when Buchanan was sworn in by Chief Justice Taney as the fifteenth president of the United States. That very public meeting was mere prelude to a far more consequential political convergence. The chief justice chose to await the new president's inauguration before issuing his infamous decision in *Dred Scott v. Sandford*. In an ignominious start to what would be among the two or three most disastrous presidencies in American history, President Buchanan applauded the decision for bringing an end to years of political conflict over slavery. Of course, *Dred Scott* did nothing of the sort.

Roger B. Taney was born on a tobacco plantation in Calvert County, Maryland, in 1777. He was the third of seven children in a Catholic family whose Maryland roots stretched back to the seventeenth century. His eldest brother, Michael, inherited the family estate. Roger and his brother Augustus would pursue law careers, while the youngest son, Octavius, became a medical doctor. Michael Taney Sr., the family patriarch, upheld the image of Chesapeake planter—slave owner, gentleman, and obsessive attendant to his sons' educations. Among his son's tutors, one of them, Princeton graduate David English, advised Taney senior to lose no time advancing young Roger to college. After gaining assurances about the boy's well-being from Charles Nisbet, principal (as the president was called) of Dickinson College, in 1792 Michael Taney sent his fifteen-year-old son north to Carlisle to matriculate in the town's celebrated new college.

Exactly why Roger attended Dickinson is unknown. The elder Taney was reassured by Nisbet, a recent Scottish immigrant and noted Presbyterian theologian, but the decision may also have had something to do with the college's young Latin and Greek tutor, Charles Huston, himself a recent Dickinson graduate. Later in life, Roger remembered Huston with particular fondness, perhaps because Taney's career path would so closely resemble his former teacher's. While Roger was still a student, Huston left Dickinson to establish a law practice in rural Lycoming County, and after serving on the state circuit court, in 1826 he was appointed to the Pennsylvania Supreme Court. Taney graduated from Dickinson in 1795 and in the spring of 1796 began reading law with Annapolis judge Jeremiah Townley Chase. After three years of study, Taney was admitted to the Maryland bar. He briefly practiced in Calvert County before relocating to Frederick, where he would spend more than twenty years, ultimately becoming one of the town's leading attorneys and a figure known throughout Maryland for his skill before the bar.[1]

Taney's dear friend Francis Scott Key, another Frederick lawyer and eventual author of "The Star-Spangled Banner," may have invited Taney to Frederick, or it may have been that Taney was following his heart. In early 1806, having established himself in Frederick, he married Key's sister, Anne, whom Taney had initially met in Annapolis. Anne was Protestant and she and Roger raised their children as Protestants, but Roger never abandoned his Catholic faith. He helped found a new Roman Catholic church in Frederick and would continue to practice Catholic rites for the rest of his life. Reverend John McElroy, who became the priest at Taney's Frederick church, remembered that Taney's "well-known humility made the practice of confession easy to him. Often have I seen him stand at the outer door leading to the confessional, in a crowd of penitents, a majority colored, waiting his *turn* for admission."[2] This latter assessment was very likely part of a decades-long attempt by friends and fellow jurists to restore Taney's reputation after his death in 1864, just days before Maryland abolished slavery.

Far from a crude, inveterate racist, this refurbished Taney was a racial ecumenical, prepared to stand in line with his Black neighbors awaiting common absolution. Taney almost certainly was racist—a typical member of the borderlands white population, fearful of free Blacks, but not entirely comfortable with slavery. This background was not what animated the urge to cleanse his reputation. That came from his work as chief justice of the US Supreme Court, especially the majority opinion he wrote in *Dred Scott v. Sandford*, by far the most infamous Supreme Court decision of the antebellum era, and one that not only exacerbated political tensions preceding the Civil War but also asserted, in no uncertain terms, a constitutional doctrine of racial caste. In his majority opinion, Taney effectively denied all Americans of African descent, whether free or slave, the rights of full citizenship, and he did so on crudely racial grounds. Taney's path to *Dred Scott* was not foreordained. The opinion, which in its efforts to adjudicate the question of whether or not Dred Scott, an enslaved African American from Missouri, was entitled to file suit in federal courts, sits awkwardly with elements of Taney's early legal career.

As might be expected of a law office near the Mason-Dixon Line, Taney's was occasionally engaged in legal action involving free and enslaved Blacks. For the most part, Taney's legal work reflected the views of his friend Key, an ardent colonizationist and local defender of accused runaways. Taney took several cases in defense of free Blacks, some kidnapped in Pennsylvania, others accused of crimes in Maryland—the accusations a frequent ploy to justify reenslavement. Taney also intervened on behalf of Blacks caught in the borderlands' bewildering web of race and miscegenation laws. In order to preserve the marriage of a free Black man and his enslaved wife, Taney and an associate purchased the woman. As a means of reimbursing the purchase price of his wife, the woman's husband, Harry Peter, had himself bound to Taney and his legal associate for a ten-year term, on the condition that the couple be freed at the end of the term. The scheme was not exactly a financially daring proposition for Taney, but nonetheless typical of antislavery activism in the borderlands. Insofar as freedom for enslaved Blacks could be achieved at little or no cost, or even with some clear financial benefit to the white manumitters, it was a matter of routine. It would, however, be wrong to say that Taney was unwilling to bear any cost for his antislavery leanings. At one time he owned seven slaves: Clarissa and her infant daughter Mary Anne; Polly, whose youngest daughter was Elizabeth and who had three older children, Mary, John, and William, all of whom Taney also owned. In 1818, Taney completed manumission proceedings, allowing these slaves to be freed by 1836. In 1820, he and his younger brother Octavius also arranged for the manumission of two additional slaves who had been owned by their father, Michael.[3]

Taney continued to oppose slavery and its expansion following his election to the Maryland state senate in 1816. He voted with the minority in opposing an 1820 resolution supporting Missouri's admission to the Union as a slave state, and in 1821, his last year in the Senate, he again voted with the minority to uphold limits on the importation of slaves into Maryland.

By far the best-known illustration of Taney's early position on race and slavery occurred in his capacity as attorney and involved the 1819 legal defense he waged on behalf of the Reverend Jacob Gruber, a Methodist preacher from Carlisle, Pennsylvania. Maryland authorities accused Gruber of sedition after he attacked the sin of slavery during an outdoor campfire sermon. The sermon may have gone unnoticed had Gruber preached it anywhere but far western Washington County, a portion of Maryland heavily influenced by neighboring Virginia. For slave owners in his audience, Gruber's message hit altogether too close to home, and local authorities charged him with inciting slave rebellion. Gruber's local Maryland counsel, Roger B. Taney, dismembered the case against his client. Although Gruber was an abolitionist, Taney explained to the court, he was also a gradualist. Nothing in his prior conduct suggested any interest in extrajudicial destruction of slavery. His views of "those reptiles, who live by trading in human flesh, and enrich themselves by tearing the husband from wife—the infant from the bosom of the mother" could hardly be called controversial. In characterizing Gruber's views, Taney himself asserted, in no uncertain terms, that slavery was an "evil" and a "blot on our national character," and that propounding these widely held views, as Gruber had done, demonstrated no intent to incite rebellion. The Frederick County jurors concurred and returned a verdict of not guilty.[4]

Taney's reputation only grew after the Gruber trial, and he moved his practice to Baltimore. In 1827, he became Maryland's attorney general and his antislavery views began giving way to his state's political reality. At Taney's direction the state defended a Baltimore merchant and shipbuilder accused of violating federal laws prohibiting the transatlantic slave trade.

John Gooding, the defendant in the case, was accused by federal authorities of outfitting a ship with the intent of carrying slaves from Africa to Cuba. Taney attacked the prosecution's case, noting that short of showing Gooding himself acquiring captives on Africa's west coast, the federal government could not demonstrate his intent to engage in the transatlantic slave trade. The argument does not suggest an entirely clear path from the antislavery Taney of Frederick to the Taney of *Dred Scott v. Sandford*. But it does suggest that Taney's opposition to slavery had limits—even if those limits were politically driven. As chief law enforcement officer for the state of Maryland, Taney would have paid a steep political price for advancing an antislavery agenda. The slaveowning planters of the tidewater remained a powerful voting constituency. In this particular case, the politics afforded a convenient middle path. Few could fault the attorney general for defending Baltimore's merchants from intrusions by the federal government. In some ways, this was an entirely predictable position for someone with Taney's history. Slavery may have been odious, but any assault on the commercial vibrancy of greater Baltimore was more odious. As attorney general of the largely proslavery administration of Andrew Jackson, Taney defended avowedly racist policies. In the most notorious such case, he defended a South Carolina statute that allowed authorities to detain all Black seafarers arriving in Charleston Harbor, whether free or slave.

President Jackson rewarded his attorney general in 1835 with a nomination to replace retiring associate justice Gabriel Duvall on the Supreme Court. After this nomination failed to gain Senate approval, Jackson again nominated Taney, this time to serve as chief justice following the death of John Marshall. In March 1836, the Senate confirmed Taney as the new chief justice.[5]

By far Taney's most important legal action on the issue of slavery before *Dred Scott* was his concurrent opinion in the Supreme Court's *Prigg v. Pennsylvania* decision. The case involved Marylander Edward Prigg, a constable from Harford County, who had traveled to York County to claim runaways Margaret Morgan and her children, allegedly owned by a Harford County associate of Prigg's. Although a justice of the peace issued a warrant for the arrest of Margaret and her children, no Pennsylvania court authorized their rendition as required by the state's personal liberty law. Prigg, uninhibited by the particularities of Pennsylvania law, carried his captives back to Maryland.

The tangled legal status of Margaret and her children was typical of free Blacks in the borderlands. The owner of Margaret's parents had allowed them to live in Harford County as free Blacks without ever formalizing their manumission. Margaret, raised as a free Black in a free Black household, eventually married another free Black, and later moved with her family to York County, just north of the Line. At least one of Margaret's children was known to have been born in Pennsylvania. After her kidnapping, Margaret filed a freedom suit in the Harford County court, but the jury decided against her, and she and her children, even the child born in Pennsylvania, remained enslaved in Maryland.

A Pennsylvania grand jury, meanwhile, indicted Prigg for kidnapping. Maryland authorities refused an extradition request, and after five years of wrangling, the case made its way to the Supreme Court—and would be the Court's first direct ruling on the fugitive slave problem. The 1842 opinion, written by Justice Joseph Story, a former Harvard law professor and opponent of slavery, found Pennsylvania's personal liberty law to be unconstitutional and overturned Prigg's indictment. Story's opinion noted that the Fugitive Slave Law of 1793 affirmed slave owners' right to their property in human beings. It also affirmed Congress's jurisdiction in matters related to fugitives from slavery. In giving local magistrates control over the persons of accused runaways, Pennsylvania's 1826 law clearly violated both provisions. Story had long aligned himself with former chief justice John Marshall, at least on issues of federal power. His opinion reflected that pedigree. Here was a bold, unalloyed assertion of the supremacy of federal law in matters related to fugitives from slavery.

Although Story found in favor of Prigg, his opinion infuriated the Court's proslavery justices. Federal law may have guaranteed slave owners the right to carry their states' slave law anywhere in the United States; it may also have afforded Congress legislative supremacy on matters related to extradition and rendition; but in doing so, it absolved states from any clear responsibility for fugitives from slavery. In effect, the decision thereby rendered null the principle of comity on the issue of fugitives from slavery. States' laws may have remained valid across state lines, but since some of those laws fell under the jurisdiction of Congress, they would be enforceable only under federal auspices.

In his concurrent opinion, Taney placed himself squarely in the Court's proslavery camp. The chief justice agreed with Story's overall assessment of Pennsylvania's personal liberty law—it was unconstitutional. Where Taney disagreed was in his colleague's explanation. In fact, Congress's supremacy was only partial. True, it had unique authority to legislate when it came to matters of interstate fugitives and runaway slaves, but this in no way absolved states from responsibility for fugitives from slavery. The 1793 act indicated that fugitives from slavery "shall be delivered up." These words could have no other purpose, Taney noted, than to "impose it as a duty upon the people of the several states to pass laws to carry into execution, in good faith, the compact into which they thus solemnly entered with each other."[6] In other words, federal jurisdiction over the fugitive slave problem was entirely consistent with the basic principles of comity. States remained obliged not only to accept the laws of other states, so long as those laws were constitutional, but also to make law enabling the enforcement of those other state laws.

It is difficult to see in Taney's opinion anything less than a full-throated affirmation of a proslavery constitutionalism. Whatever the United States may have been, it was a society that protected the right to property in human beings—and it did so not as a matter of passive compliance but as an active condition of the "compact" uniting the several states. This interpretation was not entirely incompatible with Taney's earlier antislavery actions. Like many proponents of gradual abolition, Taney had been perfectly comfortable with the idea that the nature of the national compact implied comity when it came to property in human beings. States were, as a constitutional matter, obliged to protect property rights, regardless of the nature of the property. What is somewhat harder to square with Taney's earlier positions are the implications of his opinion for free Blacks. In overturning Pennsylvania's personal liberty law, the court took a bold stand against anti-kidnapping statutes. If, as Taney's opinion seemed to suggest, Pennsylvania was now obliged to enact new laws consistent with Maryland's proslavery law, free Blacks, some of whom Taney himself defended in kidnapping cases, would face a situation not unlike what they faced before the passage of the personal liberty law. Unless and until Congress intervened, the Line would effectively be obliterated and free Blacks would have no more rights north of it than they did to its south.

James Buchanan was born on a farm in far western Franklin County, Pennsylvania, in 1791, the child of Presbyterian Scots-Irish parents, his father a recent immigrant and his mother the daughter of immigrants. A few years after James's birth, the family relocated to Mercersburg, just north of the Line, where the family's dry goods business flourished. James enjoyed an education consistent with his family's new upper-middle-class station. Much of that education was the work of Elizabeth, James's mother, whose fondness for poetry meant she "could repeat with ease all the passages in her favorite authors," John Milton and Alexander Pope among them. James remembered his mother reciting verse and debating weighty theological and philosophical issues with her sons. Because "what she read once, she remembered forever," she was, he recalled, "a delightful and instructive companion."[7]

The young Buchanan left for Dickinson in 1807 but struggled against youthful temptations—temptations Buchanan later blamed on the college. "There was no efficient discipline, and the young men did pretty much as they pleased," Buchanan recalled. "To be a sober, plodding, industrious youth was to incur the ridicule of the mass of the students. Without much natural tendency to become dissipated, and chiefly from the example of others, and in order to be considered a clever and a spirited youth, I engaged in every sort of extravagance and mischief in which the greatest proficients of the college indulged." Buchanan's many infractions infuriated the college's principal, Robert Davidson, and were it not for the intervention of Dr. John King, pastor of the Buchanan family church, James would have been expelled after only a year.

Although Buchanan was able to complete his studies at Dickinson, he never overcame the animus engendered by his earlier reputation, and the faculty denied him commencement honors, leaving him, he later explained, with "little attachment towards the Alma Mater."[8] In 1809, Buchanan moved to Lancaster to study law in the office of James Hopkins, the county's most prominent attorney. As the United States began its second war against Great Britain in 1812, Buchanan was admitted to the Pennsylvania bar. After the sacking of Washington, DC, in August 1814, he heeded the call to arms and joined Lancaster volunteers sent to reinforce the defenses of Baltimore. The mission was a short one—not long enough for Buchanan to witness the September 14 shelling of Fort McHenry in Baltimore Harbor, the event that prompted Roger Taney's friend Francis Scott Key to pen "The Star-Spangled Banner." Later in life Buchanan remembered with pride his service in Baltimore and observed that he felt an affinity for that city, far more than Philadelphia, and had "selected it as the place where to practice my profession," but was prevented by "invincible reluctance, at the last moment, to leave my native State."[9]

Within weeks of completing his military service, Buchanan began a long and distinguished political career. Though he had stood before the county's bar for only a few years, Buchanan's reputation had risen high enough to earn his fellow citizens' confidence, and in October 1814, he was elected to represent Lancaster County in the state assembly. Buchanan's political successes nourished his legal ones, as was typical, and by the early 1820s he had amassed a small fortune. His personal life was not nearly so successful. In an episode that has long been at the center of Buchanan's biography—he was the only bachelor ever to serve as president of the United States—Buchanan suffered devastating personal heartbreak. His engagement to Ann Coleman, daughter of a wealthy Lancaster ironmaster, was broken off for reasons that remain unclear but very likely had to do with Buchanan's legal work. The engagement and its interruption took place in 1819, a year of national financial panic and a year when Buchanan's legal business was all-consuming.

Ann left for Philadelphia, where she would visit relatives and find distraction from the heavy emotional toll of a broken engagement. On the night of December 9, shortly after arriving, she died of a sudden illness. Some thought it was grief-induced suicide, but the cause has never been determined. For Buchanan's official biographer, the episode was the defining event of the future president's early life: "It became a grief that could not be spoken of; to which only the most distant allusion could be made; a sacred, unceasing sorrow, buried deep in the breast of a man who was formed for domestic joys; hidden beneath manners that were most engaging, beneath strong social tendencies, and a chivalrous, old-fashioned deference to women of all ages and all claims . . . It is certain that this occurrence prevented him from ever marrying."[10] Less than a year after Ann's death, Buchanan was elected to the US Congress, where he would serve until 1831, eventually joining Andrew Jackson's Democratic Party. Representing a state with few vocal proslavery partisans, but one that remained a center of antislavery activism, insofar as he made his early views on slavery known, Buchanan generally hewed to the antislavery side. In an 1826 speech on the floor of the United States House of Representatives, he proclaimed slavery "a great political and a great moral evil," but an evil whose consequences were borne mostly by others: "I thank God, my lot has been cast in a State where it does not exist."

But Buchanan would find it ever more difficult to insulate himself from slavery and its manifold evils. Lest his southern brethren mistake his views for the antislavery views so widespread in his home state, Buchanan also stood firm in his hatred of radical abolition. For "there are portions of this Union, in which, if you emancipate the slaves, they will become masters." The best course would be to adhere to what Buchanan believed the Constitution said on the issue: the legality of slavery should remain a state matter. Opponents of slavery simply inspired in the slave "false hopes of liberty, and thus make him disobedient, and discontented with his condition." Such vain hopes only "compel the master to use more severity, than would otherwise have been necessary." Hedging ever closer to the line of his proslavery southern Democratic colleagues, Buchanan ultimately concluded there were evils far worse than slavery. The nation's best path through the slavery problem, he would write years later, when he received his party's nomination for the presidency, must involve "putting down the fanatical and reckless spirit of Abolition."[11]

Buchanan's position on slavery was similar to the position Roger Taney took in his *Prigg v. Pennsylvania* opinion: the Constitution gave states power over slavery, but any laws states made with respect to slaves and slavery could not usurp the laws of other states. Nor could such laws supersede a federal constitution that, as far as these leaders were concerned, guaranteed the right to property in human beings. Neither the antislavery states nor the federal government had the power to eradicate slavery where it already existed. If this national evil was to be addressed, it would only be done in the most incremental fashion possible. For both Taney and Buchanan, that meant gradual solutions along the lines of those supported by colonizationists. Manumitters should be compensated for their liberated property, and freed Blacks, for their own welfare, should be assigned to a lower social caste, separated from white Americans by law and geography. Buchanan showed his bona fides in this extreme gradualism when he campaigned for the Senate in 1834. His party, the Democratic Party of Andrew Jackson, was the party of the vast majority of southern slave owners, but Pennsylvania's legislature remained staunchly antislavery and US Senators were elected by their states' legislatures.

As his campaign for the Senate progressed in the summer of 1834—if the internal party machinations and parliamentary maneuvers that led to a vote for the US senator from Pennsylvania can be called a campaign—Buchanan acted to insulate himself from the worst of his party's proslavery taint. He traveled to Greensburg, southeast of Pittsburgh, the hometown of his sister Harriet and her husband, the Reverend Robert Henry. Buchanan had learned that members of Henry's family, then living in Shepherdstown, Virginia, owned two slaves. As one biographer has written, "This was political dynamite." To avert disaster, Buchanan purchased the two slaves, Daphne Cook, aged twenty-two, and Ann Cook, aged five, and granted them their freedom in Pennsylvania. In a process typical of manumission proceedings and entirely in keeping with Pennsylvania law, Daphne would serve a seven-year term of indentured servitude and Ann, as a minor, would be bound until age twenty-eight.[12]

Following his election, Senator Buchanan would abandon even his already limited antislavery leanings and become the paradigmatic doughface, as the unprincipled and craven northern apologist for the dominant southern wing of the Democratic party came to be known (symbolized by a readily molded dough mask). Buchanan's doughface bona fides were firmly in place by 1845, when he left the Senate to become secretary of state for President James K. Polk. Although Polk regarded him as a profoundly ineffective diplomat, Secretary Buchanan stood firmly by the dominant southern faction of his party. He supported their schemes for annexing Cuba, and opposed a proposal, put forth by his fellow Pennsylvanian and Democrat, Representative David Wilmot, to ban slavery from territory acquired in the Mexican-American War. As a counter-proposal, Buchanan suggested the extension of the Missouri Compromise line to the Pacific Coast, paving the way for the western expansion of slavery. In 1820, as a condition for admitting Missouri as a slave state, Congress prohibited slavery in any territory north of the 36°30′ parallel of latitude. At the time, this compromise line included only territory acquired through the Louisiana Purchase. But the Mexican War introduced new possibilities for slavery's expansion. In consummate doughface fashion, Buchanan now invited the extension of slavery in former Mexican territory south of the 36°30′ line.

As he campaigned for his party's presidential nomination in 1847, Buchanan warned Pennsylvania Democrats that the question of slavery in western territories put the unity of the Democratic Party at risk. The best path forward was strict construction, affirming the rights of the states to determine the legality of slavery. "A sacred regard for the Federal Constitution and for the reserved rights of the States," Buchanan explained, "is the immovable basis on which the party can alone safely rest." Those like David Wilmot who insisted on raising the question of slavery in newly acquired territories demonstrated profound disdain for this most sacred of constitutional ideals. For in the end, agitation over the matter, "however honestly intended, can produce no effect but to alienate the people of different portions of the Union from each other; to excite sectional divisions and jealousies; and to distract and possibly destroy the Democratic party." Instead of aligning the party with deranged and radical abolitionists, as Wilmot's Proviso promised to do, better to fall back on hallowed constitutional tradition. For Buchanan, the Missouri Compromise represented a great and noble affirmation of that tradition, for "its adoption in 1820 saved the Union from threatened convulsion." Now that convulsion threatened again, but an easy alternative presented itself. By extending the 36°30′ Missouri Compromise line "to any New Territory which we may acquire," the country will "secure the like happy result."[13]

Buchanan's support for the limited western extension of slavery did little for his campaign. The Democratic nomination for president went to Senator Lewis Cass of Michigan, and Buchanan retreated to his Lancaster home.

Roger Taney and James Buchanan had known each other at least since their days in the administration of Andrew Jackson, and Taney was partly responsible for Buchanan's appointment as Jackson's minister to Russia.[14] As political creatures, they occupied the same doughface ground. Both regarded any overt antislavery politics as a species of radical abolitionism and a direct threat to the Union. Both claimed to favor a doctrine of states' rights even though in their opposition to personal liberty laws they opposed a bold assertion of states' rights. Taney's views on these laws became clear in his *Prigg* dissent. Buchanan's were slower to materialize. As part of a United States Senate far more interested in the problem of sectionalism than the problem of fugitive slaves, and as secretary of state, Buchanan had been able to do what so many national politicians had done for so long—avoid the fugitive slave problem. But after the *Prigg* decision, avoidance became more difficult, especially for a politician seeking national office.

As Taney had predicted, northern states responded to *Prigg* with a raft of new laws prohibiting state and local officials from intervening in support of fugitive slave claims. Pennsylvania's law, enacted in 1847, contained these prohibitions and also prohibited state and local jails from being used to house accused runaways. Slave catchers would find no aid in Pennsylvania—and that passive posture would be a matter of state law. Insofar as government officials would enforce federal fugitive slave statutes, the work would have to be done by a small and largely powerless cadre of federal marshals. In addition, in a bold assertion of Pennsylvania's antislavery traditions, the 1847 law affirmed the state's right to protect free Blacks. As had been the case under the 1826 personal liberty law, the state's judges would still be able to issue writs of habeas corpus "and to inquire into the causes and legality of the arrest or imprisonment of any human being within this commonwealth." Although local sheriffs and justices of the peace would no longer be responsible for the rendition of accused fugitives, the law was unambiguous in its assertion of their jurisdiction over kidnapping cases. In this sense, as its southern neighbor very soon recognized, *Prigg* would be rendered moot. In addition to legal barriers very similar to those preceding the decision, slave catchers would now face a state law enforcement apparatus prohibited from applying comity in runaway slave cases. Without positive, statutory requirements that states enforce the federal fugitive slave law, Story's *Prigg* decision, in short, seriously weakened slaveholders' right to recapture fugitives.

Following Taney's reasoning, in early 1848, delegates to the Maryland Assembly issued a demand that Pennsylvania replace its unconstitutional 1826 personal liberty law with "such a law, as will further aid and protect the lives and persons of our citizens, whilst lawfully securing their slaves." Needless to say, Pennsylvania authorities were unmoved. The days when a delegation from Maryland could visit the Pennsylvania statehouse and demand redress for the loss of fugitives from slavery had long passed, and for the first time since 1793, whatever redress the state would gain would have to come from the federal government.[15]

Federal intervention would never have happened had the national political climate been more placid. After the discovery of gold at Sutter's Mill, an influx of tens of thousands of prospectors and their families, along with bankers, dry goods merchants, and assorted con artists and shysters, accelerated the push to bring the state of California into the Union. Since most of the far western territory's new immigrants were northerners, there was little chance of California becoming a slave state. For Democrats, a free California raised the fearful prospect of an entirely free-soil West, leaving the country's proslavery party a permanent minority party. The ensuing crisis reeked of a horror Buchanan and other doughface Democrats had long feared: disunion.

In a last-ditch effort to avert catastrophe and placate southern lawmakers, Kentucky senator Henry Clay introduced a series of proposals to appease proexpansionist, proslavery southerners while affording political cover for their northern free-soil opponents. California would be admitted as a free state, while no restrictions on slavery would be imposed in the federal territories of Utah and New Mexico—a complete rejection of Wilmot's Proviso. Perhaps most symbolic of all, at least insofar as it addressed what had for antislavery activists been among the most infuriating of all American hypocrisies, another of Clay's resolutions banned the slave trade in the District of Columbia. After months of wrangling, versions of all these provisions were enacted, along with a second Fugitive Slave Law. For the first time in more than half a century, Congress intervened in a problem that national lawmakers had previously strenuously avoided.

The Fugitive Slave Law of 1850 had no other purpose than to defuse southern sectionalism by addressing the slave South's oldest grievance. The law came at a high constitutional price. In accepting Justice Story's premise that the fugitive problem was fundamentally a problem for the federal government, the new law affirmed the end of comity, at least with respect to this issue. Congress could, and indeed would, be responsible for fugitives from slavery. A corps of federal commissioners would assist federal judges in doing what state magistrates were now refusing to do: they would hear claims for the recovery of runaways, issue warrants for the arrest of alleged runaways, and grant writs ordering the return of accused runaways. The exact scope of the new commissioners' responsibilities was never clearly defined—in some cases they acted as summary judge and jury for southerners' claims, while in others they presided over jury trials. One thing is clear: corruption was sure to follow the act. The federal magistrates were political appointees and were paid fees for each adjudicated case, with the highest fees for cases finding in favor of claimants.

The statute would also stipulate the terms by which those commissioners granted slave owners and their agents possession of alleged runaways, and those terms unambiguously favored claimants. An affidavit or sworn testimony from white witnesses was all that was needed to justify rendition of runaways. The accused had no right to habeas corpus and no formalized basis for legal defense, although some commissioners did hear testimony from defendants and their attorneys. The law also required existing federal agents, who included federal marshals, magistrates, court clerks, and even postmasters, to assist in the recovery of runaways. Any who failed to do so faced fines as high as $1,000. Federal marshals, responsible for serving arrest warrants, faced additional potential sanctions. Should a runaway escape federal agents' custody, the agent would be responsible for his or her full market value.[16]

For James Buchanan, at home in Lancaster as the new laws made their way to President Millard Fillmore's desk, the compromise represented clear progress in the battle against sectionalism and its fanatical apostles. "During that period," he explained to a group of Philadelphia antiabolitionist partisans (who referred to themselves as Friends of the Constitution and the Union, and many of whom would eventually support a new Constitutional Union Party),

> I have often sounded the alarm; but my feeble warnings have been disregarded. I now solemnly declare, as the deliberate conviction of my judgment, that two things are necessary to preserve this Union from the most imminent danger:—
>
> 1. Agitation in the North on the subject of Southern slavery must be rebuked and put down by a strong, energetic, and enlightened public opinion.
>
> 2. The Fugitive Slave Law must be executed in its letter and its spirit.

The alternative, for Buchanan, was dire. From the time he served the Jackson administration, Buchanan recalled, "the agitation in the North against southern slavery has been incessant, by means of the Press, of State Legislatures, State and County Conventions, Abolition Lectures, and every other method which fanatics and demagogues could devise." The effect of all this divisive abolitionism "has been to create geographical parties, so much dreaded by the Father of his Country." Without determined action, George Washington's fear that the nation would be wrenched apart by faction would be realized. The American Union's future, Buchanan pronounced, would depend on Pennsylvania, the old "Keystone of the Arch." For Pennsylvania "stands as the talisman between the North and the South, and can lay her hand on either party, and say, thus far shalt thou go, and no farther." A moderate, middle-tempered Pennsylvania would be the "just and equitable umpire between the extremes." Of course, as Buchanan well knew, Pennsylvania had long been as divided as any state in the Union. What Buchanan was less attuned to was the fact that on the central political problem of the day, his home state was growing less divided.[17]

CHAPTER 12

Border War along the Underground Railroad

WILLIAM PARKER WAS born into slavery in Anne Arundel County, Maryland. Although his first master was, by the standards of slave owners, not especially cruel, Parker's childhood scarred him deeply. He was an orphan. His mother died when he was very young, and he never seems to have known his father. He had two brothers, John and Charles, but saw little of them. William's grandmother lived nearby, but he rarely saw her. With no parents or older siblings, Parker had no protectors and was relentlessly bullied. He learned to fight and became so proficient that his owner forced him into prizefighting. Beginning in the early 1830s, when Parker was around ten or eleven, he took note of the agonies brought by the slave trade. He witnessed horrifying scenes of masters wined and dined by designing slave traders while slave families were torn apart. After his best friend, Levi Storax, was sold, Parker obtained a forged travel pass and in 1839 escaped with his brother Charles to Baltimore. The two fugitives then made their way north and west, crossing the Mason-Dixon Line somewhere below York.

Parker had been told that his best hope for refuge lay on the other side of the Susquehanna, in Pennsylvania's more antislavery east. He and Charles left York for Wrightsville. From there, the two crossed the river to Columbia, where they were taken in by the town's free Blacks. Parker found work as a laborer and married another self-manumitted slave, Eliza Ann Elizabeth Howard. Sometime in the late 1840s, the Parkers settled outside of the small town of Christiana (no connection to Swedish Fort Christina), where, with their two children, they shared a rented home with Eliza's sister Hannah and her family.[1]

Parker's 1866 autobiography recalled the discovery that life in the North involved its own particular terrors. In 1839 and 1840, while living with a Quaker family about fifteen miles north of the Line in Lancaster County, Parker came to see that "kidnapping was so common . . . that we were kept in constant fear. We would hear of slaveholders or kidnappers every two or three weeks; sometimes a party of white men would break into a house and take a man away, no one knew where; and again, a whole family would be carried off. There was no power to protect them, nor prevent it." The kidnapping problem in southern Lancaster County was among the worst anywhere along the Line, in part because the area was patrolled by the local Gap Gang, a band of Scots-Irish proslavery insurgents who took their name from the Gap Hills, where most lived. To call the group a "gang" is, perhaps, to attribute greater coherence than is warranted. This assemblage of vigilantes, who also tended to congregate at the Gap Tavern, not far from Christiana, was more an accidental posse of hard-drinking white supremacists. For kidnappers entering the region, gang members were reliable spies and informers. But the gang's primary function was to terrorize African Americans.[2]

In the face of incessant racial torment, as far as William Parker was concerned, the law did little to protect free African Americans, even before *Prigg.* "Whether the kidnappers were clothed with legal authority or not," he wrote, "I did not care to inquire, as I never had any faith in nor respect for the Fugitive Slave Law." Whatever the law's letter may have said, its spirit was obviously bankrupt. After all, "the insolent and overbearing conduct of the Southerners, when on such errands to Pennsylvania," hardly suggested anything that could be defended as lawful: "They did not hesitate to break open doors, and to enter without ceremony the houses of colored men; and when refused admission, or when a manly and determined spirit was shown, they would present pistols and knock down men and women indiscriminately."[3]

Where the law was so obviously inadequate, Parker resolved to take matters into his own hands. Sometime in the early 1840s, he and a group of other free Blacks formed a mutual defense patrol. Their purpose, unapologetic in its willingness to meet force with force, was to end the reign of terror

Lancaster County's African Americans had so long endured. The group had tacit support from antislavery whites, but it was a Black organization, and by 1850 William Parker, now in his late twenties and widely known as "the Preacher," had become its leader. Every Sunday the group met at the Parker family farmhouse near Christiana and, according to a young neighbor named Peter Woods, its members were "sworn to keep secret what we knew."[4] Oaths and secrecy were essential since so many of the group's members were, like Parker, refugees from slavery. Although its membership was intended to be as secret as its meetings, the activities of the mutual defense patrol were hard to conceal, and William Parker came to be known throughout southern Lancaster County for his heroics. Some decades later, a Quaker antislavery activist from the region recalled Parker's "wonderful force of character" as well as his "resolution, courage, and action." Southern Lancaster County's Blacks, this admirer recalled, regarded Parker "as their leader, their protector, their Moses, and their lawgiver all at once . . . he was the Toussaint L'Ouverture of his people," a reference to the great liberator of the slaves of Saint-Domingue.[5]

During his first decade of freedom, Parker's reputation was local. He worked and lived in Lancaster County, and it was in Lancaster County that he supported the struggle against slavery and kidnapping. On September 11, 1851, events at Parker's home would make his name familiar throughout Pennsylvania and Maryland, although far better known would be the Maryland farmer and slave owner Edward Gorsuch, who was killed that day.

Gorsuch owned an estate in Baltimore County on land his family had occupied for generations. The farm, just off the main road between Baltimore and York, produced grain and livestock for markets in nearby Baltimore. In addition to the family farm, Gorsuch owned as many as twelve slaves, making him one of the largest slave owners in rural Baltimore County. At a time when farmers relied primarily on wage labor, owning slaves was something of a luxury—more a matter of status than economic necessity. For Gorsuch, it was also a way to display generosity of spirit and paternal affection, something familiar among the patriarchs of the plantation South but a far more mannered posture for borderlands farmers. Gorsuch burnished his paternal bona fides with a commitment to the gradual freeing of his slaves. Rather than turn them out, innocent children confronting the hazards of freedom, he released them as they reached their majority. These freed men and women had grown accustomed to life on Gorsuch's farm and most remained, now paid for their work. One of these freed slaves, Jarret Wallace, demonstrated unusual business acumen and was employed by Gorsuch as his "market man" in Baltimore. So valuable an employee had Wallace become that by 1849 Gorsuch had begun building him a home on the Gorsuch property.[6]

In November 1849, as the fall harvest was ending, rumors began spreading among the enslaved men still working the Gorsuch farm that the master had discovered a theft. A local miller reported suspicious transactions involving a free Black. Gorsuch concluded that the transaction involved wheat stolen and sold by one of his slaves. Word of their master's suspicions reached Gorsuch's slaves, who, aware that any infraction, but especially petty theft, could justify a visit by slave traders and a sale downriver, began considering their prospects. Four of them, George and Joshua Hammond, Nelson Ford, and Noah Buley, were in their twenties, making them prime targets for the slave trade. Although Gorsuch had long assured them they would be freed upon reaching their majorities, the men still had several years of enslavement ahead of them and had no way of knowing whether Gorsuch would forgive the theft. To await his judgment was to risk a fate that had befallen too many Maryland slaves. The only alternative was flight, and on November 6, the four made their way to Pennsylvania. There is no record of how they traveled. They might have made their way to Baltimore and then north, or they might have just fled north to York, either by foot or perhaps even aboard a northbound train. The men eventually settled in southern Lancaster County, near Christiana.

After learning of the fugitives' location, Gorsuch petitioned the governor of Maryland to invoke the state's extradition agreement. Following the logic of the second Fugitive Slave Act, Pennsylvania authorities deferred to the federal government, and Gorsuch reverted to the old habits of the slave catcher. On September 8, 1851, he took the train to Philadelphia, where he met with the new federal fugitive slave commissioner, Edward D. Ingraham. Officious and obliging, Ingraham readily issued arrest warrants for the runaways while a slave-hunting posse consisting of Gorsuch's son, nephew, cousin, and two neighbors organized itself to hunt down the fugitives. The posse met Gorsuch and US marshal Henry H. Kline in Philadelphia, and the party then made its way by train to Lancaster County. Also making his way west with word of the impending slave-catching raid was Samuel Williams, an African American tavernkeeper, Underground Railroad conductor, and member of the Philadelphia Vigilance Committee, another African American anti-kidnapping force. Williams's warnings, Parker recalled, spread through the Christiana Black community "like a fire in the prairies." By the evening of September 10, seven members of the local vigilance committee had assembled at the Parkers' home. Among the assembled were two of Gorsuch's former slaves.[7]

Around dawn on September 11, Gorsuch and Kline entered the Parker home and presented a federal warrant for the arrest of the two alleged runaways. Parker refused to comply, and over the course of the morning a crowd of proslavery white men began assembling outside his home. A large group of allies also began to converge on the home. The latter, Quaker abolitionists and local Blacks, many of whom were armed, had likely been urged to act by the Quaker postmaster and storekeeper Elijah Lewis. At some point shots were fired. Kline and the other slave catchers fled, but Gorsuch, who was heard pleading for the cooperation of his former slaves, was killed. His son Dickinson, whose brother John was a graduate of Dickinson College, received multiple gunshot wounds, and Gorsuch's cousin Joshua suffered a near fatal head injury.

For William Parker, the Christiana incident would mark the start of a new ordeal. Within days he had left for Canada, joined by his brother-in-law Alexander Pinkney and by Abraham Johnson, a free Black who had assisted the fugitives from Gorsuch's farm. After two days' travel, the men reached Rochester, New York, where they were received by Frederick Douglass as "heroic defenders of the just rights of man against mansteelers and murderers." After a number of anxious hours, Douglass was able to help the fugitives board a steamer bound for Kingston, Ontario. The men eventually reached Toronto, where, several months after leaving Pennsylvania, Parker would be joined by his wife, Eliza. After the Parkers' children arrived, the family settled in a community of refugees from slavery near Buxton, Ontario, outside of Windsor.[8]

Of the range of problems that shaped the federal Union in its first half century, the fugitive slave problem was, by design, of relatively minor significance. To be sure, Americans fought bitterly over the question of slavery in federal territories, and this had some bearing on how fugitives from slavery were treated. But until 1850, the problem of interstate fugitives remained a state problem. In no two states did that problem have a longer history and a deeper political legacy than in Maryland and Pennsylvania. And yet, despite decades of legal wrangling, the clash between these two states never erupted into anything approaching the sort of border war that had occurred in the eighteenth century. With economic ties came political ones, and the problem of fugitives from slavery had never come anywhere near rupturing the ties that bound the mid-Atlantic to the northern Chesapeake.

This is perhaps why Lancaster County's most famous political figure, James Buchanan, left no substantial public remarks about the Christiana events. This silence is most obviously not because he was somehow unaware. Within days, headlines about the "Christiana murders" and the "Christiana tragedy" blazed across Pennsylvania's newspapers. To the conservative Unionist press, there could be "no difference of opinion concerning the shocking affair which occurred at Christiana on Thursday—the resisting of a law of Congress by a band of armed negroes, whereby the majesty of the Government was defied and life taken in one and the same act." The "atrocity," it was clear, was instigated by abolitionists, "advising the negroes to 'stand their ground,' that is, to resist—to arm and fight." In this view, it was abolitionist influence that elevated a mere "servile insurrection" to an act of treason. To the antislavery press, the "tragedy" at Christiana was just "another campaign of the slave-hunting war, begun last winter under the Fugitive Slave Law . . . opened upon us, threatening quiet homes and peaceful communities with the midnight incursions of man-hunters, with their treacheries, stratagems, their ruffian outrages . . . menacing the defenseless people of color with a 'reign of terror.'"[9]

For Buchanan, there would obviously be no gain from weighing in on a matter so divisive. It was a delicate balancing act for a local politician with national aspirations, but it would become even more delicate in the following days as the administration of Whig president Millard Fillmore brought the might of the federal government to bear on the accused perpetrators of the so-called Christiana Riot.[10] For the first time since the federal government had sent troops to suppress the Whiskey Rebellion, federal military personnel would be sent to the borderlands.

The precise legal grounds for such broad federal action were never clear. Murder, a capital crime, would be prosecuted in the courts of Pennsylvania.

Interfering with a valid claim for the recovery of a runaway slave was now a federal crime, punishable by fines of up to $1,000 and six months in jail but hardly warranting the deployment of the United States Army. The new federal fugitive slave bureaucracy, such as it was, attracted gung-ho, gun-slinging antiabolitionist partisans. Even before federal reinforcements arrived in Christiana, Kline began arresting alleged rioters. Claiming to have witnessed the frenzied and chaotic murder scene, the US marshal identified seventeen rioters, all of whom local authorities charged with "aiding and abetting in the murder of Edward Gorsuch." In addition to fifteen local Blacks, two of those charged were white men—Elijah Lewis and a miller who lived near the Parkers, Castner Hamway. Both turned themselves in. To Kline, the two were clearly sympathizers, as responsible for Gorsuch's murder as those who actually killed him.

On Saturday, September 13, a federal force including a detachment of forty-five marines from the Philadelphia Naval Yard, a detachment of Philadelphia police, and US fugitive slave commissioner Edward D. Ingraham arrived from Philadelphia. This force joined several dozen proslavery vigilantes, mostly from Baltimore County but also including Pennsylvanians, possibly members of the Gap Gang, lending the entire federal force an air of hideous vigilantism. According to one Pennsylvania newspaper, the motley band "of armed ruffians from Maryland, assisted by the lowest ruffians this region can furnish, are prowling around the country." Another noted, "There never went unhung a gang of more depraved wretches and desperate scoundrels than some of the men employed as 'officers of the law' to ravage this country and ransack private houses, in the man-hunt which followed the affray." The uniformed military was little better. A local schoolmistress was told by a US marine that he was in Christiana "to arrest every nigger and d——d abolitionist."[11]

Although seventeen accused rioters had been initially charged, dozens more were rounded up and brought before local magistrates. As had been the case in so many other acts of vigilantism in the borderlands, this one had as much the appearance of civil disturbance as of any kind of formal federal legal process. "A local reign of terror" followed this antiabolition force. For "the tendency of 'a little brief authority' is toward abuse of it; and the class of persons easily secured for the service then required of temporary officers of the law was not such as to insure delicacy in the treatment or tender consideration for the objects against whom their summary processes were directed. Whites and blacks, bond and free, were rather roughly handled; few households in the region searched were safe from rude intrusions." With the support of federal troops, the posse brought the accused to Lancaster, where they were arraigned before Judge Franklin Reigart, who ordered most of them remanded to Lancaster's new city prison. Exactly what they would be tried for was unclear.[12]

What was clear was that the administration of Millard Fillmore, a New York Whig with deep southern sympathies and profound anxiety about the stability of the Union, would never leave prosecution to Pennsylvania magistrates. In a public letter to the president, Maryland's Democratic governor, Enoch Louis Lowe, left little doubt about Democratic strategy: "I do not know of a single incident that has occurred since the passage of the [1850] Compromise measures, which tends more to weaken the bonds of union, and arouse dark thoughts in the minds of men, than this late tragedy. Nor will its influence and effects be limited within the narrow borders of our State. They will penetrate the soul of the South. They will silence the confident promise of the Union men and give force to the appeals of the Secessionists."[13] With Democrats happy to raise the specter of disunion in response to fanatic northern abolitionists, Fillmore simply could not risk exoneration of the alleged perpetrators by an antislavery Pennsylvania jury. Against strenuous opposition from John W. Ashmead, the US attorney at Philadelphia, US attorney general John J. Crittenden determined to prosecute the Christiana rioters for treason against the United States.

The lead attorney for the defense, Lancaster County congressman and ardent antislavery Whig Thaddeus Stevens, reminded the jury in his opening remarks that "the great question to be considered by this court, and especially by the jury is, what brought together [the accused], some armed and some unarmed?" The federal government's case, as the defense saw it, depended on very elusive evidentiary prey: it would have to demonstrate the defendants' intent to "levy a war against the United States." In fact, all the evidence suggested a different interpretation, an interpretation that any Pennsylvania jury would have instantly recognized: that the accused were simply acting against the crime of kidnapping. In a clear reference to the Gap Gang, Stevens explained that "a gang of professional kidnappers" lived near Christiana. "In the dead of night," these kidnappers invaded the homes of free Blacks and of whites where other Blacks resided. They carried off these innocent souls "without authority from any person on earth." After watching their kin stolen in the dark of night, Christiana's Black citizens were surely justified in their state of alarm. Whether self-defense resulted in the crimes of rioting and murder was for another court to decide. This court, Stevens reminded his audience, was there to learn why "a whole neighborhood might be ready upon a given notice . . . to go to a place" to battle illegal kidnapping. Stevens's remarks, a clear appeal to the spirit behind Pennsylvania's personal liberty laws, would demonstrate that the actions of the people of Christiana had nothing to do with war against the federal government and everything to do with battling a well-known, age-old scourge. The treason charges were dropped, and a Lancaster County grand jury failed to indict any rioters for the murder of Edward Gorsuch.[14]

As a legal matter, Christiana's impact was significant. Whatever federal law may have said about fugitives from slavery, the Constitution offered the federal government few tools for enforcing that law. Along the Line, the fugitive slave problem would remain, at least in de facto terms, a state and

Samuel Hopkins (wielding a corn-cutter) and Peter Woods, veterans of the Christiana Riot, outside the remains of the Parker family home, 1896.
Reproduction courtesy of Moores Memorial Library, Christiana, Pennsylvania.

local problem. As a political matter, the legacy of Christiana is more difficult to assess. Southern Democrats and their northern allies obviously saw
in it useful propaganda in their antiabolition campaigns, but in the paradox
that haunted antebellum constitutionalism, the outcome could be seen as
a triumph for the doctrine of states' rights. Federal authorities ultimately
did little to enforce the barrier between slavery and freedom, allowing the
scourge of kidnapping along the Line to persist. For James Buchanan, a
Democratic politician who was from the nation's oldest antislavery state and
who had national political aspirations, slavery had become, above all, a
political lodestone, dividing his party and forcing upon its candidates for
national office a hopeless game of avoidance. The political problem of slavery,
Buchanan hoped, would be eliminated once and for all with a decision issued
by the nation's highest court, now presided over by his fellow borderlander
and Dickinson graduate, Roger B. Taney.

The case behind that decision had no connection to the Line. It originated
in a question about the status of an enslaved man, Dred Scott, who had
lived with his master, an army physician, at Fort Snelling, located in federal
territory that would eventually become the state of Minnesota. Scott, with
his wife and daughter, also enslaved, had similarly lived with his master in
Illinois, a free state. After the death of the Scotts' owner in 1846, Scott sued
on the grounds that since he had lived both in federal territory and in a state
where slavery had been prohibited, he and his family were entitled to their
liberty. The argument rested on a distinction present in American law from
the founding of the republic. Both the Pennsylvania Abolition Act of 1780
and the Northwest Ordinance had provided for sojourners—slaves could
be carried through free territories or reside in them temporarily. But slaves
could not be introduced to and held in either federal territory or Pennsylvania. In legal terms, the case centered on a distinction between domicile
and sojourn. The former, which declared that local law applied to all persons
domiciled in a given state or territory, was an accommodation southerners
had long been prepared to tolerate. The latter allowed slaveholders to
travel through antislavery states under the terms of the law of their home
state. A Missouri court agreed with Scott: his family's owners had obviously
not been sojourners. But John Sandford, brother-in-law and executor of
the estate of the Scotts' former owner, appealed the decision to the Missouri

state supreme court. The proslavery court found in Sandford's favor. The Scotts and their lawyers appealed the decision in a federal district court, which also ruled in Sandford's favor. Following another appeal, on December 30, 1854, the case entered the docket of the United States Supreme Court, presided over by Chief Justice Taney.

The case took more than two years to rise to the top of the Court's docket; by the time it did, Taney, nearly eighty and in failing health, was grieving the deaths of his wife and daughter. The distinguished American jurist had in him one final push to reshape the national constitutional order. Taney had come to believe that that order, a patchwork of compromises between state and federal authority, between proslavery and antislavery laws, all designed to keep the nation from breaking apart, was unsustainable. Dramatic constitutional change was needed. In *Dred Scott v. Sandford,* Taney finally had the opportunity to transform his concurrent opinion in *Prigg* into settled law. It was a decision, it turns out, very much on the mind of the newly elected president of the United States.

By the time the Court began preparing its opinion, James Buchanan had become president-elect. Through correspondence with his old friend Associate Justice John Catron of Tennessee, Buchanan learned that, as part of the *Dred Scott* case, the Court was reconsidering the legality of the most vexing legacy of the Missouri Compromise: a prohibition of slavery above the 36°30′ parallel. For Buchanan, a decision on the matter would pay enormous political dividends. Although Congress had rejected the ban as part of the Kansas-Nebraska Act of 1854, Buchanan's opponents in the recently founded Republican Party had achieved national prominence with a platform that included new statutory restrictions on slavery's expansion in the West. Buchanan and the southern justices, Taney included, had come to believe that the best defense against further congressional meddling, and a potentially fatal blow to the antislavery Republican Party, would be a ruling that established once and for all the unconstitutionality of any statutory ban on slavery in federal territories. "In a single stroke," the historian Michael Holt has written, the Court "threatened to destroy the [Republican] party's principal reason for being."[15]

To achieve such a clear political aim, Justice Catron urged Buchanan to lobby another Dickinson College alum and fellow Pennsylvanian, Justice Robert Grier. In full violation of the separation of powers, Buchanan followed through on his friend's suggestion. Justice Grier replied to Buchanan that he and Taney "fully appreciate and concur in your views as to the desirableness at this time of having an expression of the opinion of the Court on this troublesome question." But Grier wanted Buchanan to know that, whatever political value such a decision might have for the newly elected president, for the Court a decision on slavery in the territories would have to be carefully formulated lest it "appear that the line of latitude should mark the line of division in the court." Given the increasingly sectional character of the nation's leading political parties, a Court divided along sectional lines could hardly claim to be above party. Grier was also mindful that the Court's decision would raise more immediate problems for the president-elect. Should the decision come before his inauguration, especially if accompanied by dissent from one or two extreme southern justices, the ensuing firestorm would surely drown out whatever limp gesture of Unionism the new president might offer. The Court, Grier promised Buchanan, would issue no ruling until after he entered office.[16]

It was the perfect day to swear in a new president. The sun shone across the low early March sky, cutting through the winter chill, a faint glimmer of warmer days to come. President-elect Buchanan stood in front of the east portico of the Capitol, surrounded by hundreds of spectators, most all of them attired in the same black suit and top hat worn by Buchanan. The first-ever photograph of a presidential inauguration shows the crush of onlookers as Buchanan prepared to take the oath of office. The whole scene has an improvised feel about it. Onlookers spilled out the windows of the Capitol building; others stood atop a temporary raised platform built over the portico's stairs. Looming above it all, at the top edge of the photograph, can be seen evidence that the ceremony was taking place as the Capitol itself was being transformed. The old dome atop the rotunda had been dismantled and was being replaced by a new fireproof cast-iron structure. Spars of the steam-powered derricks used for lifting all the new structural iron into place are visible at the top of the photograph. No bunting or flags festooned the speakers' platform, and the dark-clad crowd gives the whole scene a funereal air. At the center stood two Dickinson College men, President-elect James Buchanan and the man who would swear him in, Chief Justice Taney.[17]

The solemnity of the occasion was warranted; the United States was in crisis. The Republican Party, whose candidate John C. Frémont lost to

James Buchanan inauguration, March 4, 1857. In this first known photograph of a presidential inauguration, neither President-elect Buchanan nor his fellow Dickinson College alumnus, Chief Justice Roger B. Taney, is identifiable. Photograph by John Wood.
Library of Congress, Manuscript Division, Montgomery Meigs Papers.

Buchanan, built its following through opposition to the Kansas-Nebraska Act and the extension of slavery in the West. The old world of parliamentary procedure, legislative compromise, and parties above sections had vanished. For southern Fire-Eaters, proslavery Democrats who saw little hope for the survival of the Union, the rise of the Republican Party merely confirmed the long-suspected northern conspiracy to deny southerners their right to property in human beings. What would supplant the old politics of sectional compromise was unclear, but whatever did, most remotely aware observers agreed, would involve the dissolution of the American Union.

Before Justice Taney administered the oath of office, Buchanan delivered the customary inaugural address, punctuated with well-rehearsed pleas for unity and the similarly familiar affirmations of the sacred bonds of constitutional union. Buchanan also acknowledged the profound division within the American body politic. That division was a division over slavery, but in the aftermath of the Kansas-Nebraska Act, it had moved from the realm of politics to that of law. Whether Kansas entered the Union as a slave state or a free state, adhering to the proslavery constitution written by Kansans at the territorial capital of Lecompton or an antislavery one written by Kansans meeting in Topeka, was now also "a judicial question, which legitimately belongs to the Supreme Court of the United States, before whom it is now pending, and will, it is understood, be speedily and finally settled." Should the Court follow the path he already knew it would follow and declare the original ban on slavery in federal territory unconstitutional, Buchanan's presidency would be liberated from the age-old fight over slavery in western territories and the Republican Party's ambition to overturn the Kansas-Nebraska act would be forever defeated. "May we not, then," Buchanan asked, "hope that the long agitation on this subject is approaching its end, and that the geographical parties to which it has given birth, so much dreaded by the Father of his Country, will speedily become extinct?" The Republican Party, a baldly sectional party malignantly rejecting President Washington's Unionism, would lose the entire justification for its existence, freeing the country from the scourge of radical abolitionism, "the prolific source of great evils to the master, the slave, and to the whole country."[18]

Two days later, a frail, sunken-eyed Chief Justice Taney emerged into the Supreme Court's central chamber to read his opinion for the majority in *Dred Scott v. Sandford*. The decision represented the culmination of Taney's borderlands jurisprudence. As long as Blacks remained rights-bearing citizens in Pennsylvania and other northern states, the recovery of runaways, whatever action Congress took to address the problem, would be needlessly difficult. The incessant legal wrangling, the cruelty and violence of kidnapping, and eruptions of collective violence in the borderlands offered ample illustration of the impotence of existing law. Now, with *Dred Scott*, Taney had an opportunity to do what *Prigg* had failed to do, albeit through egregiously contorted legal reasoning. Although *Dred Scott v. Sandford* concerned the question of whether the Scotts, having been domiciled in free federal territory and a free state, were entitled to their freedom, the Court also took up the issue of whether or not the Scotts had the right to a hearing in federal court. Because people of African descent, whether slave or free, had had no role in the framing of the United States Constitution, Taney argued, they could claim no rights under the Constitution's privileges and immunities clause, including the rights to file suit in federal court. Taney's argument was manifestly unfounded. At the time of ratification, property-owning African American males were legally entitled to vote in many states, including Delaware, Maryland, and Pennsylvania. Those qualified to vote thus had as much of a role in framing the Constitution as did any single ordinary white voter. Untroubled by historical truths, in denying all Americans of African descent recourse to federal judicial process, the Taney Court essentially abolished Black citizenship, preparing the way for the abolition of the crime of Black kidnapping. In a federal republic whose constitution denied Americans of African descent any protection under the law, the principle of caption would most likely prevail again, allowing southerners to pursue fugitives from slavery as their forefathers had pursued lost livestock.

As a political matter, a far more provocative part of the ruling rejected federal power to exclude slavery from unincorporated federally controlled territories. There could be no question about reversing the Kansas-Nebraska Act, the ruling held, because what that act itself had reversed—the Missouri Compromise—had been unconstitutional. Congress had no authority to exclude slavery north of the 36°30′ parallel. The significance of this part of the ruling was lost on almost no one. With the power to establish slave states in all new western territories, it would only be a matter of time before a United States Congress dominated by the much-expanded slave power used its constitutional authority to reverse remaining state antislavery law. In the words of Frederick Douglass, the *Dred Scott* decision meant "that slavery may go in safety anywhere under the star-spangled banner; that colored persons of African descent have no rights that white men are bound to respect; that colored men of African descent are not and cannot be citizens of the United States."

An outraged Thaddeus Stevens informed supporters at the Lancaster County Republican Party convention that whatever the Supreme Court may have said, the fact remained that "Congress had absolute control over the territories, and that Congress should so legislate to keep [slavery] out of the territories forever." Stevens was aware that some notable locals would be alarmed by his radical rejection of the Court's ruling. But he assured his audience that principle would prevail and that there would be no love lost between him and one of those locals, James Buchanan: "I may come in contact with the worthy President, who claims this city as his home, and oppose his measures . . . and also say something against him; but if saying that he is the *meanest* man that has ever occupied the Presidential chair, in having violated all the pledges he has ever made, and that he is the greatest despot we have ever had . . . brings his displeasure upon me, *then I shall say it.*" Stevens was elected to represent Pennsylvania's Ninth Congressional District in the United States House of Representatives, a discouraging sign for James Buchanan's Democratic Party.[19]

In his inaugural address, Buchanan had promised that his would be a one-term presidency. In taking the highest office in the land, he told his audience, he had no motives other than preserving the Union and upholding the Constitution. And while Buchanan kept that promise to remain in office for only one term, he would find little quiet repose in retirement. Although he ended up supporting President Lincoln and the Union cause, he never supported Lincoln's policy of emancipation, one of the reasons his critics hounded him until his death. He had, they believed, failed to preserve the Union and failed to disavow the institution that brought its collapse. Buchanan died on June 1, 1868, at his estate near Lancaster.

Two months after Taney issued his infamous decision, John Sandford died in a New York insane asylum. Sandford's sister, the widow of the Scotts' prior owner, Dr. John Emerson, had remarried Massachusetts Republican congressman and abolitionist Calvin C. Chaffee. Embarrassed by revelations of their connection to the Scotts, Chaffee and his wife arranged to transfer ownership to Taylor Blow, the youngest son of Peter Blow, Scott's original owner; Blow, enabled by Missouri law, granted Dred, Harriet, and Eliza Scott their freedom. Dred worked as a hotel porter, but in September 1858, sixteen months after his manumission, he died of tuberculosis. Little is known about the fate of Harriet and Eliza, but there is some suggestion that both had died by 1862. Lizzie, the Scotts' younger daughter whose legal status was never fully resolved, is thought to have lived out her life in St. Louis. Her descendants were present at centennial observances of the infamous Supreme Court decision bearing her family's name in 1957.[20]

Chief Justice Taney never showed the slightest remorse for his *Dred Scott* opinion and was utterly unrepentant even as the country exploded in civil war. What views he did express suggest he had become a Peace Democrat, favoring any accommodation to avoid war. In the North, not surprisingly, the chief justice's death on October 12, 1864, was widely celebrated. The

Chicago Tribune condemned the Taney Court as "the temple of the man-stealers" and expressed the relief shared by so many of its readers that its "ancient High Priest lies cold at the altar." In fact, the Court had begun abandoning its angry, embittered chief justice well before his death. Lincoln appointed four justices in three years, but the president's decisive imprint would come with Taney's death. To replace the old chief justice, Lincoln nominated Salmon P. Chase, his former treasury secretary and the most ardent proponent of emancipation in his cabinet.[21]

CHAPTER 13

Borderlands into Border States

THE PRESIDENTIAL ELECTION of 1860 propelled a former state assemblyman and corporate lawyer from Illinois into the White House. Other than a single two-year term in Congress, Abraham Lincoln had no national political experience. In the months leading up to the Republican Party nominating convention in Chicago, he had campaigned widely, but remained a dark-horse candidate. After a series of contentious nominating votes, Lincoln prevailed over better-known candidates, including Senators Salmon P. Chase of Ohio and William H. Seward of New York. As is well known, Lincoln's opposition to slavery and its expansion would make him the most divisive presidential candidate since the founding of the Republic—a fact made abundantly clear by the 1860 electoral map. Lincoln received only a tiny number of votes in the slave states but won every free state with the exception of New Jersey, where he still gained four of the state's seven electoral votes.

Although sectionalism had been a fact of American life since the Revolutionary era, a two-party system, animated primarily by recognition that control of the federal government would fall to the party best able to generate support in both sections, kept this troubling fact just below the electoral map's surface.[1] What had been true of the country as a whole had long been true of the counties of the borderlands. They were separated by the Mason-Dixon Line, but voting along the Line reflected a common

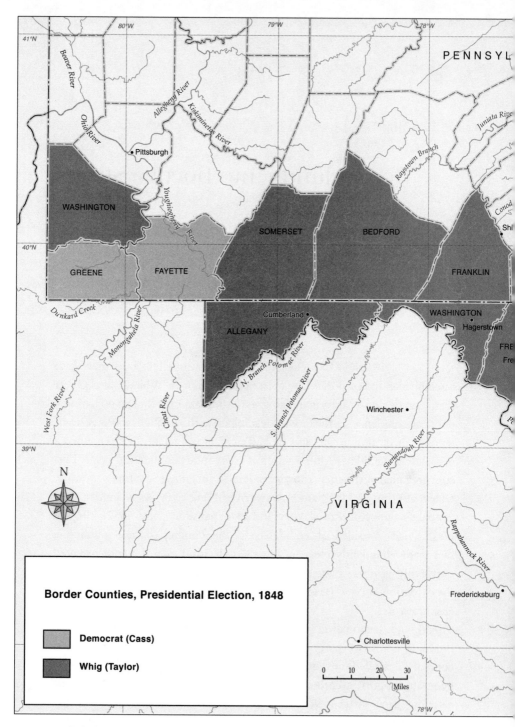

Border Counties, Presidential Election, 1848

Border Counties, Presidential Election, 1848

Democrat (Cass)

Whig (Taylor)

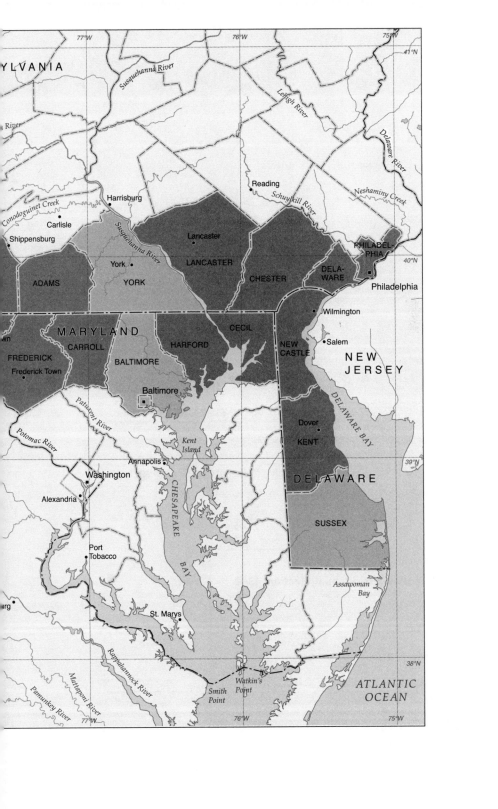

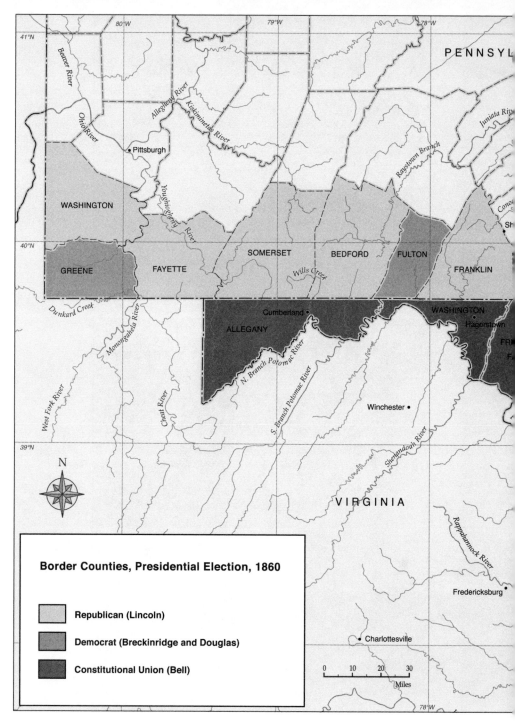

Border Counties, Presidential Election, 1860

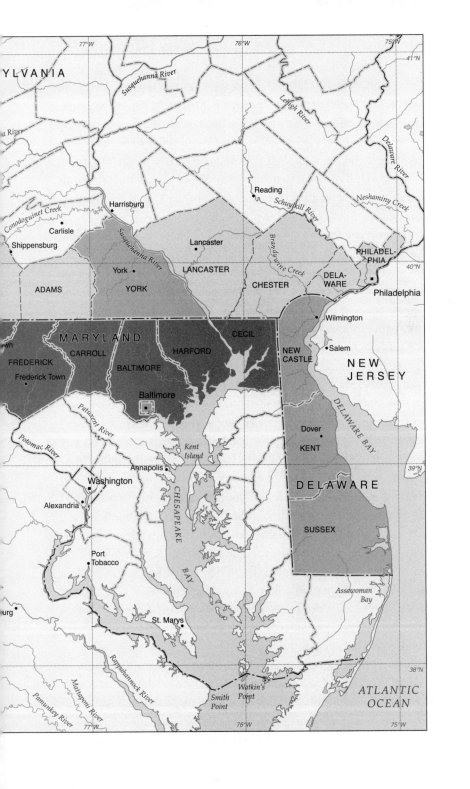

borderlands politics. Much as in newer western border regions, voting in borderlands rarely reflected any clear pro- or antislavery consensus, especially in national elections. This was partly because national political parties had struggled at least since the Missouri Compromise to occupy some sort of middle ground between their pro- and antislavery wings, but it also reflected its own kind of borderlands political logic. Rather than confront the stark legal divide separating the states south of the Line from Pennsylvania, borderlands voters reverted to a convenient Unionism.[2]

As the Democratic Party's 1856 presidential nominee, James Buchanan campaigned as standard-bearer for this borderlands politics. Whatever his opponents might have suggested, Buchanan was no doughface apologist for slavery and its ruthless political wing. He was an apostle of the reasonable middle—reasonable, in Buchanan's telling, insofar as it was prepared to look past the problem of slavery to the greater good of Union. That reasonableness, that politics of middle-ground moderation, was as authentic as the candidate's geographic roots. At a gathering of Baltimore Democrats, the old Pennsylvania pol explained that he was "born in Franklin County, Pa., on the borders of Maryland; and the trade and intercourse of that county was chiefly with Baltimore." Buchanan was now convinced that the boundary-defying commerce of greater Baltimore had become the nation's path away from disunionism: "Maryland and Pennsylvania . . . are both rapidly blotting out Mason and Dixon's line. The enterprise of your sons has penetrated [Pennsylvania] in every direction, and you are reaping the rich fruits of that enterprise from the valleys and the mountains of the Keystone State. . . . The day has passed when any jealousy should exist between us—a jealousy always injurious to both parties." The moderate, middle-of-the-road Unionism of the borderlands would be the divided republic's salvation. And Buchanan, child of the nation's first and oldest section-defying region, urged his Baltimore audience to see him as the apostle of this pro-Union politics. For Pennsylvanians, most of whom voted for Buchanan, the message of moderation was persuasive.[3]

As an electoral strategy, Buchanan's claims to the reasonable middle failed completely in Maryland. By a substantial majority, Maryland voters supported former president Millard Fillmore, candidate of the new American Party. The failure of Buchanan's message in the southern borderlands is notable for one reason: for the first time in its history, the Line corresponded to a clear line on the electoral map. Buchanan won both Delaware and Pennsylvania, with especially strong showings in the latter's southern and eastern counties. In Maryland, he only carried Allegany, St. Mary's, Prince George's, and Charles Counties. Baltimore had already given the anti-immigrant Know-Nothings a majority in the Maryland House. In support of the same nativist party, rebranded the American Party, the city would hand the state's electors to the doomed Fillmore—Maryland would be the only state the American Party carried.

With the election of 1860, a borderlands long unified in its Unionism, if not in its precise party affiliations, would finally give way to the realities of national sectionalism. Lincoln won all but three counties on the Pennsylvania side of the Line. York and Fulton were won by the northern Democrat Stephen Douglas, and the majority of Greene County voters, in the state's far southwestern corner, supported the southern Democratic candidate John C. Breckinridge, a Kentucky congressman and James Buchanan's vice president. The entire state of Delaware lined up behind Breckinridge as well. The new Constitutional Union Party and its candidate, John Bell of Tennessee, a former proslavery Whig who lost his seat in the Senate after fighting to defeat the Kansas-Nebraska Act, won most counties in Maryland, including all the counties of greater Baltimore. Unionism remained as potent as ever, but the American Party, whose members overwhelmingly threw their support behind Bell, drove the state's Catholics and Germans to Breckinridge. Because of this, more than his proslavery stance, Breckinridge picked up voters in the border counties of Allegany and Frederick as well as in Baltimore, which he nearly won. In a race decided by a mere 522 votes, Maryland threw its support to Breckinridge.

For the first time in the Line's history, political alignments reflected in the starkest terms the national sectional conflict. A majority of Pennsylvanians now supported a national political candidate openly opposed to slavery; a majority of voters in Delaware and Maryland, in contrast, supported a defender of slavery. Accounting for this electoral shift is as difficult as accounting for the shifting views of individual voters. Exactly why, after decades of Unionist dominance, so many voters on the Line's north side abandoned Unionism for Lincoln remains to be fully explained. But one borderlands event seems to have had at least some influence on voters, although that influence was far less decisive in the borderlands than it would be else-where in the country.[4]

Chambersburg, the seat of Franklin County, Pennsylvania, had long been a western crossroads. Iroquois warriors passed through the area in the eigh-teenth century, traveling along creeks and footpaths linking the Susquehanna portage north of Conestoga, near present-day Harrisburg, to the Potomac and Shenandoah Rivers. By the late 1850s, the town was a fully integrated commercial hub on the far western fringes of greater Baltimore. With the completion of the Cumberland Valley Railroad in 1837, it had rail service to Carlisle, Harrisburg, and points east. A southern extension, completed a few years later, connected Chambersburg to Hagerstown and the Baltimore and Ohio rail network. By 1860, one could readily travel west from Chambers-burg to Missouri and Kansas, and east to every major eastern city.

The Iroquois travelers who once passed through the Chambersburg area reached the Shenandoah at its convergence with the Potomac near a spit of land that eventually bore the name of Robert Harper, owner of the lease for a ferry linking western Maryland to northern Virginia. The town that grew around the ferry's southern landing, Harpers Ferry, had also long been a regional crossroads. In 1794, President Washington identified it as an ideal location for a new national armory and arms depot. Far enough inland to avoid foreign naval bombardment, but readily accessible by busy water routes linking the Chesapeake to the Appalachian Mountains and the Ohio country, the Harpers Ferry Armory began manufacturing weapons in the early nineteenth century, and by the 1850s, this federal installation had trans-formed remote Harpers Ferry into one of Virginia's most heavily industri-alized towns. At its peak production, on the eve of the Civil War, the armory employed more than 250 workers and was producing more than ten thou-sand rifles and muskets per year. At this point in its history, Harpers Ferry remained protected from the sort of naval threats that had concerned Washington, but it was hardly a remote outpost. Two of the mid-Atlantic's busiest transport arteries—the Baltimore and Ohio Railroad and the Ches-apeake and Ohio Canal—served Harpers Ferry.[5]

The proximity of Chambersburg to Harpers Ferry (they are about fifty miles apart) is the reason a transient businessman began living in the Penn-sylvania town in the summer of 1859. Dr. Isaac Smith and his associates spent several weeks at the Chambersburg train depot unloading supplies and crates marked "hardware." The "tall, spare, plainly-clad and heavily-bearded man" was "boarding with a widow who lived quietly away from the center of the town." Smith told several townsmen he was preparing for a mining expedition to mountainous western Virginia. No one thought anything of Smith. Men on the make were everywhere in greater Baltimore; most amounted to nothing, and many were just passing through, heading somewhere remote in search of mineral riches. It had been barely more than a decade since gold was discovered at Sutter's Mill, and 1859 was the year the public learned of the Comstock Lode, a massive silver find in western Nevada.[6]

In fact, Smith and his helpers were not so typical. They were paramilitary revolutionaries, and they were stockpiling weapons—rifles, revolvers, and 950 iron pikes. Isaac Smith was an alias used by the abolitionist and freedom fighter John Brown. Brown planned to lead his band of insurgents into Maryland, where they would arm supporters, most of whom would be slaves and free Blacks. After gaining control of the federal arms depot at Harpers Ferry, the insurgents would disseminate weapons to enslaved Virginians, who would join Brown's abolitionist army, and then retreat to strongholds deep in the southern Appalachian Mountains. From remote mountain hideaways, the antislavery fighters would descend across the South, inciting the slave rebellion to end all slave rebellions. A fierce Calvinist, Brown was as comfortable with martyrdom as he was with his ludicrously outsized scheme. After centuries of slave rebellions, Brown had a single example of success that came anywhere near matching what he hoped to achieve—the Haitian Revolution, led by the former slave Toussaint Louverture.[7] Brown was not one to let history, never mind doubt, intrude, nor was he without a level of discipline consistent with his devotion. His planning was meticulous. In coordination with a secret abolitionist network, he secured funding and recruited free Black freedom fighters throughout the American and Canadian North. An assiduous student of asymmetrical warfare, Brown had honed his skills fighting proslavery settlers in a divided Kansas. Once his army of slaves had been assembled and armed, he planned to train it in the guerilla tactics he had used so effectively in Bleeding Kansas.

In preparation for the great war against slavery, Brown had held a series of secret recruiting meetings near Buxton, Canada, the runaway slave enclave where William Parker and his family had settled. As part of those meetings, Brown and his local supporters, who included Harriet Tubman,

ratified a constitution outlining the governing principles of the new abolitionist army. Twelve whites and thirty-four Blacks signed the Chatham
Constitution. Parker was not one of the signers, but he surely knew of the
meetings and perhaps even met Brown. Few would have been better placed
to advise the antislavery fighter about the troubles he would face in the borderlands. But Brown, his Chatham compact in hand, expected to succeed
where eighty years of antislavery activism had failed.[8]

At Brown's request, Frederick Douglass, who had learned of aspects of
Brown's plot well before the summer of 1859, met with Brown outside Chambersburg. Douglass concealed the true purpose of his travels in the region by
delivering a public lecture, something he did at great personal peril in cities
and towns throughout the North. A local free Black and abolitionist sympathizer, Henry Watson, escorted Douglass to his rendezvous with Brown,
where Brown laid out his battle plan. He hoped Douglass would join the
fight, but instead, as Brown revealed the full quixotic scope of the plot, a
mortified Douglass begged him to reconsider. For Brown was "going into
a perfect steel-trap, and . . . once in he would never get out alive."[9]

Douglass's assessment was, of course, entirely accurate. An early sign
of trouble was the absence of any great upwelling of support from free
Blacks. Only five joined the twenty-one men who assembled with Brown at
a farmhouse on the Maryland side of the Mason-Dixon Line. On October 16,
Brown led his band of fighters the few miles to the undefended town of
Harpers Ferry. There they easily overpowered the single watchman guarding
the federal armory. After securing a few dozen hostages, Brown sent representatives to liberate slaves and initiate rebellion at a nearby plantation. Although a few slaves took the opportunity to flee servitude, the hundreds
Brown expected to join his insurrectionist band never materialized. The day
after the raid, local townsmen began firing on the invaders, killing eight of
them and forcing the survivors and a few hostages into a brick fire-engine
house. Trapped by locals and arriving Maryland and Virginia militiamen,
Brown and his army could do little but await their fate. On the night of
October 17, US marines commanded by Colonel Robert E. Lee and Lieu-
tenant J. E. B. "Jeb" Stuart overwhelmed the sad remains of Brown's army.
Several more of Brown's men were killed, including two of his sons, and
Brown himself, wounded but resolute, was taken captive. On December 2,
after being summarily convicted by a Virginia court, Brown was executed
for treason.

The failed raid on Harpers Ferry aroused much condemnation across the country, but in the borderlands that condemnation was more universal and more vocal. No public figure, no newspaper, nobody dared endorse Brown's actions. To the editors of Chambersburg's Democratic newspaper *Valley Spirit*, Brown was nothing more than a "bloody murderer," an "old scoundrel who has just expatiated his unparalleled crimes on the gallows." Only a mad abolitionist, a person of the lowest character, would conceal himself among the innocent people of Franklin County before he "stole upon their neighbors at the dead hour of mid-night and killed them without the smallest provocation."[10] For Republicans, Brown's actions were equally appalling. In a public "People's Meeting," the Republicans of Bedford County lost little time in proclaiming, "There is no party to whose principles and purposes the mad scheme at Harper's Ferry is more abhorrent than to the Republicans of Bedford County, Pennsylvania, and they will go as far as the farthest not only to condemn insurrection in the slave states, but to suppress it." In a declaration sounding similar notes, Chambersburg's Republican *Franklin Repository*, stood up for the entire town, Democrats and Republicans:

> From what we have heard, it appears our Southern neighbors of Maryland and Virginia, bordering on Pennsylvania, are very indignant at the citizens of Chambersburg—regarding them as the most fanatical "abolitionists" with which the country is troubled; and as thoroughly identified with "Old John Brown" and his crazy followers, in their late fool-hardy attempt at stirring up insurrection among the slaves at Harper's Ferry. . . . But because our people love Liberty more than Slavery, is no reason why they should be charged with a knowledge of the doings or designs of the Harper's Ferry insurrectionists, or that any, even one, of our citizens, was in on the secret; and to suppose that they would, in the most remote degree, countenance or favor, or "aid and abet" such a ruthless and murderous plot, or anything even slightly approximating to it, with a view to the wiping out of their "peculiar institution," is ungenerous—nay, it is cowardly. Had our people had the least inkling of the designs of these deluded men, they would have nipped the plot in the bud; but

THE AGE OF THE MASON-DIXON LINE

> being as ignorant of their designs as were the people of
> Harper's Ferry, it is folly for them, in their blind rage, to be
> heaping execrations upon our community, as being, in any
> manner, cognizant of their proceedings.

Pennsylvania's Democrats, desperate to quiet growing disunionist rumblings in their party, were in no mood to forgive and forget. "The Republican journals in this State, and many of them elsewhere, pretend not to approve of old Brown's armed invasion of Virginia," wrote the editors of the *Valley Spirit,* but those pretensions could hardly persuade when "New England public meetings, presided over by very prominent Republicans, have endorsed the murderer's conduct and taken measures to provide for his family as a special mark of their admiration for the man." The choice for the people of Chambersburg was clear: "All who do not want to involve us in war with our neighbors across the line must put down . . . crazy and malignant Republicanism."[11]

Over the course of the following year, as the presidential election grew closer, the rhetoric only grew shriller: the *Valley Spirit* implored its readers to vote for a "Union, and not a sectional president," unless, of course, they "desire to see the soil of Pennsylvania made the battlefield for the contending armies of the North and the South." The ultimatum was, of course, profoundly disingenuous. Whatever one may have thought of the martyred Brown, the reality was that Fire-Eating southerners had long disguised their intransigence over slavery's expansion with a rhetoric of desperation, as if disunionism was a last resort in the face of relentless northern aggression. Brown's raid was the perfect deus ex machina for disunionist southerners: abolitionism's lust for southern blood could no longer be hidden behind liberty's veil.

As the war of words took hold in the borderlands, a pall of anticipatory gloom settled over much of the rest of the country. From Washington, DC, one reporter wrote,

> I am no alarmist—not one of the despairing kind—but, on
> the contrary, am always hopeful, and disposed to look on the
> favorable side of things: but I cannot shut my eyes to the pros-
> pect before us, and I do assure you I speak the Words "of truth
> and soberness." The time of *reasoning* with these people at the
> South has gone by. They are no longer accessible to argument.

> They say that slave property is no longer safe in the Union,
> and refuse to acknowledge what is so obvious that the pro-
> posed *remedy* is ten times worse than the *disease.*

With Lincoln's election, disunionist Fire-Eaters had begun administering their frightful remedy. Barely a month passed before South Carolina seceded from the Union. By the time of Lincoln's inauguration on March 4, 1861, six more southern states had seceded.

Along the Line, southern secession was accompanied by a new source of terror. Not only did white borderlanders have to fear abolitionist fanatics and their vengeful Black associates, but they also had to fear enraged enemies of the American Union. Never before had crossing the Line represented the slightest danger to a free, law-abiding, able-bodied, employed white man. But suddenly these men confronted what African Americans had faced for generations. To cross from the North to the South was to face mortal danger. Whether or not the danger was real, partisans made much of the claim. Benjamin Wade, a Republican senator from Ohio, complained that northern men "have no security in travelling nearly one-half of this confederacy." The Unionist and Democratic Harrisburg *Patriot* acknowledged Wade's concerns but attributed them not to southern Fire-Eaters but to "abolitionist emissaries [who] have invaded the Southern States under various pretenses, as men of business, schoolmasters, & co., enticing away the slaves or inciting them to insurrection, until the Southern people know not who to trust." Faced with such a relentless abolitionist onslaught, could southerners do other than treat northern travelers with suspicion?[12]

No American would have a clearer sense of the new perils of border crossing than President-elect Lincoln. On February 11, his train left Springfield, Illinois, for a thirteen-day tour of the northern states. The journey was treacherous from its start. Rumors of assassination plots had begun swirling not long after Lincoln's election and only grew more threatening as Inauguration Day approached. Northern newspapers documented thousands of dollars pouring into the pockets of would-be assassins, and southern betting parlors accepted wagers on Lincoln's life. Given how effective southerners had been at reaching deep into the North to retrieve their slaves, few had any doubt they could reach Lincoln, even if he steered well clear of slave states. And even this would be feasible only for the early legs of the journey. Lincoln's itinerary still required him to pass from Pennsylvania across the Line to Baltimore and then to Washington, DC. As the Baltimore *Sun* reminded its readers just before Lincoln was to arrive in Maryland, "He will thus put his foot upon Southern soil, and enter that section of territory . . . from which he received not one electoral vote."[13]

While Lincoln's train encountered hazards—before it even exited Illinois, a railroad worker discovered rail equipment blocking the tracks, obviously intended to destroy the train and maim its human contents—and while Lincoln encountered unruly and threatening crowds, no part of the journey worried his security detail more than its final leg. The president-elect's train was to travel south from Harrisburg to Baltimore and then on to Washington. Dorothea Dix, a New Englander who had been touring the country advocating on behalf of the mentally ill, encountered an alarming sight while traveling by train through Maryland to Baltimore. Militiamen were drilling alongside the tracks, obviously in preparation for an assault on Lincoln's train. In December 1860, Dix held a secret meeting with Samuel Felton, president of the Philadelphia, Wilmington and Baltimore Railroad to warn him of the impending catastrophe. Felton hired Allan Pinkerton, a Chicago detective, to help secure the railroad from Confederate saboteurs.[14]

The risk to Lincoln was great, but his assassination was simply one of the looming perils the country faced following his election. For the most ambitious southern plotters, far more important than ridding the country of the president-elect was the annexation of Washington, DC. As southerners well knew, the national capital was located in the slave South. Three sides of the District adjoin Maryland, and the fourth adjoins the Potomac and Virginia. Were those two slave states to join the other seceding southern states, now unified as the Confederate States of America, the city would lie deep within enemy territory. Confederate pressure on Maryland's leaders was, accordingly, intense and unrelenting. But any remotely aware Marylander recognized the hazards of secession. "Maryland is a border State," observed its governor, Thomas Hicks, a slave owner who professed southern sympathies. "With only an invisible line between her territory and the free States," Maryland's slaves were already fleeing in great numbers. The federal government's efforts to arrest this illicit traffic would come to an immediate end with the dissolution of the Union. "In my opinion," Hicks explained to readers of the Easton *Gazette*, "if a separation should take place, in ten years there will not be a slave within [Maryland's] limits," and the state of Maryland would "become the battle ground of the hostile sections, subject to all the horrors of border war."

Hicks was an unlikely ally for Lincoln. In language that would have been utterly familiar to generations of borderlanders, he described his politics to a congressional subcommittee: "I was born in Maryland and raised there. My sympathies are with the South—I say this to the world. But I am a Union man, and would live in the Union, and die for it if necessary." Much like Lincoln, Hicks could not make this last claim lightly. To prevent a vote for secession, he repeatedly delayed convening the state assembly, infuriating the state's secessionist minority. He told his congressional interlocutors of a December meeting with southern sympathizers in Baltimore where "allusions [were] made to my personal safety, and the hazard I would run if I persisted in declining to convene the Legislature."[15]

Given Maryland's febrile political climate, and given the threats of violence, it was no wonder Lincoln's security detail was growing increasingly apprehensive. After a busy day of speeches and rallies in Cleveland, the president-elect and his entourage began learning the details of an elaborate and particularly terrifying assassination plot. Allan Pinkerton had discovered that assassins planned to kill Lincoln while he changed trains in Baltimore. Pinkerton and Felton urged the president-elect to avoid the city, but Lincoln was unmoved.[16]

What little support Lincoln had in Maryland was mostly confined to Baltimore. Any hope of rallying that support on behalf of the Union cause, let alone gaining the confidence of other Maryland Unionists, would surely be squandered if the president-elect avoided Baltimore. But the pressure to choose survival over politics was building. Kate Warne, one of Pinkerton's detectives, met Lincoln in New York City, bringing new details about the Baltimore plot, and Pinkerton himself met Lincoln in Philadelphia with additional intelligence. A group of New York City police detectives, working independently of Pinkerton, had discovered the same plot. William Henry Seward, Lincoln's Republican primary opponent, was briefed on the matter and immediately sent his son Frederick from Washington to Philadelphia to warn Lincoln. Lincoln the attorney, now presented with a preponderance of evidence, recognized that whether or not Maryland stayed in the Union could no longer depend on a rally in Baltimore. He would have to pass through the state in total secrecy.

While Lincoln slept in his Philadelphia hotel, Pinkerton prepared for the president-elect's journey across the Line. Lincoln would proceed the following day as if nothing had changed—after delivering an address at Philadelphia's Independence Hall, he would travel by train to Harrisburg, where he would consult with the Pennsylvania governor about general political matters. He would then address the state assembly, exuding the steady moral certitude that had propelled him to the presidency. Under cover of night, Lincoln would then leave his Harrisburg hotel and return to Philadelphia, where he would catch a scheduled night train to Washington, DC. Pinkerton accompanied Lincoln, as did Lincoln's old friend and personal bodyguard, Ward Hill Lamon. The night of February 22, Lincoln's train traveled east to Philadelphia. A disguised Lincoln and his two escorts transferred to the last southbound train of the night, where several of Pinkerton's agents had staked out a sleeping car for the secret entourage.

While his escorts chatted away, Lincoln slept through the night, his train rumbling south from Philadelphia, along the Delaware River, across the Delaware curve, and into Wilmington, and then southwest, across the Eastern Shore, through the far northeastern corner of Maryland. With no rail bridge, the trains were ferried across the Susquehanna to Havre de Grace. Insofar as Pinkerton and Felton knew of planned attacks, they involved the tracks between Havre de Grace and Baltimore. That John Wilkes Booth's hometown, Bel Air, was about ten miles from the rail line in Harford County may be considered coincidental. But the fact that Pinkerton's men had identified a large southern militia drilling near the rail line in southern Harford County was not. The area was widely known for its southern sympathies. The other problem, not unrelated to the proslavery, southern-leaning sentiment in the region, was the many rail bridges built over the inlets and small waterways that fed the Chesapeake Bay. Each one presented opportunity for sabotage. In what must be counted as among history's great episodes of good fortune, Lincoln's train somehow made it safely across the Line and into Baltimore.

Since locomotives were not allowed to pass through the city center, the cars from the train were pulled by horse across town from the Philadelphia, Wilmington and Baltimore Railroad's President Street station to the Baltimore and Ohio's Camden Street station. By 6 A.M., Lincoln's train was pulling into the Baltimore and Ohio Railroad depot in Washington. Pinkerton and Lincoln made a still-perilous short trip to the Willard Hotel, which would be the president-elect's base of operations for the nine days until his inauguration.[17]

In the four and a half years after Lincoln's election, Washington and the District of Columbia remained part of the United States, in no small measure because Maryland remained part of the United States. Without direct federal intervention, the latter might not have happened. Had Maryland seceded, the way would have been prepared for Delaware to contemplate the same path. But unlike Maryland, Delaware never faced a serious secessionist threat. For this reason, the state willy-nilly provided Maryland Unionists with a model for border state politics, a model that married Unionism with antipathy toward the new Republican administration.

In the decades before the Civil War, the former Lower Counties became effectively two states. In one, corresponding to the borders of New Castle County, a rapidly industrializing Wilmington attracted migrants from the countryside. In 1790, about a third of Delaware's population lived there; by 1860, almost half did. The other Delaware, composed of the two southern counties of Kent and Sussex, saw much slower population growth. Between 1850 and 1860, New Castle County's population grew by almost a third; Kent and Sussex Counties grew by about 22 percent and 14 percent, respectively. With the shifting locus of population, what had been true of Delaware since the beginning of the nineteenth century became even more true: slavery was primarily a phenomenon of its southern counties. In 1860, fewer than 1,800 slaves resided in Delaware, and 75 percent of them resided in the state's southernmost county, Sussex, placing them closer to Maryland's Eastern Shore than to Delaware's industrial capital at Wilmington. Residing in New Castle County, meanwhile, were only 254 slaves, or 14 percent of the state's total. Slavery in Delaware had become so marginal that in 1847 the legislature considered formal abolition. The initiative failed, but it generated a report whose findings were unmistakable: "Slavery in Delaware, so far as it regards the number and condition of our slaves, is rather nominal than a real evil." No wonder this labor system was associated solely with "the careless, slovenly and unproductive husbandry visible in some parts of our State." The authors of the report were obviously referring to Kent and Sussex Counties. Estimates of land values from 1860 suggest that land in New Castle County was worth four to five times that in

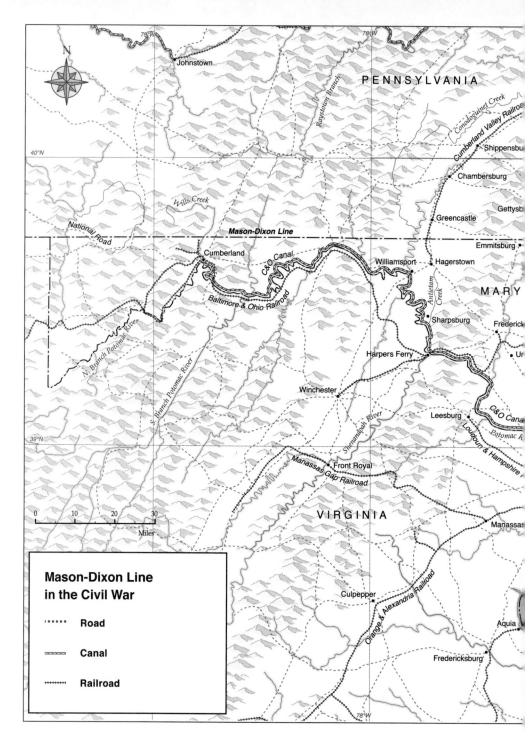

The Mason-Dixon Line in the Civil War

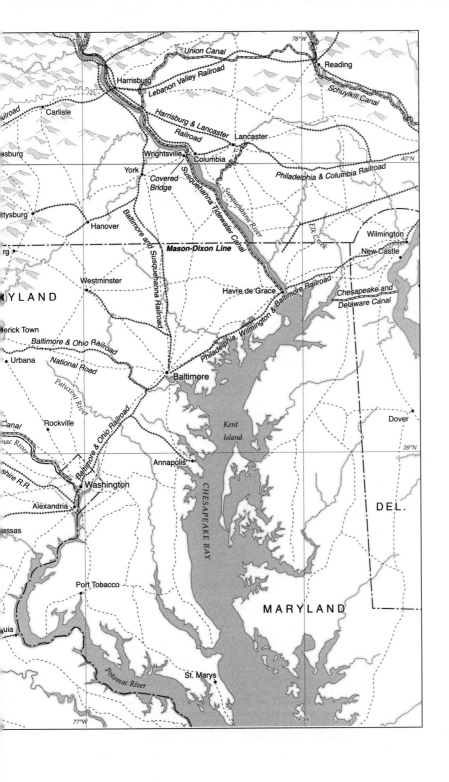

Union Canal

Reading

Harrisburg

Lebanon Valley Railroad

Schuylkill Canal

Carlisle

Harrisburg & Lancaster Railroad

Lancaster

Wrightsville

Columbia

York

40°N

Covered Bridge

Philadelphia & Columbia Railroad

Susquehanna Tidewater Canal

Susquehanna River

tysburg

Hanover

Elk Creek

Wilmington

Mason-Dixon Line

New Castle

YLAND

Westminster

Havre de Grace

Chesapeake and Delaware Canal

erick Town

Baltimore & Ohio Railroad

Philadelphia, Wilmington & Baltimore Railroad

Urbana

National Road

Patuxent River

Baltimore

rg

Canal

Rockville

Dover

ac River

Kent Island

39°N

shire R.R.

Annapolis

Baltimore & Ohio Railroad

Washington

Alexandria

DEL.

assas

CHESAPEAKE BAY

uia

Port Tobacco

MARYLAND

Potomac River

St. Marys

77°W

76°W

Kent and Sussex. Delaware's economic divisions were reflected in its political divisions. By 1860, the Democrats were dominant in Sussex and Kent Counties; in New Castle County, an agglomeration of former Whigs and Know-Nothings, known locally as the People's Party, had gained a majority. And yet, for all its demographic and political division, for all its obvious divisions over slavery, when it came to the looming matter of secession, the state was unified by an especially noxious form of Unionism.[18]

Unlike the other border states, Delaware was never home to a substantial disunionist faction. As a strategic and military matter, Delaware would have been unlikely to survive secession. Even were Maryland to secede, Delaware's security would have depended on its capacity to defend a northern border and an eastern coast, and given the limited rail access to the Delmarva Peninsula and the proximity of the state's primary rail hub to Pennsylvania, marshaling such a defense would be difficult, especially since Delaware offered little if any real strategic value for Confederate war planners. Even for Delaware's proslavery, southern-leaning Democrats, in sum, survival and Unionism were of a piece. "The perpetuity of the Federal Union, to all a matter of deep interest, is to us of Delaware an absolute Necessity," pronounced Sussex County native and Democratic governor William Burton in his 1859 inaugural address. With secession, Burton continued, "our separate existence as a State must cease, and Delaware become a dependency of some hostile but more powerful neighbor." That neighbor, Pennsylvania, already exerted a disproportionate influence over Delaware's economy. With secession would come occupation, and with occupation Delaware would, as it had been during its colonial history, be the consort of its much larger and more powerful neighbor. [19]

It is not surprising that, forced to play across his state's divergent sections, Governor Burton would have reverted to Unionism, but a similar posture prevailed in Delaware's statehouse, even among southern representatives who had no particular need to reach across the aisle. In January 1861, Judge Henry Dickinson, a secessionist envoy sent by Mississippi to lobby the state legislature, ran into a brick wall. Although the legislature was sharply divided—in the Senate, there were five Democrats and four Republicans; in the House, there were ten Democrats and eleven representatives from the People's Party—the response to Dickinson could hardly have been more definitive. With no discussion, the legislature unanimously rejected Dickinson's secessionist plea and passed a formal resolution asserting "our unqualified disapproval of the remedy for existing difficulties suggested by the resolutions of the Legislature of Mississippi."[20]

Unionism in Delaware was unquestionably proslavery Unionism—a position ideal for southern Democrats in a vulnerable border state. Proslavery Unionism also had powerful advocates in Washington—a crucial source of legitimacy for Delaware's Democrats. "Noble little Delaware," as Lincoln called it, would initially follow the path associated with former attorney general, Kentucky senator, and Constitutional Unionist John J. Crittenden. Although one of a group of senators supporting a final, desperate compromise with the slave South, Crittenden allowed his name to be attached to a plan put forth in December 1860. The so-called Crittenden Compromise proposed a constitutional amendment that would restore the Missouri Compromise line by prohibiting slavery north of 36°30′; it would also implement a series of draconian restrictions on the federal government's powers to interfere with slavery where it already existed—effectively providing southern slaveholders the constitutional protections for property in human beings they would include in the constitution of the Confederate States of America. Delaware's politicians rallied around the plan, and in mid-January 1861, by overwhelming margins, the state's legislature formally endorsed it and instructed Delaware's congressional delegation to do the same. To Republicans, the Crittenden Compromise was repugnant appeasement—particularly repugnant when embraced by north-facing Delaware. The *Philadelphia Inquirer* offered a fierce assessment of this feckless brand of border politics: "The State of Delaware, in 1850, with a population of 91,532, had 18,073 free colored persons and 2,290 slaves, and now, with 112,353 inhabitants, it has only 1,805 slaves—and yet this is called a Slave State, has slave laws, and its two Senators and its former representative in Congress (and some say its Governor and Secretary) are *violent pro slavery peace men*," the latter phrase a reference to Peace Democrats, also known as Copperheads, those northerners favoring an end to war even at the cost of appeasement of the slave South.[21]

Because there were so few slaves in Delaware, because the state's economic locus was for all intents and purposes in southeastern Pennsylvania, and because secessionism was so weak, few thought the state's intransigent attachment to slavery anything other than political posturing. After the war, Lincoln's secretaries, John Hay and John G. Nicolay, recalled believing that Delaware was "allied to the South rather by tradition than by present interest." This sense that Delaware's political alignments were largely a function of its slave-owning history rather than its predominantly free-labor present account for the state's prominence in what would be President Lincoln's first attempt to initiate state-level abolition.[22]

As a candidate, Lincoln had gone to great lengths to distance himself from abolitionism. His aim, he proclaimed over and over, was fully in line with the Republican Party platform. He had no intention of interfering with slavery where state law protected it. He did, however, intend to stop its expansion; if that could be done without interfering with the property rights of current slaveholders, Lincoln pledged to do that. By the summer of 1861, the first battles of the US Civil War having been fought, the political formula that propelled Lincoln to the White House had begun to fray. Seizing on the disruptions of war, enslaved people had begun seeking refuge behind Union lines. Encouraged by his military advisors to provide formal support for these refugees, in August 1861 the president signed into law the First Confiscation Act authorizing military emancipation. Union military leaders now had formal authority to seize rebel property, including slaves. For the abolitionist wing of the Republican Party, the act was indicative of the president's excessively incremental approach to slavery. In rebelling, southerners had forfeited any right to federal protection of their enslaved property and licensed the executive to take whatever measures were needed to suppress the rebellion, including a blanket proclamation liberating slaves in rebelling states. The argument would eventually lead the president to enact the Emancipation Proclamation. That it took him another year and a half to issue the proclamation was a function of the border states. Should the federal government endorse the seizure of slave property, Lincoln explained to his friend and fellow Illinois attorney Orville H. Browning, "the very same arms we had furnished Kentucky would be turned against us," and with Kentucky gone, "we can not hold Missouri, nor, as I think, Maryland. These all against us . . . we would as well consent to separation at once, including the surrender of this capital." However useful the First Confiscation Act was as a military matter, and whatever the legality of such a wartime proclamation, the political path to full unconditional emancipation remained unclear to the president, and yet the pressure to achieve a clear and unambiguous victory against slavery mounted.[23]

By the fall of 1861, Lincoln had begun to look for some incremental so-lution to the problem of slavery in the border states. An astute student of slavery's political economy, he turned his attention to the one border state where slavery, at least as a functioning labor system, was weakest and where secession was least likely. Delaware would be the test case for a new feder-ally sponsored abolition program. Should such a program fail, the military consequences were unlikely to be serious; should it succeed, the political payoff would be immense. Growing abolitionist ranks in the Republican Party would be momentarily reassured, and border states would have a template for ending slavery without forced emancipation.

George P. Fisher, Delaware's one member of the House, and Benjamin Burton, the state's largest slave owner, met with Lincoln to discuss the plan in November 1861. Although Burton owned twenty-eight slaves, he was a committed Unionist, and Lincoln calculated that should the state's most heavily invested slave owner agree to sacrifice his property for the Union, Delaware's other remaining slave owners would follow suit. After receiving assurances that any plan would involve compensation and include provisions to care for the children of slaves, Fisher and Burton agreed to support gradual abolition. Lincoln's secretaries then drafted two proposals. Both provided for the immediate emancipation of all slaves over thirty-five and all slaves born after the passage of a state abolition statute. To counter the tired old refrain that large-scale manumission would produce a burdensome new class of indigents, both provided for apprenticeships for children born to enslaved mothers. And both allowed slave owners to retain slaves in the prime of their working lives. The two plans differed primarily in the length of time until total emancipation—one stipulated a phased emancipation, achieving the abolition of slavery by 1867, while the other, favored by Lin-coln, achieved total emancipation by 1893. Because both plans promised compensation to slave owners, funded by the federal government in install-ments, the last of which would be paid upon the complete emancipation of all the state's enslaved, the two plans also differed in the time the federal government would have to pay off a debt Lincoln's administration estimated at $719,200. This may have been why Lincoln favored the second plan: it allowed for thirty-one payments of $23,200 as opposed to five yearly install-ments of $143,840.[24]

There was precedent for what Lincoln proposed. The British abolition of slavery in the West Indies in 1834 involved compensated emancipation, as did much abolition in Latin America, and American antislavery activists had long incorporated compensation into plans to end slavery. Similarly, statutes gradually ending slavery were obviously as old as antislavery law in the United States, dating back to Pennsylvania's 1780 gradual abolition law. In effect, what Lincoln's plan proposed was that Delaware enact some version of that very old law. To avoid the perennial constitutional questions surrounding federal power and slavery, Lincoln's plans rested on state statute—any act for the abolition of slavery in Delaware would be the work of the Delaware legislature, albeit enabled by a federal statute that allowed federal monies to cover the costs of emancipation. Here, too, Lincoln's plans carefully skirted age-old constitutional questions: rather than paying former slave owners directly, the federal government would be compensating the state. The aim of this complex gambit was clear: provide the Lincoln administration constitutional cover by leaving the ultimate act of abolition to the state legislature.

The weakness in Lincoln's scheme was also its strength. Even with federal incentives, the politics of abolition at the state level—even compensated abolition—were deeply unfriendly to Lincoln's proposals. As so many observers assumed, there was little to suggest Delaware's politicians had any ideological attachment to slavery. What they did have was a clear hostility to Black voting rights. Manumission, so proslavery partisans had long feared, was a step toward Black enfranchisement.[25]

The Republican Party was not strong in Delaware, but it was gaining strength, primarily in populous and wealthy New Castle County. While free Blacks were still denied the vote and had been since the state's 1792 constitution assigned voting rights exclusively to white males, Democratic politicians recognized that barriers to Black voting helped secure their long-term hold on the state. A surge in new Black voters, enabled by Republicans eager to attract their vote, could spell disaster for Delaware's Democrats. By February 1862, gradual abolition in Delaware was dead, the bill sponsored by Fisher having never even been formally brought before lawmakers. In 1863 the Delaware legislature betrayed its true concern, upholding the ban on Black voting. The state's frustrated Republicans decried the "miserable lie that the supporters of Lincoln and [Vice President Hannibal] Hamlin desire to place the negroes on an equality with the white men," but the lie proved a powerful one, one the Democratic Party would nurture for the better part of a century. In tying the defense of slavery to the defense of white electoral supremacy, Delaware's Democrats found a winning formula—but it was a formula possible only because proslavery politics in Delaware could never be secessionist politics. The situation would have been very different had Maryland's secessionists been more successful. But fortunately for Delaware, that was not to be.[26]

Lincoln approached his inauguration with grave concern for the fate of Maryland. He had an ally in Governor Hicks, but the governor's powers to restrain secessionists in his state's legislature were on the wane, partly because of Lincoln himself. Precisely as the president-elect had feared, his avoidance of Baltimore proved costly. Reports referred to Lincoln's "Underground Railroad Journey," signaling disdain for the so-called Black Republican, deemed too fearful to face his southern detractors. "Had we had any respect for Mr. Lincoln," the editors of the Baltimore *Sun* noted just a few days after Lincoln was to have visited their city, "his career and speeches on his way to the seat of government would have cruelly impaired it; but the final escapade by which he reached the capital . . . utterly demolished it." Lincoln had acted on "a lie, a gross and shameless lie, concocted with a view to shield from the ignominy of his disgraceful flight of the President elect of the United States at the expense of the people of Baltimore."[27]

On April 12, almost six weeks after Lincoln delivered his inaugural address, Confederate guns fired on Fort Sumter. Lincoln responded by calling up seventy-five thousand federal troops, many of whom would travel through Maryland to the nation's capital. As the realities of war descended on the nation's capital, there was little sign that Washington's neighboring states were any closer to casting their lot with the Union. "Well advised parties here," wrote a Baltimore reporter for the *New York Herald*, "express the conviction that Maryland and Virginia have both been boldly committed to secession from the beginning, and their apparent hesitation has only been worn as a mask, to throw the North off its guard." Military reinforcements were urgently needed "or the federal capital will be lost. Every hour is important." Should secession succeed in Maryland, those reinforcements would be forced to march through enemy territory. Even should Maryland somehow elect to stay in the Union, there were few guarantees that federal troops would be able to pass safely through the state. After Virginia militiamen seized the federal armory at Harpers Ferry, Lincoln's government had to

face the threat of Maryland's secession by force. Rumors were swirling that
from Harpers Ferry, the Virginians planned to invade Maryland, "making
Mason and Dixon's Line the line of warfare." For Lincoln, this dire prospect presented a dilemma almost as serious as the attack on Fort Sumter—
perhaps even more so, since it could bring the surrender of the federal
capital. The danger was so serious that when Lincoln began calling up federal
troops, Governor Hicks traveled to Washington for an emergency meeting
with the president, Secretary of War Simon Cameron, and General Win-
field Scott, the Virginia-born commander of the Union Army. To further
forestall the march to secession, Hicks convinced military officials to deploy
Maryland's Union Army contingent solely for defensive purposes and solely
in Maryland and contiguous Washington, DC. To ask citizens of his state
to raise arms against their southern brethren would, Hicks insisted, lead
headlong to secession. The political problem of deploying Union soldiers
from Maryland was, alas, not the governor's only problem.[28]

Maryland's contributions to federal forces would be significant but nowhere near adequate to protect the national capital. Many more would be
needed for that—and nearly all would have to come from north of the Line.
Not only would they have to pass through Maryland, but they would also
have to pass through the rail depots of Baltimore. Flying their palmetto flags,
symbols of solidarity with South Carolina, and holding secessionist meetings with such unambiguously grandiose titles as the "Southern Rights Convention," Baltimore's secessionists were unrelenting. On April 17, news
came of Virginia's decision to secede from the Union. Fearing this would
further embolden the city's secessionists, Governor Hicks and Baltimore's
mayor, George William Brown, issued a series of proclamations demanding
restraint, but these had little effect. With large deployments of federal troops
about to pass through a city crawling with Confederate sympathizers, violence was beginning to appear unavoidable.

On the morning of April 19, a troop train from Philadelphia pulled into
Camden Street station loaded with seventeen hundred Union soldiers, including the Sixth Massachusetts Regiment. The arrival of uniformed and
armed Union troops was provocative enough, but the idea that many came
from Massachusetts, an abolitionist stronghold, was a provocation Baltimore's southern sympathizers refused to ignore. The soldiers would have
to traverse the same route Lincoln traveled as his cars were pulled by horse
nearly a mile and a half from the President Street depot to the Camden Street

depot. Unlike the president-elect's train, the Union soldiers' trains would be pulled through the city in the middle of the day, along the swarming waterfront. As Maryland authorities anticipated, crowds pelted the railcars with paving stones and eventually pulled up the tracks linking the city's rail depots. The final groups of transiting troops were forced to march through central Baltimore. Crowds converged, and the terrified soldiers opened fire. The mayor and chief of police intervened and managed to stop the violence, but four Union soldiers were killed and several dozen injured; countless rioters had also been injured and around twelve killed.[29]

Hicks and Brown begged Lincoln to stop the transit of troops through the city. Putting the matter in its baldest terms, Mayor Brown explained to Lincoln, "It is not possible for more soldiers to pass through Baltimore, unless they fight their way at every step."[30] Maryland's Unionists, meanwhile, saw in Baltimore the beginning of the end for peace in the state. The Cumberland *Weekly Civilian* warned its readers, "Maryland is doomed to be the great slaughter house of this unnatural civil war."[31]

Maryland's internal struggles left both Governor Hicks and Lincoln with no clear path forward. War in Baltimore would leave Washington more vulnerable and further embolden Maryland's secessionists. But without massive reinforcements, the capital would surely fall. On the night of the Baltimore riots, Lincoln's personal secretary John Nicolay contemplated the anxious anticipation that had settled over Washington:

> We have rumors that 1500 men are under arms at Alexandria, seven miles below here, supposed to have hostile designs against this city; and an additional report that a vessel was late this evening seen landing men on the Maryland side of the [Potomac] river. All these things indicate that if we are to be attacked at all soon, it will happen to-night. On the other hand, we have some four or five thousand men under arms in the city, and a very vigilant watch out in all the probable directions of approach. The public buildings are strongly guarded; the Secretary of War will remain all night in his Department.[32]

As a means of assuaging Baltimoreans fearful of the impending bloodbath, a desperate Hicks ultimately agreed to the demolition of railroad bridges above the city. Meanwhile, the secessionist drumbeat continued.

In a final desperate bid to help Maryland's Unionists, Lincoln agreed to a new troop transit plan. Trains from Philadelphia would unload troops at Perryville, across the Susquehanna from Havre de Grace. From there, the soldiers would be transported by ferry to Annapolis, and then west by rail or wagon through Anne Arundel and Prince George's Counties to Washington. Life would have been much easier for Governor Hicks had there been some way to keep Union soldiers off Maryland soil entirely, and he struggled in vain to prevent Union forces from disembarking at his state's capital. To a committee of Baltimore officials, who implored Lincoln to find an alternative, the president replied, "I must have troops to defend this capital. Geographically it lies surrounded by the soil of Maryland. . . . Our men are not moles, and can't dig under the earth; they are not birds, and can't fly through the air. There is no way but to march across, and that they must do." Baltimore might be avoided, but beyond that, Maryland faced a stark choice. "Go home and tell your people that if they will not attack us," the president explained to the officials, "we will not attack them; but if they do attack us, we will return it, and that severely."[33]

By late April, reports indicated that the new strategy was paying political dividends. The Stars and Stripes was replacing the palmetto flag, and overt displays of Unionism were growing commonplace, so much so that by late May the *Sun* could report the convening of the Maryland State Union Convention, an attempt by state politicians to capitalize on the state's Constitutional Unionist pedigree. Much as had been the case during the 1860 campaign, Constitutional Unionism remained an unapologetically border-state ideology. It was as fervent in its quest to preserve the Union as in its rejection of the Republican Party's positions on slavery. While its newest iteration "concurred with the present Executive of the United States that the unity and integrity of the national Union must be preserved," in its perspective on "the nature and true principles of the constitution . . . as it relates to, and affects the question of slavery," Maryland's new Union Party "is directly opposed to the view of that Executive." The politics were old, the formulation as familiar as the endless borderlands struggle to fend off the political problem of slavery. But secessionism in Maryland pushed Unionism in a radical new direction—a point made clear in the Union Party's demand for the South's "compulsory submission to the powers of the government." A month earlier, these words would have ignited violent public unrest. That they did not in late May was thus not simply an indication that, as the *Frederick Examiner* proclaimed, "secession is a sick man in Maryland." It was also an indication that the old doughface politics of the borderlands would be very difficult to sustain as the secession crisis erupted into full-blown war. But like all ideologies of convenience, noxious Unionism would not go quietly.[34]

In the early months of the war, it surfaced in calls for some sort of armed neutrality, but geography swiftly did away with this last-ditch attempt to save the old proslavery Unionism of Taney and Buchanan. None of the other border states faced so stark a reality. "Maryland of all her sister [border] states occupies a position the most delicate," wrote Thomas Swann, former mayor of Baltimore, in a letter to Salmon Chase a few months before the senator from Ohio was appointed Lincoln's treasury secretary. The problem, Swann explained, was that Maryland was "situated upon the borders of Pennsylvania, exposed upon an extent of coast beyond her ability to adequately protect," and, perhaps most devastating of all, drew most of her trade "from the West by a line of intercommunication which has cost her more than $30,000,000." That costly line was the Baltimore and Ohio Railroad—effectively, as one historian has described it, "a Maryland public work." As the central artery linking Baltimore to its hinterland, the railroad had obvious economic importance. But its destruction would mean much more than the loss of Maryland's most important industrial concern. It would mean total economic calamity. The city of Baltimore owned shares in the railroad, as did the state. Most, however, were owned by ordinary Marylanders.[35]

After the war, Confederate vice president Alexander Stephens recalled that in the months after the fall of Sumter, the failure of secessionism in Maryland was "largely because of the fact that the overwhelming influence exerted by the Baltimore and Ohio was exerted in favor of the Washington government." Stephens was correct, but only partly so. The Lincoln administration, with the active support of John W. Garrett, the railroad's president, systematically shifted Maryland's political order.[36]

In the summer of 1861, that shift seemed some way off. Following a Confederate victory at the Battle of Manassas, not far from Washington, emboldened secessionists initiated a special session of the Maryland legislature at Frederick. For Republicans, Maryland's actions were as alarming as any since the start of the secession crisis. For Pennsylvanians, the possibility that a state with which they shared so long and undefended a border might be hijacked by Confederate sympathizers, let alone by the actual Confederacy, could hardly have been a more serious crisis. "Everyone knows," Thaddeus Stevens reminded Congress, "the Legislature of the State of Maryland is a Legislature of traitors—a rebel Legislature . . . deeply imbued with the very principles that have created this terrible war." Should Maryland join the Confederacy, the *Philadelphia Inquirer* asked, "is there any Northern man hardy enough to say the Southern boundary of the United States . . . would not be Mason and Dixon's line," rendering Pennsylvania "the Border State upon whose soil the future battles between the North and South would be fought, and the fair city of William Penn . . . liable to a sudden attack at any moment?" Even should wider war be avoided, secession would do what two generations of legal conflict had failed to do: it would destroy whatever remained of greater Baltimore. "The unrestrained free trade which has made the commerce between the several States so profitable to all parties would be put an end to," observed the *Inquirer,* "and duties . . . upon exports and imports, would have to be paid . . . whilst the Southern boundary of our State would be lined by the revenue stations of the two nations."[37]

Fortunately for Pennsylvania's Republicans, and fortunately for Lincoln, Pennsylvania's interests and the federal government's interests were in very close alignment. To defeat secessionism in Maryland, Lincoln ordered federal forces to surround Frederick, and took a series of legal actions that allowed the military to detain thirty-one secessionist lawmakers and their allies, including Mayor Brown of Baltimore. The detainees were held for several months—some released only after swearing allegiance to the United States. The legality of the federal government's action was almost immediately challenged. Among those arrested was the prominent secessionist and would-be Confederate cavalry officer John Merryman. Merryman appealed his case to a federal court in Baltimore, presided over by Justice Taney. Not surprisingly, the chief justice issued a sympathetic decision, ordering federal authorities to bring Merryman before the bench and show just cause for his imprisonment. Since Lincoln had suspended habeas corpus for rebels, Union military authorities refused to comply, prompting a lengthy court battle between Merryman's lawyers and the Lincoln administration.[38]

As a legal matter, Lincoln's actions remain a source of controversy. But as a military matter, they had the desired effect. Although Maryland Democrats delighted in castigating the tyrannical new president and his apparent contempt for fundamental rights, never mind states' rights, their claims ultimately had little effect. With many of Maryland's most ardent secessionist politicians in prison and many of their supporters out of the state fighting for the Confederacy, the elections of November 1861 effectively anointed Maryland a single-party state. The new Union Party, composed of Know-Nothings, Constitutional Unionists, and a small number of disillusioned Democrats, gained control of every branch of the Maryland state government—and did so in the most sweeping imaginable fashion. The opposition States' and Southern Rights Party, cobbled together from the remains of Maryland's Democrats, carried only a few voting districts in southern St. Mary's, Charles, and Calvert Counties.[39]

The history of the Mason-Dixon Line is inseparable from the American Civil War. But as the trials of the Line's southern states make plain, the connection is an awkward one. By the time war erupted, the Line had become much more than a boundary between Maryland, Delaware, and Pennsylvania, let alone between slavery and freedom. As the Maryland colonizationist and historian of the Line John H. B. Latrobe reminded his readers, there were two Mason-Dixon Lines. There was the "Mason and Dixon's line of geography," and there was the Mason-Dixon Line of politics. The former "will continue to be that whose heraldic insignia are still to be found in field and forest"; the latter, a metaphor for a nation divided. Latrobe's account predated the secession crisis by five years, so he could not have anticipated the struggles to come. As border states, Maryland and Delaware may have continued to embody the Line's early history—they were, after all, still bounded by the Line. But with these states remaining in the Union, could the Line still be understood as emblematic of the sectional crisis that had brought civil war? In fact, the very existence of the border states, especially Delaware and Maryland, confirmed the persistence of the sectionalism that had brought the war, a sectionalism that persisted despite the convenient fictions of Unionist politicians. The United States, Abraham Lincoln's United States, remained a house divided—if not quite half slave and half free, then part slave and part free.[40]

CHAPTER 14

The End of the Line

WITH THE LATE 1865 ratification of the Thirteenth Amendment, the slave labor system sustained by the legal regimes of Pennsylvania's pro-slavery southern neighbor states came to an end. In the stark formulation of Massachusetts senator Charles Sumner, "Freedom National," the long-sought abolitionist ideal, prevailed over "Slavery Sectional." The Line would still mark territorial and jurisdictional limits, but much as it had been for white Americans until the Civil War, those limits would impose no restrictions on the movements of rights-bearing citizens of a federated American republic.

The wartime path to Freedom National was not straight. The failure of compensated abolition in Delaware meant the secession crisis and the border state problem had no immediate impact on the laws of slavery along the Line. As the war progressed, however, and as the Union military and the United States government came to view the abolition of slavery as essential to the restoration of the Union, legal change would begin. The military, through policies that treated freed people as wartime contraband; Congress, through acts that established military contraband policy as federal government policy; abolitionists, through relentless pressure on the Republican Party; Union soldiers, especially Black enlistees, through acts of liberation and patriotism; and Abraham Lincoln, through the executive order emancipating slaves of rebel masters—all fed the wartime momentum toward a national act of immediate abolition. The culmination of this momentum would be the Thirteenth Amendment to the Constitution, but even before the federal constitutional abolition of slavery, states began for the first time in decades to consider constitutional bans on slavery. In fall 1864, over a year before the ratification of the Thirteenth Amendment, Maryland became the seventh state in the Union—following Vermont (whose 1777 constitution actually preceded formal statehood), Ohio (1802), Indiana (1816), Illinois (1818), Arkansas (1864), and Louisiana (1864)—to ratify a constitutional ban on slavery. Delaware did not follow its proslavery neighbor, and although the Thirteenth Amendment made freedom national, the smallest border state would refuse to join the majority of states in ratifying the amendment until 1901.[1]

For some African American observers, the wartime path to slavery's end only made clear what had been the case since the country's founding. As long as the United States was a capitalist nation, with little regard for the welfare of laboring people, Freedom National would be a damning fiction. In August 1864, almost two years after Lincoln issued the preliminary Emancipation Proclamation, and several months before Maryland ratified its new antislavery constitution, the radical Black physician James McCune Smith explained the full depth of the problem to readers of New York's *Weekly Anglo-African*, a leading African American newspaper: "There is neither in the political, nor religious, nor philanthropic worlds of the American people, any agency at work which can compass the entire abolishment of slavery," and yet "there are many who will persist in prophesying the certain downfall of slavery, as an outgrowth of this war."

Smith saw nothing in the actions of President Lincoln and the United States government, or the governments of the states, to justify such prophecy. The problem, Smith explained, was one of political economy. Liberal abolitionists, Harriet Martineau among them, had long assumed the logic of markets would eventually do to slavery what it did to other artifacts of a preindustrial, feudal economic order. The lure of wages and a natural human acquisitiveness would displace coercion and cruelty as the drivers of human labor. As an expanding supply of free labor allowed capitalists to reduce labor costs, inefficient slavery would suffer its deserved extinction. To Smith, this old canard was precisely what allowed even the most philanthropic Americans to believe that war would bring a final and definitive end to slavery.

War would surely blow apart the slave power, that deeply rooted, corrupt political conspiracy that had for so long insulated slavery from markets. Where liberal philanthropists erred, Smith explained, was in the belief that the end of the slave power would mean the end of slavery. This hopeful view misunderstood the problem of slavery as a fundamentally political one. In fact, what sustained slavery was not a corrupt politics, struggling against liberating market forces. What sustained slavery were those very market forces. "The main support of slavery before the war," Smith noted, "will be strengthened rather than weakened at the end of the war" for one very simple reason: in America "capital owns labor." In generating colossal fortunes, the war only made the problem worse. Those fortunes would be invested in land, both in the North and in the South, "and, owning the land, the ownership of labor also will speedily accrue to" the nation's capitalists. Opponents of slavery, hopeful that national catastrophe would be justified by the liberation of the nation's enslaved, had been lulled into a somnambulant belief that declarations abolishing slavery, whether issued by the executive branch of government or enshrined through statute or constitutional amendment, produced fundamental structural change.

In fact, these acts were nothing more than linguistic games. "The word *slavery* will, of course, be wiped from the statute book," Smith wrote, but he reminded his readers that the institution "can be just as well maintained by cunningly devised laws. In fact, the word 'slave' was already dying out of the Southern vocabulary; it was 'my servant' and 'my people.'" Whatever the war's political outcomes, its social and economic ones were clear: "The white man, owning the land, the capital and the lawmaking, already owns labor. In deference to the world's opinion, capital may for a few years, after the war ends, deck its victims with the garlands of freedom," but those garlands would soon give way, and "capital, aided by the government (which is, in wartime, the minion of capital), pursues its ownership of labor, and whatever the condition of the freedman today under the biting necessities of war, that condition will not be bettered after peace." War might destroy the slave power, but it would only strengthen capitalism, leaving all laboring Americans little better off than they had been before the national catastrophe. Much like his contemporary Karl Marx, Smith had little use for the liberal piety that a market society was, by definition, a free society. Abolition would simply enable slavery by another name. Freedom National, in Smith's telling, was another way of saying Capital National. And Capital National was unlikely to tolerate the liberation of laboring Americans, especially laboring Americans of African descent.[2]

Few African American commentators saw the prospects for national abolition in quite these terms. While most acknowledged the near universality of white American racism, many saw in the abolition of slavery a truly revolutionary aim. George E. Stephens, a Philadelphia cabinetmaker and another correspondent for the *Weekly Anglo-African,* wrote at great length about his home state's strange attachment to retrograde, racist politics despite nearly a century of antislavery lawmaking. The problem was not capital's war on labor, or even its war on Black labor. The problem lay with that "hateful political reptile, the copperhead," more innocuously known as the Peace Democrat. As sly and venomous as their reptilian namesake, the Copperheads boldly and pompously declared their opposition to war and their veneration for America's constitutional union. This political flimflam, Stephens reminded his readers, was simply white supremacy by another name. In Pennsylvania, although a majority Republican state, it proved startlingly persistent. No clearer indication was needed than the response to calls for the mobilization of African American soldiers. Stephens would eventually join the Fifty-Fourth Massachusetts, the Union's first and most famous Black regiment, but not before attempting to mobilize African American troops in his home state. His efforts met with an eruption of old-fashioned race-baiting. Pennsylvania's Peace Democrats were not about to tolerate displays of Black patriotism or Black military skill—precisely because these were well-known and long-trod paths to citizenship. With African Americans overwhelmingly supportive of the Republican Party, full Black citizenship would only further weaken the Democratic Party in Pennsylvania.

The malevolence of Peace Democrats was especially evident in proposed legislation to stop Black migration into Pennsylvania, flagrant confirmation that "there is no meaner State in the Union."[3] Representatives from Pennsylvania's border counties had long worked to restrict Black immigration. A proposed restriction on Black migration was nearly enacted at the time of the Missouri Compromise. Fearing that subsequent efforts by Virginians to drive free Blacks from their state following John Brown's Harpers Ferry raid would create a refugee crisis, opponents of Black migration began once again to petition the legislature for a new raft of anti-Black-immigration laws. The campaign culminated during the war, in the spring of 1863, when both the state house and senate considered a law prohibiting Blacks from coming "into this state from any other state or territory, with the intention of making it their temporary or permanent place of residence." The proposed law would have required state law enforcement officers to apprehend, imprison, fine, and expel Blacks unable to prove prior residency in Pennsylvania. Although the bill stipulated a "fair and impartial hearing" for those accused of being in the state illegally, it offered few details about exactly how such hearings would function. With limited access to property and the documented citizenship it conferred, and excluded from state regiments and state quotas for military recruitment, Black Pennsylvanians had few methods for documenting this state citizenship beyond direct witness testimony, itself subject to the vagaries of racist politics. Fear and intimidation would surely silence some who might testify on behalf of free Black neighbors.

As was the case in Illinois, Indiana, and Oregon, three states with constitutional prohibitions on Black immigration, the law proved precisely the point Stephens had been making. To forestall the growth of the Republican Party, Peace Democrats were prepared to block any step towards Black citizenship. In debates over the new immigration bill, Benjamin Champneys, Republican representative from Lancaster County, reminded fellow lawmakers how often they were told "that the blacks are to overrun us and that white labor will be crushed to the earth." In fact, given the "immense number who have gone into the ranks of the army . . . the demand for labor, instead of diminishing, has increased." For Republicans, this latest effort to expand the state's Black Code was nothing more than a supreme illustration of the race-baiting politics of the state's Democrats. The bill passed the Democratic state house of representatives, fifty-two to forty, but was tabled in the state senate after a committee report concluded that "there has not been, nor is there now any cause to apprehend the influx of any perceptible number of blacks and mulattoes into this State . . . though thousands of slaves have been liberated."[4]

The state senate committee's assessment was not entirely candid. Hundreds if not thousands of freedmen, mostly from Virginia but also many from Maryland, had been crossing the Line at least since the spring of 1862. The divergent views of Republicans and Democrats had obvious political origins, but as is so often the case, there were varying representations of a bewildering reality. The flight of refugees from slavery into Pennsylvania was the result of two different but related processes. On the one hand, there was direct military emancipation. In May 1861, Union general Benjamin Butler had declared fugitives seeking refuge from slavery to be wartime contraband, liable to legal seizure by federal forces. Butler's practice became official US military policy in August with the passage of the First Confiscation Act. In late April 1862, the Frederick *Examiner* reported that "a number of contraband slaves, property of Virginia rebels, had passed through Maryland, under a military escort on their way to Philadelphia." Here was a case of refugees clearly under military control.[5]

But these were the exceptions. Most came under their own control. In June 1862, the *Lancaster Intelligencer* published a report from Chambersburg noting that "the roads leading from the Virginia line to this place have been black with 'contrabands,' making their way North. . . . [S]ome of them have passed through but many are still quartered among the negroes of the town— some of the houses being crowded almost to suffocation."[6] These refugees were in Wolfstown, Chambersburg's Black neighborhood, but this offered little consolation to the town's panicked white population. One local paper complained that the refugees "added to our colored population already too numerous." Another, from nearby Waynesboro, reprinted an account of contrabands from Essex County in Virginia "in a fine buggy, drawn by a splendid horse," and "the whole party were well dressed, and had plenty of money." That this family was prepared to care for itself was immaterial. The refugees were assumed to be thieves, and this reminded the editors of the "old Jews when about to make their exodus from Egypt, they borrowed all they could from the Egyptians, before they left for the promised land of Canaan, never intending to return a single article." The idea that refugees were somehow opportunists, eager to exploit northern beneficence, made for good press but very bad social science. There were few obvious paths to well-being for wartime refugees from slavery. With a disdainful and suspicious white population, charity was mostly limited to what a small number of northern Blacks were able to provide. Access to gainful employment was also limited. A report from Johnstown, east of Pittsburgh, recounted the woeful plight of several contrabands employed at the Cambria Iron Works at the miserable rate of twenty-five cents a day. The "regular hands in the mill took offence" and stopped working until the contrabands were dismissed.[7]

The dire circumstances of contrabands above the Line were ideal fodder for a Democratic Party struggling to preserve its support among working-class immigrants. Before the eruption of war in Virginia, the *Compiler,* a Democratic paper published in Gettysburg, the seat of Adams County, warned of the dangers of being situated "as we are, on the border, where these slaves, if let loose would congregate," adding to "the vagabond free negro population of Pennsylvania" and bringing "calamity from which her people may well pray to be delivered." Lest this feared influx of "non-producing population" overwhelm the charitable instincts of Pennsylvanians, "a heavy capitation tax, upon all abolitionists," should be levied "to defray the expense of transporting them to Liberia."[8] But the real disaster, according to an April 1862 *Lancaster Intelligencer* story entitled "An Inundation of Negroes," was not that "these escaped Negroes will fill our poor houses and increase our taxes." The real problem was that "many of them will learn trades, as they are already doing in Philadelphia," pushing "white men and white women . . . out of employment." It was not in slavery that Democrats identified the chief danger to America's working people, but in race. What the refugee crisis in the borderlands demonstrated, as George Stephens so clearly grasped, was that the scourge of racism, inflamed and exploited for political gain, placed barriers before Americans of African descent unknown to white working people. Capital's indifference to slavery—whether chattel slavery or wage slavery—simply could not explain the full depth of dislocation and alienation faced by all Black Americans.[9]

A year of war had ravaged the Virginia of General Robert E. Lee, commander of the Confederate Army of Northern Virginia. Frustrated by the wreckage and desolation Union forces had left in his home state, Lee hoped to bring the same fury to the northern heartland. "I propose to enter Pennsylvania," Lee informed the Confederacy's president, Jefferson Davis. If in bringing the brutality of war north Lee's army also liberated Maryland and captured greater Baltimore, the economic lifeline of the federal capital and the Union's massive Army of the Potomac, the bold strategy would, Lee believed, give the Peace Democrats the upper hand in the elections of 1862. With a majority in the US House, they would bring the war to a swift and favorable end.[10]

By early fall 1862, Lee's designs on Union territory were widely known. General George McClellan, Lee's highly controversial young nemesis in Virginia and Commander of the Army of the Potomac, urged Pennsylvania governor Andrew Gregg Curtin to concentrate the state's soldiers near the border towns of Chambersburg and Gettysburg. "Call out the militia," McClellan pleaded, "and do everything in your power to impede the enemy." McClellan assured Curtin that he would follow the enemy "as closely as I can, and fight them whenever I can find them. It is as much my interest as yours to preserve the soil of Pennsylvania from invasion, or, failing in that, to destroy any army that may have the temerity to attempt it." McClellan was as good as his word, and within a week he would encounter Lee's army about fourteen miles south of Hagerstown, near the village of Sharpsburg. The ensuing battle resulted in the single bloodiest day in American history and the bloodiest single day of the Civil War. On September 17, twenty-three thousand men died at the Battle of Antietam, named for Antietam Creek, the tributary of the Potomac that passed just east of Sharpsburg. The Mason and Dixon borderlands had never before seen such carnage.[11]

For African Americans near the Line, Antietam was the start of the war's darkest year. Until the following summer, when Lee's army would be repelled at Gettysburg, Confederate forces engaged in some of the most ruthless and large-scale slave raiding in the Line's history. In response to northern contraband policy, the Confederate army had made a business of recapturing suspected fugitives from slavery. Until the invasion of Maryland in the fall of 1862, the practice involved scattered Union encampments, often left vulnerable by sudden troop movements. Now the Confederate military was effectively following refugees into foreign territory.[12]

The first chapter in this grim story took place at Harpers Ferry. To secure his rear, Lee ordered General Stonewall Jackson to capture the heavily defended federal armory and arms depot, which now included an encampment of at least a thousand contrabands. A military chaplain from Massachusetts recalled that "when the rebel army captured Harper's Ferry it seized all blacks, and they are still in the hands of the men-stealers." Stonewall Jackson's troops made no distinction between free and slave, carrying "many freemen into slavery." Blacks elsewhere in the borderlands would soon face similar peril.[13]

The invasion of Maryland was an incursion into Union territory, but Confederate troops had not yet crossed the Line. Less than a month after Antietam—a battle devastating to both armies but, to Lincoln's great frustration, one that had allowed Lee's battle-weary force to escape—about twelve hundred Confederate cavalrymen under the command of Jeb Stuart descended on a lightly defended Chambersburg, Pennsylvania. The invaders' primary mission was to destroy the nearby rail bridge linking Chambersburg to Hagerstown and Harrisburg and commandeer military stores, foodstuffs, and desperately needed draft animals. As Stuart's troops rampaged the countryside between Mercersburg and Chambersburg, his adjutant general, Channing Price, described the "ludicrous" and "extreme" response of "old Dutchmen as their horses were taken in every variety of circumstances," in exchange for nothing more than "a receipt to the effect that the horses were taken for the Army of the Confederate States, to be paid as damage by the U.S. Government." To feed their plundered horses, the raiders dispensed with military formalities and "took corn right from the field, having no trouble about a Qr. Master buying forage."

The morning after the raiders' arrival in Chambersburg, another of Stuart's men recalled, "the public stores were opened & I procured myself a splendid black army overcoat, bleached castile soap, teaspoons, bridle, boots, canteens, a beautiful pocketbook." According to a report from Carlisle, the town of Chambersburg "was converted into one vast dressing room. On every hotel porch, at every corner, on the greater portion of the street doorsteps, in fact, all over town might be seen Rebel cavalry donning Yankee uniforms and throwing their own faded and worn-out garments into the street." It was all a great bounty for the Confederate raiders—they gained for their army more than eight hundred horses, destroyed a million dollars' worth of armaments and industrial machinery, and carried off as much booty as their stuffed saddlebags could hold.[14]

Although the plunder was extensive, and although there are plenty of accounts of Confederate raiders appropriating uniforms and arms from the federal depot, the raiders seem generally to have abided by Lee's prohibition on "individual plunder for private use." In a widely published account, a local federal military official, Colonel Alexander McClure, who was also a Chambersburg newspaper publisher and the town's leading Republican, described the orderly and civil ways of Stuart's men. "The brilliant audacity of the rebels" left the people of Franklin County "confounded with astonishment." But what was most striking was that Stuart's force also showed consummate discipline, generally leaving the small shops and private homes of Chambersburg untouched. On the few occasions where men took private property, they were arrested and punished. The raiders left Chambersburg with the same swift tact they had shown on their entry. "But for the fact that

I can't find a horse about the barn, and that my fence is stripped of paling to remind me of the reality of the matter," McClure noted, "it would seem like a dream."[15]

While evidence of any response to the raid by Chambersburg's Black community is scarce, there is enough to suggest that for this group, there was nothing remotely dreamlike about the raiders' conduct. The rebels made no systematic effort to round up contrabands or to take prisoners of war; in fact, they granted parole to a few local militiamen and a few hundred Union soldiers, most of whom had been convalescing in Chambersburg. McClure nonetheless noted an obscure episode that suggests the town's African American population was in grave danger. At about 1 A.M. the morning after the raid, McClure welcomed into his home a group of Confederate officers. The men spent several hours with McClure in his library, drinking tea and coffee while warming themselves by the blazing hearth. It was all very convivial, so much so that the guests and their host were able to discuss such explosive issues as Lincoln's preliminary Emancipation Proclamation. McClure felt comfortable enough to acknowledge his Republican Party affiliation and his support for the president's antislavery initiative. None of this provoked any particular ill will or hostility. Had he not seen the men for himself, McClure wrote, he might "have supposed that I was having a friendly confab with a little knot of Pennsylvania Breckenridge politicians." On politics, there was little agreement. Regarding the civilities of tea and coffee in the home of a prominent Pennsylvanian, all appeared utterly routine.

McClure's account nonetheless shows that there was an additional distinction between these Confederate officers and Pennsylvanians. Before the men would settle down in McClure's library, they required "a treaty . . . on behalf of the colored servants." McClure says nothing about the precise nature of the treaty, but we can infer it involved a demonstration that his servants were not contrabands. For the servants, the transaction was surely deeply alarming, and it may have been even more so in light of an incident reported by an elderly Chambersburg diarist, William Heyser. On the day of the raid, Heyser remembered, the raiders "did take eight young colored men and boys along with them, in spite of their parents pleading." Heyser had little doubt about the victims' fate. "I fear we will never see them again," he concluded, "unless they can escape."[16]

Robert E. Lee had no intention of limiting his army to small raids of little military significance. By the spring of 1863, he was again proposing invasion as a solution to the Confederate Army's mounting problems. Losses in the West suggested that without additional victories on the scale of Lee's triumph in early May 1863 at the Virginia town of Chancellorsville, the Confederacy would soon lose its capital at Richmond, Virginia. Time was not on Lee's side. As his army struggled to recover from a long winter of scarcity, the Army of the Potomac continued its rampage across the Virginia countryside, destroying farmlands and burning fence posts for warmth, all the while enjoying open supply lines to America's original heartland. With the Virginia countryside devastated and with no significant foreign aid, the already faltering effort to feed and clothe the Army of Northern Virginia would only become more desperate.

The least bad option for the Confederacy, Lee concluded, was a bold strike at the heart of the Union. There would be no strategic stop in Maryland—no attempt to "liberate" a border state. Instead, Lee's forces would move directly from Virginia through Maryland and across the Mason-Dixon Line into south-central Pennsylvania, brushing aside hapless local militias during its march to Harrisburg. For Lee, the cost in northern morale and Republican political capital made the price of so bold a plan easily justified. Success would revive the Confederacy's foundering diplomatic efforts in Britain and Europe and, more importantly, divert the bounty of greater Baltimore west and south down the Shenandoah River Valley to Virginia. Confederate control of greater Baltimore would also mean Confederate control of the area's rail lines. Denied its northern supplies, the insatiable Army of the Potomac, now under the command of the popular Joseph "Fighting Joe" Hooker, would surely collapse, opening the way for Lee's triumphant march into Washington, DC.[17]

By mid-June, Lee's army had begun crossing the Potomac into Maryland north of Harpers Ferry. The Confederates would move through the countryside, approach Hagerstown, and then head north, crossing into Pennsylvania near the small border town of Greencastle, just over the Line in Franklin County. The previous fall, when Lee's troops crossed into Maryland, they could have been forgiven for believing they were welcomed as liberators, freeing southern brethren from the Union yoke. Admiring crowds cheered the troops and offered up desperately needed food and clothing. An engineer who crossed into Maryland with Stonewall Jackson's army at White's Ford, about forty miles northwest of Washington, told his wife that news of the invasion "spread rapidly, and young men & old flocked to see

Gen. Jackson, whom they look upon as their deliverer." Although the Maryland countryside failed to disgorge the expected army of Confederate loyalists, Confederate sympathy remained widespread, even in the state's far north. As they rode through the border town of Emmitsburg, Jeb Stuart's troops were received as saviors. One of Stuart's men recalled, "Such enthusiasm as we witnessed here . . . you can form no idea of." Another found the town "as true south as Charleston, S.C. The ladies came on the street & cheered us most lustily. Some of the men were so much overjoyed that they cried & wept."[18]

Although the first invasion of Maryland failed to arouse a new push to leave the Union, let alone to take up arms for the Confederacy, the state displayed sufficient pro-South sentiment to afford Confederate commanders at least some hope of resurrecting its secession movement. But the politics, as Lee was now fully aware, were complex. Despite the display at Emmitsburg, Unionism was dominant in the Maryland borderlands. Any hope of enlisting what remained of sympathetic Marylanders meant avoiding conduct that would strengthen the hand of Unionists.

In its second invasion of Maryland, Lee's army thus conducted itself with rare decorum. Confederate commanders generally enforced Lee's order that they "repress marauding." According to a report in the Baltimore *Sun,* "there was no property destroyed in Hagerstown or in the vicinity." Another newspaper reported that "horses and property taken from citizens of Maryland, have been returned to them, and every effort has been made to make their stealing as little offensive as possible." The Confederate soldiers also returned fleeing slaves. "The hope of obtaining recruits in Maryland," this report concluded, "is no doubt the secret of this conciliatory policy."[19]

To Pennsylvanians, there could be little doubt that whatever restraint Lee's army exercised in Maryland would evaporate the minute it crossed the Line. The resurgence of Confederate forces in the Shenandoah Valley, where they routed Union general Robert Milroy's forces at the Second Battle of Winchester, was an obvious prelude to a march north and a subsequent reign of terror. The day after Milroy's defeat, William Heyser confided to his diary, "We all feel Pennsylvania will be invaded." Families evacuated to Shippensburg, Carlisle, and Harrisburg; schools and shops closed; the few remaining holdouts buried or otherwise stashed valuables; factory owners and warehouse managers hid goods in the countryside. A widely circulated news report from Shippensburg, just northeast of Chambersburg, described "considerable excitement . . . created in this place by the arrival of farmers from the neighborhood of Chambersburg, who brought all their stock of horses in anticipation of an advance of the rebels. The town is one vast stable." With so many evacuating the central Pennsylvania borderlands, with rail service interrupted and telegraph lines sabotaged, preparations were guided by the most fragmentary intelligence. Philip Schaff, a seminarian from Mercersburg, about fifteen miles southwest of Chambersburg and just a few miles north of the Line, worried that "we are cut off from all communication and dependent on the flying and contradictory rumors of passengers, straggling soldiers, run-away negroes and spies." For the region's Black communities, the intelligence, fragmentary as it may have been, was unambiguous. Grave danger was imminent. Another witness at Mercersburg reported that the town's Blacks "are trembling like leaves and flying with their little bundles 'to the mountains,' especially the numerous run-away slaves from Virginia, from fear of being captured as 'contrabands,' and sold to the South." On the railroad, between Shippensburg and Harrisburg, "there are hundreds of contrabands proceeding . . . to escape the rebel grasp."[20]

Initial confederate forays looked much like Stuart's earlier raid. Small detachments of cavalrymen rode into towns, commandeering horses, cattle, and other stores, but this time there was no mistaking the invaders' determination to recapture contrabands. The first invaders of Mercersburg carried off several African American boys. Over the course of the next few days, subsequent waves of invaders only became more brazen. Upon encountering four wagonloads of Black women and children captured by Confederate raiders, a farmer living near the Maryland border asked "why they were taking off the children, even the babies?" The presiding officer answered, "Oh, they will bring something."[21]

Rachel Cormany, whose husband enlisted in the Pennsylvania cavalry and who had recently moved to Franklin County from Canada, was horrified by what she saw: the Confederates "were hunting up the contrabands & driving them off by droves," showing little regard for the fact that "some of the colored people . . . were raised here." To seminarian Philip Schaff, the behavior of subsequent bands of raiders suggested that conditions would only worsen as the invasion progressed. In the days following the initial incursion, Mercersburg was raided by "an independent guerilla band of cavalry, who steal horses, cattle, sheep, store goods, negroes, and whatever else they can make use of." When it came to contrabands, these marauding bands were "on a regular slave-hunt, which presented the worst spectacle I ever saw in this war." The raiders were not small packs of bandits and displayed none of the illicit tendencies of slave raiders and man-stealers from the age of the Cannon-Johnson Gang. Nor did they make any effort to depict themselves as lawful slave catchers. They were marauding, terror-spreading militants in ruthless pursuit of their quarry. They threatened and terrorized whites who concealed local Blacks. They captured Black women and children, showing little concern for their legal status or family ties. They rampaged through neighborhoods and homes, indifferent to the legal niceties of peacetime slave catching. No magistrates were consulted; no constables were enlisted; no effort was made at any due process whatsoever. The raiders' indifference to the actual legal status of local Blacks only heightened the anguish endured by Black families since the passage of the second Fugitive Slave Act. Schaff's family, he wrote, "is kept in constant danger, on account of poor old Eliza, our servant, and her little boy, who hide in the granary during the day, and return under cover of the night to get something to eat." Some of the victims of rebel slave raiding Schaff knew "to have been born and raised on free soil." In Chambersburg alone, it was estimated that 250 African Americans were captured and sent south.[22]

The fate of captives is difficult to know. A small number, perhaps as many as forty, were sent to Castle Thunder, the Confederate prison in Richmond. Records indicate that Confederate authorities were aware that some captives were free Blacks, but little was ever done to repatriate them. With the help of well-connected Pennsylvania merchants and a Richmond minister, Amos Barnes of Franklin County was able to regain his freedom months after his capture—but Barnes seems to have been the exception. Most Castle Thunder captives spent the war as slave laborers, building defensive earthworks surrounding Richmond and serving as orderlies in Confederate hospitals. As Union forces closed in on Richmond late in the war, some of the captives seem to have been relocated to Confederate prisons in North and South Carolina. The fate of these Pennsylvanians is unknown. That Confederate prison authorities made no effort to repatriate more free Blacks may have been a consequence of Confederate prisoner exchange policies. Following the collapse of a general prisoner exchange agreement, the Confederate government decreed that all Black Union soldiers would be treated as fugitive slaves, their commanders as abettors of slave insurrection; Lincoln responded with a complete suspension of prisoner exchanges. Unable to repatriate soldiers, Confederate authorities had little incentive to countenance the freedom of any prisoners.[23]

In the two weeks after the initial invasion, the exodus from the Pennsylvania borderlands continued. By late June, with the Confederates reaching Carlisle, preparations were under way in Harrisburg to remove the contents of the state library, official state papers, and anything else of value. Military preparations, meanwhile, had been shambolic, in part because of old intrastate sectionalism. State authorities, recognizing the limits of local military resources, employed a defensive strategy whose primary bulwark would be the Susquehanna River. As a political matter, the strategy was disastrous. Recruits from the western borderlands proved reluctant to join a force whose strategy involved, effectively, surrendering their homeland.

By the end of June, Lee's army had forced the surrender of Mercersburg, Chambersburg, Carlisle, York, and Wrightsville, leaving most of greater Baltimore in rebel hands. To the invaders, the economic abundance of the Pennsylvania borderlands confirmed what Lee had assumed: spared the fury of warfare, the region looked much as the fertile valley of western Virginia once looked. "The Valley of Pennsylvania, through which my command marched," recalled one of Lee's deputies, Major General John Brown Gordon, "was a type of the fair and fertile Valley of Virginia at its best, before it became the highway of armies and the ravages of war had left it wasted and bare." Could there be any wonder that the invasion brought "a touch of sadness" to Gordon's troops, as they contemplated the same "broad green meadows with luxuriant grasses and crystal springs" that once filled Virginia's valleys? As a strategic matter, Lee's invasion appeared to be succeeding brilliantly. What his army lacked in the Shenandoah Valley, it now found in Pennsylvania's heartland. Abundant livestock, grain stores, and horses would allow the Army of Northern Virginia to replenish itself after a difficult spring. By the end of June, the Confederates had seized as many as 50,000 head of cattle, 35,000 sheep, and another 20,000 horses and mules, in addition to countless chickens, turkeys, and tons of salt, flour, bacon, cheese, butter, pickles, jam, and other foodstuffs.[24]

Among the targets of Confederate raiding was an ironworks on South Mountain, just was of Gettysburg. The ironworks, owned by Congressman Thaddeus Stevens, was seized by a Confederate raiding party under the command of General Jubal A. Early. In a letter to his law partner, Simon Stevens (no relation), Thaddeus enumerated the losses. They included the usual mules and horses, "even the crippled horses," about four thousand pounds of bacon, several thousand dollars' worth of milled grain and corn, and extensive stocks of bar iron. Much as had been the case in Chambersburg, the Confederate raiders also took aim at industrial infrastructure. After burning the ironworks's furnace, sawmill, two forges, rolling mill, bellows, and bellows houses, Early and his men "slept in the office and store-room," and then, upon awakening the next morning, burned them and their contents, which included all the business records of the works. According to the manager, John Sweney, the rebel raiders "expressed great regret that they were not so fortunate as to meet the owner."[25]

Lee had never seen the invasion in simple material terms—it was about much more than acquiring vitally needed stores and damaging the industrial lifeline of the Army of the Potomac. Insofar as it assisted Copperhead opponents of the war, damage to the borderlands economy was of great political benefit to the Confederate war effort. If the economic damage sustained by the borderlands reverberated across the North, so much the better. As General John Brown Gordon, one of Lee's most trusted lieutenants, understood it, "a defeat of the Union army in territory so contiguous to" Washington, Baltimore, and Philadelphia would "cause financial panic in the commercial centres, and induce the great business interests to demand that the war should cease." Shortly after the surrender of York, Lee thus ordered Gordon and his two thousand men to press on to Philadelphia. This would involve a crossing of the Susquehanna on the mile-long covered bridge between Wrightsville and Columbia. From the Columbia side of the bridge, Gordon anticipated a two-day march through Lancaster to the outskirts of Philadelphia. Eastern Pennsylvania would be as endangered as the western part of the state, and all Pennsylvanians would be made to fear the wrath of the Army of Northern Virginia. The plan ended in tactical failure, however. At Wrightsville, Gordon's men battled local militiamen, at least fifty-three of whom were African Americans from Columbia. Unable to hold off the rebel advance, the Pennsylvanians retreated back across the Susquehanna, having suffered one dead, a Black soldier killed in a Confederate artillery barrage. Anticipating the loss of

Wrightsville, carpenters had prepared sections of the Columbia-Wrightsville bridge for demolition. Local militia commanders hoped this would allow most of the bridge to be preserved, but the onslaught of Gordon's army was too great for any kind of precision demolition, and the bridge was torched, igniting much of Wrightsville as well. Before he and his men were able to get across the Susquehanna, Gordon received orders to reverse course and head forty miles west and south to another small border town, Gettysburg. There, on July 1, Gordon's men would encounter the Army of the Potomac on the first day of the Battle of Gettysburg.[26]

In the weeks before the battle, the Confederates continued their search for contrabands, but they found very few. The vast majority of African Americans had evacuated the border towns. The town of Gettysburg had a prewar Black population of 186, out of a total population of around 2,400. By 1863, the Black population had fallen to less than 70. According to white travelers, there were no barbers, cooks, or porters in south-central Pennsylvania because the African Americans who normally did this work had left. Far from a vestige of earlier times, the Underground Railroad and its pathways remained busy during the war years, assisting Black refugees in their escape from the slave South. Now those same paths were also being used by refugees from south-central Pennsylvania. Many traveled across the Susquehanna to the evident safety of Harrisburg, and others trekked much further afield. Many refugees simply camped in Philadelphia's public spaces, churches, and courthouses; one estimate places the number at close to two thousand. Some refugees made their way to Camp William Penn, a new federal military installation just north of Philadelphia—two walked to the camp from Lancaster, and others arrived from Bedford and Huntingdon Counties, in the south-central part of the state. As Lee's army poured into Pennsylvania, the US War Department had established the camp to train three new regiments of African American troops. Although none of the Fort William Penn troops completed their training before the Gettysburg campaign, some would join the Army of the Potomac the following spring and summer.[27]

The flight of so many African Americans in the days before the battle at Gettysburg did little to deter Confederate slave raiders. William S. Christian, a colonel in the 55th Virginia, noted that on June 27 his regiment "took a lot of negroes." How many of these captives were actually sent south is unknown, but Christian suggested that mitigating circumstances had begun to intrude on Confederate slave raiding. When his men offered him a choice of the captives, most likely women and children, Christian acknowledged that "I could not get them back home," and in any case "they were so scared that I turned them all loose." These "poor devils" had very likely been hiding in the hills near South Mountain, along the route Christian and his command had followed as they marched from Chambersburg toward Gettysburg. The group may have included the wife and children of an employee of Stevens's South Mountain ironworks who Stevens believed had been sold into bondage.[28]

For Lee and his army, Gettysburg was supposed to be just another way station on its rampage through the borderlands in preparation for the march to Philadelphia. Even were Union commanders to grasp the full scope of Lee's Pennsylvania campaign—something made difficult by Confederate destruction of rail and telegraph lines—the massive Army of the Potomac would be too unwieldy to respond in any kind of timely fashion.

But Lee had miscalculated. In a stunning logistical feat following the disaster at Chancellorsville in Virginia, the Army of the Potomac's hard-drinking commander, General Joseph Hooker, marched his war-weary force of nearly ninety thousand men north, across the Potomac, to the outskirts of Frederick, Maryland. An oblivious Lee, meanwhile, sent three regiments to Gettysburg to seize a supply of shoes. They expected little resistance—at worst the kind of ragtag militias encountered in Pennsylvania's other border towns. Instead, they were met by a Union cavalry detachment under the command of General John Buford. Lee immediately ordered his entire army to head to Gettysburg. Frustrated with Hooker's cautious tactics, Lincoln replaced him with George Meade, a civil engineer and veteran of the Mexican-American War. Although little known outside the ranks of those who had already served under him, Meade proved a decisive and effective leader. Acting on fragmentary and imprecise intelligence, he ordered his men to move north, hoping to catch the bulk of the Army of Northern Virginia somewhere near Gettysburg.

For the first three days of July, 160,000 soldiers fought just outside the small Pennsylvania border town. Following an artillery bombardment so massive the ground trembled a hundred miles away, on the afternoon of July 3, in the culminating maneuver of the battle, 12,500 Confederate infantrymen under the command of General George Pickett threw themselves at the center of Union lines. What has come to be known as Pickett's Charge would be among the costliest moments in Confederate military history. Half of those under Pickett's command were killed or wounded. Overall, Confederate losses at Gettysburg were catastrophic: about 28,000 killed, captured, wounded, or missing. Lee's officer corps was decimated. Roughly a third of his fifty-two generals were killed or wounded. Union losses were hardly less shocking: 23,000 casualties. Although Lee's forces were ultimately routed, his army lived to fight another day. The remains of the Army of Virginia retreated, leaving hundreds of wagonloads of wounded and dead along the roads of central Pennsylvania and western Maryland.[29]

Union forces had defeated Lee's last, boldest effort to carry the fight into enemy territory—although it did not end those efforts entirely. On July 30, 1864, two brigades of Confederate cavalrymen, about three thousand horsemen in total, raided and burned that old Confederate target, Chambersburg. But nothing on the scale of the Gettysburg campaign was ever again attempted. As a strategic matter, Lee's invasion of Pennsylvania ended in disaster. Although collateral damage was widespread, Union communications channels were readily restored and the economy of greater Baltimore suffered no lasting damage. As a political matter, the invasion also achieved little. No silent majority of Peace Democrats rose up and took control of the Pennsylvania statehouse and Maryland's Unionists maintained control of their state's government. Nonetheless, to Lincoln's great frustration, plunder extracted from the borderlands proved vital for the survival of Lee's army through the summer of 1863.

As long as the Confederacy continued to fight, the abolitionist wing of the Republican Party continued its ineluctable march from the party's periphery to its center. "No peace can come without emancipation," wrote Thaddeus Stevens in early fall 1863, and "no peace can be maintained without the perpetual prohibition of Slavery in the fundamental Law of the Nation." The Copperhead mantra, "The Union as it was, and the Constitution as it is," had proven its bankruptcy in the Pennsylvania borderlands. There could be no reconciliation with "Southern Traitors." The Confederacy and the slave system on which it stood had to be destroyed. Referring to the destruction of his ironworks, Stevens noted, "I have been among the people whom they robbed in their late invasion of Penna in Franklin & Adams Counties." These southern raiders were mere "thieves, robbers, traitors kidnappers! . . . I would as soon acknowledge fellowship with sooty demons, whose business and delight it is, to torture the damned!" The Thirty-Eighth Congress, which began its first session in December, demonstrated the unmistakable assimilation of Stevens's message. In an effort to transform wartime expedient into statute, one bill after another emerged from Republican congressional ranks, all with the purpose of securing the permanent liberation of contrabands. Few of these bills succeeded, mostly because they defied the long-standing Republican position that the Constitution empowered only the states to abolish slavery.[30]

The resilience of the Confederate military may have had a role in strengthening the abolitionist wing of the Republican Party, but it was surely less consequential than the direct actions of American slaves and northern free Blacks. As hundreds of thousands of self-manumitted former slaves fled to Union encampments and willingly labored to support the Union war effort, Union doubts about the military necessity of abolition grew ever more aberrant. These former slaves volunteered their labor in a host of essential trades: they worked as teamsters, stable hands, boatmen, butchers, cooks, laundresses, nurses, carpenters, coopers, blacksmiths, and common laborers. More than 135,000 African American soldiers, enduring some of the war's most brutal combat and cruelest wartime deprivations, similarly stood as a clear refutation of Copperhead questions about African American loyalty and made President Lincoln's reluctance to embrace immediate, principled abolition very difficult to defend.[31]

In an August 1864 letter to the editor of the *Weekly Anglo-African*, "Africano," pseudonym of a volunteer in the 5th Massachusetts Black cavalry regiment, decried Lincoln's "fickle-minded" attitude toward slavery and urged those northern Blacks who could vote in the coming presidential election to cast their votes for John C. Frémont, nominee of a new proabolition Radical Democratic Party. "While we thank Mr. Lincoln for what the exigencies of the times forced him to do," Africano wrote, he insisted his fellow Blacks "censure him for the non-accomplishment of the real good this accursed rebellion gave him the power to do, and which if he had done . . . the world would have looked upon him as the magnanimous regenerator of American institutions, and the benevolent protector of human freedom."[32] A vital election loomed, and Lincoln could ill afford to lose even marginal members of the Republican coalition. Nor could he afford to lose the border states, especially Maryland.

Much as had been the case with the secession crisis, the president's approach involved a combination of political suasion and rump politics—all designed to bring about state-by-state constitutional prohibitions of slavery. This may have avoided the difficult constitutional question of whether the federal government had the power to abolish slavery, but as a political strategy it seemed maddeningly indolent to Lincoln's antislavery allies, even though by 1864 it had begun to pay dividends. In March, loyal voters in Arkansas ratified a new antislavery constitution, and in September, a tiny loyal electorate in Louisiana ratified that state's new antislavery constitution. In both of these cases, military imperative substantially strengthened the administration's hand. In his capacity as commander in chief, Lincoln set the conditions for readmission of former Confederate states to the Union. Among those would be formal affirmation of wartime proclamations, including the Emancipation Proclamation, through the ratification of antislavery constitutions. With the preservation of nominal state authority and no formally proclaimed military occupation, no such imperative existed for the border states. Lincoln was the president of those states, but he was not their military governor.

These facts make Maryland's path to abolition all the more remarkable. In a striking rebuke to the southern slaveholding counties, in February 1864, the state's voters endorsed the formation of a constitutional convention. Given the extent of federal intervention, the results hardly demonstrate a transformation in Maryland's position on slavery. The Baltimore newspaperman and Confederate sympathizer William Wilkins Glenn recalled that Maryland's tidewater slaveholders made every effort to stop the push for constitutional change, but "it was a useless endeavor, for the election was under military control." As a final, desperate ploy, Wilkins Glenn recalled, the benighted slave owners, required to swear "a strong anti-Southern oath" before casting their votes, resorted to deplorable "false swearing." The strategy failed, but just barely.[33]

During its six months of deliberations, from April to September, the convention drafted an unqualified pro-Union and antislavery constitution. The twenty-fourth article of the new charter's Declaration of Rights was nearly identical to the Thirteenth Amendment, drafted by the Republican-dominated US Senate the previous spring: "Hereafter, in this State, there shall be neither slavery nor involuntary servitude, except in punishment of crime, whereof the party shall have been duly convicted; and all persons held to service or labor, as slaves, are hereby declared free."[34] Abolitionists and free Blacks hoped Maryland's new constitution would secure full African American citizenship, including voting rights, but the pro-Union framers were unwilling to go that far. A vote to end slavery, Allegany County anti-slavery Unionists explained, was far from a vote for "negro equality at the ballot-box, in the jury box, on the witness-stand, or elsewhere."[35]

Even the abolition of slavery nearly proved too much for the state's voters. Initial polling for ratification indicated 27,541 in favor and 29,536 opposed. As expected, the margins in the tidewater counties were over-whelming. In Charles County, barely 1 percent of voters supported the new charter. In St. Mary's, Calvert, and Prince George's Counties, no more than 10 percent favored it. These margins were made up for by the city of Balti-more, which cast more than 80 percent of its nearly twelve thousand votes for the new constitution. In the eastern border counties, the votes were much closer—Cecil, Baltimore, and Carroll effectively split their votes. In Har-ford County, opponents far exceeded supporters: about 60 percent voted against the new constitution. Substantial majorities in Frederick, Wash-ington, and Allegany Counties, in the western part of the state, voted in favor. But in the end, only the late-arriving ballots of several thousand sol-diers would finally enable ratification—by a margin of merely 375 votes.[36]

When she learned of the Maryland vote, the author and abolitionist Lydia Maria Child was said to have remarked, "If I had acted out my im-pulses, I would have swung my bonnet, and given three hurrahs; but it is not proper for women to obey their impulses, you know." For the nation's oldest abolitionist newspaper, the *Liberator*, "it was a close contest, hardly and stubbornly fought; but Freedom and Union have clearly and rightfully won, and the good old State rids herself of the life-long incubus of slavery." Although the manipulation of voter rolls "took power away from the slave counties and gave it to Baltimore and to the counties which are populous with whites," the ratification of Maryland's antislavery constitution was no small act of gerrymandering: "The Convention was one . . . of revolution. They went to the bottom of the State's ills. Their aim was to get rid of slavery, and, as the enemies of 'the great evil,' they were . . . determined not only to destroy it, but to sponge out its marks, and to make a fundamental law suited throughout to the new order." Revolution, not reform. The aim of immediate abolitionists had finally been achieved in the nation's second-oldest slave state.[37]

The day of the Maryland vote, the state's most influential defender of slavery, Chief Justice Roger B. Taney, breathed his final breath. In the words of New York diarist George Templeton Strong, "two ancient abuses and evils were perishing together."[38]

With the end of slavery in Maryland, the Line remained as a demarcation between slave and free states for more than another year. Delaware proved as intransigent about state abolition as it had been about compensated abolition. As of 1860, the state was home to fewer than two thousand enslaved Americans. Following the election of 1864, Democrats controlled the state's legislature, its US Senate seats, and its seat in the US House. State abolition in Delaware was a dead letter. The state's ratification of the Thirteenth Amendment was equally unlikely. The position of Delaware's Democrats was more the stuff of farce than even the rudest form of political posturing. In his January 1865 state of the state speech, the state's Republican governor, William Cannon, declared that with their state "surrounded by free territory inviting on all sides the escape of our slaves" and a national constitutional ban likely, the institution of slavery was effectively at its end. "There is now neither market nor demand for this species of property," leaving Delaware's slave owners with all of slavery's disadvantages and none of its advantages. Cannon's words had little impact, although he would not live to see their full impotence. He died two months after proclaiming slavery's de facto death in his state. With Secretary of State William Seward's certification of the ratification of the Thirteenth Amendment on December 18, 1865, slavery's death in Delaware and in the only other holdout, Kentucky, became de jure.[39]

The end of slavery in Delaware could hardly be mistaken for a revolution. Through the amendment process, the federal government had altered the law of the Line's last slave state—though the state itself made no actual alteration in its legal code. Despite what abolitionists may have said, the end of slavery in Maryland was hardly revolutionary either. The Line's defining slave state only abolished slavery after four years of martial law and de facto federal military occupation.

Epilogue

THE CIVIL WAR WAS the first American war to leave an extensive photographic record. Much of that record was the work of Mathew Brady. One can hardly conjure the American cataclysm without bringing to mind Brady's images. Owing to the slow exposure time of mid-nineteenth-century photography, those images mostly capture aftermaths: denuded battle-fields strewn with the bodies of men and horses, railcars cast off their tracks and lying chock-a-block across the adjoining sidings, the ruins of cities and towns, and many desolate faces. Some of those faces appear in group portraits of military officers, ordinary soldiers, and contrabands. Others are in the carefully staged studio portraits that were the stock in trade of the mid-nineteenth-century photographer: Ulysses Grant, Major General Philip Sheridan, President Lincoln, and countless others, including a defeated Robert E. Lee. After the war, Brady's studio in Washington, DC, respon-sible for so many masterpieces of midcentury photography, photographed military veterans and celebrities, all for display in Brady's gallery on Pennsyl-vania Avenue.

In early 1871, three prominent journalists sat for a group portrait in Brady's studio. At the time the portrait was taken, the least well known was David Gray, editor of the *Buffalo Courier*. Much better known was the man at the center of the picture, the essayist, travel writer, and humorist Samuel Clemens, whose pen name was Mark Twain, and whose celebrated novels

George Alfred Townsend (left), usually known by his byline, Gath, sat for this 1871 portrait with his friends Mark Twain (Samuel L. Clemens) and Buffalo newspaperman David Gray. Photograph from the Studio of Mathew Brady, between 1865 and 1880.
Library of Congress, Manuscript Division, Brady-Handy Collection.

had yet to be published. But the most famous of the three was George Alfred Townsend, known by his byline, Gath. As a young reporter for the *New York Herald* and the *New York World*, Gath had traveled with the Army of the Potomac during the pivotal year of 1862, and through April and May 1865 he reported on the pursuit and capture of the assassin John Wilkes Booth. Gath's war reporting earned him national acclaim, and following the war his syndicated column appeared in more than one hundred papers.

Much like Twain, Gath had literary aspirations and turned to poetry, short stories, and novels. And much like Twain, his literary aspirations reflected a new conception of the United States. No longer a nation of sections, North and South, the country was now a place of regions—New England, the Great Plains, the West, the South. Twain's regionalism centered on the Mississippi River, the anterior artery of a United States haunted by the ghosts of racial caste and carried away by a torrent of trade and imperialist cant. Gath, too, was a regionalist. And Gath, too, was consumed with the ghosts of his nation's divided past. But Gath's metaphor for that past had long since lost the immediacy of a churning, unstoppable Mississippi. Once the divide of a nation, the Line had become a quaint remnant, better suited to Gath's romantic longings than anything so transcendent as the quest to understand modern America.

Gath was born in 1841 in the small village of Georgetown, Delaware, north of what remained of the Pocomoke Swamp. His childhood was a peripatetic one. The family followed Gath's father Stephen, a Methodist minister, as he moved between pulpits in Maryland, Delaware, and Pennsylvania, finally settling in Philadelphia. After graduating from high school, Gath went to work for the *Philadelphia Inquirer* and then reported on the war for the *New York Herald*. Gath briefly abandoned the field of battle to work as a foreign correspondent in Europe, but he returned to report on the war's final year and the aftermath of Lincoln's assassination. In 1867, Gath and his young family settled in Washington, DC, where he continued to work as a political correspondent.

Although his writing was far-ranging, including biographies of Lincoln and the Italian revolutionary Garibaldi, Gath's literary inclinations drew him back to the borderlands of his youth. His *Tales of the Chesapeake*, a collection of prose and poetry published in 1880, bore a dedication to the Reverend Stephen Townsend, "whose ancestors explored the Chesapeake Bay in 1623, and were settled on the Pocomoke River Almost Two Hundred Years." Those same ancestors, the weary survivors of Old World religious strife, brought to America a familiar combination of Protestant piety, frugality, and steely-eyed strength of character. But these were not the peaceful, quietist Quakers of Pennsylvania and New Jersey. For a "long boundary quarrel" had made the subjects of Gath's fiction a "predatory . . . though God-fearing people," prepared to "fight with all their religious intensity for their right in the land and the dominion of their particular province." That Old World fervor was now gone, destroyed by the intertwined forces of slavery and capitalism, leaving in its place little more than haunting, spectral remnants of Gath's ancestral past.[1]

"The Ticking Stone," the second story in *Tales of the Chesapeake*, describes a mysterious stone near the graveyard of a Newark, Delaware, Baptist church. The stone emitted "an audible, almost tangible ticking, like that of a lady's watch" and, according to a mysterious local storyteller, marked the grave of Fithian Minuit, a Revolutionary War veteran and celebrated local watchmaker. The many who had traveled to Minuit's shop learned that "this henchman of time and minute-hand of diligence drew his power from doubtful sources." His pulse had a "metallic beat." The watchmaker's peculiar physiognomy originated with familiar figures, if not with complete historical accuracy:

> In the year 1764 the comparative solitude of this region was broken by a large party of chain-bearers, rod-men, axe-men, commissaries, cooks, baggage-carriers, and camp-followers. They had come by order of Lord Baltimore and William Penn, to terminate a long controversy between two great landed proprietors, and they were led by Charles Mason, of the Royal Observatory, at Greenwich, England, and by Jeremiah Dixon, the son of a collier discovered in a coalpit. For three years they continued westward, running their stakes over mountains and streams, like a gypsy camp in appearance, frightening the Indians with their sorcery. But, near this spot, they halted longest, to fix with precision the tangent point, and the point of intersection of three States—the circular head of Delaware,

the abutting right angle of Maryland, and the tiny pan-handle
of Pennsylvania.

All the while, as he and his party divided America, Charles Mason had been
pursuing his own solution to the famous longitude problem and had created
a fine and delicate chronometer. In a cruel twist, Fithian Minuit, child of a
friendly fishmonger, swallowed the watch. Minuit's grave, not far from
stones placed by Mason and Dixon, continued to pulse, a vigilant remnant
of the Line, up to which had so long "flowed the waters of slavery."[2]

A few years later, Gath published *The Entailed Hat,* a novel inspired by
his mother's stories of Patty Cannon, the local man-stealer who died in the
Georgetown jail. The novel was a romance with "much local truth," but that
local truth was not the story of Georgetown, or even Delaware. It was "the
story of a large region comprehending three state jurisdictions, and also that
period when modern life arose upon the ruins of old colonial caste."[3] For
Gath, Cannon's exploits demonstrated the collapse of a hard-won colonial
order—the quietude and calm built by Gath's puritanical ancestors, destroyed by the cruelty and criminality possible only in a nation beholden to
the business of slavery.

In 1884, the year Gath published *The Entailed Hat,* his research for a new
novel took him to the western borderlands. He was stunned by their natural
beauty, so much so that he built a hundred-acre summer retreat there, about
twenty miles southeast of Catoctin Mountain, the Maryland side of Pennsylvania's South Mountain, and the setting for Gath's Civil War epic,
Katy of Catoctin, or: The Chain-Breakers. Here was Gath's Civil War, from
the raid at Harpers Ferry to Lincoln's assassination, set in the Arden-like
forests of western Maryland. We encounter Gath's pet themes: a verdant
and bounteous borderlands populated by descendants of the author's pious
ancestors, now confronted by slavery, the monstrous evil embodied not in
the sufferings of the enslaved or their descendants but in the slovenly slave
owner with his "Judaic nose . . . and wad of grizzly hair above his grizzled
updrawn eyebrows." The hard-won and very godly purity of Gath's colonial ancestors, much as it had been on the Eastern Shore of Gath's earlier
work, was gone, swept away by greed and its chief appurtenance: the trade
in enslaved human beings.

Katy of Catoctin's protagonist, a young hunter from Baltimore, Lloyd
Quantrell, also happens to be the nephew of a well-known Baltimore slave

trader. He is told by western Marylander and slave owner Isaac Smith that the rise of slavery had little to do with slave owners, and everything to do with calculating converts to capitalism. "If nobody could be found to trade in slaves," Smith reminded the young hunter, "the evils of slavery would be small, because they would not be sent to great distances and worked up on the plantations. It would not then be profitable." The novel follows the young Quantrell's romance with Katy, daughter of a Pennsylvania Dutch family, members of a group the nativist Quantrell dismisses as knowing only "saving and slaving."[4] Katy and her family, with their frugality and fierce Protestantism, struggle to redeem the wayward Quantrell from the foul seductions of drink and Know-Nothingism, but their efforts are mostly for naught. Quantrell is mesmerized by the southern nationalist John Wilkes Booth and chooses to leave Maryland for Confederate Virginia.

For Gath, the Line had become a metaphor less for a nation divided by slavery than for the destruction of an ancient colonial world. There is no ethnic slaughter and no horse-trading colonial lords in Gath's vision; there are only refugees from Old World strife, facing nature and their colonial rivals in a determined quest for peaceable, pastoral civilization. With Mason, Dixon, and their line came that ticking of time, the rhythm of modernity, and the loss of a fictive colonial world. The Line and its borderlands had become little more than remnants of battles fought and lost. There was no place in this history for the Native peoples who first cleared the lands Gath's ancestors farmed. Nor was there any place for the thousands of enslaved and free Blacks who transformed the Line into a border between slavery and freedom. Insofar as slavery figured in Gath's romances, it stood as yet one more symptom of a lost world, blown apart by the hideous trade in Black captives.

That Gath's fiction is now so little known has much to do with its lumbering and crudely romantic storylines. But it also has to do with its failure to speak to subsequent generations of American readers. Unlike his friend Twain, Gath's America was riven by time, not race. The Line, for Gath, defined a region, but it also explained the disappearance of that region, consumed by many of the very same forces that created a greater Baltimore, forces that for Gath also explain slavery's devastating power: technology, markets, and the decline of authentic faith. Little more than a ticking remnant, the

Line stood as a reminder of Gath's border-hardened colonial ancestors. In effect, all of America had become greater Baltimore—and, much as in greater Baltimore, in the postwar United States there was no place for borders between states.

Gath's nineteenth-century readers had embarked on a great national project of forgetting. The Line, much like the strife that made it a national symbol, was best dead and forgotten. To a cheering audience at Philadelphia's Hibernia Club, the Alabamian and former Confederate Army officer Hilary Herbert, appointed secretary of the navy by President Grover Cleveland, declared that the "tramp of armies to an' fro across Mason and Dixon's line had opened the eyes of the South to the fact that there were no natural barriers separating the South from the North, that this country is geographically one country." Just a few years after Herbert's address, as the country prepared for the Spanish-American War, the *Idaho Statesman* offered a most satisfying observation about the state of the country: "It would be difficult to tell whether loyalty to the Union is greater north or south of Mason and Dixon's Line." There could be no doubt that "our government is one that people of all sections are proud of." Reporting on the stunning congressional unanimity behind a massive new military spending bill, the reporter Isabel Worrell Ball concluded that "Mason and Dixon's line has been covered up with Old Glory." The United States had become a single nation; sectionalism a dim memory from that nation's violent founding. "Nothing short of an archaeological society will be able to locate Mason and Dixon's line after this," observed a Detroit newspaper. At the Iowa Republican Party convention of 1899, the convention's chair, Charles E. Pickett of Waterloo, congratulated his party for "the obliteration of Mason and Dixon's line from the map of our country."[5]

This triumphalism was, of course, pure cant. No longer a border between slavery and freedom, the Line had become a border between citizenship and other forms of servitude. For Blacks south of the Line, the national project of forgetting involved not just the erasure of the Line but the reconstruction of white supremacy. In 1887, the citizens of Baltimore's Mt. Vernon Place unveiled a bronze statue of Roger B. Taney; the statue was a recasting of a Taney monument commissioned by the state legislature and erected at the statehouse in Annapolis a few years earlier. Taney's resurrection in his home state foretold the national resurrection of Taney's jurisprudence. In 1896, the Supreme Court found in favor of the defendants in *Plessy v.*

Ferguson, a case brought by Homer Plessy, a New Orleans activist and shoemaker who described himself as having one-eighth African ancestry. After his arrest for violating a Louisiana law by sitting in a whites-only railcar, Plessy's case made its way to the Supreme Court. The Fourteenth Amendment, Plessy argued, prohibited such segregation on the basis of race. Given the long reign of de facto segregation in the South, the Court's majority concluded, the state was entitled to require segregated railcars so long as accommodations were equal. In his lone dissent, Justice John Marshall Harlan compared the decision to the *Dred Scott* decision, excoriating his colleagues for permitting "the seeds of race hate to be planted under the sanction of law."[6]

By the time *Plessy v. Ferguson* was decided, Baltimore's Daughters of the Confederacy had begun pushing to erect monuments to putative Confederate veterans from Baltimore. In 1899, their efforts yielded support from the Baltimore city council for the construction of a Confederate soldiers' and sailors' monument.[7] For the African American press, these monuments and legal segregation were of a piece. The United States was once again two nations, and the Line stood as the starkest reminder of this truth. "The southern states are in revolt—in almost open war with the colored population," noted the Topeka *Plaindealer.* The Republican politicians who had in 1896 "wept over Mason and Dixon's Line, at their national convention in St. Louis, had to quarter their colored delegates in railroad cars rather than eat with them at the hotels where colored cooks prepared the food and colored waiters brought it to the table." Confronting the Democratic Party's vigorous new efforts to disenfranchise Black voters, the Indianapolis *Freeman* urged its readers to "hold disenfranchisements in abeyance at the 'Mason and Dixon's' line" by uniting behind the Republican Party. For in the end, as readers of Chicago's *Broad Axe* knew all too well, their fellow citizens "have taken away from the Negro almost every vestige of his civil and political liberty below Mason and Dixon's line."[8]

The resurrection of the Line had nothing to do with Gath's Line, or the Line of Charles Mason and Jeremiah Dixon. But it had everything to do with what that line had become: a national shame, where African American citizenship dropped away and civil rights once again became a matter of race. As a border, the Line remained an artifact of an increasingly distant past.

There was no illicit trade in human beings across the Line; there were no magistrates prepared to interrogate and arrest free and fugitive Blacks; the states adjoining the Line had long since given over questions of interstate commerce and comity to a powerful federal state; and although extrajudicial violence against African Americans in the South had become epidemic, the Line itself no longer marked profound legal divergence among American states. Insofar as the United States was a nation of borders, it had become like so many others around the world. As borders between states fell away, international borders would come to define the American nation.

The 1893 annual meeting of the American Historical Association, held in Chicago to coincide with the greatest-ever celebration of American nationhood, the World's Columbian Exhibition, would come to represent another pivotal moment in the forging of an American territorial nation— defined less by borders within than by borders without. In a bold attempt to recast his nation's history, the young Wisconsin historian Frederick Jackson Turner reminded his audience that the American frontier, that unconquered wilderness where Old World peasants became New World democrats, had itself become a historical artifact. From the Atlantic to the Pacific, the American continent had been conquered. What would now shape the United States would be the forces shaping all other nations—empire and the global competition on which it rested.

Until the Mexican Revolution in 1910, there was no border between the United States and Mexico west of the Rio Grande. The region had been controlled by the Apaches, and other than a few border towns visited by the occasional customs official, the United States had done little to mark its territory off from its southern neighbor. The Mexican Revolution and World War I brought new tensions, prompting the construction of a new militarized border. For a Democratic Party defining itself in part as the party of southern segregationists, the need to defend the Mexican-American border offered rich new opportunities to justify racial caste. Could African American soldiers be trusted to defend American interests, or would they be seduced by Mexico's revolutionaries and drawn into an insurgency against their own country? Loyal service in the Civil War and the Spanish-American War meant nothing. Old shibboleths about Black loyalty remained powerful political lucre. The absurdity of these tired claims made little sense on their face, but for some African American commentators, radicalized by unrelenting racial injustice, they were beginning to raise important questions. "Suppose," a writer for the *Washington Bee* asked, "Mexico says that the American Negro should enjoy all the rights and privileges that other citizens and nations enjoy and the Negro knows that he is being oppressed, what will be his attitude? That is the question that should occupy the minds of his oppressors in the South." For at the end of the day, whether the US-Mexico border would become another Line between slavery and freedom was a question of whether Americans of African descent would, everywhere in the land, enjoy the rights of citizenship. "The Negro is willing and ready to serve his government," readers of the *Bee* were reminded, but only "if his government is willing and ready to protect him."[9]

The signs were not promising. A 1916 NAACP pamphlet entitled *"Life, Liberty, and the Pursuit of Happiness" on Our Own Side of the Border* described the lynching of Jesse Washington, a disabled sixteen-year-old convicted by a Waco, Texas, jury of raping and murdering his employer's wife. A white mob "unsexed" Washington and burned him alive in the town square—this while thousands watched in approval. Meanwhile, south of the border, "the gallant Negro Troopers of the Tenth Calvary were on their way" to the Mexican town of Carrizal to capture the revolutionary Pancho Villa.[10]

ABBREVIATIONS

AAN   *African American Newspapers, Series 1,* https://infoweb-newsbank-com
.proxy.lib.fsu.edu/apps/readex/?p=EANAAA

AHN   *America's Historical Newspapers,* https://www.readex.com/products
/americas-historical-newspapers

AM   *Archives of Maryland Online,* http://aomol.msa.maryland.gov/html
/volumes.html

BAP   *The Black Abolitionist Papers,* ed. C. Peter Ripley (Chapel Hill:
University of North Carolina Press, 1985–1992)

CRP   *Colonial Records of Pennsylvania* (Harrisburg: T. Fenn, 1831–1853)

CSP   *Calendar of State Papers: Colonial Series, America and West Indies*
(London: Her Majesty's Stationery Office, 1860–1994), British History Online,
https://www.british-history.ac.uk/search/series/cal-state-papers—colonial—
america-west-indies

CVSP *Calendar of Virginia State Papers and Other Manuscripts,* ed. Sherwin
McRae (Richmond: A. R. Micou, 1886)

CW   *The Collected Works of Abraham Lincoln,* ed. Roy P. Basler (New
Brunswick, NJ: Rutgers University Press, 1953)

FCA   *Foundations of Colonial America: A Documentary History,* ed. W. Keith
Kavenagh (New York: Chelsea House, 1974)

JMD   *The Journal of Charles Mason and Jeremiah Dixon: Transcribed from the
Original in the United States National Archives* (Philadelphia: American Philosophical Society, 1969)

MHM *Maryland Historical Magazine Online,* https://www.mdhistory.org
/publications/maryland-historical-magazine-online/

MPCP *Minutes of the Provincial Council of Pennsylvania*

PA   *Pennsylvania Archives*

PBF   *Papers of Benjamin Franklin,* https://franklinpapers.org/

PCM   *Proceedings of the Council of Maryland*

PH   *Pennsylvania History*

PMHB *Pennsylvania Magazine of History and Biography*

PNA   *Pennsylvania Newspaper Archive,* Penn State University Libraries, https://panewsarchive.psu.edu/

PWP   *The Papers of William Penn,* ed. Mary Maples Dunn and Richard S. Dunn (Philadelphia: University of Pennsylvania Press, 1981–1987)

SPTS   *The Selected Papers of Thaddeus Stevens,* ed. Beverly Wilson Palmer et al. (Pittsburgh: University of Pittsburgh Press, 1997)

VOS   *The Valley of the Shadow* (archive), Virginia Center for Digital History and the University of Virginia Library, https://valley.lib.virginia.edu /VoS/choosepart.html

WMQ *The William and Mary Quarterly*

NOTES

PROLOGUE

1. *JMD*, 63.

2. George Francis Beaven and Henry J. Oosting, "Pocomoke Swamp: A Study of a Cypress Swamp on the Eastern Shore of Maryland," *Bulletin of the Torrey Botanical Club* 66, no. 6 (1939): 367–389.

3. [Captain John Smith], *The Generall Historie of Virginia, New-England, and the Summer Isles: with the Names of the Adventurers, Planters, and Governours from Their First Beginning Ano 1584 to This Present 1626* (London: n.p., 1627), 24; James D. Rice, *Nature and History in the Potomac Country: From Hunter-Gatherers to the Age of Jefferson* (Baltimore: Johns Hopkins University Press, 2009).

4. Francis Jennings, "Glory, Death, and Transfiguration: The Susquehannock Indians in the Seventeenth Century," *Proceedings of the American Philosophical Society* 112, no. 1 (Feb. 15, 1968): 15–53.

5. *JMD*, 66–67.

6. *JMD*, 111.

INTRODUCTION

1. In the context of North American history, the term "borderlands" originated as a means of characterizing the contested frontiers of Spanish North America—areas from Florida to northern Mexico and California. The layered, negotiated legal and political regimes of the Spanish-American borderlands signify something somewhat different from what I mean by "borderlands" in this book. "Bordered lands," a term employed by Jeremy Adelman and Stephen Aron to describe territories adjoining formally recognized international borders, is perhaps more accurate for my purposes but still not precisely applicable. In the end, neither term is ideal, but "borderlands" seems to me the less cumbersome of the two. Jeremy Adelman and Stephen Aron, "From Borderlands to Borders: Empires,

Nation-States, and the Peoples in between in North American History," *American Historical Review* 104, no. 3 (June 1999): 814–841.

2.   John H. B. Latrobe, *The History of Mason and Dixon's Line: Contained in an Address, Delivered by John H. B. Latrobe* . . . (Philadelphia: Press of the Society, 1855), 6–7.

3.   For a recent exploration of the roots of this historical amnesia, see Greg Grandin, *The End of the Myth: From the Frontier to the Border Wall in the Mind of America* (New York: Metropolitan Books, 2019).

4.   Here I am indebted to scholars of the Revolutionary era who see the American founding as the struggle for union as much as an ideological struggle. See Peter Onuf, *The Origins of the Federal Republic: Jurisdictional Controversies in the United States, 1775–1787* (Philadelphia: University of Pennsylvania Press, 1983); *Statehood and Union: A History of the Northwest Ordinance* (Bloomington: Indiana University Press, 1987); and, with Nicholas Onuf, *Nations, Markets, and War: Modern History and the American Civil War* (Charlottesville: University of Virginia Press, 2006). More recently, see Eliga Gould, *Among the Powers of the Earth: The American Revolution and the Making of a New World Empire* (Cambridge, MA: Harvard University Press, 2012), and Max M. Edling, *Perfecting the Union: National and State Authority in the US Constitution* (New York: Oxford University Press, 2021).

5.   I am not suggesting a complete absence of spatially bounded forms of territorial control. But the mechanisms for establishing that control were mostly passive; their function was not so much to police the movement of citizens / subjects as it was to secure control of the land and its resources. For an important counterargument, see Juliana Barr, "Geographies of Power: Mapping Indian Borders in the 'Borderlands' of the Early Southwest," *WMQ* 68, no. 1 (Jan. 2011): 5–46.

6.   This is not to say that British subjecthood or US citizenship was universal for white Americans—or that the conditions for subjecthood and citizenship were uniform in the American colonies and United States. Liberty varied from colony to colony and state to state, and liberties afforded able-bodied white men were very often denied white women, children, the disabled, and paupers, whether at a colonial / state level or an imperial / federal level. I am saying that territorial demarcations had relatively little bearing on individuals' legal status in the period covered by this study—except in the case of African Americans. On that legal status, see Kunal M. Parker, *Making Foreigners: Immigration and Citizenship Law in America, 1600–2000* (Cambridge: Cambridge University Press, 2015); Barbara Young Welke, *Law and the Borders of Belonging in the Long Nineteenth Century United States* (Cambridge: Cambridge University Press, 2010). On state citizenship, see Kate Masur, *Until Justice Be Done: America's First Civil Rights Movement, from the Revolution to Reconstruction* (New York: W. W. Norton, 2021).

7.   John Michael Huffman, "Americans on Paper: Identity and Identification in the American Revolution" (PhD diss., Harvard University, 2013). See also

Craig Robertson, *The Passport in America: The History of a Document* (New York: Oxford University Press, 2010); and John Torpey, *The Invention of the Passport: Surveillance, Citizenship, and the State* (Cambridge: Cambridge University Press, 2000). For a discussion of border proceedings in Napoleonic Europe, see, for example, Michael O'Brien, *Mrs. Adams in Winter: A Journey in the Last Days of Napoleon* (New York: Picador, 2011), 268–269.

8.   Yair Mintzker, *The Defortification of the German City, 1689–1866* (Cambridge: Cambridge University Press, 2012); Lewis Mumford, *The City in History* (Harmondsworth: Penguin, 1973), 350.

9.   Peter Sahlins, *Boundaries: The Making of France and Spain in the Pyrenees* (Berkeley: University of California Press, 1989), 6.

10.   See, for example, *John Ledyard's Journey through Russia and Siberia, 1787–1788: The Journal and Selected Letters*, ed. Stephen D. Watrous (Madison: University of Wisconsin Press, 1966), 201–232.

11.   J. H. Elliott, *Empires of the Atlantic World: Britain and Spain in America 1492–1830* (New Haven, CT: Yale University Press, 2006), 267.

12.   Edward G. Gray and Mark Peterson, "Border Troubles in the Land of Euclid: How the Revolution Empowered Imaginary Lines" (paper presented at the conference Writing to and from the Revolution, Fred W. Smith National Library for the Study of George Washington, Mt. Vernon, Mar. 18–19, 2016).

13.   On the growth of lineal borders, see Sahlins, *Boundaries*, ch. 5; Charles S. Maier, *Once within Borders: Territories of Power, Wealth, and Belonging since 1500* (Cambridge, MA: Harvard University Press, 2016), esp. ch. 3; Jordan Branch, *The Cartographic State: Maps, Territory, and the Origins of Sovereignty* (Cambridge: Cambridge University Press, 2014); and Jürgen Osterhammel, *The Transformation of the World: A Global History of the Nineteenth Century* (Princeton, NJ: Princeton University Press, 2014), ch. III, esp. 107–113.

14.   Patrick Spero, "Creating Pennsylvania: The Politics of the Frontier and the State, 1682–1800" (PhD diss., University of Pennsylvania, 2009). For a similar argument about another corporate entity, see Philip J. Stern, *The Company State: Corporate Sovereignty and the Early Modern Foundations of the British Empire in India* (New York: Oxford University Press, 2011).

15.   Lauren Benton, *A Search for Sovereignty: Law and Geography in European Empires, 1400–1900* (Cambridge: Cambridge University Press, 2010).

16.   Samuel Moyn, *Not Enough: Human Rights in an Unequal World* (Cambridge, MA: Belknap Press of Harvard University Press, 2018).

17.   Representative titles include Kathleen Duval, *Independence Lost: Lives on the Edge of the American Revolution* (New York: Random House, 2015); Brian Delay, *War of a Thousand Deserts: Indian Raids and the US-Mexican War* (New Haven, CT: Yale University Press, 2008); Steven Hahn, *A Nation without Borders:*

The United States and Its World in an Age of Civil Wars, 1830–1910 (New York: Viking Penguin, 2016); Daniel Immerwahr, *How to Hide an Empire: A History of the Greater United States* (New York: FSG, 2019); Mark Peterson, *The City-State of Boston: The Rise and Fall of an Atlantic Power, 1630–1865* (Princeton, NJ: Princeton University Press, 2019); Alan Taylor, *American Colonies: The Settling of North America* (New York: Viking, 2001); and Alan Taylor, *American Revolutions: A Continental History, 1750–1804* (New York: W. W. Norton, 2016). The last comprehensive history of the origins of the Line appeared in 1909 as part of the last full survey of the Line, commissioned by the governors of Pennsylvania and Maryland: Mason and Dixon Line Resurvey Commission, *Report on the Resurvey of the Maryland-Pennsylvania Boundary Part of the Mason and Dixon Line* (Harrisburg, PA: Harrisburg Publishing Company, 1909).

1. LORD BALTIMORE'S NORTHERN PROBLEM

1. John Lathrop Motley, *History of the United Netherlands* (New York: Harper & Brothers, 1861), 359.

2. Gaillard Thomas Lapsley, *The County Palatine of Durham: A Study in Constitutional History* (London: Longmans, Green, 1900), 3.

3. Viola Florence Barnes, "Land Tenure in English Colonial Charters of the Seventeenth Century," in *Essays in Colonial History Presented to Charles McLean Andrews by His Students* (1931; reprint, Freeport, NY: Books for Libraries Press, 1966), 4–40; Albert J. Martinez Jr., "The Palatinate Clause of the Maryland Charter, 1632–1776: From Independent Jurisdiction to Independence," *American Journal of Legal History* 50, no. 3 (July 2008): 308–309; Francis A. Mullin, "The Palatinate of Durham," *Catholic Historical Review* 21, no. 2 (July 1935): 186.

4. Quoted in Charles M. Andrews, *The Colonial Period of American History: The Settlements, Volume I* (New Haven, CT: Yale University Press, 1934), 310.

5. Antoinette Sutto, *Loyal Protestants and Dangerous Papists: Maryland and the Politics of Religion in the English Atlantic, 1630–1690* (Charlottesville: University of Virginia Press, 2015), 23–24.

6. Charles M. Andrews, *The Colonial Period of American History: The Settlements, Volume II* (New Haven, CT: Yale University Press, 1936), 279.

7. Bernard Bailyn, *The Barbarous Years: The Peopling of British North America: The Conflict of Civilizations, 1600–1675* (New York: Knopf, 2021), 194–197; Ralph Davis, *The Rise of the Atlantic Economies* (Ithaca, NY: Cornell University Press, 1973), 176–185; Andrews, *The Colonial Period of American History: The Settlements, Volume II*, 279–280, 284; Jonathan I. Israel, *Dutch Primacy in World Trade, 1585–1740* (Oxford: Clarendon Press, 1989), 161–163.

8. "Charter of Maryland Granted to Lord Baltimore June 20, 1632," *FCA*, vol. II, part 1, 757–759.

9. Sutto, *Loyal Protestants*, 33–37.

10. *FCA*, vol. II, part 1, 757.

11. Russell R. Menard and Lois Green Carr, "The Lords Baltimore and the Colonization of Maryland," in *Early Maryland in a Wider World*, ed. David B. Quinn (Detroit: Wayne State University Press, 1982), 189–190.

12. Robert C. Ritchie, *The Duke's Province: A Study of New York Politics and Society, 1664–1691* (Chapel Hill: University of North Carolina Press, 1977), 23–24; Jean R. Soderlund, *Lenape Country: Delaware Valley Society before William Penn* (Philadelphia: University of Pennsylvania Press, 2015), 112.

13. When in 1678 the Lords of Trade queried Charles Calvert, the third Lord Baltimore, about the precise boundaries of his colony, he in fact referred them to Herrman's map. Christian J. Koot, *A Biography of a Map in Motion: Augustine Herrman's Chesapeake* (New York: New York University Press, 2018), 202. More generally on Herrman, Blathwayt, and the Board of Trade, see Koot, *Biography of a Map in Motion*, 200–203. Also see Koot, "The Merchant, the Map, and Empire: Augustine Herrman's Chesapeake and Interimperial Trade, 1644–73," *WMQ* 67, no. 4 (Oct. 2010): 603–644.

14. Bailyn, *Barbarous Years*, 319–320.

15. *AM, PCM*, vol. V, 55–56.

16. Lovelace to Calvert, Aug. 22, 1672, Lovelace to Carr, Oct. 17, 1672, in *Annals of Pennsylvania: From the Discovery of the Delaware, 1609–1682*, ed. Samuel Hazard (Philadelphia: Hazard and Mitchell, 1850), 398–399, 402.

17. Lovelace to Carr, Oct. 17, 1672, *Annals of Pennsylvania*, 403, 402.

18. Leon De Valinger Jr., "The Burning of the Whorekill, 1673," *PMHB* 74, no. 4 (Oct. 1950): 481–482, 480.

19. Andros to Blathwayt, Oct. 12, 1678, in *Documents Relative to the Colonial History of the State of New York*, ed. E. B. O'Callaghan (Albany, NY: Weed, Parsons, 1853), vol. III, 272–273.

20. Paul A. W. Wallace and William A. Hunter, *Indians in Pennsylvania*, 2nd ed. (Harrisburg: Pennsylvania Historical and Museum Commission, 2005), 12; James D. Rice, *Tales from a Revolution: Bacon's Rebellion and the Transformation of Early America* (New York: Oxford University Press, 2012).

21. *AM, PCM*, vol. V, 138–139.

22. Lorena S. Walsh, *Motives of Honor, Pleasure, and Profit: Plantation Management in the Colonial Chesapeake, 1607–1763* (Chapel Hill: University of North Carolina Press for the OIEAHC, 2010), 372.

2. WILLIAM PENN'S UNLIKELY EMPIRE

1. Christopher Hill, *The World Turned Upside Down: Radical Ideas during the English Revolution* (1972; pbk. ed., London: Penguin Books, 1988), 37.

2. *The Diary of Samuel Pepys: Daily Entries from the 17th Century London Diary* (https://www.pepysdiary.com), Aug. 19, 1664, and July 5, 1662.

3. Penn to Mary Pennyman, November 22, 1673, *PWP*, vol. I, 264–265.

4. *PWP*, vol. I, 264.

5. "An Account of My Journey into Holland & Germany," in *PWP*, vol. I, 476–477; *Diary of Samuel Pepys*, Dec. 29, 1667.

6. Quoted in Hill, *World Turned Upside Down*, 245.

7. Richard S. Dunn, "Penny Wise and Pound Foolish: Penn as a Businessman," in *The World of William Penn*, ed. Richard S. Dunn and Mary Maples Dunn (Philadelphia: University of Pennsylvania Press, 1986), 40–41.

8. Edwin B. Bronner, ed., *The Peace of Europe, The Fruits of Solitude, and Other Writings* (London: J. M. Dent, 1993), 97.

9. Dunn, "Penny Wise and Pound Foolish," 41.

10. Charles M. Andrews, *The Colonial Period of American History: The Settlements, Volume III* (New Haven, CT: Yale University Press, 1939), 281–285.

11. Sir John Werden to William Penn, July 16, 1681, *PWP*, vol. II, 103. During the dispute over their colonies' shared boundary, Penn and Baltimore began referring to the Lower Counties as Delaware. See Lord Baltimore to William Blathwayt, December 7, 1683, *AM, PCM*, vol. V, 402; Penn to the Governor and Council of West New Jersey, June 4, 1683, *PWP*, vol. II, 399.

12. Robert Barclay to Penn, Apr. 15, 1681, in *PWP*, vol. II, 90–91; "Deed for New Castle," in *PWP*, vol. II, 281–284.

13. Commission to William Markham, in *PWP*, vol. II, 86; "To the Inhabitants of Pennsylvania," Apr. 8, 1681, in *PWP*, vol. II, 84.

14. Penn to Charles Calvert, 3rd Lord Baltimore, Apr. 10, 1681, in *PWP*, vol. II, 87; [Letter to Maryland Planters], Sept. 16, 1681, in *PWP*, vol. II, 112.

15. Bronner, *Peace of Europe*, 294.

16. "To the Inhabitants of Pennsylvania," *PWP*, vol. II, 84; Dunn, "Penny Wise and Pound Foolish," 48–49.

17. Penn to Gulielma Penn and Children, Aug. 4, 1682, *PWP*, vol. II, 270–273.

3. THE BATTLE FOR MARYLAND'S FAR NORTH

1. Petty to Penn, Aug. 14, 1682, *PWP*, vol. II, 279.

2. On the Pennsylvania-Ireland contrast, see Robert David Sack, *Human Territoriality: Its Theory and History* (Cambridge: Cambridge University Press, 1986), 138–140.

3.   Penn to the Lenape, Oct. 18, 1681, *PWP*, vol. II, 128; John Smolenski, *Friends and Strangers: The Making of a Creole Culture in Colonial Pennsylvania* (Philadelphia: University of Pennsylvania Press, 2010), 91. My interpretation follows Francis Jennings, "Brother Miquon: Good Lord," in *The World of William Penn*, ed. Richard S. Dunn and Mary Maples Dunn (Philadelphia: University of Pennsylvania Press, 1986), esp. 196; Thomas J. Sugrue, "The Peopling and Depeopling of Early Pennsylvania: Indians and Colonists, 1680–1720," *PMHB* 116, no. 1 (Jan. 1992): 3–31.

4.   "William Penn's Purchases from the Indians, 1682–1684," in *William Penn and the Founding of Pennsylvania: A Documentary History*, ed. Jean R. Soderlund (Philadelphia: University of Pennsylvania Press, 1983), 159; "Instructions given by me William Penn Proprietor and Governr of Pennsylvania . . . ," Sept. 30, 1681, *PWP*, vol. II, 120; Charter for the Province of Pennsylvania, Feb. 28, 1680/81, *FCA*, vol. II, part 1, 849.

5.   Gary B. Nash, *Quakers and Politics: Pennsylvania, 1681–1726* (Boston: Northeastern University Press, 1993), 49–50; D. W. Meinig, *The Shaping of America: A Geographical Perspective on 500 Years of History: Volume I, Atlantic America, 1492–1800* (New Haven, CT: Yale University Press, 1986), 131–134.

6.   William Penn, "A Further Account of the Province of Pennsylvania," in *Narratives of Early Pennsylvania, West New Jersey, and Delaware*, ed. Albert Cook Myers (New York: Charles Scribner's Sons, 1912), 261; Nash, *Quakers and Politics*, 56–63.

7.   "Petition for Act of Union," Dec. 6, 1682, *PWP*, vol. II, 318; "Naturalization of Swedish Inhabitants," Jan. 11, 1683, *PWP*, vol. II, 337, 339n16.

8.   Mary K. Geiter, "Notes and Documents: London Merchants and the Launching of Pennsylvania," *PMHB* 121, nos. 1–2 (Jan. 1997): 101–122; Nash, *Quakers and Politics*, 19–22, 67–69; Nash, "The Free Society of Traders and the Early Politics of Pennsylvania," *PMHB* 89, no. 2 (Apr. 1965): 147–173.

9.   Penn to the Earl of Rochester, Feb. 5, 1683, *PWP*, vol. II, 351; Delaware charter quoted in Charles M. Andrews, *The Colonial Period of American History: The Settlements, Volume III* (New Haven, CT: Yale University Press, 1939), 295n2.

10.   Penn to Augustine Herrman, Nov. 9, 1682, *PWP*, vol. II, 309.

11.   *A Counter-Blaste to Tobaacco* (1604; reprint, Edinburgh: E. & G. Goldsmid, 1885), 32.

12.   James Horn, *Adapting to a New World: English Society in the Seventeenth-Century Chesapeake* (Chapel Hill: University of North Carolina Press for IEAHC, 1994), 186; Russell R. Menard and Lois Green Carr, "The Lords Baltimore and the Colonization of Maryland," in *Early Maryland in a Wider World*, ed. David B. Quinn (Detroit: Wayne State University Press, 1982), 191.

13.   Alvin Rabushka, *Taxation in Colonial America* (Princeton, NJ: Princeton University Press, 2008), 245–247, 258; Horn, *Adapting to a New World*, 142–143,186.

14.   Menard, "Farm Prices of Maryland Tobacco, 1659–1710," *MHM* 68, no. 1 (1973): 80–85; Paul G. E. Clemens, *The Atlantic Economy and Colonial Maryland's Eastern Shore* (Ithaca, NY: Cornell University Press, 1980), 34–35; Lorena S. Walsh, *Motives of Honor, Pleasure, and Profit: Plantation Management in the Colonial Chesapeake, 1607–1763* (Chapel Hill: University of North Carolina Press for the OIEAHC, 2010), 178–179.

15.   David W. Jordan, "'The Miracle of This Age': Maryland's Experiment in Religious Toleration, 1649–1689," *The Historian* 47, no. 3 (May 1985): 345–346.

16.   Rabushka, *Taxation in Colonial America*, 256–261; Paul Musselwhite, *Urban Dreams, Rural Commonwealths: The Rise of Plantation Society in the Chesapeake* (Chicago: University of Chicago Press, 2018), 129–139.

17.   Baltimore to Earl of Anglesey, June 6, 1681, *AM, PCM*, vol. V, 279; Rousby deposition before the Commissioners of the Customs, Apr. 29, 1781, in *AM, PCM*, vol. V, 290–291. The best treatment of Maryland's troubles with its customs agents in this period is Antoinette Sutto, "'You Dog . . . Give Me Your Hand': Lord Baltimore and the Death of Christopher Rousby," *MHM* 102, no. 4 (Winter 2007): 240–257.

18.   Colonial Entry Book, no. 106, Jan. 23, 1681/2, *AM, PCM*, vol. V, 305; Paul D. Halliday, *Disembodying the Body Politic: Partisan Politics in England's Towns, 1650–1730* (Cambridge: Cambridge University Press, 1998), 26–27; Jennifer Levin, *The Charter Controversy in the City of London, 1660–1688, and Its Consequences* (London: Athlone Press, 1969).

19.   Penn to Baltimore, Apr. 10, 1681, *PWP*, vol. II, 87, 88n1; Penn to Planters in Maryland, Sept. 16, 1681, *PWP*, vol. II, 112; Baltimore to Markham, June 5, 1682, *PWP*, vol. II, 259; Charles II to Lord Baltimore, Apr. 2, 1681, *CSP*, vol. XI, 25–37.

20.   Andrew Murphy, *William Penn: A Life* (New York: Oxford University Press, 2019), 109, 111; "A Conference Held between the Right Honorble the Lord Baltemore Proprietor of Maryland and William Pen Esqre . . . 13th of December 1682," in *Narratives of Early Maryland, 1633–1684*, ed. Clayton Colman Hall (New York: Charles Scribner's Sons, 1910), 426, 432, 430.

21.   Baltimore to Penn, June 24, 1683, *PWP*, vol. II, 408. Penn clearly recognized that the demand to exchange the Lower Counties for a Susquehanna corridor was impossible. Penn response to Talbott queries, Oct. 31, 1683, *AM, PCM*, vol. XVII, 148.

22.   Charles Dutrizac, "Empire, Provinces, Frontier: Perspectives on the Pennsylvania-Maryland Boundary Dispute, 1681–1738" (Ph.D. diss., University of Western Ontario, 1986), 62–64; Jean R. Soderlund, ed., *William Penn and the Founding of Pennsylvania: A Documentary History* (Philadelphia: University of

Pennsylvania Press, 1983), 336–338; Francis Jennings, *The Ambiguous Iroquois Empire: The Covenant Chain Confederation of Indian Tribes with English Colonies* (New York: W. W. Norton, 1984), n6.

23. Talbott commission, *AM, PCM,* vol. XVII, 145–149.

24. Penn to the Duke of York, Feb. 2, 1684, *PWP,* vol II, 518.

25. Talbott Commission, *AM, PCM,* vol. XVII, 149–150.

26. Penn to Duke of York, June 8, 1684, *PWP,* vol. II, 560; Welch to Penn, Apr. 5, 1684, *PWP,* vol. II, 547–548.

27. Penn to Duke of York, June 8, 1864, *PWP,* vol. II, 560–561.

28. "Mr. Blackston's Letter of Complaint against Lord Baltemore's Officers," Apr. 20, 1685, *AM, PCM,* vol. V, 438; Sutto, "'You Dog,'" 240–257.

29. Nicholas B. Wainwright, "The Missing Evidence: Penn v. Baltimore," *PMHB* 80, no. 2 (Apr. 1956): 234; *CSP,* vol. XII, 99–123.

30. *CSP,* vol. XII, 168–182.

31. James T. Lemon, *The Best Poor Man's Country: A Geographical Study of Southeastern Pennsylvania* (New York: W. W. Norton, 1976), 54–55, 58–59.

4. THE SQUATTERS' EMPIRE

1. Patrick Griffin, *American Leviathan: Empire, Nation, and Revolutionary Frontier* (New York: Hill & Wang, 2007); Eric Hinderaker, *Elusive Empires: Constructing Colonialism in the Ohio Valley, 1673–1800* (Cambridge: Cambridge University Press, 1997); James Merrell, *Into the American Woods: Negotiators on the Pennsylvania Frontier* (New York: W. W. Norton, 1999); Jane T. Merritt, *At the Crossroads: Indians and Empires on a Mid-Atlantic Frontier, 1700–1763* (Chapel Hill: University of North Carolina Press for OIEAHC, 2003); Patrick Spero, *Frontier Country: The Politics of War in Early Pennsylvania* (Philadelphia: University of Pennsylvania Press, 2016); Peter Silver, *Our Savage Neighbors: How Indian War Transformed Early America* (New York: W. W. Norton, 2008); Alan Taylor, *The Divided Ground: Indians, Settlers, and the Northern Borderlands of the American Revolution* (New York: Alfred A. Knopf, 2006). For a probing critique of this scholarship, see Rob Harper, *Unsettling the West: Violence and State Building in the Ohio Valley* (Philadelphia: University of Pennsylvania Press, 2018).

2. James Logan to John Penn, June 26, 1727, quoted in Alan Tully, *William Penn's Legacy: Politics and Social Structure in Provincial Pennsylvania, 1726–1755* (Baltimore: Johns Hopkins University Press, 1977), 210n25.

3. Council Minutes, Nov. 5, 1722, *CRP,* vol. III, 225–226.

4. Culver H. Smith, "Why Pennsylvania Never Became a Royal Province," *PMHB* 53, no. 2 (1929): 141–158.

5.　Council Minutes, Feb. 15, 1717, *CRP*, vol. III, 27.

6.　Council Minutes, Oct. 28, 1718, *CRP*, vol. III, 51–52.

7.　William H. Egle, ed., *The Breviate: In the Boundary Dispute between Pennsylvania and Maryland*, vol. XVI of *PA*, 2nd ser. (Harrisburg, PA: Edwin K. Meyers, 1891), 726–727.

8.　Council Minutes, May 28, 1722, *CRP*, vol. III, 185.

9.　Council Minutes, June 16, 1722, *CRP*, vol. III, 192–195. On Springettsbury, also see George R. Prowell, *History of York County Pennsylvania* (Chicago: J. H. Beers, 1907), vol. I, 24–27.

10.　Council Minutes, June 15, 1722, *CRP*, vol. III, 191–192; Daniel K. Richter, *The Ordeal of the Longhouse: The Peoples of the Iroquois League in the Era of European Colonization* (Chapel Hill: University of North Carolina Press for IEAHC, 1992), 238–240; Merrell, *Into the American Woods*, 115–121; Francis Jennings, *The Ambiguous Iroquois Empire: The Covenant Chain Confederation of Indian Tribes with English Colonies from Its Beginnings to the Lancaster Treaty of 1744* (New York: W. W. Norton, 1984), 278, 290–291.

11.　Quoted in Richter, *Ordeal of the Longhouse*, 241.

12.　Council Minutes, June 16, 1722, *CRP*, vol. III, 193; *The Case of Isaac Taylor and Elisha Gatchel, Two Officers of Pennsylvania, Made Prisoners of the Government of Maryland* (Philadelphia: Andrew Bradford, 1723), 1.

13.　Maryland Council Proceedings, Nov. 4, 1722, *AM, PCM*, vol. XXV, 396; Dulany Opinion, *AM, PCM*, vol. XXV, 416.

14.　Council Minutes, Nov. 5, 1722, *CRP*, vol. III, 224–225.

15.　Council Minutes, Nov. 19, 1722, *CRP*, vol. III, 228.

16.　James T. Lemon, *The Best Poor Man's Country: A Geographical Study of Early Southeastern Pennsylvania* (Baltimore: Johns Hopkins University Press, 1972), 48; Russell R. Menard, "Five Maryland Censuses, 1700 to 1712: A Note on the Quality of the Quantities," *WMQ* 37, no. 4 (Oct. 1980): 616–626; George Johnston, *History of Cecil County Maryland, and the Early Settlements Around the Head of the Chesapeake Bay and on the Delaware River* (Elkton, MD: George Johnson, 1881), 478–479.

17.　Benedict Leonard to Charles Calvert, Oct. 29, 1729, *AM, PCM*, vol. XXV, 602; Clarence Pembroke Gould, "The Land System in Maryland, 1720–1765" (PhD diss., Johns Hopkins University, 1911), 90–92; Frank W. Porter III, "From Backcountry to County: The Delayed Settlement of Western Maryland," *MHM* 70, no. 4 (Winter 1975): 329–349.

18.　Nicholas B. Wainwright, "Tales of a Runaway Cape: The Penn-Baltimore Agreement of 1732," *PMHB* 87, no. 3 (July 1963): 251–293.

19.　Petition quoted in Jerome H. Wood Jr., "The Town Proprietors of Lancaster, 1730–1790," *PMHB* 96, no. 3 (July 1972): 347; Ken Miller, *Dangerous*

Guests: Enemy Captives and Revolutionary Communities during the War for Independence (Ithaca, NY: Cornell University Press, 2014), 8–9.

20.   Lawrence C. Wroth, "The Story of Thomas Cresap; Maryland Pioneer," *MHM* 9, no. 1 (Mar. 1914): 1–37.

21.   Blunston to Robert Charles, Oct. 3, 1731, *PA*, 1st ser. (Philadelphia: Joseph Severns, 1852), vol. I, 295; Prowell, *History of York County*, 146. The absence of references to Springettsbury is a puzzle. One researcher has suggested that the initial survey was never formally submitted to the Pennsylvania land office. See William H. Kain, "The Penn Manorial System and the Manors of Springetsbury and Maske," *PH* 10, no. 4 (Oct. 1943): 229–231; also Prowell, *History of York County*, 26–27.

22.   Tully, *William Penn's Legacy*, 153–155.

23.   Blunston to Charles, *PA*, 1st ser., vol. I, 295; "Further Propositions of the Govr of Virginia made to the five Nations of Indians, Septr 11. 1722," in *Documents Relative to the Colonial History of the State of New York*, ed. E. B. O'Callaghan (New York: Weed, Parsons, 1855), vol. V, 674, 676, excerpted in "Early Recognized Treaties with American Indian Nations," University of Nebraska–Lincoln, Center for Digital Research in the Humanities, http://treatiesportal.unl.edu/earlytreaties /treaty.00001.html#n660.01.note; Richter, *Ordeal of the Longhouse*, 237–241.

24.   Allan Kulikoff, *Tobacco and Slaves: The Development of Southern Cultures in the Chesapeake, 1680–1800* (Chapel Hill: University of North Carolina Press for IEAHC, 1986), 328–329.

25.   Dutch to Governor of Maryland, *PA*, 1st ser., vol. I, 493.

26.   Tully, *William Penn's Legacy*, 8; Paul Doutrich, "Cresap's War: Expansion and Conflict in the Susquehanna Valley," *PH* 53, no. 2 (Apr. 1986): 89–104; Spero, *Frontier Country*, esp. ch. 4.

27.   Council Minutes, Oct. 14, 1736, *CRP*, vol. IV, 92–93.

28.   Council Minutes, Oct. 9 and 12, 1736, *CRP*, vol. IV, 86–88; Indian Deed, Oct. 11, 1736, *PA*, 1st ser., vol. I, 495.

29.   Indian Deed, Oct. 11, 1736, *PA*, 1st ser., vol. I, 494–496; Richter, *Ordeal of the Longhouse*, 275.

30.   Council Minutes, Feb. 8, 1737, *CRP*, vol. IV, 153–154.

31.   Council Minutes, Mar. 1, 1737, *CRP*, vol. IV, 155–156.

32.   *Journals of the Board of Trade and Plantations: Volume 7, January 1735– December 1741, Journal, June 1737: Volume 46*, June 2 and 9, https://www.british -history.ac.uk/jrnl-trade-plantations/vol7/pp188-204.

33.   May 25, 1738, from the king via the Board of Trade, *AM*, *PCM*, vol. XXVIII, 145–146.

34.   May 25, 1738, from the king via the Board of Trade, *AM*, *PCM*, vol. XXVIII, 147–148.

5. AN AMERICAN BLOODLANDS

1.   "Witham Marshe's Journal of the Treaty Held with the Six Nations . . . in Pennsylvania, June, 1744," *Collections of the Massachusetts Historical Society,* ser. 1, vol. VII (Boston: Samuel Hall, 1801), 171–178.

2.   "Witham Marshe's Journal," 178; Indians present at the treaty held at Lancaster in June 1744, *PA,* ser. 1, vol. I, 656–667. See also James H. Merrell, ed., *The Lancaster Treaty of 1744: With Related Documents* (Boston: Bedford / St. Martin's, 2008).

3.   "Marshe's Journal," 173–174. Frank Porter notes that quitrents rather than clergy taxes were the principal deterrents to settlement in Maryland: "From Backcountry to Country: The Delayed Settlement of Western Maryland," *MHM* 70, no. 4 (Winter 1975): 336; Alvin Rabushka, *Taxation in Colonial America* (Princeton, NJ: Princeton University Press, 2008), 686–687.

4.   One estimate says that by 1790, 60–70 percent of the population of Frederick County in Maryland were Pennsylvania Dutch. James D. Rice, "Old Appalachia's Path to Interdependency: Economic Development and the Creation of Western Maryland, 1730–1850," *Appalachian Journal* 22, no. 4 (Summer 1995): 351.

5.   Paul G. E. Clemens, *The Atlantic Economy and Colonial Maryland's Eastern Shore: From Tobacco to Grain* (Ithaca, NY: Cornell University Press, 1980), 174–183; John J. McCusker and Russell R. Menard, *The Economy of British America, 1607–1789* (Chapel Hill: University of North Carolina Press for IEAHC, 1985), 204–205.

6.   James T. Lemon, *The Best Poor Man's Country: A Geographical Study of Early Southeastern Pennsylvania* (Baltimore: Johns Hopkins University Press, 1972), 202–204; Marc Egnal, "The Economic Development of the Thirteen Colonies, 1720–1775," *WMQ* 32, no. 2 (Apr. 1975): 202–203; Arthur L. Jensen, *The Maritime Commerce of Colonial Philadelphia* (Madison: State Historical Society of Wisconsin, 1963), 8.

7.   Aaron Spencer Fogleman, *Hopeful Journeys: Germain Immigration, Settlement, and Political Culture in Colonial America, 1717–1775* (Philadelphia: University of Pennsylvania Press, 1996), 8; Council Minutes, Apr. 22–25, 1745, *CRP,* vol. IV, 756; Porter, "From Backcountry to Country," 346.

8.   Gary B. Nash and Jean R. Soderlund, *Freedom by Degrees: Emancipation in Pennsylvania and its Aftermath* (New York: Oxford University Press, 1991), 32–35. Although focused on four Chesapeake Bay counties, a pattern similar to Pennsylvania's is suggested by Russell R. Menard in "The Maryland Slave Population, 1658 to 1730: A Demographic Profile of Blacks in Four Counties," *WMQ*

32, no. 1 (Jan. 1975): 49. Also see Max Grivno, *Gleanings of Freedom: Free and Slave Labor along the Mason-Dixon Line, 1790–1860* (Urbana: University of Illinois Press, 2011), 11. One historian has estimated that Frederick County, Maryland's slave population on the eve of the Revolutionary War was around 10 percent of the total population, the lowest percentage of all Maryland counties. Ronald Hoffman, *A Spirit of Dissension: Economics, Politics, and the Revolution in Maryland* (Baltimore: Johns Hopkins University Press, 1973), 11.

9. On the quote, Lemon, *Best Poor Man's Country*, 229n1; James Merrell, *Into the American Woods: Negotiators on the Pennsylvania Frontier* (New York: W. W. Norton, 1999), 283–284.

10. Daniel K. Richter, "A Framework for Pennsylvania Indian History," *PH* 57, no. 3 (July 1990): 248–249; Eric Hinderaker, *Elusive Empires: Constructing Colonialism in the Ohio Valley, 1673–1800* (Cambridge: Cambridge University Press, 1997), 27–28.

11. On the Maryland planter class, Trevor Burnard, *Creole Gentlemen: The Maryland Elite, 1691–1776* (New York: Routledge, 2002), esp. ch. 6.

12. Rabushka, *Taxation*, 679–682.

13. Lorena S. Walsh, *Motives of Honor, Plea, and Profit: Plantation Management in the Chesapeake, 1607–1763* (Chapel Hill: University of North Carolina Press for OIEAHC, 2010), 625.

14. Aubrey C. Land, "Economic Base and Social Structure: The Northern Chesapeake in the Eighteenth Century," *Journal of Economic History* 25 (1965): 648–649; Aubrey C. Land, *Colonial Maryland: A History* (Millwood, NY: KTO Press, 1981), 219.

15. Reply to Governor, Aug. 19, 1755, *PA*, ser. 8, (Harrisburg: Pennsylvania State Library, 1931), vol. V, 3997–3998.

16. Gottlieb Mittelberger, *Journey to Pennsylvania*, ed. Oscar Handlin and John Clive (Cambridge, MA: Harvard University Press, 1960), 77.

17. Franklin to Richard Partridge, Oct. 25, 1755, *PBF*, vol. VI, 230.

18. Hinderaker, *Elusive Empires*, 24, 40–45.

19. Council Minutes, Sept. 6, 1756, *CRP*, vol. VII, 242; "Petition of the Inhabitants of the Town and County of York," *CRP*, vol. VII, 233–234; *Penna Gazette* quoted in David Dixon, *Never Come to Peace Again: Pontiac's Uprising and the Fate of the British in North America* (Norman: University of Oklahoma Press, 2005), 162; Philadelphian quoted in Matthew C. Ward, *Breaking the Backcountry: The Seven Years' War in Virginia and Pennsylvania, 1754–1765* (Pittsburgh: University of Pittsburgh Press, 2003), 57.

20. Ken Miller, *Dangerous Guests: Enemy Captives and Revolutionary Communities during the War for Independence* (Ithaca, NY: Cornell University Press, 2014), 27.

21. Franklin to Robert Hunter Morris, Jan. 14, 1756, *PBF,* vol. VI, 357.

22. Council Minutes, Apr. 13, 1756, *CRP,* vol. VII, 87–89.

23. Council Minutes, Apr. 10, 1756, *CRP,* vol. VII, 80.

24. Peter Silver, *Our Savage Neighbors: How Indian War Transformed Early America* (New York: W. W. Norton, 2008), 161–162.

25. Hinderaker, *Elusive Empires,* 147–149.

26. Patrick Spero, *Frontier Country: The Politics of War in Early Pennsylvania* (Philadelphia: University of Pennsylvania Press, 2016), 151–152.

27. Merrell, *Into the American Woods,* 282–288; Kevin Kenny, *Peaceable Kingdom Lost: The Paxton Boys and the Destruction of William Penn's Holy Experiment* (New York: Oxford University Press, 2009), 127–129.

28. Two Indians, Michael and Mary, who had lived at some prior date at Conestoga, were known to have continued living in Lancaster County with members of the Hershey family, perhaps as servants. Kenny, *Peaceable Kingdom,* 235–236.

29. Penn to Governor Cadwallader Colden, Jan. 5, 1764, *CRP,* vol. IX, 112.

30. Matthew Smith and James Gibson, *A Declaration and Remonstrance of the Distressed and Bleeding Frontier Inhabitants of the Province of Pennsylvania . . .* (1764), in *The Paxton Papers,* ed. John Dunbar (The Hague: Martinus Nijhoff, 1957), 102–103.

31. Gage to Penn, Mar. 10, 1766, *CRP,* vol. IX, 307; Alden T. Vaughan, "Frontier Banditti and the Indians: The Paxton Boys' Legacy, 1763–1775," *PMHB* 51, no. 1 (Jan. 1984): 6–7; Kenny, *Peaceable Kingdom,* 209; Patrick Spero, *Frontier Rebels: The Fight for Independence in the American West, 1765–1776* (New York: W. W. Norton, 2018).

32. Gage to Penn, Dec. 7, 1767, *CRP,* vol. IX, 403.

33. [Benjamin Franklin], "Cool Thoughts on the Present Situation of Our Public Affairs," Apr. 12, 1764, *PBF,* vol. XI, 153.

34. Quoted in James H. Hutson, *Pennsylvania Politics, 1746–1770: The Movement for Royal Government and Its Consequences* (Princeton, NJ: Princeton University Press, 1972), 216.

35. In October 1764, John Penn reported to Thomas Penn that, prompted by Franklin, the Maryland assembly was preparing to submit a petition to the Crown requesting "a Change of Government." I can find no evidence of this actually happening, although in "Cool Thoughts" Franklin did suggest that the Maryland and Pennsylvania governments were "both at this Instant agitated by the same Contentions between Proprietary Interest and Power, and Popular Liberty." Penn may have been reacting to a deliberate misinformation campaign by Franklin and his allies or he may have seized on innuendo to inspire his uncle to draw Lord Baltimore into a battle for proprietary governance. William S. Hanna, *Benjamin Franklin and Pennsylvania Politics* (Stanford: Stanford University Press, 1964), 168.

6. THE SCIENCE OF BORDERS

1.   Francis Vesey, ed., *Reports of Cases Argued and Determined in the High Court of Chancery, In the Time of Lord Chancellor Hardwicke, from the Year 1746/7 to 1755* (Philadelphia: Robert H. Small, 1831), vol. I, 446.

2.   Vesey, *Reports of Cases,* 444, 446.

3.   Mason and Dixon Line Resurvey Commission, *Report on the Resurvey of the Maryland-Pennsylvania Boundary Part of the Mason and Dixon Line* (Harrisburg, PA: Harrisburg Publishing Company, 1909), 173–175.

4.   Vesey, *Reports of Cases,* 454, 450.

5.   Bill Hubbard Jr., *American Boundaries: The Nation, the States, the Rectangular Survey* (Chicago: University of Chicago Press, 2009), ch. 1.

6.   Lewis Evans, *Geographical, Historical, Political, Philosophical, and Mechanical Essays* . . . (Philadelphia: Franklin, Hall & Dodsley, 1755), 5–6.

7.   Sharpe to Lord Baltimore, Dec. 20, 1760, *AM,* vol. IX, 469–471.

8.   Calvert to Sharpe, July 20, 1763, *AM,* vol. XIV, 106.

9.   *JMD,* 58.

10.   Calvert to Sharpe, July 20, 1763, *AM,* vol. XIV, 106.

11.   Quoted in Thomas D. Cope, "Degrees along the West Line, the Parallel between Maryland and Pennsylvania," *Proceedings of the American Philosophical Society* 93, no. 2 (May 1949): 127.

12.   *JMD,* 129.

13.   Sharpe to Johnson, Dec. 15, 1766, *The Papers of Sir William Johnson,* ed. Milton W. Hamilton (Albany: University of the State of New York, 1957), vol. XII, 231.

14.   Boundary Commissioners to Mason and Dixon, June 18, 1767, in *JMD,* 177. On wage labor in Pennsylvania: Mary M. Schweitzer, *Custom and Contract: Household, Government, and the Economy in Colonial Pennsylvania* (New York: Columbia University Press, 1987), 49–56.

15.   Carl N. Everstine, "The Potomac River and Maryland's Boundaries," *Maryland Historical Magazine* 80, no. 4 (Winter 1985): 356–360.

16.   *JMD,* 178, 184, 187.

17.   *JMD,* 187, 147 (on setting eastern stones). Between 1991 and 2016, the Mason and Dixon Line Preservation Partnership prepared an inventory of the remaining stones: https://www.mdlpp.org/stone-inventory.

18.   George Croghan to Franklin, Feb. 12, 1768, *PBF,* vol. XV, 42.

19.   Gage to Penn, Dec. 7, 1767, *CRP,* vol. IX, 403–404; Penn to the Assembly, Jan. 5, 1786, *CRP,* vol. IX, 407.

20.   Assembly to Penn, Jan. 13, 1768, in *CRP,* vol. IX, 408–411.

21.   Deposition of William Blyth, Jan. 19, 1768, in *CRP*, vol. IX, 414–415; Kevin Kenny, *Peaceable Kingdoms Lost: The Paxton Boys and the Destruction of William Penn's Holy Experiment* (New York: Oxford University Press, 2009), 209–216; Patrick Spero, *Frontier Country: The Politics of War in Early Pennsylvania* (Philadelphia: University of Pennsylvania Press, 2016), 187–193.

22.   Council Minutes, Feb. 8, 1768, *CRP*, vol. IX, 460–461.

23.   Johnson to Penn, Mar. 16, 1768, *CRP*, vol. IX, 495.

24.   Council Minutes, Feb. 24, 1768, *CRP*, vol. IX, 481–482.

25.   Kayashuta to Pennsylvania Indian Agents Frazer and Thompson, May 9, 1768, *CRP*, vol. IX, 542.

26.   Quoted in James Kirby Martin, "The Return of the Paxton Boys and the Historical State of the Pennsylvania Frontier, 1764–1774," *PH* 38, no. 2 (Apr. 1971): 127–128.

27.   Nicholas B. Wainwright, "Mason and Dixon's Map," *Princeton University Library Chronicle* 45, no. 1 (Autumn 1983): 28–32. Also see Pamela Young, "Conserving the Mason-Dixon Map," *Colonial Williamsburg Journal* 28, no. 1 (Winter 2006), 74–79; Thomas W. Streeter, "Princeton's Mason and Dixon Map," *Princeton University Library Chronicle* 16, no. 2 (Winter 1955): 97–99.

28.   Dorothy Twohig, Mark A. Mastromarino, and Jack D. Warren, eds., *The Papers of George Washington*, Presidential Series, vol. 5, *16 January 1790–30 June 1790* (Charlottesville: University of Virginia Press, 1996), 293–296; Mary Mason to the Commissioners of the Board of Longitude, March 5, 1791, Papers of the Board of Longitude, University of Cambridge Digital Library, https://cudl .lib.cam.ac.uk/view/MS-RGO-00014-00012/99.

7. THE MAKING OF STATES, FREE AND SLAVE

1.   *The Journal of John Woolman and A Plea for the Poor*, introduction by Frederick B. Tolls (New York: Corinth Books, 1961), 49–52, 57.

2.   Gary B. Nash and Jean R. Soderlund, *Freedom by Degrees: Emancipation in Pennsylvania and its Aftermath* (New York: Oxford University Press, 1991), 7; John J. McCusker and Russell R. Menard, *The Economy of British America, 1607–1789* (Chapel Hill: University of North Carolina Press for IEAHC, 1985), 134–136; Ronald Hoffman, *A Spirit of Dissension: Economics, Politics, and the Revolution in Maryland* (Baltimore: Johns Hopkins University Press, 1973), 11.

3.   Jean R. Soderlund, *Quakers and Slavery: A Divided Spirit* (Princeton, NJ: Princeton University Press, 1985).

4.   Alexander Hamilton, *A Gentleman's Progress: The Itinerarium of Alexander Hamilton, 1744*, ed. Carl Bridenbaugh (Pittsburgh: University of Pittsburgh Press, 1948), 14–15. The association of a dissolute Maryland with slavery persisted after the

Revolutionary War. See, for instance, Jacques-Pierre Brissot de Warville, *New Travels in the United States of America: Performed in 1788* (London: J. S. Jordan, 1792), 424.

5. Ira Berlin, *Many Thousands Gone: The First Two Centuries of Slavery in North America* (Cambridge, MA: Harvard University Press, 1998), esp. 7–10. The demographic vitality of the Mason-Dixon borderlands is suggested by immigration data compiled by Bernard Bailyn. Of 9,364 English and Irish immigrants to British North America (including Canada and the West Indian colonies) between December 1773 and March 1776, 3,742, roughly 40 percent, disembarked in Pennsylvania or Maryland. Bernard Bailyn, *Voyagers to the West: A Passage in the Peopling of America on the Eve of the Revolution* (New York: Alfred A. Knopf, 1986), 206–207, table 6.1.

6. In 1777, the renegade New York province of Vermont adopted a constitutional ban on slavery, but Vermont was not yet a formally recognized state. Similarly, because Vermont's was a constitutional prohibition, it did not *abolish* in the way Pennsylvania's legislative act did.

7. Arthur Zilversmit, *The First Emancipation: The Abolition of Slavery in the North* (Chicago: University of Chicago Press, 1967), 155; Gary B. Nash, *Warner Mifflin: Unflinching Quaker Abolitionist* (Philadelphia: University of Pennsylvania Press, 2017), 139–141; Manisha Sinha, *The Slave's Cause: A History of Abolition* (New Haven, CT: Yale University Press, 2016), 92–93.

8. *MPCP, CRP,* ser. 1, vol. X, 244; Lord Dartmouth to Penn, Jan. 7, 1775, *MPCP, CRP,* ser. 1, vol. X, 240; "Constitution of Delaware; 1776," Article 26, https://avalon.law.yale.edu/18th_century/de02.asp#1; Patience Essah, *A House Divided: Slavery and Emancipation in Delaware, 1638–1865* (Charlottesville: University Press of Virginia, 1996), 40–41; William H. Williams, *Slavery and Freedom in Delaware, 1639–1865* (Wilmington, DE: SR Books, 1996), 143–144; George William Van Cleve, *A Slaveholder's Union: Slavery, Politics, and the Constitution in the Early American Republic* (Chicago: University of Chicago Press, 2010), 28–31; W. E. B. Du Bois, *The Suppression of the African Slave-Trade to the United States of America* (New York: Oxford University Press, 2007), 5–8.

9. Essah, *House Divided,* 2, 6, and on percentages of enslaved Delawareans, 7; Williams, *Slavery and Freedom,* 141–144.

10. Seth Rockman, *Scraping By: Wage Labor, Slavery, and Survival in Early Baltimore* (Baltimore: Johns Hopkins University Press, 2009), 60; Du Bois, *Suppression,* 8–9; James Martin Wright, *The Free Negro in Maryland, 1634–1860* (New York: Columbia University Press, 1921), 53–61, 66; Benjamin Joseph Klebaner, "American Manumission Laws and the Responsibility for Supporting Slaves," *Virginia Magazine of History and Biography* 63, no. 4 (Oct. 1955): 443–453.

11. James D. Rice, "Old Appalachia's Path to Interdependency: Economic Development and the Creation of Community in Western Maryland, 1730–1850," *Appalachian Journal* 22, no. 4 (Summer 1995): 356.

12.   Unless otherwise noted, I rely on United States census data, accessed through https://www.socialexplorer.com/explore-tables. Graphs showing county-by-county population changes can be viewed at http://earlyamerica.create.fsu.edu/mason-dixon. Census data are imperfect, especially where they discriminate between free and enslaved African Americans. Until 1820, free Blacks were designated as "All other Free Persons," differentiating them from slaves and free whites. In 1820 census authorities introduced "Free Colored Persons" to distinguish free Blacks from other free nonwhites. For the most part, census enumerators were left to apply these designations in the field and occasionally counted free Blacks as enslaved and vice versa, especially in areas—such as the Mason-Dixon Line border counties—with extensive populations of both. Claudette Bennett, "Racial Categories Used in the Decennial Censuses, 1790 to the Present," *Government Information Quarterly* 17, no. 2 (Apr. 1, 2000): 161–180.

13.   Barbara Jeanne Fields, *Slavery and Freedom on the Middle Ground: Maryland during the Nineteenth Century* (New Haven, CT: Yale University Press, 1985), 5 and ch. 1, quote on 6–7.

14.   "The Genuine Information, Delivered to the Legislature of the State of Maryland . . . in 1787, by Luther Martin," in *The Records of the Federal Convention of 1787*, ed. Max Ferrand (New Haven, CT: Yale University Press, 1911), vol. III, 211; "Martin, Luther," in *A Biographical Dictionary of the Maryland Legislature, 1635–1789*, ed. Edward C. Papenfuse et al. (Baltimore: Johns Hopkins University Press, 1979–1985); *AM*, vol. CDXXVI, 577–578.

15.   Van Cleve, *Slaveholders' Union*, 145–146; Jonathan Elliot, *Journal and Debates of the Federal Convention, Held at Philadelphia, from May 14–September 17, 1787* . . . (Washington, DC: Jonathan Elliot, 1830), vol. IV, 26, 36. On Revolutionary politics and the opposition to the slave trade, see Steven Deyle, "The Irony of Liberty: Origins of the Domestic Slave Trade," *Journal of the Early Republic* 12, no. 1 (Spring 1992): 37–62.

16.   Nash and Soderlund, *Freedom by Degrees*, 7, table 1-2; Darold D. Wax, "The Pennsylvania Slave Trade, 1759–1765," *PH* 50, no. 1 (Jan. 1983): 38; Jean R. Soderlund, "Black Importation and Migration into Southeastern Pennsylvania, 1682–1810," *Proceedings of the American Philosophical Society* 133, no. 2 (June 1989): 144–146.

17.   Nash and Soderlund, *Freedom by Degrees*, 18, table 1-4; 80, table 3-1.

18.   Nash and Soderlund, *Freedom by Degrees*, 4–5, table 1-1.

19.   Nash and Soderlund, *Freedom by Degrees*, table 1-1.

20.   Christopher M. Osborne, "Invisible Hands: Slaves, Bound Laborers, and the Development of Western Pennsylvania, 1780–1820," *PH* 72, no. 1 (Winter 2005): 77–99.

21.   Nash and Soderlund, *Freedom by Degrees*, 18, table 1-4; 36, table 1-8.

22. Zilversmit, *First Emancipation*, 139–153.

23. For the politics surrounding Pennsylvania's first constitutional convention, see Eric Foner, *Tom Paine and Revolutionary America* (New York: Oxford University Press, 1976), ch. 4; Gary B. Nash, "Philadelphia's Radical Caucus That Propelled Pennsylvania to Independence and Democracy," in *Revolutionary Founders: Rebels, Radicals, and Reformers in the Making of the Nation*, ed. Alfred F. Young, Gary B. Nash, and Ray Raphael (New York: Knopf, 2011), ch. 4; Steven Rosswurm, *Arms, Country, and Class: The Philadelphia Militia and "Lower Sort" during the American Revolution, 1775–1783* (New Brunswick, NJ: Rutgers University Press, 1987), 100–108.

24. Gordon S. Wood, *The Creation of the American Republic, 1776–1787* (New York: W. W. Norton, 1972), 230; Thomas Paine, "Common Sense," in *Thomas Paine: Rights of Man, Common Sense, and Other Political Writings*, ed. Mark Philp (Oxford: Oxford University Press, 1995), 7.

25. *Diary and Autobiography of John Adams*, ed. L. H. Butterfield (New York: Atheneum, 1964), vol. III, 333. Other critics quoted in Wood, *Creation of the American Republic*, 233, 234.

26. On the undemocratic features of Pennsylvania's 1776 constitution, see Kenneth Owen, *Political Community in Revolutionary Pennsylvania, 1774–1800* (Oxford: Oxford University Press, 2018), 44; Terry Bouton, *Taming Democracy: "The People," the Founders, and the Troubled Ending of the American Revolution* (New York: Oxford University Press, 2007), 55–56.

27. If anything, the new constitution, which required oaths of allegiance for all elected and appointed public officials, was overt in its hostility to the Society of Friends. See Bouton, *Taming Democracy*, 56.

28. Quoted in John N. Shaeffer, "Public Consideration of the 1776 Pennsylvania Constitution," *PMHB* 98, no. 4 (Oct. 1974): 418. On the rise of plebeian radicalism in Philadelphia, see Foner, *Tom Paine*, ch. 4; Gary B. Nash, *The Urban Crucible: Social Change, Political Consciousness, and the Origins of the American Revolution* (Cambridge, MA: Harvard University Press, 1979), 378–380.

29. *Journals of the House of Representatives of the Commonwealth of Pennsylvania . . .* (Philadelphia: John Dunlap, 1782), vol. I, 390–391.

30. Nash and Soderlund, *Freedom by Degrees*, 104–108.

31. Michael B. McCoy, "Forgetting Freedom: White Anxiety, Black Presence, and Gradual Abolition in Cumberland County, Pennsylvania, 1780–1838," *PMHB* 136, no. 2 (Apr. 2012): 148; Pennsylvania Constitution of 1776, Section 36, http://www.phmc.state.pa.us/portal/communities/documents/1776-1865/pennsylvania-constitution-1776.html; Rosswurm, *Arms, Country*, 106.

32. Nash and Soderlund, *Freedom by Degrees*, 111; "An Act for the Gradual Abolition of Slavery," https://avalon.law.yale.edu/18th_century/pennsto1.asp; Stanley I.

Kutler, "Pennsylvania Courts, the Abolition Act, and Negro Rights," *PH* 30, no. 1 (Jan. 1963): 14–27.

33.   "An Act for the Gradual Abolition of Slavery"; Nash and Soderlund, *Freedom by Degrees,* 102; 111–113; Kutler, "Pennsylvania Courts," 14–15.

34.   Philip S. Foner, "A Plea against Reenslavement," *PH* 39, no. 2 (Apr. 1972): 239–241; Nash and Soderland, *Freedom by Degrees,* 114–115.

35.   "An Act to Explain and Amend an Act, Entitled 'An Act for the Gradual Abolition of Slavery,'" *Laws of the Commonwealth of Pennsylvania* . . . (Philadelphia: John Bioren, 1810), vol. II, 445.

36.   Soderlund, "Black Importation and Migration," 150–153.

37.   Gary B. Nash, *Forging Freedom: The Formation of Philadelphia's Black Community, 1720–1840* (Cambridge, MA: Harvard University Press, 1988), 71–72; Hamilton, *A Gentleman's Progress,* 4, 206n6.

38.   Rockman, *Scraping By,* 27, 34; Nash, *Forging Freedom,* 137, table 4.

8. BORDERLANDS AS HEARTLAND

1.   On the politics of austerity in post-Revolutionary Pennsylvania, see Terry Bouton, *Taming Democracy: "The People," the Founders, and the Troubled Ending of the American Revolution* (New York: Oxford University Press, 2007), esp. ch. 3.

2.   Johann David Schoepf, *Travels in the Confederation [1783–1784],* trans. and ed. Alfred J. Morrison (Philadelphia: William J. Campbell, 1911), vol. II, 10, 26.

3.   Paine to Daniel Clymer, Sept. [n.d.], 1786, *The Complete Writings of Thomas Paine,* ed. Philip S. Foner (New York: Citadel Press, 1945), vol. II, 1255–1256.

4.   *Debates and Proceedings of the General Assembly of Pennsylvania, on the Memorials Praying a Repeal or Suspension of the Law Annulling the Charter of the Bank,* ed. Matthew Carey (Philadelphia: Carey & Seddon, 1786), 65; Paine to Daniel Clymer, Sept. [n.d.], 1786, *Complete Writings,* vol. II, 1256.

5.   Thomas Paine, "Addressed to the Opposers of the Bank," in *Complete Writings of Thomas Paine,* vol. II, 434–435; *Independent Gazetteer* (Philadelphia), Mar. 12, 1787, col. 1, 3, *AHN;* Edward G. Gray, *Tom Paine's Iron Bridge: Building a United States* (New York: W. W. Norton, 2016).

6.   "Pres. Franklin to Commissioners for Improving Inland Navigation, 1785," Oct. 26, 1786, *PA,* ser. 1, vol. XI, 78; "Meeting of Counties for Improving Susquehanna River, 1789," *PA,* ser. 1, vol. XI, 626.

7.   Gray, *Tom Paine's Iron Bridge,* 196–197.

8.   Timothy J. Shannon, "Native American-Pennsylvania Relations, 1754–89," *The Encyclopedia of Greater Philadelphia,* Mid-Atlantic Regional Center for the Humanities, Rutgers-Camden, https://philadelphiaencyclopedia.org/archive/category/timothy-j-shannon/.

9.   Peter Silver, *Our Savage Neighbors: How Indian War Transformed Early America* (New York: W. W. Norton, 2008), 265–274. The Allegheny community occupied lands deeded by the state of Pennsylvania to the Seneca headman Cornplanter in payment for his services during the Revolutionary War. Keith Heinrich, "The Cornplanter Grant: The Last Native American Settlement in Pennsylvania," *Pennsylvania Historic Preservation: Blog of the Pennsylvania State Historic Preservation Office,* Nov. 14, 2018, https://pahistoricpreservation.com/cornplanter-grant -native-american/.

10.   Schoepf, *Travels,* vol. II, 20.

11.   Jacques Pierre Brissot de Warville, *New Travels in the United States of America: Performed in 1788* (London: J. S. Jordan, 1792), 232.

12.   Baltimore Grain Commissioners to Governor Lee, Jan. 14, 1780, quoted in "Provisioning the Continental Army," *MHM* 9, no. 3 (1914): 243.

13.   George Terry Sharrer, "Flour Milling and the Growth of Baltimore, 1783–1830" (PhD diss., University of Maryland, 1975), 19–20.

14.   Sharrer, "Flour Milling," esp. 29–37; Geoffrey Neal Gilbert, "Baltimore's Flour Trade to the Caribbean, 1750–1815" (PhD diss., Johns Hopkins University 1975), ch. 3 and 82–83, 121, table V-1, 123, table V-3; Brooke Hunter, "Wheat, War, and the American Economy during the Age of Revolution," *WMQ* 62, no. 3 (July 2005): 523.

15.   Max Grivno, *Gleanings of Freedom: Free and Slave Labor along the Mason-Dixon Line, 1790–1860* (Urbana: University of Illinois Press, 2011), 29–31; Sharrer, "Flour Milling," 44–46.

16.   Israel Acrelius, *A History of New Sweden: Or, the Settlements on the River Delaware,* trans. and ed. William M. Reynolds (Philadelphia: Historical Society of Pennsylvania, 1874), 165; Tench Coxe, *A View of the United States of America, in a Series of Papers, Written at Various Times, between the Years 1787 and 1794* (Philadelphia: William Hall, 1794), 313; J. Thomas Scharf, *History of Western Maryland: Being a History of Frederick, Montgomery, Carroll, Washington, Allegany, and Garrett Counties . . .* (Philadelphia: L. H. Everts, 1882), vol. I, 361; Bernard Bailyn, *Voyagers to the West: A Passage in the Peopling of America on the Eve of the Revolution* (New York: Alfred A. Knopf, 1986), 245–248; Scharf, *History of Western Maryland,* vol. II, 1170–1171; Tench Coxe, *A Statement of the Arts and Manufactures of the United States of America, for the Year 1810* (Philadelphia: A. Cornman, 1814), lxiii.

17.   "Act for the Relief of the Securities of John Ward Veazey," *AM,* vol. 24, 416–418.

18.   On Fayette and Washington County tax resistance, Bouton, *Taming Democracy,* 161–162; Michael Hahn to John Nicholson, Dec. 15, 1786, *PA,* 1st ser., vol. XI, 97.

19. Biddle to County Commissioners, July 2, 1789, *PA*, 1st ser., vol. XI, 593; Franklin County treasurer quoted in Bouton, *Taming Democracy*, 156. More generally on tax resistance, Bouton, *Taming Democracy*, esp. chs. 7, 9.

20. "An Act to Enable the Securities of Christopher Edlen," Jan. 20, 1786, *AM*, vol. CCIV, 176; Journal of the Council of Md., May 28, 1789, *AM*, vol. LXXII, 30–31.

21. "Act for the Benefit of John Frederick Amelung," May 26, 1788, *AM*, vol. CCIV, 298–299.

22. Quoted in Henry Adams, *The Life of Albert Gallatin* (Philadelphia: J. B. Lippincott, 1879), 86.

23. Federalist press quoted in Thomas P. Slaughter, *The Whiskey Rebellion: Frontier Epilogue to the American Revolution* (New York: Oxford University Press, 1986), 194–195.

24. Alvin Rabushka, *Taxation in Colonial America* (Princeton, NJ: Princeton University Press, 2008), 411, 536, 650. These taxes were imposed on spirits at point of sale, rather than point of production, as would be the case with the new federal tax.

25. Slaughter, *Whiskey Rebellion*, 3.

26. Jefferson to Washington, July 12, 1790, *The Papers of Thomas Jefferson*, ed. Julian P. Boyd et al. (Princeton, NJ: Princeton University Press, 1950–), vol. XVII, 109.

27. Hamilton quoted in Gordon S. Wood, *Empire of Liberty: A History of the Early Republic, 1789–1815* (New York: Oxford University Press, 2009), 137. On western separatism and lawlessness, Slaughter, *Whiskey Rebellion*, 32–33, 117–118.

28. "Petition against Excise," in *The Writings of Albert Gallatin*, ed. Henry Adams (Philadelphia: J. B. Lippincott, 1879), vol. I, 3–4.

29. *The Writings of Albert Gallatin*, ed. Henry Adams (Philadelphia: J. B. Lippincott, 1879), vol. III, 4–5.

30. Slaughter, *Whiskey Rebellion*, 217–219.

31. Hugh Henry Brackenridge, *Incidents of the Insurrection in the Western Parts of Pennsylvania, in the Year 1794* (Philadelphia: John McCulloch, 1795), part III, 32, 30.

32. Quoted in Stanley Elkins and Eric McKitrick, *The Age of Federalism: The Early American Republic, 1788–1800* (New York: Oxford University Press, 1993), 483–484.

33. Gallatin to Giles, February 13, 1802, *Writings of Albert Gallatin*, vol. I, 79.

34. *Report of the Secretary of the Treasury on the Subject of Public Roads and Canals* . . . (Washington, DC: R. C. Weightman, 1808), 7, 8.

35.   Traveler and *Aurora* quoted in James Weston Livingood, *The Philadelphia-Baltimore Trade Rivalry* (Harrisburg: Pennsylvania Historical and Museum Commission, 1947), 50.

36.   Billy Joe Peyton, "Surveying and Building the Road," in *The National Road*, ed. Karl Raitz (Baltimore: Johns Hopkins University Press, 1996), 138.

9. FUGITIVE DIPLOMACY

1.   Bill Hubbard, *American Boundaries: The Nation, the States, the Rectangular Survey* (Chicago: University of Chicago Press, 2009), 28–29.

2.   "Resolution of the General Assembly of Virginia, June 23rd, 1780," *PA*, ser. 1, vol. VIII, 353.

3.   Deposition of David Davis, by William McMachan, Sept. 22, 1792, *CVSP*, vol. VI, 84–86.

4.   Whitfield J. Bell Jr., "Washington County, Pennsylvania, in the Eighteenth-Century Antislavery Movement." *Western Pennsylvania Historical Magazine* 25 (1942): 135–142; W. Thomas Mainwaring, *Abandoned Tracks: The Underground Railroad in Western Pennsylvania* (South Bend, IN: Notre Dame University Press, 2018), 30–35.

5.   John Waller and Horatio Hall to Governor Randolph, of Va., Nov. 30, 1791, *CVSP*, vol. V, 402–403.

6.   "Enclosure: Statement of Conflict between Pennsylvania and Virginia, 20 December 1791," *The Papers of Thomas Jefferson*, vol. 22, *6 August 1791–31 December 1791*, ed. Charles T. Cullen (Princeton, NJ: Princeton University Press, 1986), 425–427; Richard S. Newman, *The Transformation of American Abolitionism: Fighting Slavery in the Early Republic* (Chapel Hill: University of North Carolina Press, 2002), 69–70.

7.   Washington Society to the PAS, Dec. 6, 1790, *PAS Committee of Correspondence Letter Book*, vol. I, 76, *Papers of the PAS at the Historical Society of Pennsylvania*, reel 11 (microfilm ed.); Sharon Braslaw Sundue, "'Beyond the Time of White Children': African American Emancipation, Age, and Ascribed Neoteny in Early National Pennsylvania," in *Age in America: The Colonial Era to the Present*, ed. Corinne T. Field and Nicholas L. Syrett (New York: New York University Press, 2015), 53–54; Gary B. Nash and Jean R. Soderlund, *Freedom by Degrees: Emancipation in Pennsylvania and Its Aftermath* (New York: Oxford University Press, 1991), 176–177.

8.   "Enclosure," in *The Papers of Thomas Jefferson*, vol. 22, *6 August 1791–31 December 1791*, ed. Charles T. Cullen (Princeton, NJ: Princeton University Press, 1986), 425–427; Paul Finkelman, "The Kidnapping of John Davis and the Adoption of the Fugitive Slave Law of 1793," *Journal of Southern History* 56, no. 3 (1990): 402–403.

9.   *PAS Committee of Correspondence Letter Book,* vol. I, 72, *Papers of the PAS at the Historical Society of Pennsylvania,* reel 11 (microfilm ed.).

10.   Affidavit, William Willson, Apr. 22, 1791, *CVSP,* vol. 5, 291–292.

11.   "Cornplanter & Other Indians, to the President of the United States," Mar. 17, 1791, *CVSP,* vol. 5, 315; Knox to Mifflin, May 30, 1791, *CVSP,* vol. 5, 318.

12.   William R. Leslie, "A Study in the Origins of Interstate Rendition: The Big Beaver Creek Murders," *American Historical Review* 57, no. 1 (Oct. 1950): 66.

13.   David Sheppard Lt. of Ohio County to Gov. Randolph, May 9, 1791, *CVSP,* vol. V, 301; Randolph to Mifflin, May 19, 1791, *CVSP,* vol. V, 306.

14.   Mifflin to Randolph, June 4, 1791, *CVSP,* vol. V, 320. Paul Finkelman characterizes the timing of the requests as "coincidental," but his own chronology suggests otherwise unless—hardly plausible—Governor Mifflin was oblivious to the fact that on the same day he received a letter from Secretary of War Knox denying Pennsylvania assistance for one extradition request he received a new request, endorsed by members of the PAS, for the extradition from Virginia of John Davis's kidnappers—a request on which he chose to act, even though pressure to bring the Beaver Creek murderers to justice had in no way abated.

There are several plausible explanations for the timing of the PAS request. The PAS lawyers may have believed that Randolph would have been less likely to reject a second extradition request so soon after rejecting an earlier request and, aware that the Washington administration declined to intervene in the extradition proceedings for the Beaver Creek murderers, assumed Pennsylvania's governor would now have no grounds for delaying their request. Any question about whether the extradition of indicted kidnappers remained a state matter had been answered. A second possibility is that Mifflin believed that, faced with two extradition requests, Randolph would have to act on at least one, and given the political stakes of the Beaver Creek murders, much higher than those surrounding the case of a single kidnapped Pennsylvanian, he would extradite the murderers.

There is a third possible explanation. Perhaps Governor Mifflin and the members of the PAS saw in Davis's situation a test case for American extradition law. Beyond the Indian-haters of the western frontier, few Americans saw any particular virtue in renewed Indian war. Compelling Pennsylvania and Virginia to comply with the Constitution in order to avert such a conflict was thus unlikely to carry an especially high political price—at least outside of Virginia and Pennsylvania. The kidnapping, rendition, and enslavement of a free Black was another matter. Davis's case had remained active for almost three years and was now the subject of negotiations between two state governors. Should Governor Randolph refuse to extradite Davis's kidnappers, and should Mifflin appeal once again to the Washington administration, the political stakes would be very different, for then President

Washington and his cabinet would be forced to mediate a dispute between a pro-slavery state and an antislavery state. The PAS and Governor Mifflin might well have assumed that the president and his advisors would be forced to act on so politically explosive an issue, and doing so would mean that at least one of the Beaver Creek murderers would face trial, albeit for another crime. Finkelman, "Fugitive Slave Law of 1793," 399n5.

15. Randolph to Washington, July 20, 1791, *American State Papers: Class X. Miscellaneous* (Washington, DC: Gales and Seaton, 1834), vol. I, 43.

16. *Annals of Congress*, 2nd Congress, 2nd Session, 1414–1415, in "A Century of Lawmaking for a New Nation," Library of Congress, https://memory.loc .gov/cgi-bin/ampage?collId=llac&fileName=003/llac003.db&recNum=702; Don E. Fehrenbacher, *The Slaveholding Republic: An Account of the United States Government's Relations to Slavery* (New York: Oxford University Press, 2001), 210–212.

17. David Davis deposition, Sept. 22, 1792, *CVSP*, vol. VI, 86–87.

18. "Wright v. Deacon," 1819, *The Founders' Constitution* (University of Chicago Press), vol. 4, art. 4, sec. 2, cl. 3, doc. 11, http://press-pubs.uchicago.edu/founders /documents/a4_2_3s11.html.

19. H. Robert Baker, *Prigg v. Pennsylvania: Slavery, the Supreme Court, and the Ambivalent Constitution* (Lawrence: University Press of Kansas, 2012), 56–57.

20. William R. Leslie, "The Pennsylvania Fugitive Slave Act of 1826," *Journal of Southern History* 18, no. 4 (Nov. 1952): 432–433.

21. Leslie, "Pennsylvania Fugitive Slave Act," 435–436.

22. Leslie, "Pennsylvania Fugitive Slave Act," 435–436; Joseph Kent to Gov. Shulze, Jan. 9, 1826, *PA*, ser. 4, vol. V, 628; *Laws of the State of Delaware*, rev. ed. (Wilmington, DE: R. Porter and Son, 1829), 291–292; Stanley Harrold, *Border War: Fighting over Slavery before the Civil War* (Chapel Hill: University of North Carolina Press, 2010), 74.

23. *Laws of the State of Delaware*, 292; David Skillen Bogen, "The Maryland Context of *Dred Scott:* The Decline in the Legal Status of Maryland Free Blacks 1776–1810," *American Journal of Legal History* 34, no. 4 (Oct. 1990): 404–405; Justin S. Conroy, "'Show Me Your Papers': Race and Street Encounters," *National Black Law Journal* 19, no. 2 (2005–2006): 153–154; John M. Huffman, "Americans on Paper: Identity and Identification in the American Revolution" (PhD diss., Harvard University, 2013), 265–270.

24. Thomas D. Morris, *Free Men All: The Personal Liberty Laws of the North, 1780–1861* (Baltimore: Johns Hopkins University Press, 1974), 51–53.

25. Julie Winch, "Philadelphia and the Other Underground Railroad," *PMHB* 111, no. 1 (Jan. 1987): 3–25.

26.   Quoted in Carol Wilson, *Freedom at Risk: The Kidnapping of Free Blacks in America, 1780–1855* (Lexington: University of Kentucky Press, 1994), 28.

27.   On the Cannon-Johnson gang, see Wilson, *Freedom at Risk*, 19–37; and Richard Bell, *Stolen: Five Free Boys Kidnapped into Slavery and Their Astonishing Odyssey Home* (New York: 37Ink / Simon & Schuster, 2019), esp. ch. 4.

10. THE FALL OF GREATER BALTIMORE

1.   Harriet Martineau, *Society in America* (New York: Saunders and Otley, 1837), vol. I, xiii–xiv.

2.   Martineau, *Society in America*, vol. I, 345–346.

3.   Martineau, *Society in America*, vol. I, 350, 356.

4.   Martineau, *Society in America*, vol. I, 351.

5.   Martineau, *Society in America*, vol. I, 358.

6.   Martineau, *Society in America*, vol. II, 1–2, 11–12.

7.   George Wilson Pierson, *Tocqueville in America* (Baltimore: Johns Hopkins University Press, 1996), 543; John Lauritz Larson, *Internal Improvement: National Public Works and the Promise of Popular Government in the Early United States* (Chapel Hill: University of North Carolina Press, 2001), 220–221; Martineau, *Society in America*, vol. II, 28.

8.   Harriet Martineau, *Illustrations of Political Economy. No. IV. Demerara: A Tale* (Boston: Leonard C. Bowles, 1832), 99.

9.   See, for example, Trevor Burnard, *Jamaica in the Age of Revolution* (Philadelphia: University of Pennsylvania Press, 2020), ch. 9; Seymour Drescher, *The Mighty Experiment: Free Labor versus Slavery in British Emancipation* (New York: Oxford University Press, 2002), esp. Introduction.

10.   Robert J. Steinfeld, *The Invention of Free Labor: The Employment Relation in English and American Law and Culture, 1350–1870* (Chapel Hill: University of North Carolina Press, 1991), 134–135; Max Grivno, *Gleanings of Freedom: Free and Slave Labor along the Mason-Dixon Line, 1790–1860* (Urbana: University of Illinois Press, 2011), 56–57.

11.   Larson, *Internal Improvement*, 89–91; Daniel Walker Howe, *What Hath God Wrought: The Transformation of America, 1815–1848* (New York: Oxford University Press, 2007), 254–255.

12.   Steinfeld, *Invention*, 166–170, quote from William Cranch on 167.

13.   Frederick Douglass, *The Life and Times of Frederick Douglass, from 1817–1822, Written by Himself* (London: Christian Age Office, 1882), 132–133.

14.   Douglas C. North, *The Economic Growth of the United States, 1790–1860* (New York: W. W. Norton, 1966), 260, table B-XI; on the expansion of cotton exports, Sven Beckert, *Empire of Cotton: A Global History* (New York: Alfred A. Knopf, 2014), 119; Grivno, *Gleanings*, 67, 70–76.

15. Grivno, *Gleanings*, 29, fig. 3.

16. Peter Way, *Common Labour: Workers and the Digging of North American Canals, 1780–1860* (Cambridge: Cambridge University Press, 1993), 107, 212, 283 (appendix I, table 12).

17. Asia Booth Clarke, *John Wilkes Booth: A Sister's Memoir*, ed. Terry Alford (Jackson: University of Mississippi Press, 1996), 48–50; James Shapiro, *Shakespeare in a Divided America: What His Plays Tell Us about Our Past and Future* (New York: Penguin Press, 2020), 90–93.

18. Quoted in Ronald G. Walters, *American Reformers, 1815–1860* (New York: Hill and Wang, 1978), 128.

19. Way, *Common Labour*, 182–187.

20. Asa Earl Martin, "The Temperance Movement in Pennsylvania prior to the Civil War," *PMHB* 49, no. 3 (1925): 203–206; Louis Hartz, *Economic Policy and Democratic Thought: Pennsylvania, 1776–1860* (Chicago: Quadrangle Books, 1968), 208–213.

21. Grivno, *Gleanings*, 183–184.

22. Barbara Jeanne Fields, *Slavery and Freedom on the Middle Ground: Maryland during the Nineteenth Century* (New Haven, CT: Yale University Press, 1985), 33–35.

23. Hartz, *Economic Policy*, 289.

24. Annual Message to the Assembly, 1836, *PA*, ser. 4, vol. VI, 286, 309.

25. *Proceedings and Debates of the Convention of the Commonwealth of Pennsylvania to Propose Amendments to the Constitution* . . . (Harrisburg: Packer, Barrett, and Parke, 1837), vol. II, 76, 64.

26. John F. Stover, *History of the Baltimore and Ohio Railroad Company* (West Lafayette, IN: Purdue University Press, 1987), 25–27; John Quincy Adams, diary 36, 1 January 1825–30 September 1830, p. 21 [electronic edition], *The Diaries of John Quincy Adams: A Digital Collection* (Boston, MA: Massachusetts Historical Society, 2004), https://www.masshist.org/jqadiaries/php/popup?id=jqad36_21.

27. Stover, *History of the Baltimore and Ohio Railroad Company*, 61; Diane Lindstrom, *Economic Development in the Philadelphia Region, 1810–1850* (New York: Columbia University Press, 1977), 113, table 4.6.

28. Jo N. Hays, "Overlapping Hinterlands: York, Philadelphia, and Baltimore, 1800–1850," *PMHB* 116, no. 3 (July 1992): 295–321.

29. Darwin H. Stapleton, "The Diffusion of Anthracite Iron Technology: The Case of Lancaster County," *PH* 45, no. 2 (Apr. 1978): 150–151.

30. Van Gosse, *The First Reconstruction: Black Politics in America, from the Revolution to the Civil War* (Chapel Hill: University of North Carolina Press, 2021), 119–120.

31. Quoted in Willis L. Shirk, "Testing the Limits of Tolerance: Blacks and the Social Order in Columbia, Pennsylvania, 1800–1851," *PH* 60, no. 1 (Jan. 1993): 42.

32. Thomas P. Slaughter, *Bloody Dawn: The Christiana Riot and Racial Violence in the Antebellum North* (New York: Oxford University Press, 1991), 164; Adam Malka, *The Men of Mobtown: Policing Baltimore in the Age of Slavery and Emancipation* (Chapel Hill: University of North Carolina Press, 2018), 49–50; Leon F. Litwack, *North of Slavery: The Negro in the Free States, 1790–1860* (Chicago: University of Chicago Press, 1961), 100.

33. Howe, *What Hath God Wrought*, 433–435; Gary B. Nash, *Forging Freedom: The Formation of Philadelphia's Black Community, 1720–1840* (Cambridge, MA: Harvard University Press, 1988), 273–274; citizens committee quoted in Litwack, *North of Slavery*, 101.

34. Quoted in Slaughter, *Bloody Dawn*, 171; my account relies on 164–181.

35. Seth Rockman, *Scraping By: Wage Labor, Slavery, and Survival in Early Baltimore* (Baltimore: Johns Hopkins University Press, 2009), 41–42.

36. Frederick Douglass, *Narrative of the Life of Frederick Douglass, An American Slave*, ed. John W. Blassingame et al. (New Haven, CT: Yale University Press, 2001), 67–68.

37. *Colonization: A Notice of Victor Hugo's Views of Slavery in the United States, in a Letter from John H. B. Latrobe, of Baltimore* (Baltimore: John D. Toy, 1851), 18.

38. Fields, *Slavery and Freedom*, 35.

39. "An Act Relating to Free Negroes and Slaves," Mar. 14, 1832, *AM*, vol. CCXIII, 445–451; "Supplement to the Black Code of 1831–32," Mar. 18, 1840, *AM*, vol. DC, 36–39; Ira Berlin, *Slaves without Masters: The Free Negro in the Antebellum South* (New York: Pantheon Books, 1974), 203–212; Penelope Campbell, *Maryland in Africa: The Maryland State Colonization Society, 1831–1857* (Urbana: University of Illinois Press, 1971), 203–204; Farmer quoted in Grivno, *Gleanings*, 184.

40. Patience Essah, *A House Divided: Slavery and Emancipation in Delaware, 1638–1865* (Charlottesville: University Press of Virginia, 1996), 113–116, quote on 115.

41. Bradford and Tubman excerpted in Jean M. Humez, *Harriet Tubman: The Life and the Life Stories* (Madison: University of Wisconsin Press, 2003), 182–183.

11. THE SECOND FUGITIVE SLAVE ACT

1. Bernard Christian Steiner, *Life of Roger Brooke Taney: Chief Justice of the United States Supreme Court* (Baltimore: Williams and Wilkins, 1922), 7–17; Charles Coleman Sellers, *Dickinson College: A History* (Middletown, CT: Wesleyan University Press, 1973), 94.

2. Quoted in Steiner, *Life of Roger Brooke Taney*, 46.

3. Timothy S. Huebner, "Roger B. Taney and the Slavery Issue: Looking beyond—and before—*Dred Scott*," *Journal of American History* 97, no. 1 (June 2010): 19–20.

4.   Taney quoted in Huebner, "Roger B. Taney," 25.

5.   *United States v. Gooding,* in *Reports of Cases Argued and Adjudged in the Supreme Court of the United States, January Term, 1827,* ed. Henry Wheaton (New York: R. Donaldson, 1827), vol. XII, 460–480; Huebner, "Roger B. Taney," 34.

6.   *Reports of Cases Argued and Adjudged in the Supreme Court of the United States, January Term 1842,* 3rd ed., ed. Frederick C. Brightly (New York: Banks Law Publishing, 1903), vol. XVI, 627; Robert H. Baker, Prigg v. Pennsylvania: *Slavery, the Supreme Court, and the Ambivalent Constitution* (Lawrence: University of Kansas Press, 2012).

7.   Excerpted in George Ticknor Curtis, *Life of James Buchanan: Fifteenth President of the United States* (New York: Harper & Brothers, 1883), vol. I, 2.

8.   Curtis, *Life of James Buchanan,* vol. I, 4–5.

9.   Buchanan was honorably discharged before Sept. 9, to his father's great relief. James Buchanan Sr. to James Buchanan, Sept. 22, 1814, in Curtis, *Life of James Buchanan,* vol. I, 10–11; vol. II, 26.

10.   Curtis, *Life of James Buchanan,* vol. I, 21–22.

11.   "Speech, April 11, 1826, on the Panama Mission," in *The Works of James Buchanan, Comprising His Speeches, State Papers, and Private Correspondence,* ed. John Bassett Moore (Philadelphia: J. B. Lippincott, 1908), vol. I, 202–203; Buchanan to Jones, Mar. 7, 1856, vol. XI, 509.

12.   Philip Klein, *President James Buchanan, a Biography* (University Park: Penn State University Press, 1962), 100–101.

13.   Buchanan to Charles Kessler et al., Aug. 25, 1847, in *Works of James Buchanan,* vol. VII, 386–387.

14.   Steiner, *Life of Roger Brooke Taney,* 103.

15.   *Journal of Proceedings of the House of Delegates of the State of Maryland* (Annapolis: Riley & Davis, 1847), 53.

16.   R. J. M. Blackett, *The Captive's Quest for Freedom: Fugitive Slaves, the 1850 Fugitive Slave Law, and the Politics of Slavery* (Cambridge: Cambridge University Press, 2018), 52–53; Stanley W. Campbell, *The Slave Catchers: Enforcement of the Fugitive Slave Law, 1850–1860* (Chapel Hill: University of North Carolina Press, 1968), 23–25.

17.   "Letter to a Public Meeting," Nov. 19, 1850, in *Works of James Buchanan,* vol. VIII, 393–394, 396. On the Constitutional Unionist movement, see Blackett, *Captive's Quest,* 25–32.

12. BORDER WAR ALONG THE UNDERGROUND RAILROAD

1.   William Parker relayed the story of his life in "The Freedman's Story," published in two parts in the *Atlantic Monthly* in February and March 1866 and

reprinted in Jonathan Katz, *Resistance at Christiana: The Fugitive Slave Rebellion, Christiana, Pennsylvania, September 11, 1851: A Documentary Account* (New York: Thomas Y. Crowell, 1974), chs. 1 and 2.

2.   Parker in Katz, *Resistance*, 27; on the Gap Gang, Katz, *Resistance*, 26; Thomas P. Slaughter, *Bloody Dawn: The Christiana Riot and Racial Violence in the Antebellum North* (New York: Oxford University Press, 1991), 44–45.

3.   Parker in Katz, *Resistance*, 27.

4.   Katz, *Resistance*, 28.

5.   Katz, *Resistance*, 34.

6.   On Gorsuch and his slaves, see Katz, *Resistance*, 66–71. Also see Slaughter, *Bloody Dawn*, ch. 1.

7.   Parker in Katz, *Resistance*, 81.

8.   Douglass, excerpted in Katz, *Resistance*, 260.

9.   "The Christiana Murders," *North American*, Sept. 13, 1851, 2, col. 1; "The Christiana Tragedy," *Public Ledger*, Nov. 1, 1851, 1, col. 6; "The Slave-Hunting Tragedy in Lancaster County," *Pennsylvania Freeman*, Sept. 18, 1851, 2, col. 6; all *AHN*.

10.   Although contemporaries may have referred to the events at Christiana as a "riot," suggesting little coordination or premeditation on the part of Parker and his associates, recent scholarship has suggested that in fact the community centered on Parker's home has a closer resemblance to a fortified maroon community, such as those in the Jamaican upcountry. Steven Hahn, *The Political Worlds of Slavery and Freedom* (Cambridge, MA: Harvard University Press, 2009), 41.

11.   Quotes from Katz, *Resistance*, 124–125.

12.   W. U. Hensel, *The Christiana Riot and the Treason Trials of 1851: An Historical Sketch*, 2nd rev. ed. (Lancaster, PA: Press of the New Era Printing Company, 1911), 41.

13.   Katz, *Resistance*, 162.

14.   Argument in the Christiana Riot Trial, November 29, 1851, *SPTS*, vol. I, 136–137; Slaughter, *Bloody Dawn*, 135.

15.   Michael F. Holt, *The Political Crisis of the 1850s* (New York: W. W. Norton, 1983), 202.

16.   Justice John Catron to James Buchanan, Feb. 19, 1857; Justice Robert Grier to James Buchanan, Feb. 23, 1857, in *The Works of James Buchanan, Comprising His Speeches, State Papers, and Private Correspondence*, ed. John Bassett Moore (Philadelphia: J. B. Lippincott, 1908), vol. X, 106–108.

17.   "Inauguration of James Buchanan, President of the United States, at the East Front of the U.S. Capitol, March 4, 1857," https://www.loc.gov/resource/msspin.pin2003/; "History of the U.S. Capitol Building," Office of the Architect of the Capitol, https://www.aoc.gov/explore-capitol-campus/buildings-grounds/capitol-building/history.

18.   "Inaugural Address, March 4, 1857," in *The Works of James Buchanan,* vol. X, 105–108.

19.   "The Dred Scott Decision: Speech, Delivered, in Part, at the Anniversary of the American Abolition Society, Held in New York, May 14th, 1857," in *Frederick Douglass: Selected Speeches and Writings,* ed. Philip S. Foner and Yuval Taylor (Chicago: Lawrence Hill Books, 1999), 347; "Abstract of Remarks on the Buchanan Administration, August 25, 1858, at the Lancaster County Republican Convention," *SPTS,* vol. I, 156; *Lancaster Intelligencer,* Aug. 31, 1858, 2, excerpted in *SPTS,* vol. I, 157n3.

20.   Don E. Fehrenbacher, *The Dred Scott Case: Its Significance in American Law and Politics* (New York: Oxford University Press, 1978), 568–569.

21.   Fehrenbacher, *Dred Scott,* 574–580; *Tribune* quote, 577.

13. BORDERLANDS INTO BORDER STATES

1.   There has been much debate about the so-called slave power thesis. Its modern iteration is ably developed in Leonard L. Richards, *The Slave Power: The Free North and Southern Domination, 1780–1860* (Baton Rouge: Louisiana State University Press, 2000). See a parallel thesis developed in Matthew Karp, *This Vast Southern Empire: Slaveholders at the Helm of American Foreign Policy* (Cambridge, MA: Harvard University Press, 2016).

2.   By the late 1830s, constitutional reform begun in the 1790s had effectively excluded all free Blacks from voting in Delaware, Maryland, and Pennsylvania. Martha S. Jones, *Birthright Citizens: A History of Race and Rights in Antebellum America* (Cambridge: Cambridge University Press, 2018), 25–26, 92; William H. Williams, *Slavery and Freedom in Delaware, 1639–1865* (Wilmington, DE: SR Books, 1996), 189–190; Leon F. Litwack, *North of Slavery: The Negro in the Free States, 1790–1860* (Chicago: University of Chicago Press, 1961), 84–86. For county-level electoral data, Walter Dean Burnham, *Presidential Ballots, 1836–1892* (Baltimore: Johns Hopkins University Press, 1955).

3.   "Arrival of the Hon. James Buchanan," *Baltimore Sun,* May 13, 1856, 1, cols. 3–4, *AHN.*

4.   William J. Evitts, *A Matter of Allegiances: Maryland from 1850–1861* (Baltimore: Johns Hopkins University Press, 1974), 149–150.

5.   Merritt Roe Smith, *Harper's Ferry and the New Technology: The Challenge of Change* (Ithaca, NY: Cornell University Press, 1977), 344–345, table 1.

6.   On John Brown in Chambersburg, Edward L. Ayers, *In the Presence of Mine Enemies: War in the Heart of America, 1859–1863* (New York: W. W. Norton, 2003), ch. 2, quotes on 11–12.

7. David S. Reynolds, *John Brown: Abolitionist* (New York: Alfred A. Knopf, 2005), 108–110.

8. Jonathan Katz, *Resistance at Christiana: The Fugitive Slave Rebellion, Christiana, Pennsylvania, September 11, 1851: A Documentary Account* (New York: Thomas Y. Crowell, 1974), 280; Louis A. Decaro Jr., "The Useful Frontier: John Brown's Detroit River Preface to the Harper's Ferry Raid," in *A Fluid Frontier: Slavery, Resistance, and the Underground Railroad in the Detroit River Borderlands,* ed. Karolyn Smardz Frost and Veta Smith Tucker (Detroit: Wayne State University Press, 2016), 229–244.

9. Ayers, *In the Presence of Mine Enemies,* 16.

10. Chambersburg *Valley Spirit,* Dec. 7, 1859, 4, col. 1, *VOS.*

11. "People's Meeting," *Weekly Civilian* (Cumberland, MD), Dec. 8, 1859, 2, col. 3, *AHN;* "A Word for Chambersburg," *Franklin Repository,* Oct. 26, 1859, 4, col. 4, *VOS;* "Admiration for Old Brown," *Valley Spirit,* Dec. 7, 1859, 4, col. 1, *VOS.*

12. "Prepare for November," *Valley Spirit,* Oct. 24, 1860, 4, col. 1, *VOS;* "Danger of the Union," *New York Express,* excerpted in Baltimore *Sun,* Dec. 5, 1859, 1, col. 4, *AHN;* "Wade's Speech," *Weekly Patriot and Union* [Harrisburg, PA], Dec. 20, 1860, 5, col. 2, *AHN.*

13. "Mr. Lincoln in Baltimore," Baltimore *Sun,* Feb. 23, 1861, 2, col. 1, *AHN.*

14. Ted Widmer, *Lincoln on the Verge: Thirteen Days to Washington* (New York: Simon & Schuster, 2020).

15. "Gov. Hicks' Patriotism," *Easton Gazette,* Dec. 22, 1860, 2, col. 3, *AHN;* "Abstract of the Testimony of Gov. Hicks before the Investigating Committee," Baltimore *Sun,* Feb. 21, 1861, 1, col. 6, *AHN.* Hicks was also lobbied by pro-Union representatives from Pennsylvania, although there is no evidence that they resorted to the sorts of threats and intimidation employed by their Confederate counterparts. Jean H. Baker, *The Politics of Continuity: Maryland Political Parties from 1858–1870* (Baltimore: Johns Hopkins University Press, 1973), 47–48.

16. Widmer, *Lincoln on the Verge,* 67–68, 250.

17. Widmer, *Lincoln on the Verge,* chs. 13–14.

18. *Journal of the House of Representatives of the State of Delaware* (Dover, DE: Samuel Kimmey, 1847), 195–196; Patience Essah, *A House Divided: Slavery and Emancipation in Delaware, 1638–1865* (Charlottesville: University Press of Virginia, 1996), 8, table 1; Williams, *Slavery and Freedom in Delaware,* 185–186; David Paul Peltier, "Border State Democracy: A History of Voting in Delaware, 1682–1897" (PhD diss., University of Delaware, 1967), 219, table II.

19. *Journal of the House of Representatives of the State of Delaware,* 89.

20. Harold Bell Hancock, *Delaware during the Civil War: A Political History* (1961; online reprint, Dover, DE: Delaware Heritage Commission, 2011), resolution quoted on 48, composition of legislature on 47.

21. "Annual Message to Congress," Dec. 3, 1861, *CW*, vol. V, 49; "The Rebellion.—No. 3. Pennsylvania and Her Interests," *Philadelphia Inquirer*, Sept. 20, 1861, 8, col. 1, *AHN;* Michael D. Robinson, *A Union Indivisible: Secession and the Politics of Slavery in the Border South* (Chapel Hill: University of North Carolina Press, 2017), 118–119.

22. John G. Nicolay and John Hay, *Abraham Lincoln: A History* (New York: Century, 1890), vol. IV, 92.

23. Lincoln to Orville H. Browning, Sept. 22, 1861, *CW*, vol. IV, 532.

24. "Drafts of a Bill for Compensated Emancipation in Delaware [Nov. 26, 1861]," *CW*, vol. V, 29–30.

25. James Oakes, *Freedom National: The Destruction of Slavery in the United States, 1861–1865* (New York: W. W. Norton, 2013), 282–285, 485; Eric Foner, *The Fiery Trial: Abraham Lincoln and Slavery* (New York: W. W. Norton, 2010), 181–184.

26. *The Delaware Republican* quoted in Peltier, "Border State Democracy," 257. On voting returns in Delaware, Peltier, "Border State Democracy," 257 and 269, table 1. On Black voting rights in Delaware, Williams, *Slavery and Freedom in Delaware*, 189–190.

27. "The 'Underground Railroad' Journey," Baltimore *Sun*, Feb. 25, 1861, 1, col. 2; "The Great Lincoln Escapade," Baltimore *Sun*, 2, col. 1, both *AHN*.

28. "The Position of Maryland and Virginia," *New York Herald*, April 22, 1861, 1, col. 2, *AHN;* "From Chambersburg," *Philadelphia Inquirer*, April 22, 1861, 1, col. 2, *AHN;* Evitts, *Matter of Allegiance*, 176.

29. Evitts, *Matter of Allegiance*, 178–180.

30. Nicolay and Hay, *Abraham Lincoln*, vol. IV, 125.

31. "Our Warning," *Weekly Civilian* (Cumberland, MD), April 25, 1861, p. 2, col. 2, *AHN*.

32. Nicolay personal memorandum, excerpted in Nicolay and Hay, *Abraham Lincoln*, vol. IV, 124–125.

33. Nicolay and Hay, *Abraham Lincoln*, vol. IV, 167–168; Reply to Baltimore Committee, April 22, 1861, in Nicolay and Hay, *Abraham Lincoln*, vol. IV, 140.

34. "The Maryland State Union Convention," Baltimore *Sun*, May 24, 1861, 1, col. 4, *AHN; Frederick Examiner*, quoted in Evitts, *Matter of Allegiance*, 184.

35. Swann quoted in Baker, *Politics of Continuity*, 51.

36. Festus P. Summers, "The Baltimore and Ohio—First in War," *Civil War History* 7, no. 3 (Sept. 1961): 239; Stephens quoted in Evitts, *Matter of Allegiance*, 171.

37. *SPTS*, vol. I, 213; "The Rebellion.—No. 3. Pennsylvania and Her Interests," *Philadelphia Inquirer*, Sept. 20, 1861, 8, col. 1, *AHN*.

38. Frank J. Williams, "Abraham Lincoln, Civil Liberties, and Maryland," in *The Civil War in Maryland Reconsidered,* edited by Charles W. Mitchell and Jean H. Baker (Baton Rouge: Louisiana State University Press, 2021), ch. 6; James M.

McPherson, *Battle Cry of Freedom: The Civil War Era* (New York: Oxford University Press, 1988), 285–289.

39.   Baker, *Politics of Continuity,* 67–75.

40.   John H. B. Latrobe, *The History of Mason and Dixon's Line: Contained in an Address, Delivered by John H. B. Latrobe . . . before the Historical Society of Pennsylvania, November 8, 1854* (Philadelphia: Press of the Society, 1855), 51.

14. THE END OF THE LINE

1.   James Oakes, *Freedom National: The Destruction of Slavery in the United States, 1861–1865* (New York: W. W. Norton, 2013), ix–x.

2.   *BAP,* vol. V, 299–302.

3.   George E. Stephens to Robert Hamilton, Apr. 2, 1863, *BAP,* vol. V, 199–202.

4.   *The Legislative Record: Containing Debates and Proceedings of the Pennsylvania Legislature for the Session of 1863* (Harrisburg: George Bergner, 1863), 545–547, 329; Thomas Anthony Sanelli, "The Struggle for Black Suffrage in Pennsylvania, 1838–1870" (PhD diss., Temple University, 1978), 135–138; Leon F. Litwack, *North of Slavery: The Negro in the Free States, 1790–1860* (Chicago: University of Chicago Press, 1961), 35–36, 70–71.

5.   "The Views of a Loyal Journal of a Slaveholding State," from the Frederick *Examiner,* reprinted in *The Raftsman's Journal* (Clearfield, PA), Apr. 23, 1862, 1, col. 4, *PNA.*

6.   "Swarms of Contrabands," *Lancaster Intelligencer,* June 24, 1862, 3, col. 4, *PNA;* Richard S. Newman, "The Age of Emancipating Proclamations: Early Civil War Abolitionism and its Discontents," *PMHB* 137, no. 1 (2013): 39–41.

7.   "First Installment," from *Chambersburg Spirit,* reprinted in *The Compiler* (Gettysburg, PA), June 2, 1862, 2, col. 6; "Gradual Emancipation Continues . . . ," from the *Christian Banner,* reprinted in the *Village Record* (Waynesboro, PA), July 18, 1862, 2, col. 6; "Clippings," *The Mariettian* (Marietta, PA), July 12, 1862, 2, col. 3, all *PNA.* For comparative wages, Max Grivno, *Gleanings of Freedom: Free and Slave Labor along the Mason-Dixon Line, 1790–1860* (Urbana: University of Illinois Press, 2011), 157. More generally on contrabands in Pennsylvania, Edward L. Ayers, *In the Presence of Mine Enemies: War in the Heart of America, 1859–1863* (New York: W. W. Norton, 2003), 271–273.

8.   "The War in Its Relations to Slavery," *The Compiler,* June 17, 1861, 1, col. 7, *PNA.*

9.   "An Inundation of Negroes," from the *New York Herald,* reprinted in the *Lancaster Intelligencer,* Apr. 8, 1862, 3, col. 2, *PNA.*

10.   Lee to Jefferson Davis, September 4, 1862, in *The Wartime Papers of R. E. Lee,* ed. Clifford Dowdey and Louis H. Manarin (Boston: Little, Brown, 1961),

294; James M. McPherson, *Crossroads of Freedom: Antietam* (New York: Oxford University Press, 2002), 91–95.

11.   McClellan letter quoted in Ayers, *In the Presence*, 313.

12.   David G. Smith, "Race and Retaliation: The Capture of African Americans during the Gettysburg Campaign," in Peter Wallenstein and Bertram Wyatt-Brown, *Virginia's Civil War* (Charlottesville: University of Virginia Press, 2005), 137–151.

13.   Alonzo H. Quint, *The Potomac and the Rapidan: Army Notes, from the Failure at Winchester to the Reënforcement of Rosecrans, 1861–3* (Boston: Crosby and Nichols, 1864), 234–235; Channing Price to Mrs. Thomas Randolph Price Sr., Sept. 18, 1862, in *With Pen and Saber: The Letters and Diaries of J. E. B. Stuart's Staff Officers,* ed. Robert J. Trout (Mechanicsburg, PA: Stackpole Books, 1995), 101.

14.   Channing Price to Mrs. Thomas Randolph Price Sr., Oct. 15, 1862, and Chiswell Dabney to Mrs. Elizabeth T. Dabney, Oct. 21, 1862, in *With Pen and Saber*, 107, 111; "The Daring Rebel Raid into Pennsylvania," *North Branch Democrat* (Tunkhannock, PA), Oct. 15, 1862, 2, col. 6, *PNA*.

15.   Lee quoted in Ayers, *In the Presence of Mine Enemies*, 326; A. K. McClure, "Chambersburg, October, 1862," *Carlisle Herald*, Oct. 24, 1862, 1, cols. 2–5, *PNA*.

16.   McClure, "Chambersburg," *Carlisle Herald*, Oct. 24, 1862, 1, col. 4, *PNA;* Heyser's diary excerpted in Ayers, *In the Presence*, 323.

17.   Ayers, *In the Presence*, 391–392.

18.   Confederate cavalry officer Jedediah Hotchkiss quoted in Ayers, *In the Presence*, 314; Channing Price to Mrs. Thomas Randolph Price Sr., Oct. 15, 1862, and Chiswell Dabney to Mrs. Elizabeth T. Dabney, Oct. 21, 1862, in *With Pen and Saber*, 107, 112.

19.   Robert E. Lee to General Richard S. Ewell, June 17, 1863, in *The Wartime Papers of R. E. Lee*, 518; "The Confederate Invasion," Baltimore *Sun*, June 18, 1863, 1, col. 3, *AHN;* "Operations of the Rebel," *New Haven Daily Palladium*, June 20, 1863, 2, col. 6, *AHN*.

20.   Heyser and Schaff quotes from Ayers, *In the Presence*, 395–397; "From Shippensburg," *The press*, June 20, 1863, 2, col. 6, *PNA*.

21.   "Speech on State Elections [Sept. 17, 1863 in Christiana]," *SPTS*, vol. I, 407.

22.   Cormany quoted in Ayers, *In the Presence*, 405; Schaff quoted in Ayers, *In the Presence*, 397–398, 405.

23.   David G. Smith, *On the Edge of Freedom: The Fugitive Slave Issue in South Central Pennsylvania, 1820–1870* (New York: Fordham University Press, 2013), 192–193; Chris E. Fonvielle Jr., "'Welcome Brothers!': The Union Prisoners of War Exchange in North Carolina," *North Carolina Historical Review* 92, no. 3 (July 2015): 279–281.

24.   Edwin B. Coddington, "Pennsylvania Prepares for Invasion, 1863," *PH* 31, no. 2 (Apr. 1964): 171–172, 163; John B. Gordon, *Reminiscences of the Civil War*

(New York: Charles Scribner's Sons, 1903), 140–141; Edward L. Ayers, *The Thin Light of Freedom: The Civil War and Emancipation in the Heart of America* (New York: W. W. Norton, 2017), 51.

25. Stevens to Simon Stevens, July 11, 1863, *SPTS*, vol. I, 402; Ayers, *Thin Light of Freedom*, 34.

26. Gordon, *Reminiscences of the Civil War*, 139–140; "Columbia, Pa, June 29," *The Press* (Philadelphia), June 30, 1863, 1, col. 5; "The Fight at Wrightsville, Columbia, June 29," *The Press* (Philadelphia), June 30, 1863, 1, col. 5; "The Skirmish beyond Wrightsville," *The Columbia Spy* (Columbia, PA), July 11, 1863, 1, cols. 1–2, all *PNA;* William Alan Blair, "'A Source of Amusement': Pennsylvania versus Lee, 1863," *PMHB* 115, no. 3 (July 1991): 332–333.

27. Margaret S. Creighton, *The Colors of Courage: Gettysburg's Forgotten History: Immigrants, Women, and African Americans in the Civil War's Defining Battle* (New York: Basic Books, 2005), 131–132; Jeffry D. Wert, "Camp William Penn and the Black Soldier," *PH* 46, no. 4 (Oct. 1979): 340–341; Ted Alexander, "'A Regular Slave Hunt': The Army of Northern Virginia and Black Civilians in the Gettysburg Campaign," *North and South* 4, no. 7 (Sept. 2001): 88.

28. Frank Moore, ed., *The Rebellion Record* (New York: D. Van Nostrand, 1864), vol. VII, 325; Smith, "Race and Retaliation," 143–144; "Speech on State Elections [Sept. 17, 1863 in Christiana]," *SPTS*, vol. I, 407.

29. Ayers, *The Thin Light of Freedom*, 67, 74–76; Elizabeth Varon, *Armies of Deliverance: A New History of the Civil War* (New York: Oxford University Press, 2019), 242–256.

30. "Speech on State Elections [Sept. 17, 1863 in Christiana]," *SPTS*, vol. I, 407–409; Oakes, *Freedom National*, 430–431.

31. Ira Berlin, *The Long Emancipation: The Demise of Slavery in the United States* (Cambridge, MA: Harvard University Press, 2015), 162–163.

32. *Weekly Anglo-African*, Aug. 6, 1864, *BAP*, vol. V, 277–278.

33. *Between North and South: A Maryland Journalist Views the Civil War: The Narrative of William Wilkins Glenn, 1861–1869*, ed. Bayly Ellen Marks and Mark Norton Schatz (Rutherford, NJ: Fairleigh Dickinson University Press, 1976), 167.

34. Text of the Maryland Constitution of 1864, in Edward Otis Hinkley, *The Constitution of the State of Maryland. Reported and Adopted by the Convention and Delegates Assembled at the City of Annapolis, April 27th, 1864* . . . (Annapolis: Richard T. Bayly, 1865), 16.

35. Quoted in Charles Lewis Wagandt, *The Mighty Revolution: Negro Emancipation in Maryland, 1862–1864* (Baltimore: Johns Hopkins University Press, 1964), 217.

36. Oakes, *Freedom National*, 463–467; William Starr Myers, *The Maryland Constitution of 1864* (Baltimore: Johns Hopkins University Press, 1901), appendix.

37.   "Speech of Secretary Seward," *Carlisle Herald*, Nov. 18, 1864, 3, col. 2, *PNA;* "Maryland. 'Come in, thou blessed of the Lord,'" *Liberator* (Boston), Dec. 2, 1864, 1, col. 3, *AHN.*

38.   Strong quoted in Michael Vorenberg, *Final Freedom: The Civil War, the Abolition of Slavery, and the Thirteenth Amendment* (Cambridge: Cambridge University Press, 2001), 173.

39.   Quoted in Patience Essah, *A House Divided: Slavery and Emancipation in Delaware, 1638–1865* (Charlottesville: University Press of Virginia, 1996), 182.

EPILOGUE

1.   *The National Cyclopaedia of American Biography* (New York: James T. White, 1893), 154; George Alfred Townsend, *Tales of the Chesapeake* (New York: American News Company, 1880), 33.

2.   *Tales of the Chesapeake*, 32–34, 42.

3.   *The Entailed Hat or: Patty Cannon's Times: A Romance* (New York: Harper & Brothers, 1884), viii.

4.   *Katy of Catoctin, or the Chain-Breakers: A National Romance* (New York: D. Appleton, 1887), 14, 18.

5.   "Why Is the South Loyal," *New York Herald*, Mar. 19, 1895, 7, col. 5; "National Unity," *Idaho Statesman*, Mar. 15, 1898, 2, col. 2; "It Was a Great Day," *Topeka Weekly Capital*, Mar. 15, 1898, 2, col. 2, all *AHN*. Detroit paper quoted in Edward L. Ayers, *The Promise of the New South: Life after Reconstruction* (New York: Oxford University Press, 1992), 329; "Shaw and Milliman," *Iowa State Bystander*, Aug. 4, 1899, 2, col. 4, *AHN.*

6.   Quoted in Ayers, *Promise of the New South*, 327.

7.   Robert J. Cook, "'F—k the Confederacy': The Strange Career of Civil War Memory in Maryland after 1865," in *The Civil War in Maryland Reconsidered*, ed. Charles W. Mitchell and Jean H. Baker (Baton Rouge: Louisiana State University Press, 2021), 317.

8.   "Race War—the Color Labor Line," *Plaindealer* (Topeka, KS), Feb. 9, 1900, 2, col. 5; "Let Us Reason Together," *The Freeman* (Indianapolis), Oct. 13, 1900, 4, col. 3; "The White and the Black of It," *Broad Axe* (Chicago), Feb. 21, 1903, 1, col. 6, all *AAN.*

9.   "Is He Loyal," *Washington Bee*, May 2, 1914, 4, col. 1, *AAN.*

10.   "The Waco Horror," excerpted in Herbert Aptheker, ed., *A Documentary History of the Negro People of the United States, 1910–1932* (Secaucus, NJ: Citadel Press, 1973), 143–144.

ACKNOWLEDGMENTS

I wrote this book during my tenure as FSU history department chair. That would have been impossible without the support of department coworkers and colleagues John Netter, Suzanne Sinke, Jennifer Koslow, Will Hanley, and Katherine Mooney. I am similarly indebted to the FSU College of Arts and Sciences Dean's Office, particularly now-retired Senior Associate Dean Lois Hawkes, Associate Deans Jeanette Taylor and Tim Logan, Dean Sam Huckaba, and Sam's indefatigable assistant, Sheryl Grossman. Dan Maier-Katkin, Lenin Mongerie and Dr. Paul Deitchman have also been invaluable resources.

A series of outstanding FSU graduate students supported my work as research assistants: Chelsi Arellano, Kyle Bracken, Amy Coale, Scott Craig, Emily Lu, Ed Shockley, Rhiannon Turgel-Ethier, Justin Vos, and Dragana Zivkovic.

Professor Yoshio Higomoto graciously invited me to present an early version of the book's argument at the 2014 Doshisha University American Studies Summer Seminar in Kyoto. My fellow invited speakers, Brian DeLay and David Leal, have remained good friends, intellectual compatriots, and fellow travelers.

The Introduction of this book builds on ideas first presented in "First Partition: The Troubled Origins of the Mason-Dixon Line," my contribution to *The American Revolution Reborn,* edited by Patrick Spero and Michael Zuckerman and published by the University of Pennsylvania Press in 2016.

The FSU Library staff, especially history subject area librarian Adam Beauchamp, helped locate sources and cheerfully fielded my many arcane queries.

Lisa Adams of the Garamond Agency remains a voice of calm encouragement. Kathleen McDermott of Harvard University Press took an early interest in my work, and Cheryl Hirsch expertly shepherded the manuscript through production. The book's two anonymous peer reviewers offered invaluable suggestions; I wish I could have addressed them all.

Tom Willcockson of Mapcraft created the maps for the book. This is now the third book of mine Tom has worked on. He is a genuine master of his craft.

The book builds on decades of research by the many historians of the mid-Atlantic and upper Chesapeake. I regret that I was only able to acknowledge a small fraction of that work in the book's notes.

Fellow early Americanists Lige Gould, Eric Hinderaker, Peter Mancall, and Mark Peterson read portions of an early draft and helped me think through a number of challenges. I would especially like to thank Mark, a fellow Homewood-Flossmoor High School graduate, who helped me stay the course.

Trevor Burnard and Katherine Mooney both read early versions of the entire manuscript and offered much-needed editorial counsel.

Jane Kamensky has been an unfailingly steady and generous friend and collaborator. She also happens to be the best reader in the business. Whatever coherence this narrative reflects is in large part owing to her many incisive suggestions.

Thanks to Jennifer Portman, Chris Robertson, Greg Falstrom, and Barb Shoplock for innumerable acts of kindness and friendship.

My parents, Mel and Sue Gray, my brothers, Matthew and Steven, and their families, my in-laws, Christine Bosworth and Bill and Silvia Rutledge, my brother-in-law, Bill, and his family, and the Spenard-Bosworths have been steadfast in their support over the years.

Above all, Stacey and our kids, Sophie and Tobias. Mahalo.

INDEX

Page numbers in italics refer to maps and illustrations.